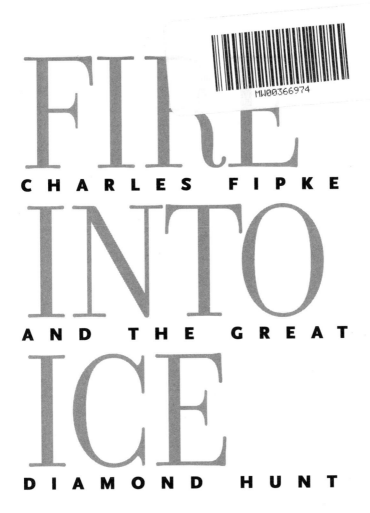

FIRE
CHARLES FIPKE
INTO
AND THE GREAT
ICE
DIAMOND HUNT

VERNON FROLICK

RAINCOAST BOOKS

Vancouver

FOR JOHNNY HARRISON, "KING OF EAGLE RIVER"
A hard-rock prospector who knew even the slightest sound was worth investigating

TO ELIZABETH AND MARK

Text copyright © 1999 by Vernon Mark Frolick
Photographs © Charles Fipke except where otherwise noted.

First published in 1999 by

Raincoast Books
8680 Cambie Street
Vancouver, B.C.
V6P 6M9
(604) 323-7100

1 2 3 4 5 6 7 8 9 10

CANADIAN CATALOGUING IN PUBLICATION DATA

Frolick, Vernon, 1950–
  Fire into ice

ISBN 1-55192-232-0

  1. Fipke, C. E. 2. Geologists—Canada—Biography. 3. Diamond mines and mining—Canada. I. Title
QE22.F56F76 1999   551′.092   C98-911173-3

Printed in Canada

Raincoast Books gratefully acknowledges the support of the Government of Canada, through the Book Publishing Industry Development Program, the Canada Council and the Department of Canadian Heritage. We also acknowledge the assistance of the Province of British Columbia, through the British Columbia Arts Council.

CONTENTS

ACKNOWLEDGEMENTS

THIS BOOK is the product of many voices and visions. To all those who generously shared their experiences and freely gave their time, wisdom and insight that this book might be written, I am indebted. I would like to express a special thanks to the following people who will see their hand in the result: Leslie Paige, Maureen Duffy-Lewis, Lynne Leydier, Anne Snyder, Mary Gibson, Valerie Bonga, Nicholas Zaseybida, Ian Gibson, Bob Stathers, Dave L. H. Snyder, Jim Kupchenko, Dr. Chris Purton, Brian Hughes, Marc Tougas, Bruce Johnson, Gerald Roach, Alphonse Witteman, Dr. Walter Nassichuk, Dave MacKenzie, Jim Eccott, Marlene Fipke, Mark Fipke, Ed Fipke, Anna Fipke, Hugo Dummett, Ray Ashley and Brian Scrivener. I would, finally, like to express my deepest gratitude to Chuck Fipke, for allowing me to share his life, and to my brother, Larry Frolick, whose tireless editing and support made this book possible.

All omissions, errors and derelictions are mine.

VMF, January 1999

I FIRST met Charles (Chuck) Fipke before the discovery of the diamond pipes in Canada's Northwest Territories that made him famous. I was a guest in his crowded, modest home in Kelowna, British Columbia. After dinner, instead of the customary drinks and postprandial conversation, he dug into a closet packed with primitive artifacts and treasures collected from the tribes of Africa, New Guinea and the Amazon to retrieve a number of drums. Of different shapes and sizes, wrapped in stretched hides and tied with gut, the drums were matched to an equally eclectic group of guests.

With no further discussion or preparation, Chuck began to beat on a drum and to dance. Left free to join in or not as we pleased, we were soon, in any event, lost to him as he danced wildly, with an intense, otherworldly abandon.

I could see him then in the heart of the Pygmy Congo, dancing before the elephant hunt, in the heat, in the night.

In the grip of some driving need, unarticulated and perhaps even unknowable, oblivious to the presence of his guests, he continued to dance, unrestrained, as the vibrations of the drums, pounding hypnotically, infused the space with a wild energy. When finally, what seemed like hours later, he stopped – his shirt wet with sweat that ran freely down his body–and looked about him as though awakening from a dream, there was on his face an expression I had never seen before. A look so unusual I didn't recognize it.

That Charles Fipke set off the greatest mining-exploration rush in history was no accident. His discovery in the Barren Lands of northern Canada of one of the richest diamond fields in the world is the product of a vision that is his alone.

There is an aspect to Chuck's character – a force – that remains obscure. Beyond culture, family and personal history, there exists in some a drive that remains inexplicable: the silence of pure experience. In countless ways, this silence passes down through generations, taking from culture, blending in and out of culture, yet remaining always distinct. To the extent that history informs the present and our roots direct our future, there may be value, beyond mere curiosity, in understanding this silent reckoning – and its power in shaping our destinies.

TREPANIER BENCH,
CENTRAL BRITISH COLUMBIA, 1965

Eᴀᴄʜ morning, with a friend in the passenger seat, he would come screaming out of the mountains like a hurricane, headed toward school. With his "new" '53 Ford, Chuck Fipke was 18 when he decided on a new challenge: to see how fast they could get down the mountain. To set a record nobody could beat. Every day, they'd test each other's mettle and flirt with fate, adding a little more speed to the ride.

With Clarence watching the speedometer and recording their times, they'd gun the car over the edge of Trepanier Bench, airborne, leaving the farm in a cloud of dust, careening sideways around corners on two wheels. The back end would slide across the road and threaten to keep going, taking them backwards over the edge. Finally they'd burst forth out of the bush onto the highway and – the absence of Mounties permitting – race away up the highway to Kelowna.

Every day they went faster still, increasing their speed until they became prisoners in a steel box hurtling nearly out of control down the mountainside. The charge – the release of stress when they touched pavement, still alive and rolling – was the reward, and they laughed, giddy from the rush, all the way into their classes.

The two boys were quite different and talked about their futures. But for a few moments each morning, when they survived on adrenaline and luck, the real world did not extend beyond the next corner and they were bonded, living on its pure energy.

PART ONE

The Hole in Time

Papua New Guinea, 1970–72

His eyes were as a flame of fire;

And his feet were like brass, as if they had burned

in a furnace; and his voice

as the sound of many waters.

—REVELATIONS, 1:14–15

CHAPTER ONE

STAR MOUNTAINS, WESTERN PAPUA NEW GUINEA, SEPTEMBER 3, 1971

Ladi Williams watched the ends of the prop blades, shimmering distortion against the green. They had blade covers on their tips, but if they hit a branch too thick to cut through, the helicopter would spin itself into oblivion.

The jungle was formidable. In this flight from their base at Ok Tedi, 20 kilometres away, through the tortured ruggedness of the Star Mountains, the forest canopy seemed impenetrable. Under the equatorial sun, receiving more than nine metres of rainfall yearly, the rainforest lay like a living thing, hunkered down, breathing its own dark spirit into the land.

Finding a way to get down through it with the helicopter was nearly impossible, but Ladi had been doing it for years. Chuck was confident he could do it again. Before Kennecott brought him out to the wilds of New Guinea, Ladi had been the best helicopter pilot in Australia.

There was a small gap in the canopy ceiling, just wide enough for them to squeeze down into. Sinking slowly through the jungle, like an insect moving through a bush, they dropped down 10 metres into the growth. Their way further down blocked by another ceiling of vegetation, Ladi backed them up under a tree, squeezing them this way and that through gaps in the foliage. Then, he took them around the tree to another hole, which got them 10 metres closer to the ground, probing their way, a dragonfly hunting prey.

It was a tricky and dangerous descent, the jungle around them an infinite unknown. Of its nearly 10,000 species of plants, Chuck knew he could never hope to recognize more than a few, yet it was a marvel to behold. The richness and diversity of life was like nowhere else on Earth. Even the people of this country were more diverse than any other. In successive waves over the ages, migrations of different races had settled here. For 20,000 years, their offspring had remained, protected and isolated from each other in countless pockets and steep valleys ringed with smouldering volcanoes. So far, more than 700 distinct languages spread among thousands of tribes had been counted. Yet that was only the beginning. Most of the island remained unexplored.

A blade hit a branch suddenly with a *whamp* – and their hearts stopped. A sound like the rapid fire of a machine gun suddenly filled the air, hammering through them over the noise of the engine.

Bamp, bamp, bamp, bamp, bamp, bamp!

They froze.

Shredded leaves and smashed branches rained down over them, cut by the ends of the blade. But they were still airborne. It had been a small branch.

Ladi held the helicopter perfectly steady, hovering until the debris cleared. Then they continued their descent, snaking their way down through the jungle toward the Earth. Again the metal tips bit into a vine. Another heart-stopping machine-gun burst.

Still they descended.

Huge trees towered around them: pines, klinki and gum, some of them 75 metres tall. Reaching up through them in a tangled net were dozens of other varieties of trees, vines and flowering plants. Rafts of epiphytes grew in wild hypercoloured profusion, covering the canopy and upper limbs. The weight of orchids, ferns and other plants was heavier than the branches supporting them.

In the rotten, feral humidity, they could now see the leaf moulds on the earth beneath them, a metre thick in places.

The helicopter could not land – there was nowhere to touch down – but it could get them close enough to allow them to leap out. Chuck looked at the Natives behind him. Huddled in the back seat, the four men were terrified – frightened enough to all jump out at once if the door were opened, resolutely throwing themselves at the ground. Even the weight loss of a single person, jettisoned suddenly from a hovering helicopter, could cause it to spring up into the trees, where it would smash itself into tangled steel and bone in seconds. Four men jumping out at once would be impossible to adjust for. There was simply no room to manoeuvre.

Ordering the men not to move, Chuck climbed out first. Balancing carefully on the skid while Ladi adjusted for the weight shift, Chuck shinnied over, opened the back door from the outside and took the others out one at a time, helping them leap from the skid down to the ground.

Once free of its passengers, the helicopter began its jagged ascent through the jungle canopy to the clear sky. It would return soon to drop the portable camp Chuck had ordered. If they were too late for the evening rendezvous with the helicopter, they would set up the camp and spend the night. Chuck didn't plan on doing this, but the distances he wanted to cover today were great, and he would not be caught out at night here without protection. Quickly setting to work with their machetes, they cleared the undergrowth beside the stream for a landing pad for the helicopter when it returned. Then, shouldering their gear, they turned upstream and started climbing up into the lush hillside.

Chuck had made ambitious plans for the day. His intent was to hike all the way to the top of Mount Ian, following the stream, collect silt samples along the way, and get back down before nightfall to meet the helicopter.

A dark and dank tunnel stretched before them. They began climbing through it. The jungle quickly closed in over them and shut out the light. If not for the water at their feet and the path the stream cut through the forest, the journey would have been impossible.

The heat and humidity were indistinguishable from each other. Four degrees below the equator, the sun's rays burned straight down through the atmosphere in searing waves of full-spectrum radiation. It scorched unprotected flesh, but it gave life. The jungle fed on it, fought for it. Thrived in it. Life crawled, climbed and choked its way to the top of the canopy to break out of the darkness into the blinding light.

Movement cross-country along the jungle floor was unthinkable. From hair's-width vines and roots to towering white giants with enormous, webbed roots anchoring them, buttressed to a wet and unstable earth, the plants elbowed and jostled into every available space. Even with steel machetes, the effort needed to chop a path through this dripping jungle would soon defeat even the hardiest local.

The New Guineans were not explorers. Left on their own for thousands of years, they preferred to stay near their villages. Their own world ended at a spear's throw – at the border with their nearest hostile neighbour. Fearful and warlike, adjacent tribes engaged each other in endless battles and defended their own territories against the constant pressure of outsiders who probed, seeking space. It was a stable, dense, hostile social environment that had remained basically unchanged for thousands of years until the arrival of the Europeans.

Chuck climbed ahead of the others. He had brought four men with him, three to cut and one to carry, but the path was open over the water. Here they could move forward without having to clear brush.

They came to a rise in elevation. Bending low at a rock wall, he let the water cascade down over his head and shoulders, cooling him off. The sensation was wonderful. A jungle waterfall climb. For a moment, his mood lightened.

Above the sound of the water, the occasional shriek of a bird broke the silence, freezing the men in position. They listened with intensity. It was not love of birdsong that stilled them but the possibility of meat. Every call was the sound of protein. Food.

The birds of New Guinea were magnificent, with the most beautiful of all the bird of paradise. Treasured by Natives, their dried, feathered skins were used as currency throughout the country long before the European craze for their feathers put them on the brink of extinction in all the areas of contact. Since early childhood Chuck had had an attraction to birds. They had always been a part of his life.

The greater bird of paradise was his favourite. Its mating was altogether a spectacle. The elaborate feathering had only one purpose. The males, splashed in colour, would gather in a proud group around a single female. As she watched, they would parade themselves about her boldly, strutting with their wings outstretched, until, at her signal, they would freeze suddenly. While they held their positions in absolute stillness, she would move through them, inspecting each one minutely, as though they are artful sculptures, until she decided on the prizewinner, allowing him to mount her.

Chuck glanced back at his men. Although older than he was, they were all young, the average life span here being only 30 years. Those tribal fighting didn't kill, disease, especially malaria, claimed.

He had taken a couple of them into the bush before. Abani and Imba were men from the Native village located beside the base camp, and they had dressed for the expedition. Wearing thick breastplates woven from tightly bound strips of cane and pale, cream-coloured penis gourds, they were ready for battle. Unlike the breastplates, which would stop arrows and might deflect spears, the long, tapered gourds were not designed to protect or conceal vulnerable organs but to display their genitals in stiffly exaggerated proportions.

With a connectedness they felt to the birds, the men moved lightly, otherwise naked, through the forest, bouncing from rock to rock up the river. Their affinity with the birds, a spirit they recognized in themselves, was a common motif in their ceremonies. Their carvings – of fantastic bird men – half-human, half-air creature – were not "art" but signposts of their spiritual world.

Chuck was wearing his heavy hiking boots with steel cleats, shorts and a T-shirt. The way to travel was Native – naked – but not through the jungle up a mountain waterfall. As the villagers moved, their penis gourds, held erect with fibrous cords tied around their waists, posed a constant threat, should they fall, of impaling them.

They were a strange people, he thought. Hiking with them through the bush, even working with them at the camp and drinking with them at night in the canteen, it was impossible to know what they were feeling or thinking. Theirs was a different reality completely, as though he had dropped down, not just through a gap in the rainforest, but through a hole in time itself, thousands of years back into the Stone Age. Theirs was still the tribal, pagan world of mystery and magic, spirits and powers, where man's role was to divine the fearful forces of the world and attempt to harmonize with them.

Hiking with Stone Age men up a jungle mountain where no one had ever gone before was an experience out of this world. Absolutely exhilarating. Except for the heat, the humidity, the pounding in the ears.

Chuck's employers, Kennecott Australasia, hunters too, were not interested in birds or antique cultures. They were on a different hunt altogether. Theirs was a search for hidden treasures of the modern kind. Nor was Kennecott alone. Several hundred kilometres to the east, on Bougainville Island, the most easterly of New Guinea's islands in the North Solomon chain, its principal competitor, CRA of Australia, a subsidiary of the British giant Rio Tinto Zinc, was developing a huge body of copper it had unearthed there. CRA had already invested over 20 million Australian dollars in development costs and had nearly 10,000 people on the payroll. Commercial production was expected to begin sometime in mid-1972.

Although controversial on independence-minded Bougainville, the project was the darling of the government of Papua New Guinea. The royalties from that one copper field would rescue the country from its dependence on foreign aid and allow it to move toward economic self-sufficiency. No small feat.

It was a good year to be a geologist. Prospectors in New Guinea were seen as modern knights. Behind their advance guard lay the whole of the modern world. Saviours and conquistadors at once, they enjoyed certain privileges. Access to the outback areas was strictly controlled by the Australian administration in Port Moresby, and in the case of the simply curious and adventuresome, typically denied. Geologists alone were allowed unrestricted movement in the trackless jungle. Kennecott had its own "hit", a promising geologic hot spot, at Ok Tedi.

In the remote Star Mountains of the central cordillera, with peaks reaching 4,600 metres and all its lower elevations under dense, impenetrable jungle, Ok Tedi was in the most inhospitable and least explored region of Papua New Guinea. The Kennecott Copper Company, through its Australasia subsidiary, had found what appeared to be another huge copper deposit. The site promised the potential of Bougainville. Perhaps even better – the associated gold results were looking almost as valuable as the copper.

In 1971 Ok Tedi was still a small, cleared field of mud at the edge of a mountain plateau, and the company was still exploring the dimensions of the deposit. Or, rather, Chuck was. His boots, now soaked, still provided protection from the sharp rocks – and the parasitic worms that would quickly eat their way through the skin of his feet, up into his body, if given a chance.

The climbing was hard. The riverbed rose steeply. The temperature in the lowlands was over 90 degrees Fahrenheit. And the humidity, the evaporation of groundwaters from rain mixing with the damp breath of expired moisture from the jungle vegetation, was so high that movement itself was restricted. The air, thick and heavy, clung to them like mucous.

Occasionally the creek's flood banks had cut back the encroaching jungle enough to let some sunshine penetrate down to the water's surface, lighting up silvery showers and pools like crystal jewels. They were too tempting to resist, and the men sunk under the inviting surface to cool off. Cicadas started up and were quickly joined by other insects in a chorus of shrill sound.

Suddenly, inexplicably, they stopped. The jungle turned silent again. As though it were listening to the human footsteps, and ever watchful.

The water they splashed through was one of the mountain tributaries of the Fly, one of the mighty rivers that drained the southern slopes of the Star Mountains. At the base of the mountains it metamorphosed from a raging mountain river to a deep, sluggish channel that wound its way for hundreds of kilometres through flat lowlands, past majestic, 60-metre-tall Erima trees – the Native favourite for dugout canoes – to the coast. There the river, a swollen stream, oozed slowly through sago and mangrove swamps infested with poisonous snakes, ticks, dengue fever and malaria. There, too, in the river's estuary, lived the world's most fearsome crocodiles, creatures that hunted men and swam far out into the blue-green waters of the Coral Sea in search of live food.

Imba, one of the village men climbing behind Chuck, was a cannibal. Perhaps they all were, or had been. Although cannibalism was now strongly discouraged and no longer widespread, it was still practised in remote areas of Papua New Guinea where a boy's rite of passage into adulthood required that he kill. Children and women, easier to kill, were the preferred targets. The eating of their flesh, following other ritual ceremonies, ensured a healthy relationship with the spirit world, but just as commonly human meat was consumed simply as food. Everything that moved was killed and eaten; protein was scarce and highly valued.

Imba had worked for Chuck before, at the camp at Ok Tedi, and had described to him the taste of white flesh. Missionary meat. It was 10, 15 years ago, but he remembered the occasion clearly. He had had some expectation that the experience would be special, something really different – only to be sorely disappointed. The white meat had a strange taste to it. And it was salty. Black meat, he said, was better. Sweeter.

At the confluence of each side creek draining the slopes, Chuck stopped to take a sample. Having had only limited contact with white men, these New Guinea warriors watched Chuck with studied interest. There was no question of his power and station. He commanded helicopters and earth machines. He had tools – the purpose of which they could not fathom – and was, in almost every way, more foreign to them than they were to him.

That he was connected to the spirit world, there was no doubt. All things were. But the meaning of the sacred rituals, the rites and practices this white man followed to live in balance with his spiritual world, was a mystery to them. When he dug out stream sediment from the earth, carefully brushing the tiniest bits of heavier black sand that clung to the shovel into the sample bag, they could only stare and wonder. Here in his "gathering of the Earth" lay some secret of the white man's magic, some spirit appeasement of which they could only remotely guess.

It was getting late. Nobody would ever accuse Chuck of not working hard enough or fast enough. It was just that the country and the conditions he had to get through were so difficult. Even simple exertions drove up the body heat tremendously. Climbing steep rock walls and scrambling over boulders, the men were sweating profusely. The heat was more of a concern than parasites, leeches and poisonous things. The heat drained off body fluids, which were necessary to keep a person's chemistry in balance. At the rate they were perspiring, a person could slip easily from exhaustion to heat stroke. Chuck knew their salt losses were extremely high.

He watched the New Guineans for a moment. They were in better shape than he was. Harder. Tougher. More able to endure. Having spent their whole lives outdoors, they were as adapted to these conditions as any man could get. That was always his ultimate standard. How were the locals faring? When the villagers crouched to drink from the stream, so, too, did he. He had not packed bottled water. He did not have to share the hardships with them, but he did. They were in this together.

Now they were all drinking from the creek. If he got ill from it, he would deal with that later. His risks were no worse than theirs, but Chuck was concerned. His was the sole reason for their being there, and the urgency that pressed him was not shared by the others.

"Em i longwe?" Imba asked him in pidgin. Is it far?

"Longwe liklik," he answered, meaning literally "long way little" but understood to mean "not too far, not near."

Perhaps "too far" would have been the better answer. If they did not return down the mountain to the landing zone by dusk, the helicopter would leave without them, and darkness arrives suddenly at the equator. But the samples were important – and the last sample the most important of all.

They moved in single file. Chuck was now in second place behind Imba but forcing the pace by pressing them on. Imba was earning his money, cutting back the jungle that overgrew the stream in places. Suddenly he stopped. Carefully he put down his machete and took off his pack. The others, behind him, waited.

Free of his load, Imba glided ahead, placing his steps carefully, catlike, stalking something he had seen. Then he pounced, scrambling wildly after a thing that splashed and squirmed, trying to get away.

His shout of triumph broke them from the spell, and they rushed to see what he had caught. It was a great, brown, wide-bodied frog the size of a small pie. Imba held it with both hands from the sides, immensely pleased with himself as his companions looked on, their own expressions difficult to read. Bringing it up level with his face, he examined it carefully from side to side and then, opening his mouth, bit off the frog's head.

Chuck could hear the brittle crunching of frog bones as Imba happily munched down on his twitching meal. The other men watched, envious now, as Imba took the next bite – removing a leg and shoulder. A bit of flesh dangled from his thick lips as he chewed to make room for it in his mouth.

Impatient to get going but fascinated, Chuck watched intently with the others as Imba finished eating the whole frog before calmly picking up his machete and his gear. Taking the lead again, he continued up the riverbed, swinging heavily into the plants that blocked their path. When he was too tired to continue, Asiwa, the next cutter, took his place, the three cutters taking turns in the lead.

Chuck needed one last sample. Each sample added to the picture of the formation, geological history and mineralization of the region they were investigating. Minerals that broke free from their original deposits, sometimes traces of the pure metals themselves, would wash away downstream. Over time, hundreds or thousands of years, water could move these particles great distances. When analyzed later, a sand sample from a river's bed revealed the secrets of the rock types it flowed over. The presence of ore minerals in it pointed to upstream deposits.

Chemistry and physics were the tools used to decipher the clues, to find the trail and follow it back to its source. Most often the samples were barren and the effort futile. Occasionally a sample "kicked" in the lab, and when the "hit" proved out with an economic ore deposit, the results could be phenomenal.

The samples themselves were all-important. They alone would determine where the search would lead and how far it would go. Huge resources were spent just to collect them.

It would be easier, instead of climbing higher, to take a sample from underfoot and then go back. To say it came from the top. Who would ever know the difference? But lazy employees with bad samples quickly exhaust the limited resources of an exploration company. Worse, the sample that was missed might have been that one in thousands that held the key to a new mine. To a new economy. To survival.

Chuck despised quitters. Worse than useless, they were bloodsuckers who cheated those who trusted them. Whatever it took to get the job done – that was his standard.

Chuck glanced again at his watch. It was almost two o'clock. Late. The sun had crossed the zenith and was now on its way down. They had set out just after first light. With only 12 hours of daylight at the equator, it would be dark again at six. Eight hours up the mountain and four down. That was their schedule. Even less. Three and a half. The chopper pilot would only wait until 5:30, then he would leave. With or without them.

Chuck pulled out his map and plotted their new position, noting the distance left to go, farther up the mountain, away from the helicopter. They had reached the point of no return. To go on now meant they could not get back in time. But to go back now, down the mountain, would only mean he would have to return another day, that he had wasted a day, and all this effort! That was a major consideration.

There were others. The work was taking its toll. Even with all the water he was drinking, he could feel his energy sapping away. He would not let it affect his performance; he had tremendous reserves of energy and, beyond that, a willpower that would never admit defeat. But the villagers, too, were showing signs of fatigue.

He had a reputation to uphold. They pressed on.

The jungle completely enveloped the creek. The higher they climbed, the closer the banks grew. Each man took his turn cutting a way ahead; Chuck's shirt stuck like a second skin as sweat drained from his neck, back and chest. As the sun's rays softened, oblique, the air above the canopy began to cool, but the air within the jungle still cooked. Later, after sunset, the moisture would lift in hot sheets off the jungle and precipitate, forming into grey fingers of mist, then settle down to cover the forest with a thick shroud, the clammy nightly embrace.

But the day was still clear, the sky almost cloudless. Chuck hoped the weather would hold. It might, but he doubted it. A rainstorm would make things very difficult. With the approach of evening and the cooling of the sun, the insect chorus was rising to challenge the supremacy of the creek; by nightfall its roar would take over completely.

Chuck and his crew were travelling light. Expecting to be back at the rendezvous by late afternoon, Chuck had packed only lunch, long since gone. No spare clothes, no wet-weather gear, no tents or sleeping bags. No mosquito nets. The Natives had been agreeable until now, but they had not counted on being away so long either.

Again one of the men asked him, "Em i longwe?"

But now Chuck answered, "Klostu." Nearby.

They were easy to persuade. He was the boss. And these men, as fierce and strong as they were, were not going to be left behind. When he pushed on, they followed. They marched silently, and their steps were becoming heavy. Rather than jump from rock to rock, covering ground quickly, they now plodded stubbornly on. Even with the gain of altitude, the air remained thick, an oppression that sucked at what was left of their energy, making them dizzy with exertion and the loss of vital fluids.

An hour later, with numb fingers they scraped together another sample of wet sand from under the bed of the last important tributary creek. They bagged it, sealed it and packed it away into the load of one of the men. Their last sample. More weight to carry.

Chuck was pleased. He had accomplished everything he had set out to do. Now they could go back. It seemed impossible, and he was not going to admit it until he had to, but they were going to try to make the rendezvous with the helicopter. Or at least make it back to the landing zone, to their supplies. That was Chuck's new goal.

There were only two hours of daylight left. And they all knew how far they had to travel. They would really have to move. Chuck led the way, setting their pace down the mountainside.

At breakneck speeds, they leaped from ledge to ledge, rock to rock, using fresh reserves of energy now that their direction was reversed. When the water or mud was too deep, they crawled around it; otherwise they waded straight through. Along the edges of the banks above them, the jungle's growth was halted only by the ripping action of the river in flood. Now it was only a stream, but if rain came, it would rage again within minutes.

Chuck was pushing them past all limits. His compact, muscled body moved with surprising ease over the land. Occasionally he glanced back to see how his companions were faring, but he did not slow his pace for them. It was for them to keep up. They, too, were anxious to get back.

They descended for an hour before he conceded they could not do it. They would never make the helicopter, he realized. Yet he did not slacken his pace. Still rushing headlong down the mountain, he was hoping they could at least make it back to their drop site before dark. There, the portable camp was waiting for them – tents, sleeping bags, food and mosquito nets. It was a haven.

If they could get there …

The moist air rising in hot waves off the jungle all afternoon had been forming overhead into dark, rolling clouds. Chuck cursed. The good weather had not held. The clouds began to leak. The rain would make little difference to their comfort – they were already drenched with sweat and river water – but they were moving through the jungle down a watercourse. It was the mountain's drainpipe, and the high-water mark was well above their heads. If the water rose and pushed them out of the creekbed, they would be trapped in the thick of the jungle – the creekbed was the only route back down the mountain. They raced desperately ahead of the prospect.

When the clouds finally burst, the torrent released from the sky crashed in sheets over them. The creek rose quickly. Brown and frothy, it swirled around their feet, flowing faster than they could move. It began to obscure details and hide the rocks, forcing them to slow down. Their descent was slippery and steep, with rock cliffs and great holes to climb down and around. Their progress became slower and slower, each step more treacherous than the last.

They were miles yet from the landing site when the last of the light failed and darkness closed in. With it, the temperature began to drop quickly while the heavy, dark, pounding rain continued to pour down.

Still they pushed on, one careful step at a time. As Chuck had feared, the flow of the creek had become a raging chute of black water that would drag a man away if he attempted a crossing. Nearing the upper bank and continuing to rise, the water pushed them closer and closer to the jungle.

Hanging on to the roots and branches that lined the bank, they felt their way through the night, one handhold after another. Exhausted and numbed, they inched down the mountain, slipping and sliding in the muck. Counting on fate for safe handholds and sure footholds, they kept going, moving at a crawl.

Although it was pitch dark, they were in no condition to camp, nor were they equipped to. There was no telling how long it would rain. Hours or days. Last year it had rained on 339 days. Intent on moving ahead through the night, Chuck ignored the messages his body was giving him to stop and rest. But he could not give in. There was no choice. The only relief lay in making it to the supplies.

The darkness was total, and the rain, cooler now, continued relentlessly. It was impossible to see. Passing a dead tree that was glowing with phosphorescence, Imba ripped off a bright branch and, holding his natural glow stick high for them to follow, took the lead.

From handhold to handhold, groping ahead in the dark, sliding in the mud, Imba kept shouting out "Lukautim gut!" – be careful! – every time his footing slipped, as their way became ever more dangerous.

"Lukautim gut!"

Chuck was concentrating on following the glow stick when it suddenly disappeared. He heard a splash and a cry. Screaming for help, Imba had fallen over a waterfall and was being washed away downstream! Imba's fist tightened on the glow stick; they could see the light wedged between some rocks and rushed down to rescue him.

It was enough. The next accident might kill them.

They climbed away from the edge of the water and, with their backs to the jungle, squatted over the ground that sloped steeply down toward the raging torrent. While the rain poured down over them, they huddled for warmth, their only comfort the heat from each other's bodies. The rank smell of sweat was overpowering. Even a day hiking the creek and showering in rainfall did not wash away a lifetime of built-up body odours.

Shivering miserably in the mud, the men knew they had no choice. They had to wait out the night in the hope that dawn would bring relief. With their bodies exhausted and immobilized, their exposed flesh now became host to legions of hungry insects, crawling and squirming through the mud to find them. Even in the rain, with the sky flooding the Earth, the lure of warm blood, the very smell of their breath, drew in flying creatures. The jungle would not leave them alone.

Weakened and dizzy, the need for continued effort gone, Chuck's body began to react. As the night wore on, the cold Earth drawing out his last reserves, his resistance slipped away, and he was grateful for the gift of body heat that came from the others, pressed tightly together. He barely noticed the mosquitoes biting. Such a minor discomfort.

What they took would not hurt him. It was what they left behind that would. Some carried the parasite *Plasmodium falciparum*, one of the world's oldest and deadliest plagues. Local mutations of the parasite in the Star Mountains of New Guinea had produced an especially virulent strain of the disease. But Chuck was not paying much attention to the mosquitoes. He was trying to control his shivering. He had a new goal: surviving the night.

CHAPTER TWO

SYDNEY, AUSTRALIA, MAY 25, 1970

Chuck's sojourn in New Guinea had begun over a year earlier, in the spring of 1970, in what seemed another lifetime, under a different sky entirely. The family had made a stop-over in Sydney, Australia, to meet Chuck's new bosses. Bob Hutchison, the president of Kennecott Australasia, had planned a reception at the American Club. Chuck was hesitant – they had a young son to look after. Bob promised a sitter.

"Well, I just got out of university," Chuck protested. "Like, I don't even have anything to wear, hey?"

Sydney required no adjustment. As they drove through the city, the young couple was constantly reminded of their last home, back in Vancouver. Like Vancouver, Sydney was a modern port with an inner harbour, exclusive oceanfront properties, shimmering sailboats and a commercial centre of towers. With nearly identical colonial influences, even the Victorian architecture was similar. To the west of the city, 80 kilometres away, the Blue Mountains rose up to conceal the secrets of the interior, just as the Coast Mountains pressed Vancouver to the sea.

"They actually turn blue," Bob explained as he gave them a quick tour of the city. Sitting quietly in the back seat of the Mercedes, Chuck and Marlene were feeling distinctly out of place. Bob was in black tie and his wife in a formal evening gown. Chuck was wearing the only jacket he had ever owned: the sports coat he was married in. Over the years, it had gotten a little threadbare and its fit somehow too tight.

"They're covered in eucalyptus and turpentine trees," Bob was saying. "And when the sun bakes down, they cook, releasing a blue vapour which fills the forest. Quite dangerous, really. On extremely hot afternoons the gas can explode. Spontaneous combustion. The trees are built to withstand the blast, but not us!"

Inside the pastel stucco club, the men wore dinner jackets and the women expensive cocktail dresses, and all were gambling – a form of entertainment Chuck had not experienced, money never having been plentiful enough to allow him the luxury of risking it to chance. When Bob dropped a coin into a one-armed bandit, Chuck's reaction was immediate.

"Careful! You might lose that!"

Dinner was Australian lobster, another new experience, and Chuck looked at his row of cutlery with some bewilderment. In Canada he had been free to eat steaks, thrown directly into a fire to cook, with his bare hands, and nothing more complicated than knives and forks had confronted him before. Marlene nudged him to use his napkin and quietly indicated the correct utensils. The battle with the lobster, though, was a difficult one, and the creature, although dead, almost finished him.

Chuck was looking forward to getting into the jungle.

Toasts to send him off and stories about the fatal Rockefeller expedition followed, with jokes about headhunters and cannibals, but it was the talk of the Kukukukus, which they pronounced cooker-cookers, that intrigued him the most.

"They're the worst," declared one of the men, an old hand in Papua New Guinea. He held the table's attention, "The most notorious killers in all the territory. Small men, almost like pygmies, they used to raid over thousands of square miles hunting people for their heads and meat! Their last mass slaughter and cannibalism was only two years ago! But they're tame now. Just don't go wandering off into the country," he warned Chuck. Some of the men laughed. They all knew he was going to be living in the bush.

Two days later, they landed in Port Moresby – the ragged port capital of Papua New Guinea, only a few degrees below the equator – their new home. A Kennecott representative picked them up at the airport for a brief tour before dropping them at the apartment the company had prepared for them.

What a dramatic change from Sydney! Marlene and Chuck looked at each other. The Australian administration kept Port Moresby well run and ordered, but still, it was a small expatriate population running a Third World country. Indeed, even "Third World" had connotations of familiar infrastructure and development. Most of Papua New Guinea was still Stone Age. The air smelled of tropical decay, diesel fumes and garbage fires.

As their driver talked, he drove them through the shantytown slums that were growing around the old city. Of a population of 40,000 Native inhabitants, nearly 10,000 were recent arrivals from "the country," he told them. Mostly young men, without wives, gardens, marketable skills or jobs, they survived by support of their own clan systems.

"Now, don't go walking about by yourself here," he cautioned. "Especially at night, when these fellows are piss-drunk; they can be pretty dangerous!"

Marlene had no intention of doing that. Even by day, white women were targets. There was status to be gained by raping one. But Chuck laughed. He'd go anywhere he wanted!

At the Native market on Koki Beach they drove slowly between rows of tall coconut palms planted by the Australians years earlier for shade. The white beach sloped gently into a small, perfect harbour sheltered by a sandy peninsula that curved gracefully around the water, protecting it. Small coastal ferries and diesel traders floated on their own reflections in the warm green water, and ringing the inside of the peninsula, pulled up to shore, were dozens of handmade Native "houseboats" festooned with bright red cloth. Large sea-going outriggers with decks made from wooden planks laid across their gunwales and extending precariously out over the sea on both sides, they were roofed over in canvas. Entire families lived, slept and cooked in these floating huts.

Under the trees, scattered over the sand, were pulpy dried-grass blankets, open tables and jerry-built stalls selling an assortment of roots: taro, sweet potato, manioc. Small piles of lumpy firewood were spread out for sale in the sand, pennies a bundle. Coconuts, oranges, bananas of all shapes and sizes, fresh fish, bunches of limes, exotic fruits and nuts still attached to their branches, squash, melons and corn – their guide pointed out the bargains as they slowly cruised by.

Occasionally, as though haemorrhaging uncontrollably in the horrible last stages of some fatal disease, a man or woman would lean over to cough and spit out a long, gelatinous string of red fluid. The Natives were rotting from the inside! As they watched, they saw more and more people who appeared to be afflicted. When the Natives opened their mouths, they exposed black teeth and blood-bright gums. It looked contagious.

"Betel nut," their driver explained – and pointed out the bunches of nuts from the areca palm. "It's called buai in pidgin. Awful stuff, really, very bitter. You chew it with lime leaves and it drugs you up. Numbs the pain … You want to stop and try some?"

Chuck didn't. Although recreational drug use had been exploding in popularity around the world since 1967, he was not particularly interested in it. Betel chewing seemed especially vile. Why would people want to tranquillize themselves, to deaden their lives? If anything, one should want to live more, harder, faster.

Chuck was extremely excited by everything he saw, Marlene less so. The faces on the streets were nearly all black, and some of the women were naked but for grass-fibre skirts. Here and there, the white face of an expat moved purposefully through the crowd. They drove past playing fields that Chuck recognized at once. They were so out of place, he had to ask to confirm it.

"Rugby?" It seemed unlikely.

"It's the national sport here," the guide answered.

With its tribal and warrior roots, it was the perfect game for New Guinea.

"We introduced it to the Natives about 10 years ago and they really took to it. Fanatics now. Hard to say who's more dangerous, the players or the fans! Sometimes the whole bloody thing blows up in your face. You never know minute from minute how it's going to turn out. You'd better just steer clear of the games, if you ask me. Not many white folk go to them anyhow. Bloody rough game!"

Raised up on stilts, as virtually every house was for ventilation and bug control, theirs was one of four apartments in a single-storey, wood-frame building. The other tenants were all company employees or, more correctly, the wives and children of employees. The men spent little time there. Chuck, like them, would be living out in the jungle.

He could hardly wait.

Two days later the plane ferrying the men to their work sites was flying low. Hugging the coast northeast of Port Moresby, around the Gulf of Papua to the huge delta swamplands of the Fly River, it turned to follow the river north into the interior. Then, for almost 900 kilometres, it traced the route of the Fly River before landing at Kiunga, where Kennecott had set up its base camp. A supply centre for the region, Kiunga was an inland port accessible by boat from the sea.

To the north, climbing above Kiunga, the land made a series of knifelike folds, rising, as though seeking flight, toward the Star Mountain Range. Spanning the border of Papua New Guinea and West Irian, this Range was part of an unbroken chain that ran the length of New Guinea from the distant Vogelkop Peninsula in West Irian to the Owen Stanley Range, southeast of Port Moresby. Accessible only by foot or helicopter, half-buried in trackless jungle, it was home to thousands of Stone Age villagers.

Waiting at the edge of the tiny airstrip was Chuck's helicopter. His pilot was Ladi Williams, an Australian who greeted Chuck enthusiastically, calling him "Bossy" for fun and mimicking a Native New Guinean. Ladi was a live wire but coolly professional, and Chuck took to him immediately.

As they climbed up out of Kiunga, Ladi filled him in on the camp gossip in a running commentary that competed with the scenery outside through their Plexiglas bubble – near-vertical rock walls that soared up to disappear into the clouds.

"The food's the shits but we managed to bang up a canteen and it's always stocked. Ah, the nights aren't so bad now. Worst of all is the bloody rain! When it's really coming down, ya can't see a fuckin' thing. Bloody dangerous flying in it, I'll tell ya' – no worries though, mate! I have a fondness for this life as if it's the only one I'll get!"

The slope below them, ragged with rocks, tilted at an impossible angle. Watered by a daily deluge of hot pounding rain and cooked in the dull insinuating heat, it was laden with a surreal growth, not a shadow of a space anywhere. There was absolutely nowhere to land the helicopter.

"Do you?" Chuck asked. He could not imagine anyone flying without good visibility, especially in this green torrent. He had flown enough in the Canadian Barren Lands and the unforgiving mountains of British Columbia to know that it wasn't always the men with mettle who survived. "Like, in Canada, hey, we say pilots are either old or bold, but never both, eh?"

Ladi shot back a knowing look and grinned. "Listen, mate, this is the best day we've had in weeks! There's no safe way to fly in this country. It never stops raining and we're out every bloody day."

As they neared the peak of Tabubil at 2,074 metres, Chuck spotted the drill camp near the top. Buzzing over it, Ladi dropped down along the mountain to the base camp far below that Chuck would be calling home for the next 18 months. At 1,200 metres, the men had a long climb each shift just to get to the drill sites.

They landed at the edge of an area of a couple of hectares had been cleared of trees and levelled along one edge to form a plateau. The camp commanded a view down the valley, over land that fell away sharply at the edge of the clearing before rising higher and steeper into the next fold of mountains towering over them.

They were just south of the mountain divide that separated the northern watershed of the Sepik River from the southern watershed of the Fly. The water running off their camp flowed south into the Alice River, a tributary of the Fly. Around them, the Star Mountain range dwarfed their "hill" with peaks rising yet another 1,800 metres higher through dark fog and cloud.

They had named their camp after the nearby native village. "Ok Tedi" (pronounced Awk-Teddy) was a collection of stick and palm huts, bamboo sheds and portable buildings flown in by helicopter along with fuel drums, spools of cable, core boxes and drill rigs. Except for the setting and the several black men walking around naked, the camp itself was a familiar scene, one that could have been lifted straight out of the Canadian bush.

Chuck was exuberant. To stand at Ok Tedi and look around, inhaling the warm, moist air, was to arrive at another world, as distant from the Western world as a person could be. Elsewhere over the ages, people had come together, willingly or not, assimilating into larger socialized communities, part of ever greater political and economic unions. New Guinea was different. Settled by successive waves of people and races as the ice ages raised and lowered the seas, it was a country whose ruggedness had kept hundreds of ancient cultures isolated for thousands of years. Of the entire total of languages still spoken in the world, fully one-third were here. Not a lost island, but an entire world. An ancient, pre-Christian, pagan world that had, until recently, routinely practised head-hunting and cannibalism.

Pressed up near the West Irian border and tucked against the Star Mountains, Ok Tedi was in one of the last blank areas in Papua New Guinea's map. From Port Moresby, Chuck had seemingly travelled backwards in time, to the point from which all humankind had sprung thousands of years ago. It was thrilling.

But now he could waste no more time in thinking about the country. He could explore later; there would be time enough for everything. His first priority was the job. He had been told he was expected to do the work of two men. That was enough of a present challenge.

CHAPTER THREE

OK TEDI

SEVERAL months before Chuck arrived, Kennecott had discovered the existence of the copper deposit at Ok Tedi. Finding it was an application of chemistry, physics, luck – and a feeling for copper.

Metals had long ago become man's most useful discovery since fire and agriculture. Demarcating a major stage of human progress over the ages, the power of copper had been one of the earliest discoveries, leading man out of the Stone Age. Industrial man had more than peaceful uses for copper. Finding and developing copper deposits had become the worldwide focus of the mining industry. The main constituent element of brass, copper was essential for the manufacture of bullet casings and other modern military projectiles. Across the China Sea to the northwest, "copper" was raining down daily over Vietnam in a raging metal storm – so much more effective than wooden spears and stone arrowheads.

Although copper was widely distributed as a fractional trace element, concentrations rich enough to warrant commercial extraction were rare. Kennecott had several advantages over its competitors. It owned the world's largest underground copper mine, at El Teniente in Chile, which provided the company with more than experience in copper: it financed new ventures. El Teniente was the source of the company's cash.

Just as important, through secret research conducted in its laboratories in the United States, Kennecott had developed, and now carefully guarded, technologies, like Jack Gower's leach-capping interpretation analysis, that allowed it to assess the commercial viability of copper deposits with a minimum of cost. It was to learn these secrets that Chuck had joined Kennecott. This was the hook that had brought him to New Guinea.

Chuck had begun his study of geology indifferent to the field, in the beginning seeing it only as a source of income. Then, year by year, experience after experience, he had been drawn in, deeper and deeper, until it had captured him completely and he had become its willing disciple; the science, his master.

For geology was not the study of a static Earth, inert masses of matter, like picking through a dead carcass. No. It was an investigation into the mysterious forces attracting elements, the chemistry of atomic particles. Science was the new realm of the explorer – perhaps it had always been. What he was now learning, day by day, was how the dynamic forces of the Earth played – ever changing and complex forces that were the key to the universe, the foundation of life itself. This Chuck had come to understand, and he had become so committed he saw no reason whatsoever not to risk his own life for an all-important sample. In him, the drive to know was surging.

In geology copper was in, and Chuck had specialized in the field of porphyry copper deposits, the type Kennecott had developed in Chile and was now exploring in Ok Tedi. In fact, his honours thesis, although still incomplete, was on just such deposits. He would complete it, he promised himself, when he had time. Right now, he had more important things to do; he had to learn his job – and quickly. He was now a boss, and the purpose of the entire operation at Ok Tedi was to explore this deposit.

As Kennecott and Chuck well knew, ore deposits worldwide were not random but followed structures or rules that, if understood, could be applied to broadly predict where other deposits might lie. Copper's primary global occurrences were along the edges of the continental plates bordering the North and South Pacific Oceans.

Knowing the genesis of copper deposits was just as important as knowing their ranges, and in the final analysis, when the whole of the South Pacific Islands chain might conceal the potential deposit, one had to learn exactly what to look for.

Like all such deposits, Ok Tedi's had as its origin a historical eruption of molten magma from deep in the Earth toward the surface but not actually extruding over it, as lava did. Under tremendous pressures and at temperatures of 1,200 degrees Celsius, the magma began to cool as it rose through the Earth. As it cooled and entered environments of relatively lower pressure, minerals with high melting points began to grow in the magma, crystallizing out of the liquid mass. As it continued to rise, cooling and expanding with the decreased pressure, new minerals formed, and when the magma was cooler still, the feldspar mineral groups, with lower melting points, crystallized – one of the principal constituents of granite. With the magma still rising and cooling, at 573 degrees Celsius, its own melting point, quartz, the other major constituent of granite, crystallized out.

However, even at this cooler temperature, the volatile elements, including the metals, were still in a liquid and gaseous state. The next transformation was the most crucial one – something no one yet knew, something key to the understanding of the nature and extent of the Ok Tedi deposit. If this mass of crystallized minerals, molten liquids and gases comprising the magma, on its way toward the surface, passed through surrounding rock that was itself porous, having been fractured along fault lines, the escape of the metal-rich vapours from the magma into the narrow, cooler chambers and cracks of the faulted host rock would allow them to build up and slowly crystallize out into rich concentrations of metals. Gold as well as copper would fill the cracks.

So there had to be a hard, broken cap over the rising magma at the right depth. Kennecott knew it was over a copper deposit, but the dimensions and extent of the ore reserves buried inside Tabubil Mountain were unknown. Whether the deposit was of a size and concentration suitable for commercial development was the issue. It had to be very rich to justify the construction of a mining city in the heart of New Guinea. The company was hoping for concentrations of copper between one and two percent. More would be fantastic, but a mine might still be feasible with a copper grade as low as 0.70 percent. No one yet knew the extent of it.

That was for Chuck to determine. It was the reason Kennecott had brought him here. He was not the only geologist working at the site – there was some rotation – but when he was, and it was often, he was in charge of up to six drill sets on the deposit site and nearly one hundred men.

He was 23 years old.

The drillers were all expats, mostly Aussies and Canadians; a few Europeans worked among them as well. The Native New Guineans assisted the drill crews and performed odd jobs around the camp. Although Chuck found them strange, distant men, they followed orders and worked without complaint. They even drank with the others nightly in the canteen, but they remained a world unto themselves, studying the behaviours and relationships of the white men they worked beside. They spoke no English, and neither Chuck nor the other expats learned the local language. It was difficult to communicate with them, let alone try to understand what the New Guineans thought.

There was, however, a common tongue: New Guinea pidgin. An invented language drawn primarily from English, it had fewer than 2,000 words, was easy to pick up and permitted communication at a basic level over a wide range of subjects. Although it was condemned by some outsiders as an insulting colonial heritage, its usefulness across a country of 700 distinct and competitive languages ensured its continued success. Everyone spoke pidgin. As a language in which to issue directions and orders, it was more than adequate.

There were five drill crews working around the clock; Chuck had to determine where they should drill, at what angle and to what depth. In order to find out the underlying geology – where exactly the intrusive granitic pluton intersected the host rock, and the nature and extent of the fault system containing the richest veins of ore – he had to strategically probe the earth with drills, examining the fault structures, mapping rock types and storing the cores. Gradually the ore body – a massive whale lying in a sea of rock – took shape. Working with Dubu Balum, a Native New Guinean from the coastal area of Madang who had been western-educated and was a qualified draftsman, Chuck also surveyed and mapped out the entire surface area. It kept him occupied.

Soon after Chuck arrived, the company flew in John Wilson, the head of Kennecott's geological research department from Salt Lake City, and a scientific crew. Kennecott's top scientists came to the jungle to share the secret of their leach-capping technology originally developed by Chuck's old professor and mentor, Jack Gower.

Pure elements like copper occur rarely in nature. Instead, a free copper atom combines chemically with other elements to form compounds. At Ok Tedi, the copper in the deposit had combined with elements of iron, sulphur, hydrogen, oxygen and calcium to form several different copper ore minerals. What Jack Gower had discovered in his original research of such porphyry copper deposits was that when the ancient paleoclimatic conditions were very hot and wet, the ore would "rust." That is, the iron and sulphur, attracted to the oxygen atoms in the water, would oxidize, combining with the oxygen to form new compounds.

Sulphur dioxide was then formed naturally, which, when combined next with hydrogen and oxygen, became sulphuric acid, itself highly corrosive and a vigorous oxidizing agent. This powerful acid would leach the copper down to the groundwater table, which then neutralized the acid, causing the copper in it to precipitate as a "blanket" of copper sulfide, which was in turn eroded down, leached and combined into new minerals.

And so the process went, a chain of chemical reactions that constantly transformed the minerals, stripping them of atoms, replacing them with others and building new compounds.

What was remarkable about the analysis was its practical application. Understanding the chemical chain of events was one thing. Much more importantly, using the methods designed by Gower, an analysis of the resulting leached surface minerals could determine or predict not only what the primary copper grade was, but also what the enrichment would be at depth – without drilling.

Gower's method was cost-effective and so accurate that the company had used it on more than a dozen copper sites in Argentina to do preliminary calculations of their copper grades. Concluding they were all too low to be of commercial value, they abandoned them. The proof came fast that it was right: every time it walked away from a low-grade deposit, a half-dozen other companies would rush in to acquire the abandoned claims, completely perplexed as to why Kennecott would drop known copper deposits without drilling them. Floating new issues of shares to raise exploration capital, one after the other these companies exhausted all their investors' money on properties that, after expensive drill programs, proved to be useless. No surprise to Kennecott. When the grades looked good – as they did at Ok Tedi – the company embarked on an extensive study of the deposit, using conventional techniques in addition to its new technology.

By the time John Wilson flew back to the United States after a couple of weeks in the jungle, leaving the leach-capping analysis of Ok Tedi for Chuck to perform, Chuck was on his way to becoming a world-class expert in the field. Adding the leach-capping study to his already heavy workload left little time for anything else. He was up before dawn every morning, barely pausing to drink in the oxygen-rich air, and he was off, with a hundred details to attend to. He understood the theories and had gained some experience as a summer student, but the hard, real challenge of Ok Tedi was to apply everything he knew. And if he did not have an answer, to find one fast.

Although he was alone in New Guinea, he knew he was being watched. How well he did here, the reputation he would earn, would become his calling card. As in all things, he was passionate about winning this play. Now that he was in the game, he was not going to quit until he came out on top. He would not allow himself to make mistakes, and with the pressures of running the camp, he did not tolerate his time being wasted. Sometimes he stepped on other people's toes.

Chuck was out searching the site for one of the drill bosses to give him the new targets he had worked out. Bad enough, he had to spend time looking for him; Chuck found him chatting in pidgin with one of the Natives. The driller, like Chuck, was wearing the camp "uniform": shorts, a short-sleeved shirt for the heat, a poncho worn loose like a cape for the ever-present rain, and heavy, steel-spiked work boots to give grip in the greasy mud. The Native was barefoot and naked except for his "penis cone".

Wasting no more time, Chuck came up between them and, avoiding pleasantries, got down to business. As he was talking to the driller, he sensed the villager standing close by his elbow. Crowding him, the man tapped at Chuck's shoulder timidly. Irritated at being interrupted while he was talking, Chuck barked at him in what had become the typical expatriate manner of dealing with Natives at Ok Tedi.

"Don't interrupt me! Me talkin!" Chuck roared, continuing his discussion with the driller until, again, he felt a gentle tap on his shoulder. The faintest touch. Furious at a second interruption, he exploded at the man.

"C'MON! DON'T INTERRUPT ME!"

In pidgin, to be sure he understood, Chuck added, "YU SAVE?"

Once more he resumed his conversation, completely ignoring the village man still standing patiently at his elbow. Only when Chuck was finished his business and stepped back away from the two men did he realize that he had been standing on the villager's foot. With his heavy soles and steel cleats, Chuck could not feel the flesh and bone under his boots. Too timid to speak out, too awed by power to protest, the villager had been standing in quiet agony as Chuck's cleats had ripped through his skin and dug into his bone.

CHAPTER FOUR

HUMAN MEAT

THE men spent their evenings in the canteen under the generator lights, out of the night, drinking SPs. South Pacific beer came in two colours. Depending on his colour preference, a man would call out for either a "greenie" or a "brownie," tell his stories and fade away. The New Guineans were paid the equivalent of only a couple of dollars a day – Australian national policy at the time. The other men all pitched in to buy them drinks, and the villagers joined them nightly.

The Australians were rough in their treatment of New Guineans: rude and forceful. Initially Chuck thought it a characteristic of the Australian male, but as time went on, working and socializing with the village men, first in the canteen and later, on occasion, in the "men's houses" in their villages, he observed that aggression had a fundamental role in their culture. The men were very aggressive with one another and particularly so toward their women. There was a total absence of the usual western courtesies and never any public display of affection. Kindness and politeness were never reciprocated – indeed, the overseer who employed them at Ok Tedi lost all respect among the Natives. Only a weak man shows gratitude and offers praise; currying favour. A truly powerful man wields power, and it was the naked display of power that impressed them the most.

What surprised Chuck was how positively they responded to being treated aggressively. As long as things were being run the way they were supposed to – as the villagers expected – relations were good. They expected to be treated the same way by their white bosses as they were by their own chiefs. Even *more* forcefully by the whites. After all, were they not more powerful than the chiefs?

Once he broke the threshold of power, by being forced to issue commands – directing orders to human beings to do his bidding – Chuck found the role comfortable. Before long it began to feel natural. Once released, his own aggressive nature and competitiveness found a perfect outlet in Papua New Guinea. It would be hard, later, when he left New Guinea, to readjust to the western rule of practising egalitarianism. For all the expatriates, the colonial experience had its own corrupting influence, and a return to civilization was never the same afterwards – from near gods to mere citizens.

Controlling the white crews was another story. As the weeks drifted into months Chuck noticed a gradual decline in morale. Their work schedule was three full weeks in, one week out; the married men generally spent the time with their families in Port Moresby, while the single men usually went to the beach at Cairns. Even after breaks, their moods hardly improved. They complained inces-

santly in the nightly canteen about the rain, the mud, the work and their meagre lives, searching constantly for a way out, dreaming about women. When they
began to show disinterest in the quality of their work and to slack off, Chuck felt
compelled to act.

It was not the prolonged periods of isolation at the camp or the oppression
of the jungle or the weather that had gotten under their skin. As he saw it, it was
a failure of leadership. The responsibility for keeping up the men's spirits and
helping them maintain a sense of pride in their work rested with the company.
The conditions in the camp were a given. They could not be changed. Only the
men's attitudes toward them could. In shoring up those attitudes, Kennecott was
failing miserably.

It was a classic case, Chuck deduced, of needing to support the troops in the
field. Sitting at the drafting table in the operations shed, with the rain hammering
down on the tin roof, he composed an angry letter to Keith Holly in Port Moresby,
Kennecott's top manager in New Guinea, blasting him. In point-blank terms,
Chuck wrote that the company's managers in Sydney had to "get off their butts
and come to Ok Tedi and see what's happening!"

"How can the company expect to run the project from a city hundreds of
miles away in another country?" he demanded. The letter went out with the regular helicopter supply run.

Chuck had another concern. The Australian mining company CRA was
already in the final phase of the exploration of its Bougainville Island copper
field. The ore reserves there were estimated to be high enough to balance the
country's budget for the first time ever, 120 million Australian dollars' worth of
ore annually. Chuck secretly hoped Ok Tedi would rival Bougainville. CRA was
certain to go ahead with its mine. His own competitive nature made him want
to push his company to redouble its efforts, to get its own mine going! But Kennecott seemed comfortable with the pace of the work and in no hurry to change
things. That, too, made him angry.

It had been four months since any of the company's senior managers had
been to the site. At least three months too long, Chuck figured. Yet, after firing
off his letter, Chuck began to have second thoughts. Perhaps he had been too
hasty? Ordering the locals around was one thing, but these were his own bosses.
He had to remind himself that he was an employee.

Within the week they arrived, wondering what the fuss was all about. The
managers looked around, met the men, patted their backs and flew back to
Sydney, not to return again for another five months. Rather than firing Chuck,
they rewarded his ambitions with new responsibilities. Annan Cook, a well-
known earth scientist and former Rhodes Scholar, was flown in to do the calculations of the ore reserves. Chuck was assigned to work with him. As well, they
granted Chuck two wishes. They agreed to allow him to assist geologist David
Jordt in running a heavy-mineral sampling program in the region and to change
his work schedule. After six months, the routine had become tedious. Three
weeks in, working at Ok Tedi, and one week out, living in Port Moresby with

Marlene, then back to Ok Tedi for three more weeks left no room for excitement. He knew his job well enough now; the pressure was off. He could do it all. In fact, he could and wanted to do much more.

New Guinea remained darkly mysterious. As he trudged up the creeks and over the mountain at Ok Tedi, he studied the countryside intently. From the air, the hidden world and strange people continued to tantalize his imagination. The desire to explore the country became an obsession. While the others wanted to get out at every opportunity – as far as they could – Chuck wanted to get deeper in. With only one week off every month, there was never enough time to explore anything but the country around Port Moresby. And he had seen that already. Doubling up his schedule, doing six straight weeks without a break, would allow him more time to get into the country, two weeks at a time.

The company agreed, and the world suddenly opened up for him.

Over the course of the next year, Chuck, Marlene and their son Mark, who had turned four in August, began exploring the interior of Papua New Guinea, travelling thousands of miles and visiting dozens of villages. With the exception of an old, used Datsun car he bought, all the money he made Chuck spent on airfare and Native carriers as they wandered through the high, dry savanna of the eastern highlands and lived with the Kukukukus in their villages. Long, slender Native dugouts took them up the Kikori River into the southern highlands. From the port city of Lae, they travelled by motorboat up the Markham River. There was nowhere Chuck would not go and nothing he would not try. If an area was closed off, deemed too dangerous by the authorities, he contrived to get into it. Secrets and forbidden zones for him held an irresistible attraction.

There were more gentle trips, too. On an invitation from Dubu Balum, the Native draftsman from Ok Tedi, they flew to Madang on the north coast and from there travelled by ocean outrigger canoe to Balum's home, an isolated village on an island lagoon surrounded by coral reefs. There, for two weeks, they slept on the floor of a palm-leaf hut, ate fish, taro root and coconut, and participated in the life of the village.

The men and women had separate lives, highly segregated, sleeping in different quarters and dancing with their own gods. Their daily routines, too, were different. While Marlene kept watch over Mark and tried to entertain herself with the other women, Chuck went off with the men – racing over the sea in outriggers, fishing and free-diving the reef.

At night, when the men produced tall, narrow hourglass-shaped drums stretched overtop with lizard skins, the drum ceremonies would begin. Several drummers played together while the men danced. Chuck had never experienced anything like it. Their music was produced solely to connect them to a strange spirit world. The drums pounded steadily, a deep, resonating booming that infused the village and the ground beneath it with a primordial energy.

Boom, boom, boom, boom.

With no variation in speed or pitch, the drummers repeated this single note, over and over again.

Boom, boom, boom, boom.

One by one, the men rose. Taking Chuck with them, they shuffled in a circle, eyes half-closed, their arms limp by their sides, moving to the pounding of the drums, animated by the vibrations.

Boom, boom, boom.

Entirely focused on the drumming, the men entered a trancelike state, hypnotized by the waves of sound and the monotony of the beat. Something internal transported them into another plane as they "danced" throughout the night until dawn.

Although Chuck stayed with these men for two weeks, their inner spaces remained completely alien as, each night, they brought down ghosts and danced with spirits.

On their return trip to Port Moresby, the Fipkes stopped over at Madang and went immediately to a restaurant. Sitting at a table next to them, a missionary couple joined them, New Guinea being a country where expats sought out each other. Otto Kowning, an evangelical minister, and his wife introduced themselves.

"We're out on break from our mission at Otsjanep in the Asmat."

The Asmat was a region in West Irian, the Indonesian-controlled western half of New Guinea. The name of the village was also familiar.

"Isn't Otsjanep the village where Michael Rockefeller disappeared?" The story was regularly talked about, a familiar tragedy in New Guinea.

Nine years earlier, in 1961, Michael Rockefeller, the son of New York's governor, Nelson Rockefeller, accompanied the Harvard-Peabody New Guinea Expedition into the Baliem Valley, in the central interior mountains of what was then Dutch New Guinea. Seven months later, young Rockefeller went alone with a Dutch anthropologist and two Natives to the Asmat region along the south coast to photograph the people and collect artifacts for the American Museum of Primitive Art and for the Rijksmuseum in Holland. While crossing the mouth of the Betsj River in a Native catamaran, they overturned in the currents. The two Natives swam to shore while Rockefeller and his Dutch companion climbed onto a raft they had been towing with the gear. The wind was against them. The raft began to float out to sea. Rockefeller, convinced his life depended on it, made a desperate bid to swim for shore. His partner, staying with the raft, last saw him swimming strongly with two empty jerry cans for flotation.

When the Dutch anthropologist was later spotted and recovered at sea, his story of Michael's disappearance galvanized America. Organizing the largest search for a missing person in Pacific history, Nelson Rockefeller flew immediately to the nearby coastal town of Merauke to personally take charge of the effort. Dozens of American and Australian journalists descended on the town, and Dutch New Guinea spent a few short days in the brilliant light of the western press. The two Natives who first swam safely to shore had made it to a Dutch coastal post, giving encouragement to the father's dream of finding and rescuing his son.

For 10 days they searched. All they found was one of the two jerry cans bumping in the water against the roots of a mangrove on the shore. When expert opinion convinced them that no man could live longer in the coastal swamp, they all left. The swamp returned to its natural state; only the hum of mosquitoes, the cry of an occasional bird and the splash of its crocodiles marred the stillness.

The official version was accidental death by drowning. Others speculated the crocodiles found him. But the eyes peering out from blackened huts raised high on stilts on a firmer bit of ground in the swamp had seen things, things they were reluctant to tell outsiders. Otto Kowning said he knew something about it. After operating his village mission for several years, his Native Christians had recently unburdened themselves to him. He received their confessions.

They had known the young Rockefeller, Kowning said. Rockefeller had lived among them, studying them. But then he encouraged them to attack their neighbours, so he could get pictures of the fighting. When they found Rockefeller alone, unarmed and vulnerable, they decided to kill him. They had other reasons, as well.

Protein deficiencies were endemic in the coastal regions. The staple food was the pithy core of the sago palm. Human flesh, when it could be obtained, was highly prized. Eaten as often for its food value as for religious reasons, it sustained numerous villages and kept the populations in check for millennia.

The young Rockefeller was cooked in the traditional way: wrapped in leaves with sago, then laid into a hot rock pit, covered over and baked.

Although Chuck doubted the complete accuracy of Kowning's story, the minister swore he had young Rockefeller's eyeglasses and his watch – taken by the villagers and later turned over to him. It was a bizarre account, especially given the events that followed Rockefeller's disappearance. While the Australians ruled Papua New Guinea, in part as a British colony from the turn of the century and in part as a former German colony (the mandate going to Australia under the authority of the League of Nations following the First World War), the western half of the island had been a Dutch colony since 1824. The Dutch had no interest in New Guinea itself and acquired that part of the country, west of the 141st meridian, solely to keep it as a buffer between encroaching British interests and its Dutch East Indies empire.

In the enlightened age of the 1960s, Australia was under intense pressure to release Papua New Guinea and give it independence. Freedom for subject peoples, without war, was the new political vision. To that end, it was actively trying to build up an economy and an infrastructure so that Papua New Guinea could stand on its own. After a heroic effort, Papua New Guinea would soon become an independent country.

Across the border, in 1961, when Michael Rockefeller disappeared, the Dutch were similarly under pressure from the United Nations to divest themselves of their last colony. Unlike Papua New Guinea, though, Dutch New Guinea remained a dark mystery. Its raw interior had never been explored. Headhunters still ruled a land that remained virtually untouched, as it had been for centuries. With the Netherlands prepared to comply with the directions of the United Nations for its colony's disposal, the obvious and enlightened route would have been to allow the two halves to be joined into an independent New Guinea. Inexplicably, however, the Americans, in a complete betrayal of democratic values and of the people of New Guinea as well as their Australian neighbours, compelled the United Nations to give Dutch New Guinea to Indonesia instead – a dictatorship with no connection at all to the country beyond a desire to build an empire of its own.

In 1963 the deed was done. The Dutch left and Indonesia became the new and brutal colonial master of the old Dutch colony. With no intention of benefiting the Native New Guineans, the Indonesians moved quickly through the few scattered Dutch coastal towns in the western Vogelkop Peninsula, stripping them of whatever of value they could find.

Renaming its new possession West Irian, Indonesia quickly sent troops into the Asmat – the very region in which Michael Rockefeller had been collecting artifacts when he disappeared. Unlike that expedition, the Indonesians were not interested in recording primitive cultures. They had come instead to crush the local people. Shooting them indiscriminately with machine guns and garrotting those they could catch alive, the Indonesians forced thousands of villagers from the Asmat to flee across the border into Australian-controlled Papua New Guinea. Next, the Indonesian troops began to intimidate their new Australian and Papau New Guinean neighbours, casting covetous eyes over the land across the border with its rich new mines, plantations and Australian-built infrastructure.

Curiously, the Indonesians reported one fact from their terror campaign to the western press, as though it alone justified all the killing. A captured Asmat chief confessed after interrogation that a cholera epidemic suffered by his people had been caused by the ghost of Rockefeller in revenge for his murder, which the chief also admitted to participating in. If American revenge were necessary for the death of Rockefeller, the Indonesian takeover was payback in plenty.

After the campaigns, the borders were sealed off and the country once again fell into darkness. Only missionaries like Otto Kowning were allowed in after the troops – people whose interests lay not in protecting the ancient cultures of West Irian or even studying them, but in tearing them down, as well.

It was a strange meeting, and the story turned Chuck's mind even more to thoughts of West Irian. While at Ok Tedi he had often looked west across the border into that country. Except for the rare jungle mission here and there – the only infrastructure the country had – West Irian remained a living, Stone Age world. So fanatical was the Indonesian hold on its little empire, no one was allowed entry. The last western expedition to go in had been Rockefeller's.

To Chuck the territory's unknown quality was irresistible. But it was a forbidden zone. Indonesian troops stationed along the border had orders to shoot to kill even the surveyors who tried to define the wild international boundary. Still it pulled him, and he began to look for openings. If any chance at all presented itself to penetrate the dark veils of West Irian, he would go. Whatever the cost.

CHAPTER FIVE

THE CANTEEN

Geological sciences are concerned with the earth and how it has changed through time. Thus by their very nature they are historically oriented, and as such they are confronted with certain kinds of problems not encountered in other, non-historical science. We should not be surprised to find that geology occupies a sort of middle ground between chemistry or physics, on the one hand, and history or sociology on the other.

—A.LEE MCALESTER, *PHYSICAL GEOLOGY*

THE Doors were playing "Light My Fire," and the lights were attracting bugs. Not just moths that bumped drunkenly around, spinning crazily in the air, but all manner of black beetles, iridescent flies and zany creatures that looked like Martian earwigs – all crawling up toward the hot bulb. Touching it, they fell, spinning down, dropping like burned-out stars onto the table below.

Nobody paid any attention to the insects. There are millions of insect species in the world, and fully half of them live in equatorial rainforests like New Guinea's. All a person could do was learn to live with them. Except when they landed inside the beer glasses! The men had better things to talk about: women mostly, and their experiences "outside". Things they could brag about.

The music, men laughing, stories, dreams and lies: the camp at night was a heady mix of realities. Penis gourds and steel-toed boots, soft flesh and cankers, goblin cannibals, pidgin and science and a lost, crazy island, cut off from everything, floating together down some dark, unknown river.

It had become their nightly routine. To sit, crowded together under the light like the insects and slowly pass into oblivion.

Chuck would have preferred scotch to beer. It was a taste acquired, only recently, by the steady paycheques from Kennecott, but the camp was "beer only." The stronger drinks stayed in Port Moresby. No one was complaining. They were grateful to have any kind of canteen. This one even had a fridge and freezer. The generator for the camp, a discreet distance away, could be heard humming gently. It was the comforting sound of the 20th century, of technology, of light in the darkness. And ice-cold beer!

Suddenly a great crashing thump erupted as the huge uncoiling mass of a python collapsed over them, smashing onto the table. Glasses and beer went flying as the men instinctively recoiled from the giant snake that had landed in their midst. More than three metres long and as thick as a man's thigh, the mot-ley-coloured monster had a black forest rat gripped tightly in its mouth. As omnipresent as the bugs hunting for food, rats were easy prey. The rat was screeching, trying desperately to tug free.

Shouting and yelling, the men pushed back away from the snake, giving it room on the floor as a couple of the Native men, machetes in hand, began chop-ping at it wildly, randomly, hitting it anywhere they could. The blows raining down on the reptile caused it to writhe up, twisting away from the pain, but it held onto the rat, never relaxing its grip until it was all over. A last whack dis-patched the snake.

For a moment, the room was dead silent. The music over, the only sounds were the distant hum of the generator and the buzz of cricket life outside. Every-one stared transfixed at the bloody body of the creature that had crawled unseen into the canteen and had lain, draped over their heads on the rafters, waiting.

"Kilim i dai!" one of the Native men announced almost matter-of-factly in pidgin. It was done. Killed dead.

Solemnly he and the other villagers gathered up the body of the snake and, without another word, filed out, subdued and somewhat fearfully, into the night. One of the men got up and put on a Rolling Stones favourite, the words famil-iar to them all: *Pleased to meet you/hope you guess my name....* Some of the men began to sing along, while others laughed maniacally. It was all so insane.

"What they gonna do with it?" A cocky young Australian driller asked of no one in particular.

Max, one of the pilots, answered him. "Eat it," he said simply. A man of 50, Max was based out of Kiunga and flew freight into Ok Tedi regularly. Tonight he had stayed to drink with the men in the canteen. Having spent two decades in New Guinea working the outback with the "Kiaps," as the field agents of the Department of Native Affairs were called, Max was an acknowledged authority. An expat with a strange mix of wisdom, humour and fatalism, he had predicted his own life would end in the country. Jungle pilots were a breed unto themselves.

"Christ, the bloody Bush Kanaka eat everything, don't they?" The driller shot back. His use of the derogatory term, although not the worst around, offended the pilot.

"Listen, you soulless bastard," Max responded, speaking slowly and pausing to draw deeply on a cigarette. After a lifetime under the equatorial sun, his face was nearly as dark as a Native's, and deeply lined. Although his words were insulting, Max kept his tone light to avoid provoking any strong reactions. He was enjoying himself.

"They may look primitive, and you can *believe* what you like, but their world's a lot more complex than *you'll ever know!* Another thing's for sure: technology sure doesn't find the depth of a person's soul! What you see's nothing – like look-ing at the outside of a house and thinking you understand the man inside! You gotta live here years before they'll let you see into their world. Even then, it's only a small part."

"So what have you seen, old man?" Another asked. The faces that remained were white.

"I've seen the exchange of souls," Max answered slowly. "I've seen a shaman trade places with a creature from the spirit world while a spirit from there possessed his body. Danced and sang all night, it did, too. Songs no man ever heard before. Then, in the dawn, when we were spent out just from watching, the shaman's own spirit returned and he 'awoke,' bloody more refreshed and alive from where he'd been than the best of you bloody blokes after a good night!" The comment drew some protest.

"Awww, how can you believe that shit?" the driller, a thin man with reddish hair, argued, but nobody was listening to him. His skin, dry and papery, was pulled too tightly over his bony frame. He appeared exhausted, perhaps ill.

"And you know why he came back, looking like he'd been in heaven?" Max asked, the question drifting through the canteen like a zeppelin. This was an aspect of spirit travelling he knew would appeal to men trapped on a mountaintop. "He'd been having sex all night with spirit women! They say spirit women are absolutely out of this world! Something to die for!"

Everybody laughed and the conversation broke into new stories of sexual conquest, the only social release young men needing women had.

"Maybe they're all hallucinating on something," one of the men suggested. "Get me some of whatever it is and I'll do more than dance with their spirit women, too!"

"Not if they look like the beauties next door!" Ladi Williams joined in.

Another chorus of boisterous laughter.

"Right you are, mate!" Another agreed. The New Guinean women, though naked, held little attraction for most of the men at the camp. While neither drugs nor alcohol could compete with the feel of real flesh, a real woman, the powerful body odours of the Ok Tedi women acted like a natural repellent. With the force of gravity on a pendulum, the conversation inevitably and inexorably found its way back to the topic of sex.

The men were waiting for Max to speak again. He looked around at the white faces gathered under the light. Outside in the darkness, black faces would be nervously congregating together, trying to peer into the unknown.

"They'll be having a seance tonight ... and the spirits will be walking among them. Everything has meaning in life, but it's never what it seems. We live on a thin edge, but there's another force. It's here now, all around us, breathing life into everything that happens."

He was starting to drift, the alcohol and his own thoughts carrying him away. They were all drifting. Reality itself seemed suddenly vaporous.

Chuck wasn't asking questions, but he, too, was listening. He had never been introspective, never dwelling on the past. Whatever unconscious motivations drove men, whatever their spiritual worlds, he was not looking to explore them. Instead, he kept his focus fixed firmly on the external world. His goals were tangible ones.

"You don't honestly believe there's any truth to it, do you?" Ladi asked.

"Is there *truth* in *anything*, Ladi?" Max replied. "And what of our own Christianity? Isn't it just another primitive, tribal religion with its own stories of miracles – creations, the walking dead, relations with gods, angels and demons. Where has *that* taken us?"

No one answered, and he kept on.

"You know what I find funny? The Natives – your primitive half humans – imagine that our every action is connected to win the favour of the spirits, our God. That all of us – we, too – are only working for spiritual harmony. They can't imagine anything else more important. Isn't that a joke? Unlike us Christians, who, let's face it, don't really believe in the existence of another reality at all, these people live it. Here everyone talks to spirits. They walk with them, dance with them, make love to them. What have we got to compete with that?"

He considered the idea for a moment himself as his foot absently traced the sticky edge of the blood trail left by the snake when it was dragged out. Someone replaced the Stones with Dylan and the deep mood vanished.

Lay lady lay / Lay across my big brass bed ...

Max was tired of defending the Natives. The worlds were too far apart and a tide of history was against him. He gave in to it, lightened up and laughed, responding to his own question.

"Work, drink and women!"

Turning to the fellow beside him, he bellowed, "BARMAN! What kind of a slack hole do you keep here, anyways? Bloody goddamned zoo! Another brew, my good man, and quick about it or I'll have your ass!"

Everybody laughed. The chairs were pulled up to the tables, feet stomped over the trail of drying blood, and the men got back to serious drinking.

Chuck walked out into the darkness, away from the light and the noise of the canteen. The night air was rife with birds skittering back and forth in the shadows. It was as if the sight of the open sky, free for the moment from clouds and filled with countless stars, had awakened a wild energy within the birds that made them want to fly up into the violet dome and play in the stars. He knew they were only feeding.

As he watched, an owlet-nightjar resting on the ground nearby rose up quickly into the air to snatch a passing insect and then, as if in victory, flew in an erratic pattern overhead, its loud churring call giving voice to the night, before settling down again to await the passage of another small life. From out of the sky came other sounds: the shrilling, burbling, chortling and hissings of other birds on the hunt.

He stood, staring up, mesmerized by the birds. One of the engineers, a New Zealander a couple of years older than Chuck, came outside for a leak and, noticing him, walked over to stand beside him.

"Quite a sight, isn't it," he said quietly. "Nowhere else on earth can you look into both hemispheres at the same time. We're on the cusp of two different worlds, standing astride them both."

"The stars?" Chuck wasn't sure what worlds he was talking about. There seemed so many. All as distant and unreachable as the points of light.

"That's Centaurus," said the New Zealander, pointing to a line of stars that contained some of the brightest lights in the sky. "You know its history?" he asked.

"Never studied astronomy," Chuck replied.

"I love the stars," the other man explained. "Keeps me going." Like the others, he was a little drunk and would get more so before the night was over. "You know Sagittarius? It's the constellation of a centaur. And this one here, watching over us, is the other centaur, Centaurus. They're both the same creature, half-man, half-beast. The Greeks identified the wild tribes in northern Europe as centaurs. Half-human … Our ancestors, eh?… Odd how constant everything is, don't you think?"

The man didn't know the extent of it. Chuck's own roots in the Germanic crusades against the pagan Preussens were preceded by earlier campaigns against the wild Germanic tribes themselves. All, in their turn, were seen by their more powerful opponents as less worthy, only half-human. Like a shock wave rippling through time and across cultures, the momentum from those distant "disturbances" continued still to push out across the world.

Searching the sky over the mountain, as though for inspiration, the New Zealander continued.

"Unlike the gods, who cared little for the plight of mortal men, Centaurus was actually moved by their suffering. As the mentor of Jason, Achilles and Heracles, he refused to forsake his friends even when Heracles wounded him by mistake.

"Another immortal, Prometheus, also took pity on man and brought us the comfort of fire he stole from the gods. For this sin, Zeus chained Prometheus to a rock, where each day the eagle would descend and tear out his liver. Unable to die, because he was immortal, each night he grew another liver for the eagle to feed on. Condemned to an eternity of suffering.

"Moved by the plight of Prometheus, Centaurus made his final bargain with Zeus – he traded his own life for Prometheus's release. Zeus wanted man never to forget Centaurus, the immortal half-beast who died for us. Because the northern sky was already full, Zeus put him over here – above the equator – to remind us forever what the beasts have to teach us."

It was a night for philosophers and shamans. The owlet-nightjar leapt up into the sky again to bring down another tasty morsel. The air was vibrating with unseen life. As Chuck walked across the camp grounds to the small quarters he shared with Fred Files, a professor of geology who had come from Berkeley to work on the project, Chuck heard the familiar cry of a nighthawk. It was the only sound he knew well in the cacophony that echoed through the night. Small creatures of the insect world crept across the floor of his room and up the walls in instinctual quests.

Under his mosquito net, Chuck slept uneasily. Usually, dreamless sleep came almost instantly, as did each morning, when he awoke, refreshed. But tonight was different. A collage of disturbing images, feelings and experiences swirled about, unsettling him.

In the middle of the night he awoke and let out a blood-curdling scream, rocketing Fred Files, asleep on the bunk beside him, straight out of his bed. The camp sprang into life. Men in underwear rushed with flashlights to the rescue, pouring into Chuck's room. With the light thrown on, they found him stretched out, wild desperation in his eyes. His arm had fallen asleep and, paralyzed and dreaming of snakes, he had jolted awake imagining himself being devoured by a huge reptile. Unable to move, he had felt himself being crushed.

The men, laughing, sauntered, back to their own beds, leaving Chuck, embarrassed, almost wishing there *had* been a real snake in his bed.

CHAPTER SIX

BAITING CROCODILES

Exercising his passion for challenges, Chuck's sorties into the jungle for the company became more daring. He willingly embraced risks other men would have quit their jobs to avoid.

The heavy-mineral studies the company was pursuing now provided him with the chance to collect a sand sample from a riverbed far to the southeast of Ok Tedi. A mere ink line on a map in an office room in Sydney, the stream drained what looked to be a promising watershed. The reality was quite another matter getting the sample might be life-threatening.

As the helicopter lifted off the ground at Ok Tedi, Chuck noticed a large New Guinea stag beetle clinging to one of the skid struts. If it got into the electrical works it could cause problems. But for now it was no threat where it was – clinging desperately to a metal nodule 300 metres over the jungle. In the light, its carapace, almost five centimetres long, was shining with a brilliant purplish blue iridescence. Chuck was glad that Ladi was the pilot. He was a good guy and, more importantly, an expert pilot.

They dropped closer to the ground as they flew south above and around low mountain peaks. The top of the forest canopy was an irregular, lumpy blanket with some species of hardwoods dwarfing others. Beneath them were stands of hoop-pine and klinki, rising straight and sturdy for some 75 metres. Sooner or later the loggers would arrive, and these would be the first to go. Clinging to the trees everywhere were magnificent bursts of epiphytes. The air plants had no root systems and were able to sustain themselves from the moisture and nourishment they took in from the air alone. All the colour missing at ground level, under the canopy, was found here at the top. Blooms of various plants streaked the forest with splashes of red, orange and yellow.

It was an impressive display of form, texture and colour. The sun's rays lit up the forest crown in a multitude of bright green shades, from lime to emerald. Nor was the animal life of the jungle to be found among its buttressed roots. It too was at the top, concentrated high overhead, out of sight, away from the dark, wet forest floor. Here, in the crowns, sang the high-pitched cicadas. Here in the treetops, too, most of the forest's kapuls and cuscuses – rather than monkeys – ran among the branches. Numerous marsupials, species common to Australia like the tree kangaroo and several types of opossum, competed in sharp-toothed hunger for space and food with the large tree rat, a relative newcomer. Fruit bats, grunting and squealing, congregated by the thousands to feed off ripening fruit trees, their excrement raining down on the earth below. Even the snakes and lizards were arboreal, the lizards living off insects and bird eggs, the snakes eating everything.

As the two men flew over the rainforest, their passage startled flocks of multi-hued birds that rose up in waves to stream away from the helicopter, kites of colour, soaring against a background of deeper jungle greens. Chuck recognized some of them as black honeyeaters and flycatchers. Flocks of scarlet parrots and green forest pigeons wheeled in formation below them. Here and there, a raptor soared effortlessly between the taller trees.

Chuck loved the birds. With more than 600 different species, this land was nearly as diverse as all of North America or Australia. If one could only travel through the treetops as they did, it would be a birder's paradise.

Ladi took them south, out of the central mountains and the foothills, to land at Kiunga. They loaded extra gas, refuelled and took off again. Chuck then remembered the stag beetle; he looked, but it had disappeared.

After Kiunga, the country changed dramatically. No longer mountain rainforest, it had levelled out into lowland jungle. From here to the coast, hundreds of kilometres to the south, the land was a swampy quagmire.

They followed the main channel of the Fly, Chuck navigating to ensure they stayed on course, while for fun Ladi took them down below the level of the treetops to skim the surface of the milky brown waters. Occasionally they passed a solitary dugout canoe drifting through the mangrove off the main river with a Native standing poised over the water, spear in hand, waiting for a fish to break.

Along a muddy sandbar, they spotted some large crocodiles sunning themselves. The sight bothered Chuck, and he tried to joke about them to put himself at ease.

"Hey, Ladi, you know the difference between a croc and an old shoe?"

"No, what is it?" he asked, expecting a punch line.

"Shit, I think you better stay inside the helicopter if we go down anywhere around here!" Chuck laughed and then, leaning over toward Ladi, he patted the pilot on the shoulder, pretending to offer him some praise as a consolation. "But, hey, like you do know how to fly a helicopter, eh!"

Chuck laughed even harder when Ladi jokingly suggested, "Maybe you should start paying more attention to the ground, in case you find yourself having to walk back!"

No one could walk through the country beneath them. It was mostly water. Swamp and mud. And then there were the crocs. Although their numbers had been depleted previously by Australian crocodile hunters, with females laying 30 to 80 eggs at a time, the creatures had quickly repopulated the territory. They were common enough to give a man in the water some concern. Growing to more than nine metres in length, the crocodiles of the river's estuary stalked villagers living along the coast and ripped fishermen out of their dugout canoes.

Chuck hoped he would not have to deal with them.

As they approached the area where Chuck was to be dropped off, his heart began beating faster. Ladi made some last-minute course corrections, slowed down, then hovered over the jungle. They had arrived.

The stream was directly beneath them, but as Chuck had feared, there was no way to get the helicopter down to it or close enough even for him to jump out. As Ladi flew the chopper in an ever widening circle, both men scrutinized the vegetation for a hole big enough to lower the helicopter into. The tangle of mangrove and sago was unbroken. Up and down the creek and over the land flanking its sides, the understorey growth was dense and impenetrable, enclosing the stream. Wherever the life-giving light touched a space, there was a plant soaking it up.

"Looks pretty bad!" Ladi said. He was waiting for Chuck to give the word. The sample was impossible to get. It was Chuck's call.

"Let's go check the swamp," Chuck responded. Anxious to know what a sample from here would reveal, he was not ready to give up. Once again curiosity pulled him, while the need to succeed – and his standard – drove him. He never missed a sample.

The creek emptied out into a huge swamp, itself the permanently flooded banks of the Fly River, a swampland that flowed along with the Fly for hundreds of kilometres before oozing out into the broad coastal swamps. Ladi slowly cruised over the edge of firm ground and out above the water, but he didn't like what he saw.

"There's no way to get down there," he argued, guessing what Chuck had in mind. Chuck was looking for a hole down into the swamp itself.

"We're not finished yet, Ladi!"

Chuck kept Ladi looking, flying farther from the creek, farther out into the swamp. Downstream from the mouth and a half kilometre from shore, they spotted a hole. A rotten tree had fallen and the space had not yet been overwhelmed. It was one and a half kilometres from the creek Chuck had to sample.

"You sure about doing this?" Ladi asked. There was no question what he thought. Chuck was firm. He wasn't going to return without the sample.

"We'll rendezvous in three hours," Ladi told him.

Chuck nodded. He knew the drill. Ladi would drop back down through the same hole to pick him up. "If you're not here, I'll leave after 10 minutes and return again in two more hours. And then, after that, in two more hours, okay?" Over the noise of the helicopter, Ladi had to shout to be heard, but Chuck was already thinking of his next step.

"And if you're still not here, Chuck, I'll try to find somebody to come in to look for you, okay?" Ladi watched Chuck climb out on the strut. They both knew that if he didn't make it back, it would be unlikely he'd be in a condition worth any rescue attempt.

Ladi brought them down close to the water's surface and Chuck lowered his feet in first. They had no idea how deep it was. The water was opaque. Black and impervious to light, it smelled of rot. Bent at the waist over the skid, with his legs dangling down into the water, he still couldn't touch bottom. Sliding off the skid

gently, using the strength of his arms, so as not to unbalance the hovering helicopter, he lowered himself slowly down into the murky water. Deeper.

Up to his armpits, almost to his chin, he settled on the bottom. He paused for
a moment to be sure of his footing so he wouldn't sink out of sight, while Ladi
expertly kept the helicopter as steady as a dragonfly. He was in. Pulling his pack
down from the helicopter, and holding it over his head he nodded vigorously to
Ladi in lieu of the thumbs-up signal. The pilot grimly shouted out "Good luck!"
then took the machine back up through the trees and flew away, leaving Chuck
alone in the swamp, standing to his neck in brackish water.

Chuck tried to imprint the spot in his mind so he could find it again and
then, his nose just above the surface of the water, he began wading carefully
through the swamp in the direction of the shore.

As soon as the wash of the helicopter had gone, the mosquitoes came out.
As well as malaria, they carried dengue fever, an illness for which there was no
cure. The best safeguard was to avoid getting bitten. The mosquitoes were relentless. The only other place on earth they were found in such numbers was the
Canadian Arctic. Unable to brush them off, he could only blink when they
landed on his eyes, shake his head as they settled down over his face to feed. His
raised arms were a sacrifice to the bugs.

Chuck tried to ignore them. With each step forward, his heavy boots sank
deep into the gumbo at the bottom, sucking him down. As he moved, disturbing the organic mass rotting under the surface, putrid odours rose up, the gas
bubbling around him.

The water was warm. Almost hot. Cooked from the top by the heat of the
tropical sun and from the bottom by decomposing vegetation, it was a dark soup
with a layer of scum floating over the surface, hiding everything beneath it.

Feeling ahead with his foot to be sure of the bottom, he slowly made his way
around the grey columns of trunks and through the mesh of roots that anchored
the trees. Trying not to make a disturbance that might attract the curiosity of
creatures larger than mosquitoes, he pushed through the swamp, wired, taut as
a piano string.

Scanning the water, he looked around for any movement – for a rippling
wave – indicating the presence of life beneath the surface. Pumped with adren-
alin, his heart was racing. He watched the trees, too, as he passed under them.
The memory of the python falling from the rafters was still sharp. Pythons were
equally at home in water, common in the swamps.

There were other snakes here. The death adder. And the taipan. Found only
in northern Australia and southern New Guinea, the taipan was the most aggressive snake in the world. Growing to three and a half metres, it would attack
humans without provocation.

In the deafening silence of the swamp – only the sound of mosquitoes and his
own pulse drumming in his head – every crack, every whisper of the trees
around him rang loud and clear. Try as he might, he was unable to control the
images of violent death that flashed across his mind. His senses were too keyed

up. Moving blind through the deep swamp touched instinctive fears. Man was never a creature of the jungle night, nor of the swamps.

Suddenly – right behind him – there was a tremendous crash! The water erupted with a violent fury as the impact of something huge and solid smacking the surface sent a wave of water cascading over him. In the same instant his heart stopped.

A surge of adrenaline carried away rational thought and fired his body with raw energy. He spun around to face his enemy. Not that it would do any good, but he would die fighting! Escape was impossible.

There was nothing there. Just the widening circle of ripples left by the impact of the tree after it had slammed down into the water behind him.

As he collected himself, his doubts about risking his life for a sample of sand for the company soared. In spite of his efforts to stay focused on his task, the question slipped out, "What the hell am I doing here?" He spoke the words aloud. What *was* he looking for that was so important he had to risk his life for it?

It was the wrong time to ask the question. Quickly Chuck pushed his doubts aside and regained control over his feelings. Fear, he knew, like doubt, could sink a man. When he made it to firmer ground, he relaxed somewhat, but the safety was relative. Next came the exhausting task of chopping his way through the roots and vines with his machete. Following the edge of the swamp to keep his bearings, he hacked his way along. It was a release for pent-up energies, although he still kept a wary eye open for snakes and crocodiles on the ground.

The air was suffocating, thick with heat and moisture. Sweat ran freely from his body. The mosquitoes that followed him through the water now discovered new areas of unresisting flesh. Chuck didn't care. He would get his sample and get out.

Finally arriving at his goal – the creek – he dug a wet sample out of the sand. After placing it inside his pack, he hoisted it, and then turned around. He had to go back. Rushing against the clock, he retraced his steps through the jungle to the spot where he had emerged from the swamp.

With a final check on the time he moved off the shore into the water. Wading in once more to his chest, feeling his way slowly around deeper holes, he carefully marked his way to find the one opening that would take him to safety.

Arriving early at the rendezvous, anxious to get out, he stood motionless, up to his chin in fetid water. Frozen in place without a sound or a ripple to give away his location, he was as still as one of the millions of trees that survived in the swamp. There he waited for the helicopter and thought. Experiences from the past began to float up, unwilled: the dry Canadian prairie, his father, other rendezvous.

Chuck couldn't help but wonder what he would do if Ladi did not show up. Once, in Canada, when the helicopter sent out to pluck him off a remote mountaintop crashed, he had been left, buried under a winter storm for days. In the jungle, too, the helicopter was a lifeline. Through no one's fault, there were mechanical malfunctions even perfect pilots could not prevent.

He started thinking about that stag beetle.

The mosquitoes were becoming intolerable and he had neither mosquito netting nor survival gear. The experts had given Michael Rockefeller 10 days to live in the swamp. Beyond that no man could survive. He had thought it too low an estimate but now, after three hours of this, he changed his mind.

When he heard the sound of the helicopter coming back at last, the relief he felt was overwhelming. This had been his worst experience collecting a sample. And yet, once enclosed in a Plexiglas bubble of safety, soaring up out of the swamp, he was filled with elation.

As he recounted his fright at the falling tree to Ladi, he began laughing heartily, the release of tension lifting him to a new high. He had survived! Another victory over fear. The smell of the swamp's mud, clinging to him, filled their craft. His life was at a peak. Fear had never turned him. Sustaining that peak meant more.

CHAPTER SEVEN

THE CENTAUR

GRADUALLY the country worked deep changes in Chuck. Professional successes raised his confidence to new highs. But there was something else. As he had in the Yukon, paired as a student with a reclusive trapper named Gunther Lishy, when he began to relax and fit in, he began to see things around him more clearly. Whatever fears he had carried from childhood were being confronted one by one and stared down.

New Guinea touched him deeper than anything else ever had. Infused with its wild energy, its unique visions and ancient values, he found not only that his aggression was being liberated, but also that new passions were being ignited. Life itself became the goal: to live fearlessly, as a man should live.

His initial impression of New Guinea, culture had been one of repression, of men dominated by their chiefs and of women dominated by their men. Women were bought by the men, traded for pigs and shells. But that was a judgement made through western eyes. For the men, their treasure, their greatest possessions, were their women. In New Guinea, women were not degraded by being bought; they were honoured. They were not enslaved by being owned; they were made secure. Both sexes had definition and role and purpose.

While superficially they appeared distant with each other and, lacking public displays of affection, seemed emotionally impoverished, the death of Odanage, an elderly local village woman, made Chuck look more carefully at their close relationships.

The depth of feeling released by her death was a complete surprise to him. The entire village went into mourning, all the people weeping openly, the young men as well as the old. The outpouring of grief at their loss was deep and genuine and unlike anything he had ever witnessed in Canada.

Unrestrained, real passion was evident. Emotionally, they were liberated. Although the Natives were hostile toward and suspicious of outsiders, within the village their feelings for one another ran deep. They had a unity, a closeness, he had never seen before.

It was not a society to which Chuck felt drawn – he could never belong, in any event – but it made him rethink his own relationships, and it raised disturbing questions about cultural values and superiority. Had western culture evolved due to social pressure for a healthier community or had it simply been driven to change by forces beyond its control? Was it guided not by enlightened visions but forced, desperately, to adjust to a shifting economy that demanded change –

for better or for worse – from the old order, dragging first men, then women and finally children into the mines and factories of the Industrial Age? Did the machine run the man and dominate the human spirit? He hadn't thought so before, but now he questioned everything. Was western culture simply mass victimization by technology?

Laurens Van Der Post, the South African romantic-historian and one of Chuck's favourite authors, had written that the roar of a wild plains lion that knew nothing of man was one of the most thrilling and awesome sounds in nature: a sound never to be heard again. These people, like those last lions, were they not, too, reflections of the human spirit as it was meant to be? As we all once were?

What superiority of spirit or moral value did the modern age have?

In all the villages he visited, the men had wives. Most often they owned their women. As many as they could afford. And they had children. But they did not always live together. Married men lived with other married men in the communal men's houses; women lived together with the children in women's houses. Bachelors, a class unto themselves, lived together in bachelors' houses.

The social unit was the village – not the family. Men and women kept to their own societies, often coming together for shared events and needs. They had different energies, roles and skills. Their spirits were different and they had their own ceremonies, their own rituals and their own gods and goddesses. In New Guinea, the Native cultures recognized the differences between men and women, honoured them and gave them the expression they needed for their fulfillment.

On a deep level, these people were content. Their societies had evolved over tens of thousands of years. "Primitive" was an adjective meant to denigrate them, to dismiss the lessons they had learned over countless millennia, as trivial and false – worse, as pagan and evil. Chuck had found a new adjective to better describe them: natural.

Man by his nature could not vary far from the human path – that was the key. The further he went, the more unnatural he became and the more repressed he felt. Freedom lay in being oneself. To go with the flow of inner energy, rather than against it.

Chuck was grateful to be in New Guinea. It had much to teach him and he was feeling more and more at home all the time. New Guinea taught him the joy of being male and allowed him to express his personality without inhibition, as only wilderness and ancient places can do. Like the plains, with roaring lions, here was a place modern man had not ventured.

Chuck was still feeling this invincible high when he went diving off the coast near Port Moresby with his friend Gus, another Kennecott employee. The two of them had gone by themselves for a day's diving off a deserted beach fringing the Coral Sea before flying back to work at Ok Tedi.

They were free-diving with snorkels when Chuck came up under a jellyfish floating on the surface. Seeing it through his mask only at the last moment, he tried desperately to stop his momentum, to back away. He was too late. He brushed up against it. As if splashed with acid, his skin burned instantly. The flesh across his chest and over his shoulder blistered into extremely painful welts.

Gus helped him out of the water and the two men bleakly looked at each other. They had identified it as a box jellyfish – one of the greatest diving dangers of the Coral Sea. To touch one was to die.

"It's up for me." Chuck quietly stated the inevitable. There was no sense in hysterics. Or action, since there was no antidote for the poison of a box jellyfish. He had only a few minutes to live. They both knew it. Chuck asked Gus to get the bottle of wine from their car. He could at least enjoy one more drink and toast an exciting life. New Guinea was but the last experience of a remarkably full life.

He sipped his wine and focused his last moments not on regrets but on the sight of the green sea stretching to the horizon. He loved the sea. He had always loved the sea. Even now …

They sat quietly, Gus leaving him to his own thoughts, as they drank their wine. Chuck was not sad. Quietly he gave a few instructions to Gus, trusting him with his last messages for his family.

Minutes passed. He remembered the flight of his falcon …

But wait! He was still alive! They both began counting the time. Ten minutes … eleven … They realized then that he was not going to die.

Not yet, at any rate. Not today.

They had misidentified the jellyfish. What Chuck had run into was a poisonous – but not deadly – bluebottle jellyfish. He had been given a new start!

Marlene did not share his humour when he arrived home, still laughing, with great swollen, purple welts across his body.

For Chuck, life was a gift. It was wonderful to be free and living the adventure.

But always there was a price to pay.

CHAPTER EIGHT

OK TEDI, SEPTEMBER 3, 1971, 6:47PM

WHEN Ladi Williams returned alone at dusk to Ok Tedi and reported that the men he had dropped had not made it back to the rendezvous, nobody was too concerned. Chuck was out with four tough village men. They could handle themselves if they ran into trouble. Chuck had even anticipated not getting back on time; he had had the foresight to have Ladi drop off a portable camp. It was a good thing, too, Ladi thought. Just as he tied down his helicopter for the night, a torrential rain poured down – as it did only in the tropics. At least they were warm and dry, Ladi thought. It made him rest easier. It was his responsibility to take the men out into the field and bring them safely back again. Their lives depended on it.

At first light, the helicopter already warmed up, he was off. The flight north to Mount Ian took only a few minutes. It took him longer to put down through the jungle. On the ground, it would take a group of men working hard with machetes three or four days to cover the same distance.

Sinking back down through the hole in the canopy – even finding the place – was an art, but he was good. Kennecott hired only the best. Ladi settled down on the ground where Chuck and the men had yesterday cleared a small landing pad. He shut down his engine. Beside him, on the ground outside, was the portable camp, exactly as he had dropped it. It had not been touched. He looked up the stream into the jungle, but he couldn't see far.

The creek was high. Much higher than it had been the day before.

Dismayed, he radioed Ok Tedi. He could hike up the mountain looking for them or wait. The message that crackled back over the radio told him to stick with his helicopter. If anything happened to him, the men left in the jungle would all be in serious trouble. A couple of hours later, Chuck and his Native team straggled out on their own. Exhausted and weak, they had the samples, but the cost had been high. Chuck was ill.

As the days passed, Chuck continued working but his condition deteriorated until, ignoring his protestations, the company decided to fly him out to Port Moresby for a proper examination. The decision could not have been more timely. As Chuck was being moved, the illness took over completely. There was no question now that he was in a serious state.

Radioing ahead, they alerted the hospital in Port Moresby. They were bringing him straight in. It was cerebral malaria – the worst case they had seen.

CHAPTER NINE

PORT MORESBY, SEPTEMBER 17, 1971, 6:35 PM

IT was already growing dark when Marlene left work, picked up Mark and got home. That was one of the worst drawbacks to living in the tropics – the early nights. There were others. The Australian authorities had some unwritten rules for European women living in Port Moresby. Women were to dress modestly, remain indoors and stay out of sight at night, in secure quarters. Kennecott's apartments and Marlene's own modesty met the requirements. The door to their apartment was burglar-proof and the windows were secured with heavy-duty steel wire mesh.

Marlene didn't share Chuck's enthusiasm for New Guinea. It wasn't just that the culture was unfriendly toward women. It was that New Guineans had little respect for another's property. All the sins and historical excesses of New Guinea were collected in the capital city. It was safe enough for a 23-year-old woman to go to the markets and back, to stay in the crowds with her son, but not for her to move off the beaten path.

When telex, a new communications technology, had been introduced to Port Moresby a few months earlier, she had been hired by Kennecott to run the company's communication system at the office there. It was better than staying in the apartment all the time, and the social interaction at work was pleasant. But the evenings were long and frighteningly lonely. Port Moresby had no nightlife, or none of the kind a lone white woman could ever participate in – or would want to. So her nights were spent quietly at home with Mark, behind locked doors and wire-meshed windows.

Marlene went outside to the porch to feed the parrots with Mark before she made supper. Recognizing them, the birds waddled over to the edge of their cage in greeting. Marlene let one out and Mark fed it some treats. In temperament the birds were as varied as dogs, and as pets they were even more capable of learning human ways. Mark's parrot was the most gentle. Even when the boy would not let it go, the bird wouldn't bite him.

Chuck had started collecting the birds soon after they arrived in New Guinea and had built a large aviary for them on the porch. A year earlier he had come home from camp with several beautiful green-and-blue fruit pigeons. Primarily arboreal, they had blown into Ok Tedi at night during a hurricane storm. Shaken loose from their roosts, unable to see in the dark, they could not land in the jungle again. Chuck had found them fluttering around, exhausted, on the ground near the lights. He had gathered them up and kept them in safety until he was able to bring them to Port Moresby.

Like the pigeons he had had in Alberta when he was a child, these fruit pigeons, too, had responded when he cooed softly to them. But these had been wild birds, and one by one they had died. They had had the right foods, but as he and Marlene had learned, it was a matter of spirit. Unlike the feral pigeons of North America, when these were caged, they lost the will to live.

The parrots she now fed were wild birds as well, but they had been caught early in their lives. Taken by the Natives as nestlings, they were comfortable among people and usually long outlived their owners. Before when Chuck was home they were allowed free rein in the apartment, chowing down on Marlene's plants, crawling up the curtains and perching over their plates at mealtime. Mark found it as delightful as Chuck to live among the birds, but when Chuck left for camp, they went back into their cages and Marlene cleaned up the mess.

Now he was home – and the birds remained outside. He was lying in the next room breathing painfully, his pallid body racked by spasms. There was no relief.

Outside a diesel cloud poured from an old truck loaded with singing passengers. New Guinea was omnipresent. Standing on the porch, she was surrounded by it. The screeching of the parrots, the sight of the steel-roofed neighbourhood, buildings on stilts trying to clear the ground, the heavy acrid burning smell of cooking fires and organic garbage, the confluence of sea and earth, the very position of the sun and the heavy purple shadows suffused her with the reality of the dark country. The land pulsed.

Inside, the apartment offered no refuge either. It was full of images, even more elemental ones, as though through its masks the true face of the country was exposed. Dark and primitive. Mudmen land.

She stood in the middle of the room and looked around. Dead birds hung on the walls, together with the painted faces of carved figures. Spears and shields, laced-cane body armour, spiked war clubs filled every corner. Ancestral figures, some larger than Mark, lined the walls, leaning against them, and stared into the room. Carved with totems and sacred images, inlaid with shells and topped with braided palm fibres or human hair, they needed only the breath of a shaman or a fretful imagination to come to life: Stone Age visions that had the power of sight.

Marlene allowed Mark to stay out with the parrots and began to make supper. There was no hurry. It was already dark and a long evening stretched before them. Sometimes in the past she had joined her neighbours for supper, the other women of the small apartment block whose husbands also worked at Ok Tedi. But tonight she and Mark would eat alone, as they had so often done.

Afterwards she would read to him before putting him to bed. Then she would sit beside her husband and think, remembering summer days in high school, Chuck's Rambler with the Pullman seats, the late nights, the excuses, the races, the university years – how it seemed they would never end – and the move to New Guinea that had excited Chuck. Now Canada was so impossibly far away.

The memories played like a favourite tune, giving continuity to her life, bringing her here, to this place, offering some explanation for it all.

When Chuck first went into the jungle at Ok Tedi and his work schedule was three weeks in and one week out, it had been a long time to wait between visits. When he changed his schedule to six weeks in and two weeks out, the wait became almost unbearable. For Mark's sake she struggled to maintain good spirits, spending all her free time with him and counting down the days – the weeks – until Chuck returned. Kennecott was good about it. It coordinated their schedules so Marlene was off when he came out.

Rather than save their money or spend it to fly to Cairns or some other civilized Australian city for a break, like everyone else, Chuck always took her and Mark deeper into the country.

He needed to see this wild land, these strange people. So they travelled up its rivers in dugout canoes, slept in village huts on mats and ate fire-blackened roots with their hands, alongside mostly naked men and women with whom they couldn't speak a word. Every six weeks there had been another trip. They had flown into Wewak and Marienberg on the north coast, sailed the Bismarck Sea in outrigger canoes, travelled up the Sepik to the Chambri Lakes and paddled into the swamplands of the Ramu River.

Marlene never complained, although there were times she refused to get into the dugouts with Mark. For the most part she enjoyed travelling with Chuck and found their adventures exciting, too.

On one of their trips together into the backcountry, a Native had approached them with the dried, feathered skin of one of the rarest and the most beautiful of New Guinea's birds, the black sickle bird of paradise. Chuck had bartered with the man for it and now it, too, was hanging on their wall, a symbol of New Guinea.

Chuck loved to sit face-to-face on the ground and bargain with the tribesmen. Marlene usually watched, along with the entire village. More than a meeting of cultures, there was in the exchange an unspoken communication of character and temperament and spirit. Every transaction held the potential for insights into the deepest nature of the people doing the trading. After every trip into the outback they returned to Port Moresby with armloads of new treasures – the artifacts that now filled the room around her. Chuck loved to collect things. Each piece had its own history, its own story.

On other trips, they had explored the island chains off the northeast coast of New Guinea: Manus, New Ireland and New Britain. The immensity of the country, its dramatic beauty and incredible diversity – from blue-green coral reefs to black mangrove swamps, from lush rainforest to dry savanna – constantly delighted both of them.

There were times, though, she would have preferred to live more of her own life – at least to do things differently. But it was difficult to get Chuck to compromise. He always did what he wanted to do. He was like that when they first met, and he had never changed. Nor, she believed, would he. He was on his own mission and could not be turned from the river that ran through him.

Marlene saw in him a spirit. He was different from other men. Emotionally he had the exuberance of youth – an unrestrained and fearless rush over new horizons, challenging everything, a passion for living that she had never seen in anyone else. He accepted no limits and, she believed, he could have achieved anything he wanted.

But she knew, too, that Chuck could only do it his way. It was his best and worst feature. On the one hand, he was not easy to live with; on the other, life with him was always exciting. She had promised years ago to love and accept him, and it was a promise she always meant to keep. Now he was dying.

When the message had come through that Chuck was being flown out of Ok Tedi with a high fever and suffering intense pain, she had braced herself for the worst. But she could never have prepared herself for what the doctor had to tell her. He could not meet her eyes.

"It's a particularly virulent strain of cerebral malaria...." He paused to let it sink in before continuing. "One, I'm sorry to say, that we haven't had any luck with."

It was too ambiguous, the implications too serious, too shocking for her to accept. One part of her hoped he only meant the pain. Pain would pass.

"What do you mean?" Marlene demanded a straight answer. "Please – you have to be clearer!"

"I'm sorry ... there is nothing we can do for him," the doctor answered. His expression communicated more than his words. There was no hope. Marlene's heart began sinking quickly.

"I'm sorry. Really sorry," he added softly.

Marlene's head began to spin. Her whole life was faltering. How could Chuck die? It was impossible. He was 24. He was invincible. She couldn't let him down. She would save him. New Guinea wouldn't. Quickly she rallied.

"THEN FLY HIM THE HELL OUT OF HERE!" Her voice had echoed in the hallway. Anywhere would be better than New Guinea, with its hostile jungles and stinking malarial mangrove swamps. Life decayed faster here than she had ever believed possible. The whole country was septic, rotting before one's eyes. And now it was killing her husband. She hated the place!

The doctor, an Australian, maintained his even tone. There was no way to break the news any more gently.

"I'm really sorry, ma'am. There's nothing anyone can do. Some tropical diseases are beyond us. This is one of them."

It was too hard to take in.

"How long?"

"Depends ... a few days perhaps. If he's strong, and has the will to fight it, maybe even a couple of weeks." Spirit, in people no less than in other creatures, determined the quality of their passing.

The company had done what it could. The senior managers from Kennecott in Australia had flown up to talk to Marlene and look in on Chuck. Calls had been made around the world looking for answers, for the best specialist in the field. But he was already in the field, in New Guinea. They had him. Chuck was beyond help. There was no effective medicine available. The pain was inside his head – intense and continuous. Unable to sleep or even rest, he quickly became delirious, moaning, trembling and crying out incessantly.

A practising Catholic, Marlene could only pray. It was not enough. Chuck continued to deteriorate. After he'd spent a few days in the hospital, she had brought him home. And here he was. Here she could at least be at his side. And he could die in his own bed, if he knew it.

Unable to focus on anything but the pain, day after day, night after night, he sweated profusely, rocked and wasted away. The days passed into nights, into mornings … it was all the same.

Marlene tried to feed him, to pour liquids into his mouth, to give his body some nourishment to fight the disease. She was losing the battle. Each day the doctor came by and offered to take him back into the hospital, to spare her this burden, this deathwatch.

Marlene refused. Each day Chuck grew thinner and weaker. After two weeks, with his flesh shrunken and his bones protruding, almost skeletal, he rallied for a moment and recognized Marlene for the first time since he had left Ok Tedi. For the first time in nearly two months, they spoke.

"Marlene." He called her name. She met his eyes and nearly burst into tears. He was back. Only his look was so far away. His voice barely audible, he spoke clearly and deliberately. "I can't stand it anymore."

Tears welled up in her eyes. He knew he was dying.

"Please, Marlene," he begged her, "you have to finish me … I can't stand it anymore."

His lucidity was only momentary. Shaking and crying out, he was slipping away again, overcome.

He was leaving her now and she wept. This was even worse than his dying. Begging her to end his pain. His last request. As a Catholic, she couldn't. As his wife, she wouldn't. Yet how could she let him suffer? For Mark, their son, a part of her would carry on. But when Chuck died, her spirit would die with him.

A man's breath escaped his body like a small dark bird. It would not be long now.

CHAPTER TEN

CEREBRAL MALARIA

THE New Guineans, like people everywhere, were creatures of habit. The attraction of familiar ground lay in the increased potential it offered for survival. To venture into new territory, to stray from the old paths, presented serious risks. To the villagers, every challenge to the natural order was dangerous. Who knew what consequences would flow from a disturbance to existing harmonies? Change was, by its very nature, destabilizing, dangerous. But the power of the newcomers was not to be challenged, and their own fear had given way to the new order imposed by the outsiders.

Their faith in the power of the White Men of Ok Tedi was shaken, however, when Chuck took ill. To the Natives, all illnesses – and every death – had supernatural causes. As the company men in camp knew, sooner or later everyone contracted malaria. Given the conditions in which they worked, in close quarters with villagers who were host to a multitude of illnesses, the spread of disease was inevitable. For all their technology and magic, the White Men were no different. They suffered the same.

New Guinea was a vast unknown. Just as there were hundreds of undiscovered human cultures scattered throughout the country, so, too, were there deadly new diseases and new strains of old ones, never encountered before, that had incubated here in isolation. The plasmodia parasites that now flowed by the thousands through Chuck's veins were on an evolutionary path of their own. Attacking the brain, they produced pain worse than any medieval torture. They ignited his nerves with pure fire, as if the sun itself had consciousness of its own agony. The only known relief was death.

In Ok Tedi, the men who knew Chuck best took the news grimly. Sullen and morose, they gathered together in the canteen each night, in the dark, drinking heavily and cursing the country, the jungle and the plagues of parasites. Their little camp steeped itself in misery and death. Especially at night, with the rain pounding down, the civilized world seemed another reality entirely, another dimension, light-years away.

Chuck's bosses from Kennecott's offices in Australia continued to fly up to look in on him or to call, offering what comfort they could to Marlene, caring for Chuck in the small apartment in Port Moresby. Hers was a heroic effort matching Chuck's desperate bid for survival, but the battle was hopeless. His resistance only prolonged the agony. In days, maybe hours, his body would finally succumb and they would have to get on with their lives.

Marlene dreaded that moment. The aftermath. She would be left alone with Mark. How could she ever live another life? Refusing to give up, she continued to nourish Chuck as best she could, a small spoonful at a time, to greet the doctor who came each day to record the course of the disease and, when he left, to pray. Sometimes she fell asleep and forgot, only to wake to the horror of her husband's slow, agonized death, fighting her own battle to keep from breaking down while she stayed by him, day after day, praying for a miracle.

It happened.

She was there beside him when he stopped moving. His body relaxed. For a moment Marlene panicked. He was so still it seemed death itself might have calmed him, but she could see his chest slowly rising and falling. He was asleep. When he opened his eyes at last and, seeing her there, called her name, she allowed herself to cry. He was very weak – but he was back.

Chuck remembered very little of his illness. Most of the time he had been delirious. He did remember the pain, a pain that had screamed in his head, that had torn him apart, never subsiding. A pain that had burned him alive and lasted an eternity. And he remembered that single lucid moment when he had begged Marlene to stop it, to kill him.

What he did not know was that she had sent Mark away so she could stay by his side, every hour of every day; that even after he had given up, begging to die, she had continued to trickle food down his throat, to give him some strength to live on; that she fought for his life. Until the illness, he had had no idea how much Marlene loved him. Becoming lucid again after two and half weeks and seeing her for the second time since he had contracted the disease, he had a new appreciation for her.

When he opened his eyes she was there again, as she had been before, as though waiting for him all that time. He understood he had never been alone. Through it all she had been right there, with him. His voice was hoarse and quiet as he acknowledged it all in one word.

"Marlene."

He was absolutely exhausted, but the storm had passed. His head was clear. "It's over," he added unnecessarily.

He owed her his life. Together they had beaten it. The doctor, surprised, confirmed it. Chuck was his first and only case to have survived the deadly strain of cerebral malaria.

CHAPTER ELEVEN

FREEDOM FOR THE BIRDS

CHUCK had not been intimidated by the possibility of death. If anything, his escape from its embrace filled him with new confidence and excitement, empowering him to go even farther afield. For him, there was no looking back, only forward. Each day was unique, offering new possibilities – not all of them pleasant.

Australian-run Papua New Guinea was now too tame. More and more Chuck was casting his eye to the Indonesian side of the huge island, to West Irian, the dark half. There, in the interior, the people had never been subdued; there tribal warfare still raged openly. There a modern man could come face-to-face with a Stone Age warrior on a battlefield littered with 20,000-year-old skulls.

Chuck longed to cross over. The lure of the distant past was irresistible. He would have given all he had to go. As impossible as it seemed months earlier, a window was now opening. The Ok Tedi project was entering a new stage. The exploration program was complete and the ore reserves had been calculated and confirmed: Kennecott had a major hit. The ore deposit was huge – on the scale of Bougainville. Assuming the tax regime did not change for the worse, Chuck and Annan Cook had calculated that the company could clear 20 percent on its investment on copper alone. But the ore body was even richer than that. It held other precious metals, gold among them. The results of those assays were being kept strictly confidential, but there was no question about it. Ok Tedi was a real prize.

All that remained was development. This would be no small task considering the conditions and location; the effort and the cost to build the infrastructure would be enormous. One day a modern mining town would rise over the mud of Kennecott's little field, but for now, given the politics – independence was coming to Papua New Guinea – it was far more prudent to wait and see how receptive the new government would be before investing in the country's future.

In the meantime Kennecott, like Chuck, had been looking across the border. Late in 1970, it had formed a new subsidiary, Kennecott Indonesia. Kennecott wanted to continue exploring west, along the same geological structure line that Ok Tedi followed – west across the border from Ok Tedi and through the central cordillera of West Irian.

Since the Indonesian takeover on May 1, 1963, though, nobody apart from a handful of Christian missionaries had been allowed in. The deadline for the people of the former Dutch New Guinea to decide their own future – to determine whether they wished to remain a part of Indonesia – had passed only two years ago without the required plebiscite. Indonesia had made it clear to the world that, whatever the wishes of the people, Irian Jaya, now called West Irian, would never be free of Jakarta's rule. No one else was going in or coming out. However, Indonesia saw a reason to make an exception for geologists. The generals had been watching the mineral wealth of Papua New Guinea build the country. Revenue from a copper mine in West Irian would enrich Jakarta.

In Papua New Guinea there remained only a small territory to the east of Ok Tedi that was officially "restricted," because it was still "wild," but most of West Irian was similarly classified. Virtually the entire interior of West Irian, the lands that Kennecott wanted to explore, had never been visited by outsiders. Kennecott Indonesia got the permits to explore and asked Chuck if he wanted to take a look.

After 18 months in Papua New Guinea with Kennecott Australasia, Chuck was transferred to Kennecott Indonesia. He and Marlene began packing at once. Marlene was also glad to leave Port Moresby. After Chuck's near-fatal encounter with cerebral malaria, Marlene came down with malaria. A less serious strain, her illness was severely complicated by the fact that she was pregnant. They had been anxiously awaiting the birth of their second child when she took ill. The baby died.

Induced to labour to deliver a stillborn, Marlene was heartbroken. She was relieved to leave Port Moresby behind forever. Chuck's last act was to set his wild green parrots free. They screeched and cawed as they found their wings and took flight. They would survive Port Moresby, too.

CHAPTER TWELVE

WEST IRIAN, 1971

CAIRNS is a seaside town on the east coast of Queensland, due south of Port Moresby. It is an old colonial settlement, and its white wooden architecture, covered sidewalks, parks and shops were completely accessible to a young woman on foot with a child. The family took an apartment there, not far from the blistering white beach, and began a new life in paradise.

Chuck shipped the rusting Datsun he had bought in Port Moresby to Cairns and they used it to explore the Australian coastline. Marlene was happier to walk. Cairns had everything anyone needed. It was a fishing town; the fleet would go out at dawn and return the same day. The Great Barrier Reef lay just off the coast, and some of the greatest marlin fishing in the world was only an hour away.

In 1971 the town had recently been "discovered" by Australian youth. Hippies had settled in, bringing their generation's influences and earthy values to the town. There were sidewalk cafes, craft shops, stalls with organic fruit and vegetables fresh from the Atherton Tablelands, and people to talk with again. Cairns was a young person's town. And white. Even the water from the taps was drinkable.

Chuck had little time to enjoy it. His new bosses, Dave Jordt and Fred Warner, were planning an exploration program on a grand scale. They intended to prospect a 48,000-square-kilometre block of the central mountain range of West Irian, beginning at the Papua New Guinea border – the very country Chuck had longingly stared at from Ok Tedi – as well as the western Vogelkop Peninsula.

Warner took on the logistics, while Jordt and Chuck worked out the sampling program. New Guinea's geological environment was unusually pure. There were very few heavy minerals in the surrounding host rock, making separation of the heavy ore minerals from the lighter sands relatively simple. Beginning with an eight-kilogram sand sample from a stream, screened through a minus-1.5-millimetre mesh sieve and hand-panned down until only a cupful of "heavies" remained, one could later determine fairly accurately in the lab, after further chemical and magnetic separations, whether or not a copper field had been exposed to the surface in the watershed upstream. There was no better nor more economical method of prospecting anywhere in the world. Utilising these methods at Ok Tedi, Kennecott could detect the copper ore deposit 48 miles downstream.

Dave Jordt and Chuck collected all the information they could on West Irian: geological data, landforms, water systems, military side-look radar aerial photographs, topographical maps. Then they began to plot out a sampling program on a very tight budget. Even Kennecott had to be cost-conscious.

While they were busy, Warner flew in to set up a base at Ok Sibel. With no local infrastructure or support systems, everything had to be supplied by the company and transported from Australia. Landing a team in the field and keeping it supplied – and alive – would be a monumental task. Jordt wanted them to be better prepared, better equipped and more mobile than the last expedition to go in 10 years ago – Rockefeller's Harvard-Peabody Expedition. It was more than a logistical problem; it was a bureaucratic nightmare. There were no airports where they were going, only small jungle landing strips, and the Indonesian army did not tolerate foreign helicopters freely crossing its borders.

Warner had to remind them that Kennecott had the power to deliver a mine like Bougainville – if the copper was there. The royalties alone could support the entire government. Jakarta expedited the permits and Warner landed in Ok Sibel, West Irian.

A Native village in the mountains near the Papua New Guinea border, due west of Ok Tedi, Ok Sibel was not pristine – a Catholic mission had been established – but its contact with the outside world was extremely limited. The occasional Indonesian army patrol also passed through it. There was an otherworldly mood to this village. Shrouded in mists in the morning, dark and dripping in the daily monsoon rains, the mountains here were lush, and the village's small clearings were forever at risk of being retaken by the jungle. At night the smell of wood smoke hung in the air and Warner heard the sound of low conversations as he walked through the huts between flickering fires. Dark faces, huddled together as though for protection from the forces of the night, peered at him constantly.

Out in the fields forming a perimeter around the village, tall sentry towers had been raised against the threat of attack. Rickety, stiltlike constructions 12 metres high, they were manned day and night.

The village was on guard. They were a people perpetually at war.

Warner set to work engaging the Natives to build Kennecott's base camp at the edge of the village: private sleeping quarters, a field kitchen, a fuel dump and a secure warehouse for supplies. He then organized a ground expedition, to explore the possibility of sampling with Native bearers. Helicopters were not then available in West Irian, and the conditions in the mountains, higher than those at Ok Tedi, made flying extremely difficult.

Surprised but pleased to see the enthusiasm the village had for the trek, Warner hired only a dozen men to cut and carry, yet the whole village seemed intent on tagging along. As he made preparations, so, too, did they. When he and his crew set off on foot along a trail leading in the direction of the next watershed, all of the men, not one content to stay behind, drained out of the village and joined them.

The mood was festive. A long line of men, some bearing gear for the expedition, others carrying spears three metres long, or bows and arrows, moved out. They all bore large, decorated, wooden shields, a metre high and half as wide – large enough for a man to hide behind in the event of a rain of enemy arrows. Cut down through the centre of the top of each shield, a narrow slit acted as a peephole.

In Ok Tedi, body armour was worn occasionally. Here, all the men wore it. Thick, woven cane strips had been fashioned into breastplates, shoulder pads and groin covers. Cross-woven so tightly no arrow could slip through, the armour was heavy enough to turn a spear – or at least lessen its impact.

Some of the men wore magnificent, spreading headdresses of bird feathers and had painted their bodies, already decorated with tattoos, with bird images in white and red, the tints derived from wild berries. As in Ok Tedi, the bird motif, carved in wood and surmounting their regalia dominated their artistic depictions of the spirit world. The image of a half-human, half-bird spirit, repeating itself down the line, followed Warner as they moved into the hinterland beyond the village.

The line of bare-footed warriors snaked its way around the edge of the mountain. Sleek and well-muscled, many of the men wore nose pieces of bone and pig tusk. Pleased with their unflagging enthusiasm, Warner led them into the next valley, now confident that with their help, the local exploration work could proceed evenly – and without a helicopter.

They were following a narrow trail and settling into the rhythm of the march when the line began moving more quietly. Warner thought nothing of it until they came within sight of a strange village and, without further warning, his men attacked.

Like Ok Sibel, this village, too, was a collection of loosely scattered huts raised from the ground with mud, sticks and palm leaves. Their garden plots, cut out of the forest, were between Warner's men and the village. As the Ok Sibel warriors charged in attack across the fields, women and children fled for their lives while their husbands, fathers and brothers rushed to the rescue.

Under a hail of arrows, he saw people go down. Women and children were preferred targets. Unable to fight back, they were easier to kill. Glory followed from sinking one's spear or arrow into an enemy's body, regardless of size or sex.

Horrified, Warner realized too late that the men of Ok Sibel believed he was leading them on a military campaign. It was war! Even the men he had engaged to come with him threw down their supplies and rushed to join the battle. Screaming at them and cursing, Warner waded into the field, pushing them back to halt the fighting. The defending villagers, caught completely by surprise, rallied quickly and formed their own line at the edge of their village, exchanging arrows and spears with the men of Ok Sibel.

The easy killing was over. Gradually the two sides moved farther apart and Warner's men withdrew at last back into the forest from which they had come. The experiment of using Native ground expeditions was over.

The Ok Sibel men were jubilant. Had they captured one of the enemy alive or recovered one of their bodies for a victory feast, it would have been a greater day. Still, it was a tremendous victory, and they rejoiced as they retreated, recounting every arrow that found its mark and identifying each warrior who had launched it. The intensity of the battle, the thrill of combat – venting their deepest feelings, expressing their most masculine nature, facing fear and death – carried them jauntily all the way back to Ok Sibel.

Once they had put away their weapons and calmed down, Warner took them all on in classic Ok Tedi style. He was the boss! More powerful than any of them, he alone commanded a helicopter. He alone had access to goods they dreamed of: axe heads and knives of steel, light in the dark, and pots and pans, salt and tobacco. And food. Strange, tinned foods the villagers coveted. All that was his. Goods they could get – only by obeying him!

There was no doubting his power. When Warner then told them there would be no more killing on his expeditions, they accepted that. Only they had already decided they were not going out with him again. What point was there to strike out beyond their own village borders unless it was to fight? They could launch their own campaigns and do their own killing without him.

When Chuck and Dave Jordt arrived in Ok Sibel late that month to begin the sampling program, the new plan was to rely exclusively on themselves and their helicopter. The Natives' war culture could not be trusted. Despite the obvious respect the villagers had for them, their easy display of wealth was too conspicuous, too powerful a lure to be resisted.

Money had no meaning whatever, and villagers were paid instead in trade. Stacked in the company warehouse were cases of boy food. To a villager, a can of boy food was a real prize. Specially manufactured for such trade and made from a mixture of cooked grain and fish, it closely resembled cat food. Chuck found it extremely unpleasant. But for those with protein-deficient diets it was a godsend, and the villagers loved it. Even an empty tin can was a prize worth fighting for.

There were easier ways to get things than to work for them. New Guinea men did not work much. Daily chores and the garden plots belonged to the women. Warriors had more important tasks to attend to. But a raid on the Kennecott warehouse carried more risk than one launched against their traditional enemies. What kind of payback would the white men with the machines mount? Fear kept them in check.

Kennecott's men were not relying exclusively for their protection on the mystique of power. In his bunk at night, secure behind a fortified door, Chuck sometimes slept with a double-barrelled shotgun beside his bed. Deliberately windowless, the warehouse, too, was built to withstand prolonged assaults with primitive tools. Still, there had to be a tolerable balance between power and access to the wealth. As long as the warriors had some control over their access to the treasure, and the choice to work honestly for it was theirs, the geologists were safe, and a working relationship developed.

CHAPTER THIRTEEN

THE FIELD

For all its closeness to Ok Tedi, Ok Sibel – a different reality entirely – might as well have been on the other side of the world. Chuck's first day out in the field revealed just how different it was. Except in the preliminary planning, Chuck had not worked with Fred Warner and his experience with Dave Jordt, sampling around Ok Tedi, had been limited. He had to prove himself. They had an assistant, Rudy, to help in the field, and a cook who doubled as camp manager and stayed near the radio at their base in Ok Sibel – their only link to the outside.

Fred, Chuck and Rudy went out together in the helicopter, piloted by Jack Riley, a man who preferred to be called by his last name. Riley had combat experience in Vietnam. A lucky coincidence for Chuck. The most economical use of their helicopter was to map a flight plan, plotting and marking all the sample sites. Dropping one man down at the first site, another at the second, and the third at the next site, the helicopter would return to pick up the first man, who, having collected his sample by that time, was ready to be flown on to the fourth site. And so it went, with the helicopter, leapfrogging the men, one at a time, along the course.

They had been out for over an hour and had each collected a sample when Chuck was picked up and dropped off again at his second site. This one was located some distance away from the others, and Chuck figured by the time the helicopter moved them and then returned to get him, a good half hour would have elapsed. He needed all of it. He had to collect conventional silt samples and identify and record all the rock types in the float. Riley had put him down where he was able to, but Chuck was not over the best sand to sample. His first priority was to locate a site with the optimum conditions for prospecting.

He looked around him. He was in a gully that normally ran with water. The mountains were so steep that the heavy rains ran off quickly and the watercourse he was on was nearly dry. The vegetation was low, low enough that Riley had been able to get down near the ground, and Chuck had dropped the rest of the distance without effort. Flanking the gully was thick forest. Here and there every 90 metres, huge trees, their webbed trunks spread out over 10 metres to support their massive weight, rose up, towering over the forest.

Chuck wasted no time with the scenery. He was here to work. The sample was the thing. He hiked a short distance up the muddy bed, found a good spot and began to dig. He was still panning the sand when the helicopter returned. Without looking up, he continued. He couldn't believe it. He had only been at this site for a few minutes. Nobody could run a sample that fast. Ignoring the pilot, Chuck rushed to complete his work. He certainly wasn't going to leave without the sample. Riley would have to learn. He was only the taxi driver – not running the show.

It was almost impossible to work under the helicopter. The roar of its engine and the wash from its prop were extremely distracting. Chuck's anger was rising quickly. The pilot was deliberately making his work more difficult. It was maddening.

Suddenly the skid of the helicopter's landing gear hit him. Riley had come down so close that as he swept sideways, the runner had caught Chuck across the top of his back and almost threw him right over his sample, spilling the whole thing.

Furious, Chuck felt like killing him; he fought to control his anger. It was only their first day in the field. He was not going to ruin it by fighting with their pilot or missing a sample. With a rapid motion he waved the pilot off and ignored the gestures Riley was making to him in return to climb back aboard. Unable to land, Riley was hovering over him, apparently anxious to get going.

Chuck cursed him again. He had never worked with such a reckless pilot! The guy was a real asshole. Determined not to be diverted, Chuck bent low over his sample and, using his body as protection, continued to work. Then, just as suddenly as it had arrived, the helicopter left. Tilting away from the mountain, it dropped off down into the valley following the ravine.

Chuck was glad of it. He did a quick separation of the sands in his pan and recorded in his notebook what was left in the float. What he was looking for in it were monzonite intrusions, quartz or evidence of chemical alteration – anything that might indicate copper mineralization. He was so absorbed in his work it never occurred to him to question why the pilot had returned so quickly or where he had gone.

Jack Riley was as furious as Chuck. He was doing his damnedest to save the Canadian geologist, but the man was making it impossible. Right after Riley dropped Chuck and was spinning away to pick up Fred Warner, he had noticed a flicker of movement far down the valley. He had an eye for detail and flew down to check it out. It was a war party. A huge group of men, nearly 60 strong, was advancing up the ravine toward Chuck!

The sound of the helicopter had stirred them up, and its near landing had brought them out to investigate. They were moving quickly up the creekbed. Primed for an attack. As Riley flew over them, some arrows bounced off the helicopter. They were shooting at him.

Natives usually fled and hid at the sight of his machine. This group was especially brazen and hostile. They must have had experience with helicopters before, thought Riley. The Indonesian army had used them to attack villagers. Whether these warriors were seeking revenge for some earlier offence against them or merely attacked anything foreign that entered their territory, he had no doubt Chuck was a dead man if they got to him.

Covered in body armour and carrying spears, bows and arrows, they showered his helicopter again with arrows, which clattered off the Plexiglas bubble around him as he buzzed them, driving them out of the creekbed and into the forest cover. Wheeling in the air, he flew back up the ravine to pull Chuck out, the warriors now only minutes away. As soon as he spotted Chuck, Riley waved at him frantically to get aboard, but the geologist waved him off and carried on working. Riley couldn't believe it. Crouching over his sample, Chuck was ignoring him.

The situation was desperate. Riley had to get the man off the ground, but in spite of all his efforts, Chuck continued to ignore him. Moving dangerously close, Riley rocked the helicopter so that his landing skid hit Chuck, almost knocking him over. Surely he couldn't ignore that!

As soon as the Canadian looked up at him, Riley waved desperately, signalling him to climb aboard. In return he was rudely motioned to back off. From his vantage point in the air, Riley saw the Natives cresting the rise in the creek. They were closing in fast. Riley flew down into them again. Battling the Stone Age with his helicopter, risking his machine and his life to a well-aimed spear or arrow, he again scattered them back into the cover of the trees and returned for Chuck.

Still Chuck wasn't ready to leave. Grateful that the pilot had left, Chuck was now even angrier when he heard him roaring around just out of sight over the crest of the hill, only to return minutes later. Chuck cursed. The man was impossible. He had to teach him a lesson. He had been hurrying until now, but Riley's attitude needed an adjustment. If he was so anxious to get going, Chuck decided he would just take his sweet time. The pilot had to learn what he was there for. The helicopter buzzed him again. Dodging the skid as it swung dangerously close to him, Chuck ignored the pilot. Angry, he slowed his work even more. He'd prospect the float thoroughly and record everything about it meticulously. No one would ever complain he didn't get his samples.

Riley, realizing he had a madman on the ground who wasn't going to get into the helicopter until he was good and ready, did the only thing he could. He swung down once again into the war party to buy Chuck time. The warriors, having survived two challenges from the aircraft without injury, were not so quick to disperse this time. Having regrouped, they stood their ground. It didn't matter to Riley. As long as they were not advancing up the creek, Chuck could finish his work.

Riley gave him lots of time before he flew back. The warriors were so close he could not risk Chuck not being ready. Fuming, Chuck grabbed onto a skid and swung up into the aircraft.

"What kind of flying was *that!* You ran right into me! We're here to work, hey, not screw around!"

Riley said nothing as they rose up above the angry warriors and Chuck's narrow escape became obvious.

The day was not over yet. Ok Sibel was south of the central mountain range and they had crossed it, flying low through narrow valleys beneath the cloud ceiling, to prospect the country to the north. Under Warner's direction they had continued sampling nearly as far as the village of Japil before he said they could return back. It was an ambitious program for one day. Warner had pushed them hard. Too hard. They were far from their base.

Driven down by the weather lower and lower into the valleys and quickly losing their light, they were skimming the ground now, flying under the dark ceiling of cloud trying to get back, when they broke through into a wide, lower canyon. It was no salvation. The clouds closed in behind them.

They were trapped, boxed into the canyon. Below them a white river was boiling up a frenzy, and above them a mass of heavy black cloud roiled. There was nowhere to land. The jungle on either side of the river was dense and high.

Warner and Riley exchanged harsh words. Darkness was taking over and they were low on fuel. Each blamed the other for the situation. Neither knew where the hell they were. Chuck said nothing and braced himself for the inevitable. They would have to face a landing in the jungle. Sitting in the back seat with Rudy, the helicopter balancing precariously in the air, he felt very fragile. Even if they survived the crash, how long could they survive the jungle? Ten days? Fourteen? And who would come looking for them?

Warner, navigating, spread out the maps across his knees and told Riley to follow the river downstream. They were looking for a landmark to reorient themselves. Warner found it. "There it is!" he yelled, pointing. "That's the stream!"

It was a small tributary flowing down the side slope to join the main current. There was not much to identify it. The clouds, sinking with the light, had pushed them right down over the frothing river, but Warner felt sure of their position. He gave Riley very specific instructions. They were going up, into the clouds.

"Climb to 5,000 feet," he said. "Straight up."

They rose, blind, through grey soup. With no points of outside reference, it was impossible to tell what their bearing was, their elevation or even their angle.

With Riley flying on instruments alone, the tension was heavy. They all sat motionless, barely breathing, staring at the instruments. Watching the dials climb in the grey void. At the elevation, Warner gave Riley a compass bearing to fly, and an air speed. Hoping the air currents were not too strong to throw them off course, Warner counted down the seconds on his watch as they crested an invisible low range into the next valley.

"Okay ... ready ... slow ... stop!" He ordered.

"Okay ... good. We should have it; let's go straight down. There's a village below us. We should hit a mission..."

Riley began the descent into the unknown. Inching down for thousands of feet. Warner, navigating completely blind, was aiming for the only safe haven in the entire region, a Christian mission. Descending through the cloud, they dropped down into a clearer pocket near the ground and, right beneath them, there it was. Warner had performed a miracle.

They landed at dusk, radioed Ok Sibel to say they were okay, refuelled from their own spare tanks and stayed the night. The missionaries were glad to see them. After a dinner under kerosene lamps of vegetables from the mission garden and a chicken killed for the occasion, they all sat out on the veranda, drank tea and exchanged stories. Chuck would have preferred something stronger. After the day they had spent, a good drink, or several, would have been welcome. But they were all grateful to be sitting in chairs, even rough-cut ones, and sleeping under a roof. It could have been worse. Listening to Riley recount the tale of fighting off Natives to save his skin, Chuck sipped his tea and laughed at his own folly. The day could have been much worse.

The missionaries, too, had a story to tell. As it unfolded, Chuck settled into his chair, relaxing and enjoying the night. The lights flickered from the village fires below them. Sounds of a thousand crickets and frogs filled the air. Breathing deeply, he inhaled the life around him. Dampness and decay, wet earth and wood smoke. It felt wonderful to drink warm tea on a porch in the heart of this ancient, forgotten land. To listen to the strangest tales, unbelievable stories. Nowhere else was life like this.

"They were our most trusted friends," the missionary was saying about three Natives they had left in charge of the mission only two weeks before, when he and his wife had left for Jakarta, their first break in years.

"What can I say? They were Christians! We trusted them, you understand. They invited some villagers from the next community to attend the departure feast ... We minister to that community as well, and they all came to see us off. It's a big event when an aircraft comes in. The whole village was out, wishing us well."

He paused, remembering it, before continuing. "It was the last pleasant memory I have of our mission. We were not in the air five minutes when we received a desperate radio message from our houseboy. As soon as we left, the entire village turned on our guests.... Horrible really! We returned immediately. The fighting was still going on but we managed to stop it and get the survivors on the trail back to their own village. And their walking wounded.... horrible! There were three people dead and another so badly wounded he should have been. He had arrows sticking into every part of his body ... truly horrible. We loaded him into our wheelbarrow and brought him into the house here. We weren't safe at all. The villagers wanted him, you see. They shot him, so he was theirs – that's their logic. I don't know if they would've attacked us. I suppose they would have, but we didn't go outside to find out. We stayed barricaded in here for three days, while they waited outside like hyenas! Then, when the poor fellow died – he was alive all that time – do you know what we did?"

He had a need to confess. But no one in his little audience could offer him absolution. The rules were different here. Transgressions more forgivable. They were not about to pass judgement on him. He had already done that himself and found his verdict impossible to live with. What he had seen was the depth of his own fear and a desperate desire to stay alive. To save himself. Even in the dim light of the kerosene, his face expressed a tortured anguish, revealing the horror this truth was to him.

"I opened the door and let them take him." His voice choked and then trailed off. His wife said nothing. Pouring the tea, she stared off into the night and kept her thoughts to herself.

"You have to understand: he was our friend. And he was killed because of us.... They had the fire ready and began cooking him right away. I gave his body to them – to eat."

They sat in silence, each with his own thoughts.

"I would have done the same," Riley said softly, kindly, after a few minutes. He had seen more death than any of the others. And fear.

"You know who the ringleaders were?" the missionary asked. Riley's response had encouraged him to finish his story.

They all guessed it.

"Our three Christian 'brothers!' They planned it – the whole thing," he said.

"Not very Christian-like," Rudy said and laughed. He had had some other comments to add earlier; prudently, he had kept them to himself. Black humour was sometimes better than none at all, but it would have been rude to insult their hosts.

"Indeed!" agreed the missionary. "It's pretty discouraging. This is what we've come to – after five years of work with them." He looked at his wife, who quietly concurred before he continued. "We're planning to close the mission and leave. We want to find another village, somewhere far away, to build our church." He took in a long, bitter breath, signalling he wasn't through yet, then paused while they waited on his words. Beyond the fields the jungle was ringing.

Finally the missionary pronounced his judgement "God doesn't live here."

CHAPTER FOURTEEN

A MISSION FOR RILEY

WARNER's group received an urgent radio communication from the missionaries sooner than they expected. It came to them while they were out in the field near the village of Naltja. Riley was alone at the base and flew to the rescue. An attack. Like old times.

Despite what they had told the company men, the missionaries had decided to soldier on with their work, even though, as they had learned, conversions were more difficult without the traditional power of the church backing them. They had left their mission and were striking out for a new, more receptive parish when the attack began.

Travelling with a large number of Native porters they had hired, they were approaching the new village they intended to make their home when the villagers, instead of welcoming them, attacked them. Surrounding the missionaries' smaller group, the villagers yelled insults and rained arrows down on them from a distance. Three or four of the attacking warriors had worked up their courage to run right to the edge of the missionaries' defensive circle and hurl a spear into the tightly bunched group.

Their own bearers were armed and holding off the villagers, but their defence would last only as long as their arrow supply. The attacking warriors were waiting for them to run out. When they did, they would all be killed. It was a massacre in the making. Already several were wounded.

Riley swooped down out of the sky. Using his landing skids as rams, he plowed through the attackers and drove them off, giving the missionaries' party a chance to escape. Then the missionaries themselves, grabbing up their most important possessions, climbed aboard Riley's aircraft and were lifted to safety above the battlefield. Riley flew them back to Naltja, their first leg out of the country. The missionaries had decided to leave West Irian for good.

It was over for them. Responsible for more killing, they had learned almost nothing of the people they had lived with for five years. Theirs was the same mistake Warner had made – only it had been his first time in West Irian.

Parties of Natives in West Irian could not travel the land without conflict. They were a people forever at war. Not for conquest or territory or slaves or treasure. They fought for glory, for the thrill of battle, for definition. Almost an art form, battle was an expression of the heroic soul – a key to their culture.

In the mountains of West Irian, it was dangerous to travel with a Native anywhere. As unnatural as it felt to be completely alone, it was the only way to follow the trails. Their strangeness – their white skin and factory clothing – was better protection than a weapon. As long as the Natives believed they were too powerful to kill, they would live.

The missionaries never understood, either, that New Guinea was not a spiritual vacuum. The New Guinea "pagans" had their own relationship with the divine. They were a deeply religious people. With their spiritual space already occupied, they were not searching for the answers modern Christianity wanted to give them.

The earlier Christian crusaders knew that conversion had to be total. To force Christianity on them, the tribal pagans of Europe had to be completely crushed. They had become Christians only in defeat, slaves of the new ruling order in empires built on serfdom. This lesson, too, had been forgotten.

CHAPTER FIFTEEN

THE WAR PARTY

On occasion, for "special protection," Chuck wore a helicopter crash helmet. Plastic and metal, it gleamed brightly, even in dull weather. When he wore it the Natives of Ok Sibel stared at him in awe: as if he were totally alien, godlike. He hoped it would have the same effect in the field.

All the villagers were not the same. From region to region, each tribal group had different roots, languages and features. West Irian, like Papua New Guinea, was a country only in western eyes. In reality it was a thousand nations, and together they represented the way the world might once have been everywhere.

Nor were all villagers aggressive. Most often as the team flew over new villages or, for the convenience of landing, settled right down in the cleared fields, the Natives dropped everything and ran for their lives, leaving behind only grunting pigs that moved quickly into the abandoned garden plots.

On one occasion Chuck examined the workmanship on a bow a warrior had thrown aside in his terror as he took to the forest. Replacing it with a sweater Marlene had knit for him for the cool nights, he took the bow and arrows. Chuck never took advantage of his situation. It had always seemed to him that to treat people fairly brought rewards that making enemies never did. The goodwill that one created inevitably came around.

Among the people of New Guinea were some whose physical characteristics were recognizable as Polynesian, Melanesian and Malay. Others might have been related once, when the seas were lower, to the Australian Aboriginals. The "Hairy Ainu" were here as well. The original inhabitants of the Japanese islands, the Ainu had virtually disappeared there, and their presence in New Guinea spoke of their wide distribution across Asia in another age. African in appearance, some tribes were physically indistinguishable from some African blacks. Whether these tribes were the offspring of an early migration across the Indian Ocean or identical influences had produced coincidentally identical results, anthropologists coined a new designation for them: the Oceanic Negro. Even the Kukukukus, the aggressive Pygmy cannibals of Papua New Guinea, were so like the Congo Pygmies in appearance and temperament that they were thought to have a common origin until this was disproved by genetic analysis.

There were other races whose origins were completely obscure, people who had once roamed Asia, perhaps farther afield, whose migrations into the mountain fastnesses of New Guinea preserved them from the fate that befell their kin elsewhere – absorption or extinction. Other races, hundreds of cultures, thousands of villages lay undiscovered in West Irian – a treasure trove for the historian of antiquity, the geneticist, anthropologists and social scientists.

Kennecott was after treasure of another sort, however, and the contact their team had with villagers was only incidental to their particular interests. Not all of the Natives fled at the company's approach. Some stood immobilized, fascinated, stunned. Others were more aggressive. It was when they did not run that the work in the field became really interesting.

The team was prospecting the country to the north, around the village of Naltja, working the watershed of the upper reaches of the Mamberamo, a huge river that drained the northern slopes of Coen Top and the mountains to the west. Rising to a peak of more than 4,500 metres, Coen Top left the jungle below, after a transitional space of thinning and stunted trees, to break out at 3,600 metres into open alpine country. It was a strangely familiar space. Broad, sweeping meadows were covered in lilies, daisies and buttercups. Fields of moss and grass, growing among low shrubbery, were nearly identical to the alpine country of British Columbia and the Yukon's Mackenzie Mountains, until one looked beyond them, down the slopes into the valleys.

Riley was putting the men down at elevations between 1,800 and 2,400 metres, in different catchments, miles apart. Sampling 50-kilometre sections of a watercourse at a time, they were keen to ensure their samples were carefully selected and concentrated.

When Riley dropped him off, over a streambed as usual, Chuck knew the pilot would not be back for an hour. The countryside was open, nearly subalpine, with spaces between the trees that Chuck could see through. Starved of nourishment, the trees were stunted and deformed by the winds that blew through the mountains. Chuck was bent over his pan, screening a heavy-mineral sample, when he became aware of movement downstream. Rising for a better look, he saw a group of men moving up the creek toward him.

As he stood they saw him as well, and froze. They were less than 45 metres away. More than 30 men. Watching him. Painted for war.

Chuck was not wearing his helmet. Nor was he armed. To fight even with a modern weapon against Stone Age men was to invite death. They were all armed; each man carried a spear or bow. The bows were all drawn taut and their arrows were aimed at Chuck.

The warriors, after their initial shock, continued to advance. There was no escape. Chuck's mind raced as he kept his body still. All they had to do was release their arrows. Relax their grip. Within effective arrow range, they stopped.

His adrenaline soared. It was his move now and the wrong one would kill him. Forcing a smile, he raised his arms out, showing he had no weapons, and slowly stepped toward them. He knew that warriors respected power and courage.

Trying to consider everything, to do the right thing, his mind continued to race. He stepped slowly toward them, into a bristling wall of death. Their faces mirrored their own emotions. Fiercely aggressive and proud, they were also frightened and curious. Or so he hoped. He waved and maintained a smile, grinning broadly, as he carefully closed the distance between them, trying to communicate confidence and power. And friendliness.

Closer. A step at a time.

He tried to read their expressions, to walk that balance between making them too fearful to kill him yet not so fearful they had to. Identifying an older man with the grandest headdress and a necklace of prized seashells as their most likely leader, Chuck locked eyes with him and approached slowly.

With the warriors' bows still drawn tightly, it was the moment of greatest danger. He didn't hesitate. Ignoring the others, he stepped into their midst, smiling, his arm outstretched in greeting. Until this moment, his heart had been pounding wildly; now he relaxed a little. He had crossed over. He was among them – and still alive.

Not one showed the slightest friendliness. Grim-faced, distant men, they demonstrated remarkable courage.

Slowly pulling off the poncho he was wearing, he held it out to the warrior and pointed to the man's own breastplate. It was an offer to trade.

Chuck had some experience with trading in New Guinea. It was more than commerce; it was the first and universal language. Denied access to another's treasures, some Natives of New Guinea would steal, and kill a man standing in the way. Chuck knew that with their fear of him under control, simple greed might also tempt them to kill him. To take not only his body as a trophy but his possessions, the value of which, to them, was inestimable.

Instead, he offered them all. In trade. He stripped off his clothes, one piece at a time, to barter for their goods. The Natives drew nearer. It was impossible to know what they saw, but gradually all the bows were lowered and their attention shifted to the items he held out. Treasures for the men's house they could hang alongside the skulls of their dead. Everything they could want – everything he had – they could get.

Chuck considered carefully each of the items they offered in exchange. Examining the workmanship, judging its value, he passed over some items, selected others. His every motion, every turn of the eye, was watched closely. Every detail was witnessed and would be remembered. With every trade he met their eyes. This was the strangest experience of all. To look eye-to-eye into their very being, glimpsing into their world.

Chuck traded it all. His metal panner, the empty bags, even the small shovel. Stripped naked, he put on the goods he had received in trade: body armour, a headdress and shell necklaces. Everything but a penis gourd.

Less strange to the men now, he had his own spears, bows and arrows. He was standing, nothing left to trade, when he heard, before the others, the distant chop of the helicopter blade echoing through the mountains. It was returning for him.

He smiled. They smiled back.

It had worked. He was alive. A white warrior among black warriors.

A moment of intense elation passed through them. They had all faced down fears, and discovered new horizons. Then it was over. The Natives heard the approach of the aircraft and, seeing it, fled. Leaving him alone.

Through the bubble, Chuck could see Riley, astonished, mouthing questions before he landed. Chuck climbed aboard and they were off. From the distant security of the trees, warriors from another age watched as the white man from Ok Sibel disappeared with the sound of thunder into the sky.

CHAPTER SIXTEEN

THE GENERALS

Every three weeks Chuck had one week off and flew back to Cairns to be with his family. The juxtaposition of images from the two worlds was impossible to reconcile. Hiking through raw mountains with spike boots and a steel helmet, swinging dangerously down through thick foliage from the skids to collect the precious samples, pig roasts and spirit ceremonies and single-note drum rhythms pounding throughout the night, dawn breaking in pink pastels off the high peak of Juliana Top, towering nearly five kilometres into the sky over Ok Sibel – these were among the strange sights and sounds of West Irian.

Cairns was sandals, a white beach, cold beer and convoluted conversations to the sound of Cream, Joplin, Hendrix, Donovan and Cat Stevens. It was a culture of an entirely different sort. Of incense and dreams, high hopes and new gods.

Each reality was completely unaware of the other. In and out of Cairns. In and out of the jungle. And back again. There was at times a quality of unreality to it all, when it was impossible to take anything seriously, as though it were all a dream. One constant was his work. The other, Marlene. Together they gave him stability and direction.

The work in West Irian was progressing rapidly. They were exploring farther and farther from Ok Sibel, establishing supply dumps to the west and sometimes overnighting in temporary field camps like Naltja or at the rare mission. Contacts with Natives continued to present risks but were always thrilling.

Occasionally his intentions were misunderstood.

One day Riley put Chuck down at the edge of an unfamiliar village. On the banks of a river from which they needed samples, it provided a perfect landing area. The village men were all gone. Off on a raid, perhaps, or a hunt. Only the women remained. Fearful but reacting without the bravado and aggression of the men, they stood, mutely staring, as Chuck, entering their village, approached them to establish a relationship before he went off to collect the river samples.

The women were wearing the smallest grass skirts he had ever seen. Barely the size of a hand, the skirts were hung by a cord around their waists to cover only a part of their pubic area, accenting rather than concealing their sexuality.

He took off his shirt and, holding it toward a young woman, pointed at the little patch of grass covering her crotch, indicating his interest "Mi laik baim." They did not understand pidgin, but it was impossible to trade without attempting to speak. The girl turned and ran into the bush, misunderstanding him completely. Whether she intended for him to follow or was protecting herself from his advances, he was unable to tell, but he had no interest whatever in the women sexually, only in what they had to trade.

He kept still; anything else might set them all to flight. Frozen in place, none of the other women moved either. They continued to watch him intently as he held out his hand with his shirt in offering.

Finally an old woman came forward, stood before him and untied her skirt. Stark naked, she handed it to him. He passed her his shirt in return and she stepped back. The group of women suddenly came to life. Pulling their skirts off, they rushed to do business. As they gathered tightly around him, he laughed as the women, not at all interested in him sexually, thrust their own skirts at him and pointed excitedly at his clothes.

The trading took some time, and when he got back to the helicopter, Riley was once again surprised and puzzled to see Chuck in Native dress, carrying an armload of skirts.

In spite of their presence at Ok Sibel, the life of the village carried on and the ancient rules remained. Before the company arrived to set up their camp, the men from Ok Sibel had raided a nearby village and killed a boy. A payback was inevitable. In a feuding system in which communities traded "hurts" while they gained glory, there was always payback. In both West Irian and Papua New Guinea, the payback systems were as complex and entrenched as a code of law, although justice involved the settlement of private scores rather than any concept of a greater social good. Tribal common law required retribution. It was only a matter of timing.

Chuck was in the village when the attack came. Sometimes the raids were by night. The occupants of a particular hut might be chosen randomly or, because of its distance from the others, be killed as they rushed out. Most often, ambushes were laid on the trails near a village's fields or streams.

This attack came in the full light of day. From their high sentry towers out in the fields around the village, the sentries gave the warning cries: high, wailing screams. The enemy was approaching. Fleeing their towers, the sentries armed themselves, joined their comrades and rushed into the field.

The whole village was in an uproar. Women were crying out desperately for their children and children for their mothers. To be caught near the enemy was to be killed or, worse, taken alive and killed later.

Men rushed about scrambling to put on their armour as they ran to join the battle. This was their moment of purpose. The men rarely worked. Their energy was saved instead for just such moments, their task to safeguard the village, to protect the women and children. They threw themselves into the role with vigour.

Chuck grabbed his camera and ran out with them into the fray. In the cleared and burnt-off hillside slopes of the village's vegetable plots, the two sides met. The men were all experts with bows and spears, and they kept their distance, hurling more insults than weapons. They were too far apart to fire accurately, and a man could avoid incoming arrows if he didn't lose sight of them flying through the air.

A young warrior, body armour and penis gourd in place, broke away from his line and rushed toward the others to get within range to shoot more accurately. Arrows rained down on him. Dodging them, he got off one of his own and fell back to his own line amid shouts of praise and encouragement from his side and taunts from the other.

How near a man dared approach the enemy depended on his agility, his courage and his rage. Risking their lives for vengeance, the men who advanced right to the front – trading insults and arrows and, if they were really courageous, spears – were wild and fierce.

Chuck moved through the battleground as though invisible, taking pictures of men at war. Even as he photographed them, the scenes seemed unreal and impossible. The two sides had approached one another en masse, but now they spread apart, across the field in a long ragged line. There was no longer one front and one battle but many. One-on-one, they faced each other and moved in closer. A dozen personal battles were going on simultaneously.

The warriors almost danced. Springing lightly on perfect muscles, they challenged each other to demonstrate their mettle. Beside him, a man yelled in rage, his body cocked, every fibre keyed to his emotions. His was an expression of complete abandon to the play of the battle.

Chuck was thrilled to be in it. The energy on the field was like nothing he had ever felt before. Electric. A number of the men had been hit with arrows, but the wounds were not fatal. The body armour protected the largest areas of vulnerability. An arrow through the arm or in the thigh was serious but not life-threatening, unless it became septic.

Gradually, as the men exhausted themselves and their weapons, the attacking villagers moved back to the forest and then quickly melted away. The Natives of Ok Sibel remained for a while longer on the field, collecting all the arrows and spears before they withdrew to the village, leaving their sentries to scale the four-storey heights of the watchtowers and resume their guard duty. One had to be forever watchful.

At night the men gathered together to recount their experiences, to recognize courage and remonstrate against cowardice. Their chanting and the beat of the drum vibrated through the still coolness of the night. When a faint drizzle began, which would slowly build into a heavy downpour, the men broke off the ceremony to sleep. They were tired, and tomorrow there might be another battle. Death lurked everywhere, even in one's dreams.

The attackers had failed to achieve a kill. They would be back: perhaps an ambush on the trail or a sneak attack into the village after dark. One never knew when, only that it would come, as would their own payback attack. The cycle was endless.

Returning to Cairns after the battle, Chuck found the problems that preoccupied people there paled in comparison with the life-and-death issues the Natives faced daily – living in constant anticipation of a deadly attack. Yet there was an artificiality to the warriors' lives as well, as though the hostilities were contrived solely to give life greater definition and meaning.

Translated to the commercial realities of business, the experiences Chuck was collecting revealed over and over to him that life imposed no limits: only people did. Understanding that the future need not be an accident of fate but an expression of free will moved him closer to taking full control of his own life.

The Native warriors were not frightening to Chuck. They would kill but not without reason, and he intended to give them no reason. Eye-to-eye, he felt a common ground with them. They were fierce and aggressive, but they were also guileless and honest. He could handle them.

Chuck could not say the same thing about the soldiers of the Indonesian army who moved in a few weeks after the attack on Ok Sibel and set up their camp right beside Kennecott's. Ill-equipped and poorly paid, if at all, they were well supplied only with weapons and bullets. These Indonesian men from outside West Irian were mostly young, brutalized and brutal. Spooked by New Guinea, hungry and armed with FN automatics, they were trigger-happy and dangerous. The army brass had come to have a look at the big American multinational operating in its backyard. As they were hostile toward and suspicious of foreign empires, big business and international conspiracies, it was impossible to know what they expected. What they found was Chuck Fipke.

Riley had flown out earlier in the day with Dave Jordt, Rudy and Fred Warner, leaving Chuck alone with only the Native cook. He had the cook put out some extra plates and invited the colonel and other commanding officers for dinner, made from the cans of food imported from Australia and some local produce, primarily banana, yam and taro, purchased in trade with the local villagers for boy food. The presence of Kennecott's food stocks excited the soldiers as much as it did the Natives.

After the officers finished dinner and left the kitchen, the soldiers roamed the camp and the village. Drunk on alcohol they had brought with them, they carried on noisily, yelling in the night and shouting at each other. When they decided to assault the warehouse, kicking noisily at the reinforced door with heavy boots, Chuck quietly barricaded himself in his room. The night belonged to the men with the machine guns.

In the morning the officers were perfect models of decorum and moved into Kennecott's kitchen with practised aplomb, attaching themselves without further invitation to the permanent guest list. Chuck didn't argue with them. In the overall budget, what they lost to thieves and necessary guests was insignificant. The charades, although distasteful, allowed them all to carry on without any major incidents.

Each night as Chuck and the officers ate together in the kitchen, the soldiers caroused outside, carrying on with impunity, acting as if their behaviour were quite normal. They would at least wait until after dinner before breaking down the warehouse door and helping themselves to whatever food they wanted.

More frightening to Chuck than their armed drunkenness and brazen disregard for the company's property was the realization that this was a company of soldiers on its best behaviour. In another village the same soldiers would not demonstrate the restraint they were showing here at Ok Sibel, in the presence of Kennecott's agents.

Once the military camp was established, flying visits from the top brass became routine events. Generals on break from more mundane tasks regularly flew in for dinner and a tour of Kennecott's operation. Having recognized the value of a mine, they had become completely supportive of Kennecott's efforts. Just as Kennecott's larder continued to supplement the diets of Indonesia's troops and its largesse to feed their officers, the larger appetites of the country's rulers were waiting impatiently to be fed.

CHAPTER SEVENTEEN

THE VOGELKOP

WORKING from dawn to dusk for three months and risking their lives almost daily, Chuck and his crew pushed each other until they finished their survey of the entire eastern and central mountain sectors. Rather than flying out their remaining food, they organized a feast for the village, distributed what was left and closed down the camp at Ok Sibel. They were moving to the other end of the country. To the west, the Vogelkop Peninsula.

Chuck was excited about the move. He had convinced Dave Jordt to hire Marlene. She and Mark were going to join him at their new base. It was not a difficult sale. By offering to give up his own leave – agreeing to work steadily with no time off at all – Chuck had saved Kennecott more than it would cost them to pay Marlene. And they got a cook and radio operator in the bargain.

Chuck was happy to pay the price. Since their arrival in Papua New Guinea nearly two years earlier, he had found it increasingly difficult to live apart. They had a history now, common memories – some painful, others sweet – that bonded them. In all the expats, the isolation of New Guinea produced a certain intensity of longing. With Chuck and Marlene, the arrangement brought them closer together, forging a new relationship.

Although Chuck had been reluctant when he married during his first year at university, it had seemed the appropriate thing to do. Marlene had come from a good family, was attractive, loyal, sexy and capable. These were good reasons for marriage. There were others. For Marlene the necessary stages after high school were a family and the working world. Most of the young women of Marlene's age and acquaintance were married or engaged to be married soon after school finished. That was the standard. More importantly, she loved him.

Chuck, however, had remained guarded. Through their years in Vancouver at university, he had kept his feelings under control and maintained a distance. He had been more willing to risk his life than his feelings, but it was Marlene's constancy that had broken through. In illness and in health, she was there for him. When he awoke from delirium, when he arrived bruised from the bush, when he sought to explore his own visions or the hard scrabble cultures of New Guinea, she was there, beside him. He had never felt so connected to another person. The painful lessons of his childhood, to be solely self-reliant, slowly gave way, with experience, to a new feeling that seeped through his emotional armour. He loved her.

It was a revelation to discover that he loved the woman he had married, that he now wanted to have her near him all the time, to share it all with her.

The need created new issues. While the pull he felt inside for complete independence continued as strongly as before, the new attraction he felt, for a home in the heart of his wife, now pulled as strongly in the opposite direction.

For Chuck there would always be this struggle between the two forces. As much as he now felt connected and committed to Marlene – striving for a unity of spirit – he was drawn to the wild side, to live with complete abandon, throwing himself into experiences without regard for consequences, trusting that whatever happened was the full measure of life. To live any other way, cautiously or fearfully, was to live within a self-imposed prison. That was something he would not do; he could not.

A balance between the two demands was difficult to achieve. He never liked to compromise. Each compromise represented a loss, a narrowing of one's life. Instead he wanted both, to embrace it all. He wanted everything.

From Ok Sibel the crew had sampled the central mountain range of West Irian. Now they were to sample the western reaches of the country, the huge peninsula known as the Vogelkop. Like the eastern highlands, the heart of the Vogelkop was mountainous, cloaked in dense, impenetrable jungle and dangerous to fly through.

Their new base was in the old Dutch coastal port of Manokwari, a rough, impoverished little town on the northeast coast of the Vogelkop. It was the main settlement in the Vogelkop, however, and they set up their base there, on the Christian mission property.

The meagreness of the town's economy reflected the total neglect of the distant colonial administration in Jakarta. Adequate food supplies were not available locally, and Kennecott flew much of the crew's food into the country together with all of their helicopter fuel. Attempts by the government to attract Indonesian settlement along the more favourable coastal regions, to build a local economy, had met with mixed success.

West Irian had been sold as a salvation. Thousands of Indonesian settlers had come, but they had arrived with high expectations. No one told them they were to be the saviours. With no skills or investment capital, they lived in squalor, unable to create an economy or any kind of infrastructure that would improve their lot. By comparison, Port Moresby was a modern haven with all the amenities, a thriving economy, a new university and a future. After Cairns, Manokwari was a grim little place, but Marlene accepted it in the spirit of adventure and moved in.

Having Marlene in the camp changed the dynamics completely. Camp accommodation was a spot on the floor of a large central hut where all the men slept together. It had not been a problem when the camp was all male. Introducing a 24-year-old attractive brunette into their midst was, as Chuck suddenly saw it, like throwing a lamb into a cage with hungry wolves. Marlene, alone, cooking for them, talking to them on the radio, sleeping next to them on the same wooden floor, created a lot of opportunity for everyone to get to know each other.

As well as the sampling crew, there were now several engineers staying at the mission and a couple of new, American pilots fresh out of Vietnam who had entertained them all – until Marlene arrived – with exciting stories of the nightlife and women of Saigon.

Although their days were planned to allow them to return to base each evening, however short their days were, they could never be short enough now. Leaving Marlene each morning in close quarters with men who lived solely for the conquest of women was maddening. Worse, on occasion, weather or distance preventing it, he could not get back to Manokwari, leaving Marlene entirely at the mercy of the "wolves".

It made Chuck frantic. With his imagination and jealousy nearly out of control, Chuck would return from the bush on a hair trigger, ready to explode at the slightest remark, joke or suggestion of interest in his wife. She was his, and he was capable of killing if any one of them ever crossed the line – even touched her.

It was an awkward situation for the whole camp and not at all what he had envisioned when he traded his free time to have her join the staff. He now worked seven days a week, with no breaks, mostly out in the field. He saw her more frequently than before, but it was often in passing and they were virtually never alone.

Gradually they all adjusted to the new situation. The other men learned to keep their distance, and the camp established a new working routine.

Chuck found the trips into the country ever more exciting. In Papua New Guinea he had spent all his money and free time exploring. The preliminary survey they were doing in West Irian, sampling broadly across nearly the entire country, put him into places no one could pay to visit. The excitement of discovery, together with the refinements of their mineral survey, combined the best of all worlds. Chuck no longer felt the need for any breaks. Nothing else could offer what West Irian gave.

The end of their operation in West Irian, though, caught them all by surprise and came from a completely unexpected source. They were sampling in the Vogelkop, nearer to Manokwari, flying across the canopy searching for a way down through it, when events on the other side of the world were unfolding that would result in the collapse of the dreams of prospectors and soldiers alike.

Rising over the jungle, towering above everything else, was a species of tree that stood like a sentinel every few hundred metres. Dropping the helicopter down and then under the canopy created by one of these giant trees, they could descend clear to the ground. They floated down on the sound of the helicopter, its main blades and rotor smashing the stillness of the jungle, following the length of the trunk. Still far from the ground, over 30 metres in the air, the crew looked out and right beside them, built into the spreading limbs of the crown, was a house. A whole complex! As they settled on the ground, they saw around the base of the tree crude gardens and rough clearings. The gardens were freshly tended.

The engine slowed to a whine and stopped. The insect life, reacting to the intrusion of sound from the helicopter, waited, motionless for a moment, then resumed its chorus, a wave of sound blanketing the air.

Nothing moved. Not a pig. Not a branch. No arrows or spears rained down on them. Carefully Chuck stepped out. The ground underfoot was slippery, the air thick with rotting vegetation.

Dangling down from the tree house was a free-swinging ladder made from woven fibres and vines. It was the only way up, and no one seemed to be at home. Chuck crawled slowly toward the top. With each handhold, every arm's length, he moved through new spaces. As he climbed up through the jungle, away from the ground, the air became fresher, lighter. Instead of the smell of decay and mould that clung to the earth, there were the delicate fragrances of new life, of flowering orchids and blooming trees. Higher and higher he climbed, until he broke out above the lower canopy, with views that swept across the land, the treetops stretching away like the surface of a wild sea.

It was breathtaking. Here, where the plane of jungle met the open sky, one felt finally the freedom of being master of the environment, high above it all.

These people, whoever they were, had found the very best their world had to offer and had integrated it into their lives. There was a quality to the space that he had never experienced in any of the villages on the ground – a gentle tranquillity. Perhaps it was the contact with the sky, perhaps the absolute security a fortress in the treetops offered. The defensive advantages were obvious. But whatever element gave this elevation its greatest appeal, this culture of tree-dwelling people lived with more beauty than any other tribe he had seen in New Guinea.

Raised higher than a 10-storey building, the handmade structure he crawled into at the top of the ladder had the advantage of the airflow sweeping through the treetops. Large enough for a clan of 20, the tree house was made of roughly hewn boards, laboriously cut with stone tools. It contained only some dried leafy stocks, a few large gourds and several woven fibre bags filled with dried roots.

The starkness of the house, Chuck knew, was typical. Home furnishings belonged to another culture and economy. On the floor by the door there was a large conch shell. Chuck was tempted to blow into it, to see what would happen. They were far from the sea and the conch was no doubt a means of communicating through the treetops. The deep ringing of a conch shell would carry a long way. What would the inhabitants think to hear their own shell being blown while they were off? Chuck took one last look around, breathed deeply of the air, then descended into the dark body of the jungle, down to its septic basement.

After collecting their sample, while the pilot waited by the helicopter, Chuck, reluctant to leave so soon this exquisite experience, followed a narrow trail through the jungle that led him to another of these huge sentinel trees. It too, had its human occupants. A swinging ladder that hung down led to another arboreal haven, a house like the first, empty, with a conch by the entrance.

Again Chuck was tempted to blow it. From this new vantage point he could see, scattered throughout the treetops, several more houses. But of their inhabitants he saw nothing. The conch might bring them home, allow him a meeting. Chuck thought better of it, put the large shell back in its place and returned to the helicopter and to Manokwari, where the news was waiting.

Worlds away, in Chile, in October 1970, Salvador Allende, who had run for the presidency on a radical platform of land redistribution and nationalization of the country's mines as well as its banks, had narrowly defeated the moderate Christian Democrats. Now, after consolidating his rule, he had made good on those promises: Chile had just nationalized all foreign-owned mines.

It was one of the risks of the mining industry. While impoverished countries like West Irian dreamed of opening a mine, and developed countries like Australia and its Papua New Guinea outpost did all they could to encourage foreign investment, there were others who saw in mining's profits the pillaging of a nation's natural resources. The huge risks associated with the discovery and development of a mine were often forgotten once the structures were in place and money was being made.

Not content with the employment, taxes and royalties Kennecott generated, the new government in Chile suddenly stripped the company of all its assets in Chile. The move shocked the business world, but no organization moreso than Kennecott. El Teniente, named "the Lieutenant" after a Spanish officer who deserted to the region when it was ruled by Spain, had been purchased by Kennecott in 1915. Developed into the largest underground copper mine in the world, El Teniente was the principal source of Kennecott's wealth. Together with the revenue from its other assets in Chile, which were considerable, El Teniente made Kennecott the world's second largest mining company, after Anaconda.

Allende's move crushed the company. It was no consolation that investment in Chile would dry up. Nor that in less than a year the nationalizations would cost the president his life.

On September 11, 1973, Allende would be in the presidential palace when the army would blow it apart with rockets. At the end of that day, Allende would be dead, reportedly from suicide, and General Augusto Pinochet would be firmly in control, in old-world style, with all democratic institutions barred. The coup, however, would not help Kennecott. Allende took the assets, but Pinochet would keep them.

Kennecott lost it all. Overnight the company went from being a major multinational to a country player. Crippled, its revenues severely reduced, Kennecott terminated its exploration project in West Irian. The entire Indonesian section was shut down. Everyone was sent home.

For Chuck it was the end of a wonderfully wild experience. He had been in places no one else ever had and had seen things nobody else ever would. He was not sorry to leave. They had been in the Vogelkop for six months. He needed a holiday. And there were other experiences waiting.

PART TWO

The Sixth Element

Alberta to British Columbia, 1947–69

To the Five Elements of Classical thought – Fire, Water, Earth,

Air and Celestial Aether – must be added the Sixth: Man.

—VLADIMIR KUPCHENKO, *A PHILOSOPHY OF UNREASON*

CHAPTER EIGHTEEN

KELOWNA, B.C., SPRING 1964

SHE was 17 and had looked out the window a dozen times that morning. Laura Marlene Pyett, known as Marlene, had been born in Melfort, Saskatchewan, in 1947 and had moved to Kelowna with her family. The daughter of a Polish mother and an English father, she came from a strict family, Catholic and hardworking.

A year younger than Chuck, she had found herself attracted to the wild boy of the school, the boy who had a shy stutter and a reputation that made the parents of young women ready to lock their doors when he came calling. Dark-haired, slim and attractive, Marlene was one of the school's "catches".

Chuck was taken by her. Under the influence of alcohol when he had met her at a dance and made the arrangements, he was not quite sure of her address, or even her correct name, when he turned down her street to take her out on their first date. All he had was a phone number left written on his hand when he woke up at Clarence's house, in no condition to have driven all the way back to Trepanier Bench the night before. When he got home, he transferred the number into his phone book and then called it.

Marlene's mother had answered. It was Saturday. Chuck had asked to speak to her daughter.

"Um, can I, hey, speak to her?"

"Who's calling?"

"Yeah, um, just a friend, hey." Chuck was always careful about identifying himself, especially to parents of prospective dates.

"Oh, really! What friend?" Mrs. Pyett had insisted.

"Um, you know, just a friend."

Mrs. Pyett was not a woman about to be sidestepped. Her voice on the telephone hardened. "Listen, young man! If you want to speak to my daughter, I'll have to know who you are first!"

An inauspicious beginning, but Chuck was determined it would improve. He and Clarence Linenko had planned a double date. At twelve o'clock Clarence Linenko picked him up in his car, a more reliable model than Chuck's, and, with Chuck navigating, they found the street. As Marlene watched from her living room window, Clarence cruised slowly past her house, turned around at the corner and drove slowly back up the road, stopping at last in front of her house. Emerging from the car confidently, Chuck walked up to the house directly across the street – and knocked on the wrong door. A woman answered.

"Hi, I'm Chuck Fipke. I'm, uh, here, hey, to take your daughter out."

To compensate for the awkwardness of the situation, Chuck spoke in short sentences. And in these circumstances he was not volunteering any information.

"Oh?" The woman was surprised.

"We've got a date, right?" Chuck explained tenuously. Blue-eyed and blond, his facial features were boyish, almost cherubic, and projected a merriment he was not, at the moment, feeling.

"Where are you taking her?" she asked, naturally enough.

"We've got a car, hey," he replied, as innocently as he could. "I just thought, like, we'd drive around and then go to a movie."

What could one say to disarm the mother of a beautiful girl? The woman looked past him at Linenko's big Rambler parked across the street with Clarence and his steady girlfriend sitting closely together in the front seat, then invited him to step in through the doorway, shutting the door firmly behind him.

Having survived the introductions, Chuck began to relax. He was inside. That was the first step! The woman, seemingly pleased that a boy had come to take out her daughter, called to her to come and meet her new friend. Chuck didn't recognize the name she used at all, even less the girl who appeared at the top of the stairs and slowly made her way down to greet him.

She was 17, with dark hair and roughly the same height and build as the girl he remembered dancing with, but it stopped there. When she began to speak – with enormous difficulty – he was floored. She was obviously handicapped.

She finished her painful effort – and she smiled at him. Chuck would have run, only his body was suddenly numbed. Had he been so drunk? As the girl waited, peering at him with a shy grin, and her mother carried on about it being Jenny's first date, Chuck's mind bolted; he was struck absolutely speechless.

It never occurred to him that he had knocked on the wrong door. Especially now as the girl's mother, having quickly regained her composure after Chuck's unexpected arrival, was getting her ready to go out with him. He was trapped.

A knock at the door saved him. Marlene tactfully explained the mix-up to her neighbours and led him safely out the door. Chuck was immensely relieved.

"You want to meet *my* parents?" Marlene asked.

It was the last thing he wanted to do.

"Naw," he replied, moving quickly toward the car. The sooner he could escape, the better.

"Unless you come in, I'm not allowed to go out with you!"

The Pyetts, it transpired, were interested in his religion, his education and his plans for the future. In that order.

"Chemical engineering, I think," he told them. Anything so long as he could roar off with their daughter to a darkened theatre for the afternoon.

Two minutes into the cartoons, before the main feature, he made his move. Sliding his arm around her shoulders, he pulled her tightly toward him and pressed his face into her hair as she quickly turned away.

Rebuked, he slid back toward his own seat. It would improve.

CHAPTER NINETEEN

THE HORSE RACE

CHUCK shot away toward the outskirts of Kelowna. He was almost 19 years old, it was summer and the air was like luminous fire.

His rugby team from Kelowna Senior Secondary had, only a few days earlier, won the provincial high school championship after playing the entire season without a single loss. It had been a grand day, the approving roar from the stands had lifted him like a tonic, and he was still floating with the feelings of that final victory. Although adopted by the famous English private school as its official game, rugby was an ancient tribal contest that pitted opposing teams in a "game" that imitated battle. It was a sport in which Chuck excelled. Unlike most other players who paced themselves, conserving their energies, he played flat out from start to finish in an impressive display of nearly inexhaustible energy. Although shorter than many of his teammates, he was compactly built, harder and more aggressive than they were. In this head-to-head contact sport played with few rules and no protective shielding, strength, determination and, most importantly, an ability to work through pain were the qualities of a good player. And he was now acknowledged as the best.

Once across the long, floating bridge he turned south, following Highway 97 past the Indian reserve, toward the historic community of Peachland. With the powerful engine of his '53 Ford running smoothly, he almost flew over the mountain road skirting the edge of Okanagan Lake.

He loved speed. The Ford was his latest acquisition: $150. Its battery was dead and its brakes mostly gone, yet it was still a good car. Faster than his old Rambler, which was still running and still making him money.

Wheeling off at the junction of the Trepanier Bench Road just before Peachland, he left the lake with its vineyards and orchards and began climbing, following the winding dirt road up out of the valley's lushly irrigated bottom into the natural, arid vegetation of the country. Sage and bunchgrass, Indian paintbrush and yellow arrowleaf covered the ground between tall aromatic pine and spruce. The land supported large herds of mule deer, small bands of sheep and numerous bear and coyote. Until the thirties, when the Canadian government rounded them all up in a bizarre gesture of apparent goodwill and shipped them to the Soviet Union as a gift to aid Soviet farmers, there had even been thousands of wild horses roaming the hills.

Open-range cattle ranching began where the irrigation pipes ended. The Ford continued climbing, above the orchards, beyond the limits of irrigation, until

Chuck reached his family's own farm, which depended on the water from Trepanier Creek – more of a brook than a creek – for its existence.

His father, Ed Fipke, had bought the property only a couple of years earlier. A decaying house beside an abandoned apple orchard at the edge of a few small grassy clearings, it was an old homestead property that had come with more than a hundred hectares of forested mountainside. It was paradise to Chuck.

After years of wandering the backroads of western Canada while his family lived in poverty on the fringe of Edmonton, Ed had finally put down roots in the land. It was a new beginning, and Chuck was determined to make the most of it. The poverty of the past few years had not crushed his spirit. It had only hardened his resolve to succeed.

Chuck pulled up in the yard next to his Rambler and began to polish it up. Getting it ready. He had a customer for it tonight and it had to look good. Chuck rented it out, usually to his teammate buddies and their friends for "special" occasions. Tonight was one of those. Friday night. The car's shine as brilliant as dull paint allowed, he turned his attention to the interior, throwing out every little bit of garbage, cleaning the ashtrays and wiping down the dust. The final details were left until last.

Opening the trunk, he carefully placed some fruit, bread and other food inside together with a couple of folded blankets for warmth: packing for a picnic. The final touch – the most important item – was a bottle of his dad's own backcountry home brew, which he carefully wrapped up in the blankets.

In large quantities strong enough to kill a man, and in smaller ones to weaken a woman's resolve, the alcohol was the key to a successful evening. And his teammates could be trusted never to reveal their sources, should official questions be asked. Rugby players were like that: loyal. And many of them had rented Chuck's car. It was not just a car for a Friday-night date he was selling – most of them had access to other cars – but an experience, a total package.

Chuck would prearrange a spot for them to park in the wilderness. He knew all the best spots – isolated, private and scenic. A secluded bluff overlooking the valley and the lake was usually the best.

The Rambler's Pullman seats folded right down, perfect for a romantic evening. In the summer of 1965, few girls were prepared to engage in intimate physical contact without considerable encouragement. Romance, particularly the fulfillment of male desires, required planning, strategy and tactics – and sometimes teamwork.

When, after an evening of controlled passion, it was time to go home, low and behold, the Rambler would not start! Try as they might to get it going, the situation was hopeless. The trick to running the engine was a deliberately well guarded secret!

Trapped on a dark mountainside far from home, what option had the hapless couple but to spend the night and wait for rescue in dawn's light? Far from civilization, with bears, cougars and all manner of other wild creatures prowling the night, it wasn't safe to venture too far from the comfort of the Pullman seats.

Huddling together for warmth and security provided opportunities most young men only dreamed of.

Even better, on exploring their resources, they would "discover" the hidden treasures in the trunk. Chuck's survival package. Blankets, food and alcohol. A stiff drink melted resolve like hot coals under ice.

In the morning, as arranged, Chuck would "happen by" in search of his stalled car to get it going and send the couple on their way with his profound apologies. Money well spent, Chuck's friends considered it. This time, though, he would have to ask Clarence Linenko to rescue the Rambler and its trapped occupants. Chuck had other plans for himself.

The Rambler delivered, Chuck turned his attention next to the main event of the weekend. It was a contest he had been anticipating for months. The Princeton horse race was set for the morning. The big race. It was not the kind of country horse race he ran with every farm boy around Trepanier Bench but a real race, on a real racetrack, with real prize money.

Chuck needed the money. He was counting on it. He had a summer job at Gorman's Saw Mill but the work was making him physically ill, and he wanted to quit it. If he won the race, he could. He was confident he would. It was not a matter of dreaming; he was not a dreamer. Chuck believed in action, in willpower. He knew what he could do. He had never lost a race with Classic Storm. In fact, he almost never lost at anything he attempted. If he wanted something he got it, and if his first effort failed, he would try again. That was his secret strength: he never quit until he won. And he never quit.

It would be easy money. His horse, a tall, gelded stallion, was a thoroughbred, a winner. Retired from the track, Storm was still a real racehorse. At $300, Storm was the most expensive purchase Chuck had ever made. Even if it was almost all of Marlene's savings, Storm was worth every penny.

His wild, headlong rides over the earth on the horse thrilled him like nothing had ever done before. After his first ride, he had been hooked. There was a problem in stopping the horse, though. If the way ahead was still open, Storm simply refused to quit. Chuck didn't care. In fact, it was that aspect of Storm's spirit that he loved most. The only truth he needed was that his horse could run like the wind, and with the determination it showed every time he took it out to race the other horses up and down the valley, he knew he would not lose. Storm was wild, but he was a winner! Spirit in creatures, as in people, was everything.

They set out early in the morning in a borrowed truck, trailering the horse behind them. Chuck, in the passenger seat, was all keyed up. Still hours away from the race, he could barely control his anticipation. His younger brother, Wayne, drove, while Marlene, their anchor and financier, sat calmly between them. She had only enough money left to pay for the gas to get them there. To get home, Chuck would have to win the race. No problem.

He was supremely confident. Marlene was going to witness the value of her investment and the glory of Chuck's first real racing victory. Easy money.

Tucked up against the innermost reaches of the Coast Mountains, near the

American border, Princeton in 1965 was a small mining town and supply centre for the cattle ranches of the high plateau of the western interior. Its summer rodeo was a big event, and its horse race this year promised to be the best ever. Usually a local race with too small a purse to attract first-rate competitors, this year's contest was different. Coincidentally, a major horse race was being held in Calgary just a few days before the Princeton race. The timing was perfect. Princeton, on the southern highway between Calgary and Vancouver, was a convenient stop for the horses returning to Vancouver and its local race an entertaining diversion for their owners. Some of the best horses in western Canada were registered to run.

When they arrived, the field was colourful and hectic. Horses and trainers, owners and riders, friends, excited fans and the curious mingled in a state of midsummer rhapsody. The smell of sizzling hot dogs and burgers, of horse sweat and old straw, of dust and leather filled the air as Wayne found a spot to park and Chuck got ready.

Surveying his competition, the riders and their horses, his confidence soared. Professional jockeys most of them, they were small, weak-looking men, seemingly effeminate and useless. Chuck was pleased. He had expected to race against real cowboys, but this was even easier – almost a joke. Looking at their tight little pants, high boots and tiny helmets, it was all he could do to contain himself, biting his tongue to keep his mouth shut as he paraded proudly through them, leading his horse toward the track. He knew as they watched him that his very presence was disturbing them. He enjoyed causing a scene and shared none of their anxiety. He was here to win, and he would.

One of the other riders, a small, frail-looking man barely five feet tall, approached from his trailer and blocked Chuck's way. Appearing a lot more concerned than Chuck felt, he had an extra saddle, he said, that Chuck could borrow. In fact, he insisted on it. He thrust it out for Chuck to take. Chuck glanced quickly at the man's saddle: a little leather pad, even smaller than an English riding saddle, with two narrow, delicate little stirrups dangling like earrings from its sides.

Chuck laughed. He would sooner ride bareback than be caught on one of those silly little things. Why, it couldn't even be called a saddle! His own horse had a real saddle. A great big western saddle with richly embossed, padded leather and thick wide stirrup straps. It was an antique but it was still beautiful, almost a work of art.

Chuck scoffed at the man's suggestion that his saddle was too heavy, that his horse would run better with one of the lighter ones. He didn't need the man's advice. And he certainly didn't need a little toy saddle to win the race. He was going to clean their clocks. They simply had no idea what his horse could do, how it could run like the wind.

Approaching the starting gate, and recognizing suddenly that he was going to race, Storm went wild. Rising up magnificently on his hind legs, the horse lunged forward, his long mane rippling, his nostrils wide and flaring, his eyes aflame. It had been several seasons since he had run a race, and the welcome familiarity of the track put him into a frenzy.

Two men grabbed him and struggled to keep him down on the ground, as Chuck, riding higher than all the other mounted men, proudly fought to control his horse. Watching from the stands, the crowd, too, rose up and cheered wildly. Here, finally, was a horse with spirit. All bets came down now on Chuck and his horse.

It was a glorious moment: his first real race, the crowd cheering him, Marlene waving from the stands. Through every muscle of his own body he could feel that Storm was ready, trembling with the flow of unrestrained energy. The crashing of boards, the smell of the horses, the riders adjusting, balancing low on their mounts, the hot sunshine and the dry dust all intensified the excitement of the moment.

The gates burst open. At the sight of the open track, his horse reared again, banged his head – and stumbled. By the time Storm cleared the gate, the other horses were 15 metres in front. Chuck didn't care; he had a winner. Still sublimely confident, he kicked in his heels and they were off at last.

Hell-bent for glory, they were racing like the wind, faster than he had ever raced before. With his eye on the horses in front of him, gauging the distance, Chuck knew he could close the gap. He would still make it. Totally unaware that he was racing against world-class thoroughbreds and professional jockeys, Chuck still believed he could beat them.

His kicked in his heels again, urging his horse to run even faster. The gap did not close. Instead, slowly but surely, the other horses pulled farther away. He fell farther and farther behind, and came in dead last.

Even his horse was crushed, its spirit, too, defeated. Humiliated and broke, Chuck had to borrow gas money from the race organizers to get home, as he swore to himself that he would be back. One day. There were other races, bigger and better races to be won.

As though he, too, were continuing to react to the loss, soon after they got back to the farm, Storm escaped and took off to the mountains. For three weeks he ran free, living on wild grasses and drinking from mountain streams, until a neighbour spotted the horse one evening high in the mountains. By the time Wayne and Chuck caught up to Storm, it was dark.

Getting the horse down the mountain to the farm was a problem. They were several kilometres from home. They had no trailer or saddle with them, so Chuck had to ride the horse bareback, with only a bridle, through the night. Storm had always been hard to control, and the open range had encouraged the wild strains in his spirit. As soon as Chuck was on his back, the horse took off.

Wayne got in front of Storm but there was no way to stop him. Galloping hard down the road, they passed Wayne driving the car. Even at 60 kilometres per hour, Wayne had a tough time keeping up with them on the rocky road. The dangerous descent had Chuck worried. He knew the road. It wound steeply down the mountain and then spilled out onto the main highway. That was where they were heading.

He grabbed hold of the horse's mane with one fist and with the other pulled back with all his might at the edge of the bridle, but he could not get the horse to respond, let alone stop. Running flat out down the mountainside, Storm, a big, powerful animal, had given himself over completely to a mindless race down the slope, the momentum of his own weight throwing him forward, hurtling him ahead, completely out of control.

There was no way Chuck could stop him. Exhausted from trying, Chuck had only two options. If the horse reached the highway and ran into the traffic, they would both be killed. Jumping off – the other choice – could be just as deadly. As they approached the highway, he made his decision. He was not prepared to stay with the horse. That was the greater risk.

Sliding his arms around the horse's neck, he slipped one leg over and immediately fell, spinning around under Storm's neck. With both his feet under the horse's chest, he did not dare let go. The horse's hooves were pounding under him and the rocky road was spinning past. Desperately he clung onto the horse's neck, holding his legs up off the ground. His body was suspended directly in front of the animal. Crazed, the horse raced on.

The risk of Storm tumbling forward and crushing him or running out onto the highway was now so great that Chuck did the only thing he could. He let go. Backwards, head first, he hit the ground.

When he regained consciousness, he saw Wayne's face looking down at him and tried to speak but had no sensation of his body at all. He was lying on the road, completely stunned. After a few minutes enough feeling returned for him to struggle into the back seat of his car before he lost consciousness again. When he came to, he saw Wayne approaching the car.

They were on some narrow backroad, the headlights probing the darkness. Chuck could feel blood trickling down his head. The engine was running.

"What are you doing, Wayne?"

"He turned down here! I think we can still find him."

"Wayne, I think I'm hurt bad. You better take me to the hospital."

Wayne peered through the dark at his brother. At 16, unaccustomed to emergencies, Wayne had been intent on continuing their mission of recovering the horse. Looking at Chuck, it was hard to believe he could be hurt. Not Chuck. He was just too tough.

The hospital found otherwise. He had suffered a serious concussion. He was lucky to be alive. His skull was fractured in three places. The hospital scheduled a long stay: at least a month.

His spirits not the least dampened by his injury, Chuck decided to make the best of it. The hospital was like a vacation – with captive young nurses. After only two days he was discharged. It was the fastest "recovery" Kelowna General had ever witnessed.

When he got home, Chuck sold Storm. Next time, he promised himself, he would get a real winner. But racehorses were expensive. And the best horses, he knew now, were very expensive.

He needed another way to make money. He didn't want to, but he turned to Ed for help.

CHAPTER TWENTY

THE FORTRESS OF THORN

BORN on the family homestead in January 1923, near the village of Leduc, approximately 30 kilometres south of Edmonton, Alberta, Ed Fipke was part of the first generation of Fipkes to be raised in Canada. Free, finally, but not unburdened, he bore the dreams of countless ancestors on his shoulders. His life would become a standard against which his own children, among them Chuck, would be forced to measure their success, just as the lives of his parents measured his. With a history that spanned seven centuries under the rule of imperial powers, his family had learned lessons that were deep and immeasurable and continued to influence the decisions of his life, perhaps even to shape the central core of his being.

In 1230 the Vistula River in northern Europe was the frontier. To the south of the river lay Poland and the other kingdoms of the Holy Roman Empire, to the north the rune-filled pagan lands surrounding the Baltic Sea. Across the Vistula River, on the north bank, the invading armies of the Teutonic Order erected a huge stone fortress, the army citadel they named Thorn. Occupied continuously by the descendants of those German-speaking farmer-soldiers who first manned it, Thorn would stand for centuries – an island, a symbol of the Church and the penetration of the German knights into the underbelly of the Old World.

Tribal people, the Baltic pagans were independent and proud. Unlike their defeated neighbours to the south who had been forced to surrender their direct relationship with the divine – their very will – to an elaborate heirarchy of priests, the pagans remained personally connected to the sacred realm. They fought desperately for their freedom. After two years of fierce resistance, their final defeat came in 1232 at the battle of the Sirgune, and with it their history, their spirituality, their language and ultimately their identity were extinguished. Forced to choose death or conversion into serfdom, fodder for the feudal system, they were thus enslaved. It was the historical consequence of defeat. For the newly conquered subjects of Prussia, no less than the old, escape then, and for the next 600 years, was impossible. Following the defeat of the Baltic tribes, the Church, the religious arm of the empire, took over, promising the new subjects that as long as they remained compliant, loyal and faithful, loved and obeyed the new king and his kin – and God – it was *they* who would win in the end: their rewards would be realized *after* they died.

The partnership of Knight and Church had proven irresistable: the armies would conquer the new lands, force the conversion of the defeated pagans to

Christian serfdom, and thereafter pass them over to the Church for continued pacification. The limits of empire continued to expand relentlessly until the entire Western world was brought under control and the State succeeded finally in eliminating all possible competition for its Church.

In a cottage at the edge of Thorn, Martin Fipke's lot had improved, however briefly, under French revolutionary rule, but the defeat of Napoleon in 1815 restored German rule. It was a painful regression. Even for the German families like the Fipkes living within the enclave at Thorn, the victory was a bitter one. With the return of the German nobility, the French land reforms were quashed, the schools were closed once more – no education was necessary for a subject people – and the country was pressed back into a state of dark feudalism. Martin's existence was a difficult one. Ownership of land, the dream of all peasants, remained the exclusive domain of the aristocracy, but even the serfs had better means to feed themselves than he had. Martin and his wife, Christiane Schultz, were simple *kaetners*, agricultural workers who depended for their survival upon finding employment on the land of others.

Martin Fipke's life and the lives of his children were owned by others. They were, however, not entirely without resources. Bootlegging and rum-running had long been one of Thorn's principal industries. Thorn sat on the river border between the Prussian and the Russian empires, and with the sale of German spirits in the Russian-controlled territories heavily taxed, a healthy black market had developed for German alcohol. Smuggling was a way of life. For families like Martin Fipke's, the brewing of quality alcohol was a skill that had passed down through generations from father to son and would continue to do so.

Martin's son, Jakob, 21 in 1844, stayed near the family and followed in his father's footsteps, as the Fipke generations had always done, but the world was rapidly changing. Industrial labourers, a new class of urban serfs, were living under even more appalling conditions than the kaetners. Many lived lives so brutal and tortured the nobility failed to recognize them as members of the same race, even the same species. In 1844 they were starving, and when food prices rose above the value of their labour, they rioted. Under Prussian rule, rebellion, whatever the cause, was deserving of no mercy. They were brutally crushed.

To enforce its rule, Prussian law required that all men perform 19 years of military duty – after which they returned to work in their landlords' fields or factories. Whether with external foes or the internal enemy, the military was forever engaged. When the potato crop failed the following year and a widespread famine led to the outbreak of plague, 30 separate revolts kept the soldiers busy obediently killing their own people.

Over the next twenty years the struggle intensified. Battles raged in Saxony, Hanover and Baden. In the subject lands of Prussia and on the streets of Berlin, desperate people rose up to protest their bondage, only to be forced, violently, to submit to new measures of repression. For the ruling class, secure in their privileges, the years were good ones; the arts were flourishing and their growing overseas empires offered exciting opportunities for new power and wealth.

For Jakob Fipke, now 43, life had recently taken a better turn. Although still a bachlor and reluctant to marry, the widow Eva Sonnenberg, née Thober (Tober), 32 and childless, could wait no longer. She was six months pregnant. They were married in January of 1866. Two months later their daughter, Melanie Friederice, was born, and 19 months after that, on October 19, 1867, their second child was born, a strong, healthy boy, Herman Gustav.

When their own neighbours, the Poles of Prussia, revolted next, rising up around them, Jakob had only to watch from his cottage to witness the campaign. After the Poles were ruthlessly reconquered by German troops, the king William I, imposed new, harsh measures of repression that allowed only bare survival.

Less than 17 months later, Eva gave birth to another boy. Named after his father, he only lived long enough to be baptized. Their fourth child, a girl, also fell ill, dying after only 18 days. Like a curse, the births and deaths, and the country's wars and rebellions continued relentlessly. The demands of empire required sacrifice. Absolute, unquestioning faith and obedience were the virtues taught by the Church. To die in the cause, for King – and God – had become the ultimate honour.

The following year in April 1871, when the German princes, victorious in their new war with France, presented the imperial crown to King William of Prussia, commencing the German Second Reich, Jakob began hunting for a way out. It was impossible to be one's own man in Prussia, but it was, nevertheless, the new ideal: to be free.

All his life Jakob had seen barges and log booms moving downriver through Thorn laden with oak trees cut in Ukraine, the raw material for the building trades and furniture shops of Germany. It was these once-forested lands in Volhynia province of northern Ukraine, due east of Thorn, that the Russian czar now opened to settlement by the Germans. Leaseholds were being granted to farm these fields of oak stumps – hardly an improvement in living conditions. However, as life in Prussia continued to deteriorate, Russian rule became increasingly attractive.

On the third of April, 1871, Jakob Fipke's wife gave birth to another daughter. Their fifth child was healthier than their previous two and, for a time, it appeared as though she might survive. She didn't. Their sixth child, too, died just before Christmas 1873, almost two years old. On October 21, 1875, Eva gave birth to yet another child. A boy, Heinrich August, he would survive. Eva and Jakob had their eighth and last child, Carl Adolf, on January 29, 1878. He, too, would live.

Two years later Jakob Fipke committed the family to a new future. With his wife and their four surviving children, they crossed the Vistula River, leaving the Fortress of Thorn and the Second Reich behind them for good. Jakob was 57 and Eva 45. With a 30 lease of Crown land in Ukraine, Jakob Fipke knew he would never return. He didn't want to.

The air over their new land was suffused with a shimmering, bright light. Rising up to the southwest, the plateau lands merged with the heavily forested peaks of the Carpathian Mountains. The waters of the Carpathians drained north

around the "farm," the Sluch River flowing right through the nearby village of
Novohrad Volynskij before merging with the Pripyat to flow east into the
Dnieper, the great river of the Black Sea.

Jakob put his head down and promptly set to work. With only hand tools,
stump farming was backbreaking labour. Still, Jakob was freer in Ukraine than
any member of his family had been in memory. Moreover, he was far from the
troubles at the war front, and although their farm was only a leasehold, he had
every expectation it would be renewed – if his children wished it. At his age, a
30-year lease was long enough for Jakob. The future belonged to his children.

Politics, however – as always – determined it for them. With the German
emperor, William II, moving Europe inexorably toward the distant Great War,
Czar Alexander III of Russia closed the doors to further settlement by Germans
and issued an edict in 1892 to the existing German leaseholders that their leases
would not be renewed. The Germans would have to leave.

Two years later, Jakob's second son, Heinrich, married Albertine Schelender,
the daughter of another German leaseholder. It was December 28, 1894, and
Heinrich was 19. The year 1910, the termination date for the Fipke farm lease,
seemed a long way off. Certainly events within Ukraine filled the time.

In liberal Ukraine the political undercurrents – never tolerated in Germany –
grew heady and talk strong. Talk of liberation. Freedom from the Czar. Of an end
to the oppression by the Church. Of a new republic, ruled by the people. Of a
free Ukraine, independent from Russian rule. The lessons of the French Revolution and the reasons for its failure were discussed in whispers.

"Kill the Czar."

It was the only way to be free, they said. Even to think the words, though, was
a terrible heresy. Like killing Christ himself. So deeply ingrained was the indoc-
trination, the beliefs in the inherent goodness of the nobility persisted. The very
word was synonymous with honour, an icon of virtue.

"Kill the Czar," they whispered, fearfully.

By 1910 it was clear that one way or another their world was going to explode.
The tinderbox had a dozen fuses.

Thousands of kilometres away in Ottawa, the small woodland capital of
Canada, a brilliant young lawyer from Manitoba, Clifford Sifton, was sick of the
talk of superior and inferior races that dominated the debates in Parliament on
the issue of immigration. Settlement of the prairie lands of western Canada was
necessary to preserve the Dominion, but immigrant British townsmen lacked
the skills or the desire. Sifton knew the answer. Bring in the men from the
Ukrainian steppe lands and the eastern European lowlands: Ukrainians, Poles,
Germans and Russians. Accustomed to hardship, they already lived with conditions virtually identical to those on the windswept Canadian Prairies.

At the end of the parliamentary debate, Sifton won and Canadian immigra-
tion agents began scouting the Ukrainian countryside offering free land in
Canada. It was the dream of countless generations: land. Land they would own.
Land they could pass on to their children. Nor were the Canadian agents alone.

Recruiters from the United States and Brazil, sometimes telling stories too good to be true, were also scouting for new citizens to settle their own vast territories.

Jakob and his wife, Eva, both dead and buried in Ukraine in the black soil of their farm, had been survived by their four children, who remained on the property for as long as they could. But when 1910 arrived, all four had decisions to make. Herman left for a place free of ice and snow. The Brazilian land agents promised him a land grant in the southern jungle near the Argentina border. Carl responded to the reports of fertile land that could be had between Chicago and Detroit. He decided to seek his fortune in America. Melanie, their sister, elected to remain in the nearby town. After 30 years, Novohrod Volynskij was her home. She would not leave. Heinrich, now 35, had already fathered seven children, five of whom survived. He alone decided, with his wife, Albertine, to accept Canada's offer.

The children of Jakob, scattering over three continents, would never see one another again.

CHAPTER TWENTY-ONE

LEDUC, ALBERTA, 1911

To the Fipkes and the thousands of others arriving with them and disembarking at Montreal, Canada was a land beyond dreams. Clifford Sifton had promised the House of Commons the newcomers would become Canadians worthy of citizenship, and the arrivals from the empires of central Europe would prove him right.

They were free for the first time in hundreds of years, perhaps millennia, to work for themselves, and their labours were prodigious. Inured as they were to extreme hardship, the conditions in Canada could be taken in stride. Free from the dictatorship of divine right monarchs, the oppression and constant political intrigue of the nobility, forced military service, famine and revolution, Canada had achieved everything the peasants and the intellectual revolutionaries alike had whispered about back home.

No one who had not lived the conditions of their lives could know the depths of their feelings. Or their commitment to their new country.

As promised, Heinrich and Albertine received a large grant of land south of Edmonton in Alberta. To make their transition easier, ethnic communities had been grouped together, and the Fipkes were among other German Ukrainian families when they arrived at Leduc to take possession of their new properties.

It was a life they would have fought for dearly. And it was handed to them! It was far more precious, in fact, than even they knew. The land grants at Leduc included all the subsurface mineral rights. Leduc sat above a buried sea of oil. The reserves of oil and gas a kilometre beneath those fields were staggering – wealth beyond belief. Only no one yet knew of the treasure buried beneath the soil.

On the farm, Heinrich kept his head down, avoided politics and worked. Of his five children born in Ukraine, the three oldest boys, Ralph, Carl (Charles) and Frederick, remembered the Old World almost as well as he. They, too, were immigrants, carrying the weight and memories of oppression and powerlessness on their shoulders. They, too, worked hard with Heinrich in their fields.

As they secretly feared, the Old World would not leave them alone for long. Germany burst out to attack its neighbours again. The First World War had begun. Canada's future was decided by Britain. Across the Prairies, as young men were called to arms, German farmers, the newcomers, were identified with the enemy. As though, in the face of all their history, their loyalty would be to Germany!

It was politics of a kind Heinrich knew well. Repression, discrimination and murder. Tens of thousands of recent immigrants from the enemy nations were suddenly disenfranchised as Canadians and reregistered as enemy aliens. Across the country, 26 concentration camps were set up. In Alberta the families were marched into barbed-wire pens at Lethbridge, Munson and Jasper and to a large outdoor prison at Castle Mountain in Banff. There soldiers shot any farmers trying to escape.

The irony of it all was that most of the prisoners – and those killed – were not even "German". They were Ukrainians. Ignorant of the nature of the European empires and the struggles of their subject minorities for independence, Canadian authorities identified "enemies" and "allies" according to their citizenship and country of departure. Citizens of the Russian empire, Ukrainians and Poles were now allies. Those of the German and Austrian empires were now enemies. Thus Poles from the German empire and Ukrainians from the territories occupied by the Austrian empire found their farms and properties confiscated. These staunchest of Canadian allies were forcibly taken away to internment, their pleas and all reason ignored.

At the same time, Germans from the Russian-controlled Ukrainian province of Volhynia were classified as "Ukrainians", therefore allies. While their Ukrainian and Polish neighbours, having escaped the repression of German rule in Europe, were being rounded up under the harsh measures reserved for Germans, a very lucky Heinrich could only keep quiet and caution his family to do the same.

For all the advantages Canada had, it was apparent to the newcomers that the governments of the New World could be just as simple-minded and dangerously capricious as the totalitarian oligarchies from which they had recently escaped. Canada was not alone in setting up concentration camps to intern its citizen-enemies. Heinrich's sister, Melanie, who had chosen to remain in Ukraine, was deported to Siberia in 1915 and disappeared forever.

When the war finally ended, a new calm settled across the Prairies. Heinrich and Albertine had four more children, while the eldest boys, including Carl, who was 19 when Germany surrendered, found their own wives and brought them to live on the farm. It was a family business. They were all in it together, and they remained as independent and as far from the politics of power and government as they could manage.

Heinrich, resolving to concentrate all his energies on building the fortunes of his family and to take advantage of everything Canada offered, raised his children, planted his crops, tended his livestock and, when prosperity allowed, acquired more land. He continued to keep his head down until he died, fearful that the bubble might burst, and he worked relentlessly for the future of his children's children – all the while unaware of the wealth beneath the surface of the land he tilled. A buried sea of oil. A treasure trove.

CHAPTER TWENTY-TWO

ED FIPKE

Eᴅ had good memories of his childhood. Even of the Depression, the "Dirty Thirties". The Fipkes were poor, but they were never cold or hungry or threatened, at least not by anything outside the family.

A dense thicket of scrub poplar grew on the farm, bush where Ed spent many enjoyable afternoons with his father, Carl, brewing the family's alcohol. For a child, the secrecy of the hidden still, the conspiracy of family against the state, was thrilling. As a business, as a source of income, it was unequalled. They called it "the cash cooker".

Strict monopolies granted to the elite of Central Canada – the Molsons and the Hiram Walkers – to brew and distill all of Canada's alcohol were enough to tolerate. But when the government declared a general national Prohibition, which excluded Quebec, in order that the entire production of the nation's distilleries could be turned into war materials like acetone, the law fell into widespread disregard. To pay good money for something that could be made at home for free was stupid. To abstain altogether merely because the government said so was intolerable. Thousands of backwoods operations immediately sprang up across the country, from Nova Scotia to British Columbia, and rum-running activities occupied most border communities.

Carl had learned the liquor trade from his father, Heinrich, who had learned it from Jakob, who had been taught by Martin, and so on back into antiquity. Under the cover of their bleached poplar forest, Carl now taught Ed.

It was a useful skill. Not only was alcohol a standard feature of life in Germany and Ukraine, but it helped ease Canadian pains and pressures just as well. Not all the alcohol was consumed in the home, however. Across the border in the United States, the Prohibition laws were even more severe. Controlled wartime Prohibition was expanded after the war and enforced until 1933.

The unequal access to alcohol across the border, as in Thorn, was a precursor to large-scale black-market smuggling. Carl's alcohol was so superior in quality to that of his competition, his entry into the American markets was easier than the old trade over the Vistula River into Russia. Everything he was able to produce was purchased by a single customer – a large American-based drugstore chain with outlets across western Canada and throughout the United States.

The alcohol the company purchased from Carl was bottled and labelled in the States, then shipped internally. Curiously, in spite of Prohibition, not all the liquor the drugstore sold was illegal. Pharmacies were among the few outlets allowed to sell alcohol – but only as a "medicinal agent" with a doctor's pre-scription. The use of the market was extensive and the demand for supplies high. At Christmas in particular, vast quantities were sold to patients whose sudden "illness" required just such medication to carry them through the holiday season.

Carl was only caught once. The Mounties, forewarned, set up a country road-block and nabbed him. Their search of the farm, however, failed to uncover the hidden still, and the children all knew better than to talk. In the end the Moun-ties could find no more than what they had seized. The trunk of Carl's car had been loaded down with his high-quality home brew – enough to warrant a harsh penalty. Carl was made an example for those who would likewise defy the law. At a time when local farm labour was making $5 a week, he was fined $100. Far worse, the judge also ordered that his car be forfeited.

To another, the penalty might have been crushing. To Carl, it meant little. Indeed what threats remained after the hardships he had known, hardships that produced a certain kind of strength in the Fipkes? The penalties of the court, even had they included jail, only hardened his resolve to be his own man.

Returning to the bush with all his children, the family camped out by the still as he worked. Within a month the cash cooker had produced enough to finance a new car. It was not only the members of the temperance movement who were dismayed when Prohibition laws were repealed.

Life on the Prairies was a close, tight world. Edmonton was the sun around which all the outlying communities revolved. Each farm was its own little planet, self-sufficient. Each family carried its own history as a soldier remembers his battles, sharing them only with those who had been there. Even when unspoken, family history was never far away. Behind every look and lesson were the expe-riences that shaped the character of the family and everyone within it.

Young Ed had a special place in his family's dreams. They had achieved sta-bility, with the farm a base from which they could take their strength, retire to or launch new lives. That was the nature of land, its gift eternal. And they had achieved prosperity. Their farm had expanded with purchases of adjoining properties, and they now owned more than a hundred hectares. Heinrich's fam-ily had grown and none of the children had died in Canada. Some were old enough to become grandparents themselves.

Born in the glacial grip of a record winter, January 13, 1923, Ed was Carl's sec-ond child. His was the first of the three generations all living on the farm to truly pioneer Canada. Heinrich and Carl had settled in Canada, but the forces that drove their lives and their world-view had been formed in the Old World. They attempted no adjustment. They simply arrived and got to work, their dreams and their standards set long before they arrived.

Ed was the true pioneer. His society was Canada. Not Ukraine. Not Germany. Not Prussia. He had a foot in both worlds: one inside the doorstep of his par-ents' and grandparents' memories, and the other outside. A new world beckoned beyond the doorway.

It was now up to Ed to take the next step. Education, reserved for the elite, had been denied his ancestors. Education allowed a man to transcend his roots. Ed resisted being tied to the land. Or to memory. He wanted to break away, to exercise his own life freely. But the new freedom did not mean irresponsibility: Ed would go to university. The family were all agreed. And afterwards? It would be up to Ed. Heinrich and Carl had carried the future this far; now it was on Ed's shoulders.

In 1939, when German militarism, the endless spiral of predator and prey, broke out to give the world six more years of venom and paralysis, Ed was 16. With the outbreak of the war, farm products – meats and grains – got good prices. For the first time in Canadian history, farming became a prosperous business. By 1941 farmers everywhere were building additions, and barn raisings became a regular feature of Prairie life. Whole communities turned out to help their neighbours.

And to dance, a happy conjunction of circumstances. Anna Tober had just turned 14 in the summer of 1941 when she met Ed Fipke, 18, on summer break before his final year at high school. It was a community barn raising at Camrose, and she was dancing with another boy when Ed cut in. He was a good dancer and he made her laugh. Ed had a wild, reckless streak. Like his father Carl, when Ed wanted to do something, he would do it. And nobody could stop him. His new dance partner liked that.

The next year, when Ed, accepted into premed sciences at the University of Saskatchewan, went off to begin his studies, Anna moved to Leduc to attend high school. Living first in a dorm on school grounds, she later moved out to share a room at a boardinghouse with Ed's sister, Edna, and, as her guest, spent part of each weekend at the Fipke farm. Ed's family made her feel welcome. She was, in fact, family. A distant cousin of the Fipkes. It was a Tober, then Thober, who married Jakob Fipke in Thorn in 1866 – so they shared the same roots. Anna's family, like Ed's, had also moved to Volhynia, Ukraine, and then to a Canadian homestead at Hay Lakes, a hamlet a few kilometres east of Leduc. It seemed the perfect match.

Ed was in his second year at the University of Saskatchewan in 1943 when news of his father's accident reached him. Carl's arm had been ripped off by a belt on a piece of heavy equipment. Ed raced home immediately across the empty prairie but he was too late. Staphylococci bacteria had gotten in, killing Carl before Ed could say goodbye. He was 44.

A few months later Heinrich, strong-willed, powerful and healthy his whole life, suddenly developed stomach cancer. Reduced to a frail and starved skeleton, he, too, became just another memory. He was 68.

His immediate link with the past broken, Ed's resolve to carry the family's dreams forward suddenly collapsed. Making a hasty decision later regretted, he quit his studies and returned to the farm. Now 20 in 1943, his father and grandfather both dead, Ed was back working the land. Now with the burden of family history weighing directly on his shoulders, the pressures were worse than ever.

A year was all he could handle. In 1944 Ed left the farm and moved to Edmonton, where he took a civilian job with the U.S. Air Force, which operated a huge American base in the city. It was part of a little-known pipeline to supply the American's Russian allies. Russian and Ukrainian aircrews, teenagers most of them, younger than Ed, would arrive, take crash courses in flying the American-made aircraft, then try to pilot them back to Russia through Alaska. Many of them did not make it.

For Ed, Edmonton was an improvement. It was life in the mainstream and the money was good. The Americans paid better than the Canadians. The canteen sold American goods at duty-free prices, alcohol was cheap and there was a dance every Saturday night. For the first time in his life, Ed was happy. He continued to see Anna, and their relationship, too, continued to improve. They were married after her 18 birthday, under a swallow-blue summer sky on June 29, 1945.

Anna also had plans for an education. The Tobers, like the Fipkes, wanted better for their children. Anna, who had skipped two grades, planned to attend normal school and to teach; her early marriage to Ed changed everything. A year later, their first of four children was born, a boy, on July 22, 1946. Charles Edgar Fipke was named after his father, Edgar, and his grandfather, Charles, better known by the name Carl. Ed called his son Chuck after an American pilot he had known, and the name stuck: Chuck Fipke.

It was a promising year. Geophysicists had been doing some work in the area of Leduc. Walking around the farms, testing the subsurface rock formations with new wartime technologies, they finally probed the depths and discovered oil. The Fipkes were suddenly wealthy!

Heinrich's land holdings had provided the means for his children to acquire their own adjoining farms. On Carl's death he owned two half-sections of land, totalling 640 acres. One he had acquired from the Hudson's Bay Company, which still owned huge tracts of land from its original British Crown grant, and the other half-section he had purchased from the Canadian Pacific Railway Company, which had also been "gifted" large land holdings across Canada to ensure its development and future prosperity. The two properties had been run separately and, upon Carl's death, Ed's brother, Irvin, took one while Ed, together with his sister Edna and their mother, shared the other farm between them.

With the discovery of oil under Leduc, land agents and oil company people swarmed the farms in search of a piece of the action. The farmers, for the most part unsophisticated, were not, however, easily intimidated. Distrustful of big-business interests, they carefully considered the oil companies' offers. The farmers could not compete with the company men. They were unable to drill their own oil. The companies wanted to buy the land outright and offered good prices – money enough to relocate elsewhere and buy twice as much land.

If they did not sell, if the farmers tried to hold out, the companies threatened to whipsaw under their farms and drain off the oil anyway – if there was even any oil to be had. It was all a gamble. No one knew the size of the oil field, how big it was, how deep, or who had it and who did not. It was exciting but extremely stressful.

The companies kept the pressure on. Their offers for cash buyouts increased.

Final offers! Take it or leave it. Ed was in a quandary. On top of the old issues, this new pressure was intense.

At the eleventh hour a third choice arrived – right out of left field. The farmers around Leduc found the offers and the companies' pressure as difficult to deal with as Ed did, and they inherently disliked the idea of selling out. Especially without knowing what they were selling. They knew the Fipkes and they knew Ed. He was the boy with an education. He had not finished, but he had at least attended university. They proposed a farmers' cooperative. A consortium. Jointly they could raise the money themselves to drill their own land.

It was a daring idea: to compete with the companies to "produce" and market their own oil. To keep their farms and to grow. They believed in Ed. He was smart. They wanted him to run it, to head their community oil consortium.

It was a future with unlimited potential. They all had faith in Ed's ability to run their own oil company, to carry them all into a bright future. But Ed had his own doubts, doubts of which only he knew the depths.

It was Canada's first major oil discovery, a huge field which would change the fortunes of the entire province and the bald face of the Prairies. But in 1946 it was mostly theory. Not until the following year would the extent of the find be made public. The oil companies were keeping their secrets to themselves.

Ed did not wait; the risk seemed too great. Speaking on behalf of the family, for his mother and his sister, he agreed instead to sell. Ed's share seemed a healthy sum at the time, but it was only a fraction of the value he might have realized had he stayed.

The following year, in 1947, as news of the Leduc oil field find was sweeping the nation and the farmers who had kept the vision grew wealthier, Ed left the province with his young wife and baby to try to start a new life, to the east, in Ottawa.

The sale of the farm, like the death of his father, isolated Ed in a cloud of icy fog. He wanted to leave the past behind, with all its memories, and as though its effects could somehow be avoided by silence, he never spoke about it again.

Finally free but landless, he found himself a man without roots. He would spend much of his life on the long Canadian roads, always working, roaming far from home as if searching for a lost dream, something never attained.

CHAPTER TWENTY-THREE

OTTAWA, ONTARIO, 1947

Eᴅ might have purchased more land, but that seemed to be going backwards. The emerging technologies of the United States were a lot more exciting, so Ed bought himself the distribution rights in Ontario for the products of a new American company that made a portable machine that could record speech. The Dictaphone offered a whole new way of running an office. Ed was gambling that it had a future.

A wave of unprecedented growth and prosperity rolled across the continent. People were leaving farms in droves and moving to cities where jobs cried out for them. Immigration, too, followed the war, with record highs not seen since the land grants at the turn of the century. Now it was industry that was fuelling the optimism. With the victory in Europe and the changes the war had brought, Canada was discovering its own power and potential. Ed bought a small house on Louisa Street in downtown Ottawa, installed the family and set about to build his business.

The following year, in 1948, as the sugar bush around Ottawa turned the countryside brilliant shades of scarlet and crimson, Anna gave birth in October to their second child, another boy, Wayne Clifford.

Ed was right about the future of the business machines: they took off. But sales were hard, the competition stiffer than he had ever imagined and profits even harder to hang on to. As he complained to Anna, "Every time I make a buck, there's 10 guys with their hands on it!" Smart but ill-prepared for business, Ed found the going tough. With the pressure building, he began to drink more heavily as his moods grew darker.

Anna, like Ed, had come from a hard-driving German family. It was a man's world, and her role, as she had been brought up to accept, was simply to be supportive, forever accommodating, regardless of the demands. Passive, she was not disinterested but she was powerless to issue the orders to bring Ed's life under her control. While Ed became increasingly angry, dictatorial and controlling, Anna remained constant, permissive and nonjudgemental. Chuck grew up in the little city as he pleased, a boy of three. Isolated and emotionally distant from his father, Chuck felt loved by Anna, but she put no limits on his behaviour either.

There was a game he liked to play. From the command of his tricycle at the crest of a steep hill where their house perched, he would survey the road that spilled down into a busy intersection at the bottom. Gliding forward, he would roll down off the hill, gaining speed till the spinning pedals blurred, laughing as he raced wildly toward the intersection. Waiting until the last moment before spilling into the steel river, he'd finally throw his feet out, slamming them down hard into the pavement, skidding to a stop at the brink.

Anna watched from the house, her heart in her throat. Marvelling at his nerve, she kept her fear to herself, and when he climbed back to the top to do it again, she would only turn away. She never stopped him. Chuck was so different from other children. It was the same trait she had seen in her husband. Neither had physical fear. It was not as if they were unaware of the risks; it was simply that pain and suffering did not frighten them.

Neither did the neighbourhood gangs. In 1951, before television lured them indoors and with few organized community sports to busy them, newly urban kids lived their lives on the concrete paths. With memories of the war – its battles and heroics – still fresh and rehashed everywhere, children's games mimicked adult wars. Rock throwing was the rage in most cities. Children would split into camps, arm themselves with a supply of rocks and hurl their missiles back and forth at each other – sometimes with serious accuracy.

Chuck's parents watched the fights. Ed, witnessing Chuck hold his own against a tough group of recent immigrant boys, noted to Anna with pride, "Our boy can sure pitch a rock!" For the children the rock wars were more real than any that came out of a box. Street gangs and rock fights grew out of the urban cultural psyche, the battles an expression of competition and fear, and an experience in camaraderie and conflict. But, most intoxicating, the wars were a demonstration of power. One could fight and win, a lesson that was not lost on Chuck.

As new products came on the market and competition for sales became cut-throat, Ed began drinking steadily. His anger quickly tapped into a rage that seemed now to dwell permanently under the surface and sometimes exploded into uncontrollable violence. By late 1951, he had had enough. He sold the business, recovered most of his investment and moved back to Alberta, to Edmonton where he took a sales job with McCulloch Tools. By painful coincidence, they supplied blasting materials and newly designed tools to the oil businesses that now proliferated in the area.

In the early '50s, 61st Avenue was the outer limit of Edmonton. On one side was a series of small wood-frame wartime houses, on the other the open prairie bush. Ed bought No. 10808. The following summer, in June, Anna gave birth to another boy, Neil.

In 1954, amid growing fears of an atomic war following the Soviet Union's explosion in 1949 of a hydrogen bomb, Canada and the United States commenced a massive engineering project, the Distant Early Warning Line. Funded by the American military and to be built by thousands of Canadians, a chain of radar stations stretching nearly 9,700 kilometres was to be constructed in three years along the Arctic coast. The DEW Line would watch the northern skies for incoming Soviet missiles or aircrafts, to allow America the chance to fire off its own rockets before the end.

Ed quit McCulloch and went north, alone, to work the DEW Line. His absence left Anna, preoccupied now with the new baby, with huge demands. But Chuck despised his father's drinking and his raging temper. With Ed away the house was at least calm. And its location, facing the prairie, made it a gate to paradise.

Free every day after school to fill his own time until nightfall, sometimes alone, sometimes with friends from a street gang he belonged to, Chuck lived his life out on the prairie. A land of peaceful wilderness, of scrub birch and poplar, of shallow marshy sloughs and open fields, the prairie teemed with life. Of all the creatures there, it was the birds that attracted him the most. Soaring freely, riding updrafts, they kept his attention for hours. He found their nesting sites and studied their family ties. With a keen ear, he became a good mimic of their song.

In particular he was intrigued by the differences between prey and predators. There was, he observed, a structure to the natural order of life, a hierarchy that he sought to understand. Somewhere in it was a role for mankind, he knew. If he could find it, he would find his own place in the world. It was to become a life-long quest.

When Ed returned to Edmonton after only a few months, he had a new partner and another business. Among them all, it was to become Ed's favourite, and he would stay with it for the next 30 years. After Ed learned everything his partner knew about photography, Ed bought him out and became sole owner of an aerial-picture business.

He would rent a plane with a pilot or, on occasion – once he understood the mechanics of flying and if no pilots were available – he would take a plane up himself to photograph farms from the air. Later, with a coloured sample to show the farmers what he could do, he would knock on their doors with the black-and-white proofs.

On one of his first trips out, he photographed a community of 23 farms just south of Wainwright, Alberta, near the Saskatchewan border. In the follow-up on the ground, he signed contracts to sell his pictures to 22 of them. Back home, he taught Anna, whom he called Ann, how to develop and enlarge film and – their chief selling feature – how to colour the prints. With special oil-based transparent paints, she could bring black-and-white photographs to life. Or even improve on it.

Taking care to enhance the farms, Anna would make the fields greener or yellower, the barns browner and the houses whiter than they actually appeared to the eye, and the farmers loved those pictures. Some of them were very specific about how they wanted their fields coloured. Depending on the farmer's preference, a brush stroke could change hay to barley, or alfalfa to yellow rape seed. Even fallow fields could look planted. For once, a farm could look prosperous and the crops all ripe at once. Barns, as important as the fields, received the same special treatment. Rusting roofs could be made to shine. White trim could be added and walls made freshly brilliant in red.

Ed knew the character of farming well. He joked himself into the hearts of the farmers, and into their pocketbooks. It was a cash business, and it gave Ed the life he needed: on the road, moving from town to town, usually far from home.

From northern Manitoba to Lake of the Woods, he flew the side roads and highways, into Saskatchewan and across Alberta, through the valleys of British Columbia to the Fraser Delta and Vancouver Island. He photographed nearly every farm in western Canada, knocking on thousands of doors, forever looking at the land from the sky and talking to farmers. What he left behind were the painted memories of a time that would vanish forever. Thousands of images of family farms, sweet memories of a rural way of life only half-remembered, treasured by aging farmers.

Left alone for weeks at a time, sometimes months, Anna had to make do with what she had in the cupboards and often what she did not have. To Chuck she became a saint, while his own sensitivity to poverty and the value of the dollar grew acute. They were frequently hungry, and sometimes sheer survival seemed to be the chief concern.

Near their house, only a few long country blocks away, was the University of Alberta's agricultural research centre. It was run like a large public farm, and Chuck began to spend a lot of time there, resourcefully expanding his horizons. One of the university's projects involved the breeding of chickens in large pens that housed hundreds of the white and brown birds. Large chickens. His interest in them, however, was not entirely biological. At 10, he understood the fundamentals of a cash economy: without cash, a person had nothing.

The idea to turn the chickens into a business happened by chance. Chuck was hunting through the prairie grasses one day for wild birds' eggs to add to his collection. He was examining a wren's nest in an old abandoned car wreck when he spotted a chicken that had escaped from the university pens. He brought it home alive, tucked under his arm, and his mother stopped him as he was going through the kitchen. She showed a keen interest in his catch.

"Chuck, where'd you get that chicken?" Chuck was caught off guard and quickly replied, "Arno's." Arno had a small farm up the road where he kept a few pigeons and laying hens. There was no reason to lie – the chicken had been there for the taking – but "Arno's" came out instead.

"How much did you pay for it?" Anna asked. Arno would not have given a bird like this one away, she knew. Chuck was stuck with the story now.

"Oh, ah, a buck," he replied, hoping it was a reasonable figure.

His mother quickly traded him a dollar for his chicken, and as she turned it into a large pot of soup, Chuck returned to the prairie fields beside the university pens, thoughts of financial freedom germinating. Business grew.

When the university patched the hole in the fence, cutting off his supply, Chuck was left with an order for two birds he had to fill and, as he saw it, a surplus of chickens in the university pens.

When Ed returned home one afternoon from an extended sales tour, he was greeted by Chuck, brimming with enthusiasm about his new venture.

"Dad, I've got a friend, like a really good friend, and like, he's got a chicken farm and … and I can buy them really cheap!"

"Is that right?" Ed was amused by his son's eagerness. There was that small acreage Arno had up the road where Chuck used to hang out. Ed guessed that was where the chickens were coming from. Chuck encouraged the idea.

"So, how much are they?" Ed inquired.

"Just a buck," Chuck replied. "A buck a chicken."

"Not a bad deal," Ed said, nodding his head. Chuck jumped at the opening to make another sale.

"You better take two, Dad!"

Ed laughed and agreed, and Chuck ran off to complete the deal, returning later swinging a pair of freshly killed chickens. The university finally took notice of the growing predation and posted guards hidden in the night, inside the pens.

Climbing the high compound fence into the grounds with Ihor Boychuk, his business partner, Chuck moved stealthily through the night toward the roosting sheds. Not much bigger than coyotes, the boys had become proficient in catching chickens. Nimble and quick, they would slip inside among the birds, grab one apiece, and rush back over the fence into the security of the prairie bushland, where they would shut the birds up in their fort, ready for their next sale – at a profit of 100 percent!

This night, though, something much larger than the outline of a chicken appeared from the corner shadows of the pen. Lights flashed. Men were lunging at them. Shouting.

A trap.

Desperately the boys dodged big outstretched arms and kicked up a cloud of squawking chickens, knocked loose from their roosts in the crash of bodies. Breaking for the fence, Chuck nearly flew to the top, trying to heave himself over in one hurdle, and snagged himself in the barbed wire. Suspended in the air, dangling by his clothes as a guard roughly grabbed his foot, he frantically tore loose, fell to the ground with the fence between them, and made a dash for the prairie and freedom.

It was close: he had lost his shoe. Breathing hard, he met up with Ihor and they quietly slipped deeper into the darkness of the black prairie night. It was the end of "Chuckie's Chickens." He never went back.

Soon after, his father disappeared again. Ed had always come and gone. When the weeks passed into months, it became clear that this time was different. The stories that filtered back said he had gone to Saskatchewan, maybe to Regina, to live. The family didn't know, only that he had never been away so long. There was no knowing when he would come back. If ever.

As the money ran out, the family's situation grew desperate. With a new baby girl, their fourth child, Carol, Anna's life became even more of a challenge. Chuck, her eldest, took some of her own feelings to heart, but he was unable to help much. Abandoned by their father, dependent upon their mother, the children withdrew into their own lives.

For a while Anna was able to make enough to support them. Her coloured photographs were so precise and lifelike that she had been asked by other photographers to paint their pictures. In autumn, when the work painting pictures dropped off and the family was left with only some celery from the garden to eat, Chuck's feelings hardened. As hunger set in, anger replaced pain. Like generations of Fipkes before him, the lesson Chuck learned was to be detached – independent and in control.

Rather than crushing his spirit, poverty began to focus it. Dependency and vulnerability were invitations to suffering. Chuck resolved never to give in. When threatened, he would fight back. However difficult life became, he would beat it. Whatever it took, he vowed to himself, he would come out on top.

There was little room left for gentler feelings. Chuck's heart was still open, but it was guarded. There was only so much a person could allow himself to endure.

In the end, as the brittle brink of a Prairie winter edged in through the walls of the frame house, a friend of Ed's rescued them. Pat McBride was living in Edmonton and, although not much better off, he, at least, was working. When he discovered the family was in need, he arrived with bags of food. Pat's kindness became an inspiration for Chuck, and long after Ed returned, his prolonged absence unexplained, Pat's influence was to have a profound effect on the family and the direction they – and Chuck in particular – would take.

CHAPTER TWENTY-FOUR

THE PEREGRINE

THERE were four peregrine young in the nest, and he took one. He had raised three other raptors, a hawk and two owls, which he kept penned behind the garage. He was ready for the falcon.

Reputed to be the swiftest creature on earth, the peregrine could attain speeds in a headlong stoop in excess of 270 kilometres an hour. With his acquisition of the wild peregrine, Chuck's interest in ornithology now grew into a passion.

The chick grew to maturity as Chuck raised it with all the devotion his hobby demanded. He planned to train his to hunt. Good-natured and easy to train, the bird was a real prize, and Chuck knew it. Peregrines were the falcon of choice for the European aristocracy. In Asia the Mongols preferred goshawks, and the Arabs the saker falcon, but the peregrine, the bird of European history, could hold its own anywhere in the world.

Chuck's love of life was at its peak. He spent many long afternoons and entire weekends wandering the fields that fall, walking through ripening grasses and, as the season changed, through billowing gales of powdery snow or, on calmer days, crunching between rushes in frozen swamps. The bird was always with him, perched majestically on his forearm, surveying with keen eyes the details of the prairie as Chuck familiarized it with the forms and shapes of the land, its seasons and its prey.

Chuck even risked his life to feed it, to teach it how to survive. Chuck didn't mind. In fact, those were his favourite lessons. Chuck's grandmother – his father's mother – had remarried after Carl died, and with the farm gone, Emily had moved to Edmonton, where she lived with her second husband near a high-level bridge. Chuck was very fond of his grandparents and often visited them in the evenings, especially the nights Ed would come home drunk, looking for a fight. After crossing the dark city, through bone-biting temperatures, it was always a relief to find their warm sanctuary waiting at the end of a road singing with ice.

But even the coldest temperatures on the blackest nights never stopped him from turning at the edge of the bridge, scrambling down to the base supports, then climbing up through the open structure of steel beams and girders to the very top. He came for the birds that roosted there at night.

In the shadowy light from the city, he could make out handholds and footholds in the supports and cross beams of the bridge. High above the ground, underneath the road surface, with the rumbling of traffic just inches above his head, he would crawl slowly along the frozen beams and snatch up scrub pigeons roosting there. Feral birds, all descended from stocks of the domestic rock dove of Europe, they were not adapted to night flying. He took them alive.

Chuck had his own pigeons at home. In fact, the entire garage had been given over to racing birds and "fancies." But those were special birds, bought and traded from around the country. Some had been bred and raised by Chuck himself. All were champions in their own right. He would never allow them to be hurt. Indeed, on cold nights he would not leave them in the garage. Cages and all, they came into the house, stacked from floor to ceiling in his bedroom until there was barely space to squeeze through to his own bed.

But the peregrine had to eat and learn to find its own food. One bird equalled one lesson. To have a wild peregrine on the arm, a powerful spirit all of its own, and to learn with it – to share its victories and its failures – was a privileged experience. It created a union of sorts between bird and boy.

Heading out into the prairie with his falcon on his arm and a pigeon in a cage stirred deep and exciting emotions in him. More than anything else, the drama of nature and his birds made him feel whole. With his falcon he was free. It was another world, of which he was master.

By early summer the boy and his bird had become a team. Beyond biology, beyond passive observation, falconry was *the Hunt*. Now he could expand the bird's training. Hunting out on the prairie, the falcon had always been given an advantage over its prey. Chuck decided it was time for the bird to make a kill on a more even field. This time the pigeon's wing was not clipped. This time it had no weight tied to its leg, slowing it down, keeping it low to the ground. This time it would fly freely, with all its ability.

The peregrine took to the air first. Rising to a point high above Chuck, it hovered there, waiting on the release. Chuck watched it. His falcon was magnificent, a great hunter; he had every confidence in its ability. He set the pigeon loose.

The bait – the prey – took to the sky, a wild bird fleeing the falcon. The pigeon had one advantage, and only one. It used it. An old bird from under the bridge, it had learned to survive from experience. Or perhaps it was simply lucky. But instead of flying away, cross-country, which would have given the falcon the opportunity to execute its attack, the pigeon flew straight up, high into the sky.

Higher and higher it flew, taking the falcon with it in pursuit. Climbing, they were almost matched. Pursued by death trailing its talons behind it, the scrub pigeon flew faster and more cleverly than any Chuck had witnessed.

Up into the sky they rose, higher and higher, until they were distant specks. As determined as the pigeon was to survive, the falcon was just as intent on the kill. Desperately, as best he could, Chuck followed. He had his lure with him but no lure was going to bring the falcon back.

Chuck kept them in sight for a few miles before he lost them completely, his sight blocked by the thick brush around White Mud Creek. When he came out of it, the sky was clear. Pale blue and empty. The emptiness of the sky was unbearable. His bird was gone. He stood on the prairie until dark, hoping against reason that the falcon might return, looking for him, its human friend.

The stars came out and he was alone in the night with his grief.

Life at home, strained at the best of times, became hardly tolerable. Gradually, pent-up feelings began to surface. Increasingly aggressive, Chuck began testing his limits, first in the family, against his brother Wayne – his rival as often as his friend. Ed did not object to Chuck's aggression outside the home. Aggression had its place; after all, he had never been one to turn away from a fight. As Ed saw it, those without the confidence to compete, those who were not aggressive, would never be successful. He would not, however, tolerate Chuck being abusive to either of his younger brothers; when he was aware of it, the strap came out and he meted out whacks across the back.

Aggressive in his own right, Wayne was not a passive victim. However, Chuck was bigger and stronger. One summer when their father was home, Chuck again beat Wayne to the ground. Only after Wayne had run off did Chuck realize the consequences of his actions. He had been warned. Rather than follow Wayne back into the house, Chuck turned and fled in the opposite direction, toward the scrub bush of the open prairie.

He knew he would have to go home eventually, but he could not face his father yet. If he stayed away long enough, maybe it would blow over or his father would leave on business; he was never home much.

Late-summer sounds of locust wings filled the air, and the afternoon passed into dusk. He tried not to think of how his father was reacting to his running away. What if it made him angrier? In the meantime there were lots of things to occupy his time. Following birds, searching for rabbits – food for his pet owls and his red-tailed hawk.

By nightfall he was hungry, but he was no more ready to go home. It was impossible to sleep, curled up in a mat of grasses. The night grew cold and the mosquitoes fierce. By dawn he was dizzy and weak. Sneaking back to the outskirts of the city, he located some of his school friends. Renewed with a meal of soda biscuits, apples and chicken, he returned to the bush with a borrowed sweater and blanket, confident that with their clandestine support he could last indefinitely. There was no reason ever to return home.

Except for his birds. The pigeons needed constant attention. His family might care for them, but he could not count on it. Wayne had good reason not to; his father, angry, was unlikely to take over his responsibilities. His mother, if she knew how, might help. But she did not know. The birds had always been his sole responsibility – one he took seriously.

Chuck had dozens of birds. Racing pigeons and fancies, some he had bought or traded for but most he had "created." The racing pigeons provided him with yet another release. Chuck loved speed, and speed combined with competition was an irresistible magnet.

But beyond breeding and business – his birds sold across the province, making him money – the pigeons were creatures Chuck could love. Not exciting the way his peregrine had been, they nevertheless had their own kind of majesty. In early mythology pigeons were descended from angels, and there were times he could almost believe it. Unlike the falcon, which lived within its own solitude, independent and proud, the pigeons were social and gregarious, even loving.

His favourite among them all was a dove he had bred himself. Where the peregrine had been fierce, she was a gentle spirit and a champion at the shows. Without food or water they would all die.

If not for his birds, he might have spent the rest of the summer on the prairie, in hiding from his father, but after three days the pressure was unbearable. He had to go back. He could not abandon his birds – whatever the consequences.

Ed saw another side to his son's rebelliousness. He knew that Chuck needed more structure in his life, more discipline. Chuck was too independent, almost a loner – and so defiant. The Lutheran Church of Pastor Reinhold Krisch had not helped. Chuck went faithfully each Sunday with his mother, even singing in the church choir. But the pastor's sermons had no more effect in taming his wild side than the evenings he spent with the Boy Scouts. Ed had another idea.

It was totally black and still when Chuck peered into the yard. Carefully, he made his way to the garage door and listened, his heart pounding. There were a few sounds from the pigeons; the house was dark. Late at night, it seemed as though the whole city were sleeping. Gently he opened the door and stepped into the garage. The cages for his pigeons were arranged in rows, stacked off the ground like shelves at a grocery store. It was a familiar, welcoming sight. As though in warm greeting, the birds began murmuring softly and stirred as he entered.

To let some light in, he left the door open. He knew the layout of the garage, where everything was situated, even in blackness. But as he poured the feed, the room suddenly got darker. Ed was in the doorway, a belt hanging from his hand. His father had been waiting for him. He was caught!

Ed began beating Chuck with the belt. *Whack!* For running away. *Whack!* For being disobedient. *Whack!* For bullying Wayne. *Whack!*

Chuck had been beaten before. But never like this. His three-day absence from the house had only aggravated his father's temper. *Whack!*

Oddly, Chuck was not feeling anything, at least not enough pain to make him cry out. Now that he was face-to-face with his father, the fear that had driven him into hiding dissipated completely. As his father whipped him, long-pent-up feelings rose from the depths of instinct with a new defiance: anger. Anger at his father's violence. Anger at his rages. Anger at his drinking. Anger at being hurt, at being afraid, at being abandoned. Anger at being unloved. At having to run away. At being beaten.

The anger gave him strength, and the fight in him rose until it broke over him. "I hate you!" he screamed. Ed struck him again. *Whack!* "I hate you!" He yelled it like a curse. Undefeated. And Ed struck him again. *Whack!* Each time Ed hit him, Chuck yelled back, "I hate you!" until, drained, his own rage spent, Ed finally quit and stomped off, leaving Chuck alone in the garage with his birds.

Chuck moved slowly to the door and turned on the light. There was no reason to remain in the dark any longer. Moving from cage to cage, he filled the birds' trays with food and water …

CHAPTER TWENTY-FIVE

TREPANIER BENCH, 1963

Eᴅ had had enough of Edmonton. City life had been too much of a struggle. They might be poor, but Ed did not know any farmers who went hungry.

His friend Pat McBride had moved to British Columbia a few years earlier. Hitchhiking to the Okanagan Valley, he had stopped in Kelowna, a town surrounded by apple orchards irrigated from the valley's deep lake, liked what he saw and stayed. With no money of his own, he found some investors, started a financial-investment company and began building homes in the orchards. Then subdivisions. Then whole neighbourhoods. Pat was on a fast track to success. It seemed the place to go.

After renting for a while, Ed found some land he, too, liked. It was an old homestead site, a ranch, southwest of Kelowna. Too far from the water to be cultivated, the dry land was mostly in its original timbered state. After driving up the mountain through large ponderosa pines and fir, alongside Trepanier Creek to a small plateau at 600 metres, the family moved into their new home. The higher wilderness behind the farm, out of which the creek flowed, was raw and nearly unbroken for more than 300 kilometres to the sea. It was central British Columbia backcountry. In all, Ed bought more than 120 hectares.

Chuck arrived in June right after school finished in Alberta and, with the farm being several kilometres distant from Kelowna, he needed a car. It was 1963 and he was 16. Old enough. His dad already knew where he could get a job to pay for one: the army. The military camp was at Vernon, 46 kilometres north of Kelowna. Discipline there would be a little more strict than what Chuck was used to.

In mid-1963, Canada still had the jitters from the Cuban Missile Crisis of October, 1962. Only eight months earlier, Kennedy and Khrushchev had put the world on the brink of atomic war over the issue of nuclear missiles in Cuba. At risk in the first strike were the eastern cities of Halifax, Montreal and Toronto. Prime Minister Diefenbaker ordered the construction of a bunker underneath Ottawa capable of sustaining a nuclear hit, while schools practised drills with the children filing out of their classrooms and crouching down in front of their lockers, so as to provide easier identification of their remains for the authorities afterwards. President Kennedy sent warships to blockade Cuba, and the Canadian government fretted and responded by quietly moving its army to "alert" status – afraid that even that gesture might tip the scales of brinkmanship and bring the missiles raining down.

Glen Ema, the Vernon military camp, was still buzzing with self-important vainglory. But infantry, the leaders knew, was no match for nuclear weapons – even if supported by armour, which was, for Chuck, the camp's only attraction: tanks, motorized cannon, field guns.

In the summer of 1963, Chuck Fipke became a militiaman in the British Columbia Dragoons at Camp Vernon. It was his first and only summer camp, and his first salaried job. Chuck loved the tanks, with their awesome power. The camp CO, to encourage them, gave the young tank crews considerable leeway in their use. But "playing tanks" was not allowed. When some students took three of them out one afternoon for a race, they were breaking the rules.

Running his tank against the other two, Chuck roared his up the slopes of the camp, ripping up the dry sagebrush. Then, going flat out, he raced across the fields, with the other two in hot pursuit. Leaving the base behind them and dragging barbed-wire fencing they had torn through unawares, the three tanks thundered along, down the next slope and right into a flock of terrified sheep. All the boys could see from inside their tanks were white bursts of sheep flying everywhere!

The farmer was not impressed. Nor was their commanding officer. Their punishment was to stand at attention outdoors all night: "To keep watch for forest fires."

No one had thought to check their canteens. To keep them warm during the night, Chuck had filled them full of rye. By morning, dead drunk, they were in no condition to recognize a fire, even if the camp itself had been in flames. For that, they were put on radios, and the tedium of being a radio operator was punishment enough for Chuck. Still, the army paid him $125 for his summer's contribution to the military – just enough money to buy his first car, a 1949 Nash Rambler.

It did not last long. Driving home soon after he got it, with his "army buddy" Clarence Linenko in the passenger seat, he was challenged by another car. The race was on! Spinning out of control on bald tires, the Rambler jumped the bank just south of the reserve, rolled five or six times and came to a rest on its wheels.

"You okay?" Chuck asked.

"I'm dizzy," Clarence replied.

It was hard for them to see each other. The roof had been crushed and was resting on the dash and the top of the seats, completely flattened. The engine was still running, though, and Chuck could see a little light through a gap in front of him between the roof and the dash. Chuck limped the car home by dawn and parked it at the edge of the orchard to scavenge for spare parts.

The original homestead cabin, its logs gone punky, was not livable, but there was a black, tar-papered shack beside the orchard that the family had moved into. Ed had plans to fix it up, maybe even build something better, when he had time and money. But they had electric power and running water, after a fashion. Trepanier Creek flowed past their place, and the creek water was potable. There was a large concrete cistern higher up the mountain and a pump at the creek to keep it full. From the cistern a gravity-fed pipe ran the water back down into the house. It worked fine, when it did not freeze. However, it only supplied the kitchen. Six people using the outhouse created a whole new set of problems. Ed was going to put in an indoor toilet, but space was at a premium. They were already so cramped there was nowhere to put it. The bathroom would have to wait until Ed got around to building an addition.

Chuck didn't mind the conditions. For Anna and the younger children life was more difficult, but there were advantages for a teenager living in the backwoods. The mountains beckoned, a new challenge.

Back in Edmonton, a year earlier, Chuck had won two victories, the first as much a surprise as an honour, for Ed and Anna. In a large public ceremony, Chuck had been presented the award of Queen Scout by the lieutenant governor, the province's highest award for Scouts, and the prize a trip to the Seattle World's Fair. After his return he quit Scouts. He continued to respect the organization, but it simply offered no further challenge.

The other was with his new dog, Trixie. After the loss of his peregrine, he had taken to hanging around a dog kennel in Edmonton that had the contract to train Edmonton's police dogs and was known for its champion German shepherds. He persisted until they took him on as an unpaid assistant, and gradually the kennel allowed him access to all their secrets. His reward after a year – a gift he did not expect – was the pick of the litter from the kennel's prize shepherd.

Thereafter he trained Trixie at the kennel and she became his constant companion. By the time Chuck was 16, Trixie was winning her own awards. When Edmonton hosted a provincial dog show, with breeders and trainers from Alberta, British Columbia and Saskatchewan, it was Chuck and Trixie who took the field. Trixie was named Alberta Grand Champion.

Now here amid the dark British Columbia mountains was a new opening. Chuck was not looking for a safe backwater to hide in, nor was his a search for tranquillity. Craving challenge, he was pushing out in every direction he could, nearly exploding with energy, riding the currents of his own desire, a fast-flowing river that carried him along. He was powerless to resist.

After the first dusting of early winter snow in the high country, Chuck found large cougar tracks crossing the orchard. With Trixie, a small survival pack and his dad's .303 Lee Enfield for protection, he set off after it into the mountains. He had no intention of shooting the cougar, one of the country's most powerful and elusive creatures; he only wanted to live in its tracks for a few days and to see it if he could.

Crunching through virgin stands up Pigeon Creek, over the crest of Lookout Mountain, then down toward Silver Lake, he tracked the big cat for three days, Trixie at his side, through dense bush and open meadow, along spiny ridges and up steep scree slopes, alone in the vast wilderness of British Columbia.

In the snow he could see where the cat had paused to sniff something, where it had lingered by a view over open country, where it had turned onto the trail of a mule deer whose tracks crossed its own, only to change its course again and move up, higher into the mountains, picking through primordial stands of timber. Where the cat rested, Chuck rested, curled up in a tarp under a lean-to, seeing what it saw, listening to the wind whistling through the evergreens.

Chuck never caught up with couger. Perhaps it knew it was being followed. It may have smelled him, or Trixie, and kept just ahead of them. Or perhaps with four powerful legs it simply moved more quickly than Chuck did on his two.

Moving on foot through the mountains, Chuck realized the limitations of travelling alone. Walking was slow. Although heavily timbered, the bush was open enough in most places for a horse to get through. A man with a horse could go anywhere. Chuck decided he needed one.

Chuck had lost the reputation for gamesmanship he had garnered at his old school in Alberta when he moved to the Okanagan. But reputations could be quickly earned and he lost no time reestablishing his. The science teachers and sports coaches liked him, but he did not fare so well with the rest – especially his English teacher, who seemed effeminate. When Chuck saw the man put his arm around one of the girls as they walked out of class, he could not help but let everyone know what he thought of that move.

"Wow! He's a poof, too!"

He meant it as a joke, a mild rebuke at the teacher's familiarity with one of the girls, a competition with the teacher for the affection of the class, in particular the girls'. A test of maleness. The teacher saw it that way, too, and Chuck failed English.

In the late spring Ed had gone north to work the Cariboo region of central British Columbia. Chuck had wanted to spend the summer in town working for Pat McBride, who had given him a job over the school year and had advanced him enough cash to buy another car – a Rambler with Pullman seats – but Ed's was the family business and it paid the mortgage on the farm. There was no choice. Sleeping in the car, occasionally taking a cheap motel room to wash up in, they photographed farms from Williams Lake to Prince George, then followed up on foot. As Ed knocked on doors and did the selling, Chuck helped every way he could: writing up the orders and driving.

Sometimes the ranchers were interested in Ed's hand-painted pictures of their farms and sometimes not, but gradually, as the summer wore on, the money owing to Chuck – as yet unpaid – grew to a sizable sum. All the while Chuck had his eye on the horses the ranchers kept.

Off the highway just outside of Williams Lake, they made one of their best sales of the summer. A successful rancher took an order for a whole series of large, expensive pictures he wanted to send off to his family abroad. As Ed was writing up the contract, Chuck was leaning against the fence of the rancher's corral. On the other side were some of the finest horses he had ever seen. The talk turned to horses and then to prices. When the rancher agreed to sell the horse Chuck wanted – for the wages Ed owed Chuck – they struck a deal.

Rather than pay Chuck, Ed would pay the rancher. The first instalment was the value of the photographs the rancher had ordered. Ed promised to pay off the balance with regular payments. The horse was Chuck's!

A mare, Cindy added a whole new dimension to Chuck's life. As he had his birds and then his dog, Trixie, Chuck looked upon the horse as a new challenge and took to it wholeheartedly. Every chance he got, he took her out with Trixie. Together, going faster and farther than he had gone before, they explored the secrets of the mountains.

With the girls, too, he was doing better. He dated several but kept coming back to Marlene. She, alone, seemed especially right.

Marlene had secured a summer job with the Royal Bank on Bernard Avenue in Kelowna, and when he was home from selling pictures, they used to get together at lunch. Afterwards he would drop her off with the big Rambler and go about his own business. They had been dating several months when he let her off in front of the bank and, running late, she hurried in. A few minutes passed. Looking sheepish, Chuck came in through the doors to get her to help him with the car. The starter was shot. As the entire staff watched through the plate glass window, Marlene got behind the car and, with Chuck, they pushed it out of sight. Although Chuck would learn to turn the Rambler's starter defect to his advantage, he never again parked in front of the Royal Bank.

With Chuck's German-Polish background, their family histories and struggles overlapped, and Marlene understood him on a deep level, almost instinctively. His intense drive, his passions and his needs were in some ways even clearer to her than they were to him. More importantly, Marlene believed in him without reservation.

The start of Grade 13 in the fall at Kelowna Senior Secondary had meant for Chuck a return to English and, painfully, the same teacher who had failed him the previous year and who still had not forgiven him. But there were compensations. His rugby teammates were older, with more mature interests than the Scouts or the members of his gang in Edmonton. When he needed their support, they came through.

Life at home, however, took a serious turn for the worse. His father's drinking had landed Ed in court, and he lost his driver's licence. Without a car he could not make any money. He drove anyway. He was caught again, and this time he went to jail. Worse, the judge ordered that his driving-prohibition period be extended. Ed could no longer pay the bills.

Without warning the family was plunged back into poverty. Released from jail only to be bankrupted and imprisoned in his own backwoods wilderness, Ed drank heavily, paced and raged. Drunk and yelling at home one night, he took on Chuck. Ed had never seen Chuck fight or play rugby. Not that it would have made any difference. When angry or determined, neither man backed down.

Ed meant to beat him and a year earlier might have done so. Like Chuck, he was compact and powerfully built. But at 41 and in an alcoholic haze, he was no match for his 18-year-old son.

At first Chuck defended himself as Ed attacked, hoping his father would stop. But when Ed, enraged, kept at him, trying to hurt him, a well of feeling flooded up and Chuck began to fight back. Locked together, each hurt the other, yet Chuck could not stop while his father pressed the attack, and Ed would not quit. Oblivious to his own wounds, Ed kept up the battle until, thoroughly weakened and injured, he finally conceded the fight.

It was a pivotal moment in their relationship. Ed would never again attempt to physically dominate his son. Chuck felt no satisfaction from it. There was no winning. It was not an act of redemption. It drew a necessary boundary for Ed, but it deepened the already wide gulf between them.

Chuck considered quitting school to help out, but his father would not allow it. It was Ed's most bitter lesson. He had left university to "save" his family and had forever suffered the consequences. Chuck could not be allowed to make the same mistake.

There was another lesson, at least as important, Ed knew. He well remembered the trips he had taken with his own father into their poplar forest to tend the still. Through the Depression of the thirties, Carl had kept the family going by brewing alcohol. It was an old family tradition, dating back generations. Ed knew almost as much as his father about distilling alcohol and making spirits. However, Prohibition was over. The government had kept the monopoly, but the markets were free. He could brew liquor, but who would he sell it to?

Ed went into the forest to set up his still while Chuck explored the markets. In 1964 and '65, everybody drank, and men drank heavily. The standard for a "good man" was how much liquor he could hold. Young men were eager to fill their boots. Especially young rugby players.

Alcohol was a test of maleness, and the lesson of drunkenness, if there was one, was that one had somehow to be tougher, more of a man, stronger than the booze. As Chuck quickly found out, there was a ready market for good alcohol and, although the cash it generated could not pull the family out of debt, being a reliable source of this illicit entertainment made him very popular, at least.

Chuck's reputation grew as his parties in the bush and in town became more wild, and the behaviour they generated more reckless. Fired by almost pure alcohol, the partyers pushed back their limits almost out of sight, and their sense of abandon even carried over into their more sober hours. They all began to think they were invincible. Chuck, too, saw no reason to slow down or show restraint. He loved the wild life, to drink heavily and party hard, to race cars and chase girls who thrilled him.

When the bailiffs from the sheriff's office came with judgements against Ed to force the sale of large pieces of their farm to satisfy the mortgage debt, the family was near ruin.

Each day after school, Chuck sought solace in the mountains, riding his horse Cindy as Trixie ran ahead. The high country, as always, was more than an escape. It was a breathing, living environment into which he could plunge his whole being. It was his true home; the house back on the slope was nothing but his father's nightmare.

When Chuck got word that the bailiff was coming to seize Cindy because his father had never paid his debt to the rancher, he panicked and took off. Hiding Cindy in the bush, he was determined they would never take her. His effort was futile. After a couple of weeks, the mare was found in its primitive log stall, seized and hauled away in a truck.

When he came home from school, weeks after Cindy had been taken, to find Trixie dead, it was too much to bear. The neighbour had carried her, covered in blood, back to the Fipkes' with his explanation. The dog had been chasing his animals, he told Anna, so he shot it. Then, wounded, it attacked him, he said, so he shot it again.

Chuck rejected the story. Trixie was not vicious. If wounded, she was more likely to cry than to attack. More likely the man simply killed her for trespassing – or target practice. At the sight of her, dead on the porch, Chuck snapped. Grabbing his father's .303, he ran across the fields to the man's house, needing to know the real reason, if there was any.

Swearing revenge if there wasn't, Chuck was prepared to kill him. He could see the man inside, peering out from behind his curtains.

Waving his gun, Chuck challenged him to come out.

"You coward! How could you kill my dog? Try someone with a gun now! Come on you coward! Come outside! Try shooting me!"

Prudently the man stayed inside. When the RCMP arrived, Chuck was still in a furious rage, planted in front of his neighbour's house.

In 1965, police who attended armed confrontations did not always draw their guns or make arrests. A humanity prevailed over police work then. The Mounties who came understood that Chuck needed to express his grief. Working patiently from each side of the story, they gradually defused the situation and took Chuck home.

Marlene did what she could to soften his hurt. There was a racehorse Chuck had found – an even better horse than the one the bailiff had seized – that she knew he would love. Chuck had no money to buy it, but she did.

It took all her savings. It was worth it. For Marlene, committed to loving him, life would be a challenge. Sooner or later, she fervently hoped, he would let down his guard and love her back. Nothing else mattered.

CHAPTER TWENTY-SIX

GEOPHYSICS

WHILE Ed was unable on his own to effect any serious change in his behaviour, an event forced him, finally, to reexamine his life. As had been his habit for almost 20 years, he was drinking heavily one night in a local tavern. Another angry soul took exception to Ed's aggressiveness; they exchanged insults, challenged one another to fight and it was on. The Oriental man was a professional fighter, an expert in martial arts and vicious. Not content to beat Ed into unconsciousness, he very nearly killed Ed, continuing the assault until other patrons pulled him off.

Ed was in a coma for days. He survived, but the experience left him profoundly changed. The transformation was dramatic. Overnight he went from being an angry man to a loving one. And the revelation of peace in love ultimately led him to join his wife in her new church. After a lifetime spent in the Lutheran Church, she had quit to become a Jehovah's Witness. It was the church that would soon be attended by all of their children, except Chuck.

The change at home was more than welcome. The children were now totally supported in their endeavours, and in the new environment, they, too, were able to concentrate more completely on their plans for the future. Not a moment too soon. It was a crucial time in Chuck's life.

For Chuck, sports and science represented the real world, a world one could see and touch and master. In Alberta he had gone to church every Sunday for years with his mother and grandmother, earning long-attendance prizes. But religion never offered him any revelations about life. To Chuck, the moralizing sermons were like bad Sunday morning daydreams. Boring. The church survived on faith, but he knew life was not a matter of faith. It was real – flesh and blood – and it was terminal. The answers he wanted lay not in faith, but in knowledge. Not in religion, but in science.

What other reality, he wondered, had the study of English at Kelowna Senior Secondary for him but this one: an effeminate teacher who lacked the courage to confront an assertive student, who wielded the power of his position instead, to ignore the challenge and fail him for a second time.

Chuck's salvation was rugby. Not only was it a release for energy, but it was a common ground with his coach. The fact he scored the highest mark in the school in chemistry was no coincidence. His rugby coach, Walter Green, was also his chemistry teacher. They liked and understood each other.

His English grades, though, posed a serious problem. The failure in English had the potential to ruin everything. Without English, he could not get into university. The authorities were even considering forcing him to repeat his entire year.

There was one last chance to pass his year, and without interference from his English teacher. The provincial departmental exams had to be written to graduate from Grade 13, to qualify for university. If he could pass the departmental English exam, he could still graduate.

After that, there was a horse race, a real one with prize money. And he had a real racehorse to run in it. A winner. A champion.

Chuck was looking forward to it. In spite of the immediate problem he had to face, it was going to be one glorious summer.

He was wrong.

Chuck failed the English departmental exam, and he lost the race. In spite of the efforts of Walter Green to have the school give him a passing grade anyway, he failed his year. Now if he wanted to finish high school, he would have to repeat it all again – his third year with the same English teacher.

After the humiliation of his experiment with professional horse racing in Princeton, Chuck needed a new angle to make money. His job at Gorman's Saw Mill, paying $1.85 an hour, was, after only three weeks, slowly killing him. Loading a conveyer belt with freshly treated wood, his body developed a constant twitch, caused by either boredom or a neurological reaction to the industrial chemicals. Ed, concerned, suggested Chuck quit the mill and come out to Vancouver Island to sell pictures with him.

Driving his Ford by day to avoid using his lights, Chuck arrived at the seaside town of Comox on Vancouver Island with a dead battery. He needed a new one.

"Well, you know," Ed said, laughing, "there are batteries for sale!"

Chuck would have to buy his own.

They were up early the next morning having breakfast in a coffee shop. Ed, who had been in the business on and off for nearly a dozen years now, was in the habit of taking it easy. Chuck was anxious to get started. When Ed ordered his second cup of coffee, Chuck tried to stop him from drinking it.

"Let's go, Dad! Let's go!"

Ed looked at his son. He had learned a little about life and people. Having lived with his son's energy and his ambitions, Ed believed Chuck would go far in life. But it would all happen in its own time. One didn't need to rush things. The sun would rise and set on its own.

"I'll have another cup of coffee first," he replied quietly. "We're going in my car, and we'll get there and back."

The farmer was standing out in his yard when they drove up to their first farm.

"There he is, Chuck – go talk to him!"

Chuck took the small black-and-white proof his father had already made of the farm from flying the area earlier and approached the farmer. Ed rolled down the window, scanned the morning paper while he listened to his son selling and laughed. Chuck came back to the car with a $20 deposit from the sale: his first.

He was pleased. The money and the working conditions were much better than at Gorman's.

At the next farm, Chuck said, "This one's yours, Dad."

"No way, Chuck! I won't be with you all the time. In fact, I'm not going to be with you at all. You're the one that's going to be doing it steady. Might as well start now."

To learn the trick of selling, Chuck expected some training by his father. But Ed had a different lesson in mind.

"Well, Chuck, I'll tell you something. Just sit down. You know, you're already trained. You're a trained young man. Life isn't that difficult. You either sell them or you don't! That's all there is to it … There you go."

Ed handed him back the $20 bill he had just received for the deposit on his first sale, drove him into the village of Courtenay and dropped him off to buy a new car battery.

It turned out Ed was right. Chuck rarely missed a sale, one day signing $1,350 worth of contracts to supply pictures. His stutter, a disability in his English class, was here an asset. The farmers were disarmed by it, and he could speak more directly, which he preferred, without seeming too aggressive.

A whole generation of farms, the Canadian rural culture – swallowed up by urban sprawl, mechanization and single-crop consolidations – was recorded by Ed's camera and transformed by the magic of Anna's paint. For the most part theirs was an easy product to sell, and the farmers themselves were quick to collaborate in the recording of their passing world. Chuck was not at all nervous about selling. As he discovered, there were no tricks, but it was important to know when to apply pressure. He quickly learned to sell not only to people who wanted to buy, but also to those who did not. It was simply a matter of will, or, rather, the lack of it, as Chuck began to read people, to gauge their strengths and weaknesses, to discover how to sell to reluctant buyers.

After only a couple of weeks, he had earned $550 in commissions, a considerable sum in 1965. Ed had an idea how he should spend it. Chuck's old Ford was a wreck.

"I know this dealer down in Victoria who has a 1957 Buick, which would be a real car for you! It has low miles and it's just like new."

Together they talked the price down from $800 to $450. Chuck bought his first "real" car, had $100 left in his pocket and was now ready, with his confidence restored, to tackle English again.

In the fall he returned to KSS. He did not feel like it. He was 19, his teammates had all moved on, and Marlene had taken a full-time job at the bank, but he could not go on feeling defeated. Especially not by English, not by the one teacher he disliked the most. He reenrolled.

His relationship with Marlene had taken a new turn over the summer. Marlene was interested now in marriage, a subject Chuck preferred to avoid, having made it clear that he considered himself too young to marry. If her goal was marriage, he had told her, she was wasting her time with him. She should find someone else. She would not.

Soon after the school year began, she became pregnant. For a young Catholic in the early winter of 1965 who was pregnant, there were only two options. Giving up the child was out of the question. The Pyetts arranged instead for the wedding. The church, the guest list, the invitations, the wedding dress, the reception party, the dinner everything was arranged. Chuck had only to show up. He did not.

Chuck had given it serious thought. For weeks it had occupied his mind like nothing before had. He weighed and reweighed the issues, determined that the decision to marry, this most important of decisions, would be the right one. And that it would be his. Not Marlene's, not the Pyetts', not his parents'. He would not be forced into anything as serious as marriage against his will.

On the day of the wedding, as the guests filled the church, Chuck made his final decision. As the wedding party waited at the church, Chuck got in his car and drove the other way.

Chuck's second year in Grade 13 was a near repeat of his first. His math and science scores were again among the highest grades in the school, and again he failed English. As before, passing the departmental exam in English would still give him the year. Whatever happened, he would not repeat it again. Ever. He studied harder than he had done for any of the sciences, wrote the exam and squeaked by.

The next step, university, was now an option, but his failing grades in English had affected his self-confidence to the point that he was not sure he was university material. Could he pass? Pat McBride convinced him to try anyway.

"It can't hurt you," Pat told him. "Go and apply; you got nothing to lose!.... And even if you get in and flunk out, so what! You're still one step ahead of all the other guys who never even went! You can always come back and log the trees on your dad's property. They'll be worth more in a year anyway."

Pat offered more than advice. As generous with his friends as with his own family, he had never coveted good fortune. A good friend to Ed and his family, he sweetened the goal of a higher education for Chuck with something tangible, even irresistible. With business interests around the country, he kept an apartment and a car in the port city of Vancouver. A brand-new, yellow Plymouth Fury Super Sport coupe with leather seats and a 383-cubic-inch motor! With his main home in Kelowna, Pat rarely used the apartment or the car.

"If you go to university," Pat told him, "you've got free use of the apartment – and my sport coupe!"

To pay his tuition and finance the year, Chuck could take out a student loan. All he had to do was attend classes, and keep the apartment clean. Still, Chuck had his doubts. University would mean several more years of hard work and poverty. Hardly a life.

After talking to Pat, Chuck turned to Marlene. Although the failed marriage plans and her pregnancy seriously complicated her life, Marlene had not ended her relationship with Chuck. They remained friends.

"Pat, hey, you know, thinks I ... I should give up the idea of logging or ... hey, put if off for a while and go to university. But, like, I … I don't know what to do."

Marlene's response was immediate and unqualified "Go to university!" She continued, as before, to remain committed, offering him whatever support she could.

Chuck drove down to the coast, applied to the University of British Columbia and was accepted into general science. He had made the first cut, but he still had no idea what to take. His love was ornithology, but when he looked into it, he found ornithology was a specialization of biology and was not even studied until the fourth year. Biology itself did not interest him. The dissection of rats stinking with formaldehyde in high school had dampened his enthusiasm. As he saw it, the university biology program was not research-oriented but simply the memorization of thousands of terms. It seemed a colossal waste of time.

In the end Chuck turned to his father for advice. Whatever their differences, Chuck always respected Ed's opinion, knew the advantage of good counsel and most importantly, knew when to follow it.

"Well, you know," Ed began in his usual, offhand way, "I talked to a fellow who told me that geophysicists are really in demand. You work out in the field, mostly by yourself. The money's good. And, he says, there are nine jobs for every graduate."

Ed's casual comments in no way reflected the deep interest he himself took in the subject, but giving advice was a lot like fishing. You could put out the best bait, but it was up to the fish to bite. A lesson that had haunted Ed for years, from another lifetime it seemed, was the discovery of the buried oil fields of Leduc, Alberta. It was geophysics that had found the oil under those farms. That science had made those who were capable of applying its potential wealthy.

Although he had no interest at all in rocks, Chuck took his father's advice and enrolled in geology. The future – at least the next year in school – was decided.

On August 24, 1966, Marlene gave birth to a boy. They named him Mark Charles Fipke. Ten days later Chuck was in Vancouver. True to his word, Pat McBride had given him the keys to his Vancouver apartment and to the Plymouth. Marlene remained in Kelowna with her family and the baby and Chuck went off to face school alone.

With a Vancouver apartment and a dream car to race back and forth to the campus in, Chuck had only to work hard and pass. Marlene's future was more uncertain, her prospects far more limited. As a woman, an unwed mother, the decisions that would govern her life were to a large degree made for her. She could not keep the child. Mark would have to be placed for adoption. When Chuck left for university her parents began to make the arrangements.

This put Chuck in a new quandary. He could not allow Mark to be adopted out. Mark was his son. But, unmarried, he had no say over the matter. It was for the Pyetts alone to decide his son's life.

In a small, private ceremony just after Christmas on December 27, 1966, he and Marlene married. Although he was still ambivalent about the marriage, it was the only way to keep his son. Yet he had other reasons, as well. His instincts told him that Marlene really loved him; she had demonstrated her devotion. The intimacy of their physical contact was enough to sustain him, and this time the decision was his.

Although Marlene remained in Kelowna with her family, the marriage had the unexpected benefit of settling a number of basic issues – allowing Chuck to move forward, completely focused on his education and, later, on his work.

He still had not developed any interest in the field he was studying. Not until the final term, when the raw Vancouver winter turned into a warm misty spring and his studies took him into the field of paleontology, did he begin to find answers to questions he had posed in his own life. Here now, not just the physical earth, but the origins of life itself were being revealed; the secrets of biology were buried in the rock.

He passed his classes. More of a surprise, waiting at the doors when the exams ended were mining companies lined up to hire summer students. Seeing them, the reality hit home. Perhaps the education he was pursuing did offer more than information to satisfy his curiosity.

What convinced him completely was the summer that followed. His first experience with a geology company quashed all doubts and ignited a new passion. Amax Exploration Company was searching for molybdenite on Hudson's Bay Mountain at the town of Smithers and to the northwest, toward Hazelton and the Seven Sisters range.

Eight hundred kilometres north of Vancouver and Kelowna, Smithers was midway up the province. And the country was wild – even more rugged and beautiful than the high country around Kelowna. The latitude brought the tree-line down to lower elevations, and there the forest gently transformed itself into sweeping expanses of open alpine country before rising even higher into craggy rock peaks and blue glaciers.

Arriving in the small European-styled town of Smithers, the visitor's eye was drawn to the base of Hudson's Bay Mountain, rising up from the end of the street 2,331 metres, to preside over the town in gentle splendour. Beginning at the edge of town, a gravel road climbed the mountain, passing ski cabins and winter lodges and, higher, winding through fields of alpine wildflowers – lupines, fireweed and Indian paintbrush – to a large cirque carved out of the rock where a summer glacier gleamed like a jewel in the sunshine.

From the top, the mountains, which stretched away to the west toward the town of Terrace and the coast, were even more dramatic and beautiful. The dagger peaks of Rocher de Boule, Kitseguecla and the Seven Sisters, with their massive rock faces and spires towering over the country, drew climbers from around the world.

The prairie sky had always been huge – wide open spaces from horizon to horizon – but here, incredibly, the spaces were even grander. Instead of a flat earth dropping out of sight below the horizon, here the ground had erupted and forced its way into the heavens. Mountain peaks 160 kilometres away were clearly visible. From on high, one could survey the whole world.

What forces had done this? Who had written the history of this land? What said the flow of the continents, the formation of the rock itself? This was the subject of his study. His first year at university had mostly been figures and slides with some facts and theory, but here was its application.

To stand upon a mountain peak and understand the nature of its existence was the goal. It was history that went beyond man, beyond all life, to the very beginning of creation. All the secrets were here, buried within the rock, in the earth. It was a world to explore for a lifetime, and even then to have only brushed the surface.

Everything about the field was perfect. As he sat on a rock ledge and watched a score of wild mountain goats pick their way carefully up a near vertical face, he delighted in his incredible good fortune. Pat McBride, Marlene and his father had all contributed to this. He could never thank them enough, and just as incredibly, there was money in this business! Amax had lots of it. More money than Chuck had ever seen. To get around from peak to peak they didn't walk; they used heli-copters. And the food! His boss was Walter Selmer, a man Chuck took to instantly, and when Selmer went shopping he took Chuck with him to buy food for the camp.

For the first time in his life, Chuck was able to pick out whatever he wanted, to eat what he pleased, day after day. It was a dream. As many pork chops and apple turnovers as he wanted. The company kept a whole warehouse full of tinned goods at their base camp, but nobody touched them. Not with fresh food available from Smithers. For breakfast Chuck loaded up at the store on his new all-time favourite cereal, Winne-the-Pooh Honey Munch. Lunch and dinner the men cooked for themselves over Coleman stoves in their mountain camps, then did their own dishes. Chuck hated to cook almost as much as he hated to do dishes. He got around it, and happily, by filling up on freshly baked apple turnovers.

Chuck was back in the Rocher de Boule mountain range cutting lines and collecting samples on Amax's claims when Walter Selmer radioed him with the news that his wife had arrived.

The summer had passed quickly. For Chuck it was nearly over. He had only a few days left with Amax before he had to head back to Vancouver to begin his second year. This time Marlene would join him; they would live together on campus. Almost a year old, Mark was now walking. Chuck was anxious to see them, but he could not just walk off his job. Walter rescued him.

"Tell you what I'll do, Chuck. I'll trade you jobs!" Walter spoke to him over the radio. "I'll fly up and take your job, and you work here and run the warehouse."

When Chuck got down, Walter had already installed Marlene and Mark in one of the company's resort cabins on their property on Lake Kathlyn. After he walked in, the TV dinner in the oven started to burn, but even the smoke that slowly filled the cabin to linger for days afterwards did not distract them from one another.

Chuck was in the warehouse the next day when one of the company's chief exec-utive officers dropped in out of the blue with his new girlfriend and told Chuck to order them up a helicopter. He wanted to fly to the mine site on Hudson's Bay Mountain. Chuck did not know him. Besides, the order was too extravagant.

"Well, no," Chuck answered. "We don't do that, hey! There's a road right up there. You just drive to it."

Wanting to impress his girlfriend, the man, growing testier, insisted Chuck order a helicopter for him. Chuck continued to argue. To compensate for his stutter which he was working to get under control, he avoided long discourses.

"And, furthermore, hey, I don't know you from Adam! You'll have to show me some identification.... Like, helicopters are really expensive, eh!"

The fellow again told Chuck who he was. Chuck didn't recognize the name. The man claimed to be one of the company's top bosses.

"Well, you've got to prove it," Chuck insisted.

Rifling through his wallet, the only Amax identification he had was an airline travel card. Chuck recognized the card. Used to book airline tickets for the company, it was a form of credit card. Chuck knew they weren't given out freely.

"Will this do?" the man asked. It was the only company identification he had.

"Well," Chuck considered it carefully, "I guess to get one of those, hey ... you must have some pull."

So Chuck got him a helicopter. In return, they took Marlene and Mark for a helicopter ride. Even better, there was a gift waiting for him when, a few days later, his job ended and it was time for Chuck to return to university. Impressed with his integrity, the executive officer left Chuck the keys to the warehouse and an offer of employment for the next summer.

To help Chuck get through the school year, the company offered him all the tinned goods from their own stores that he could carry away. Chuck had the big '57 Buick with him, and when they finally said goodbye, there wasn't an inch of empty space in the car. With the car packed to the ceiling with canned food, they left Smithers, riding low on the springs, and carefully made their way back to Vancouver.

It had been the best summer of his life. Now Chuck wanted to be a geologist.

CHAPTER TWENTY-SEVEN

UNIVERSITY OF BRITISH COLUMBIA

ALONG a track in the university's undeveloped lands stood a row of ramshackle old shacks. With leaky roofs and paper-thin walls, they were scheduled for demolition. Until then, they were to be rented out at a nominal rate to the married students.

Chuck was used to living in difficult conditions. Most of the summer had been spent in a sleeping bag on the ground. The family home by Trepanier Creek was not much better: only three rooms for six people, its uninsulated outside walls had never been finished. Covered first with a roll of black tar paper and then with a few sheets of silvery paper stapled here and there overtop – which mostly had come loose and flapped against the house in the wind – it was cold in winter and offered only basic shelter for the rest of the year.

By comparison, for Chuck the university shack was not that bad. With the wet, coastal weather of Vancouver it leaked constantly, but other than that, it had warm running water and an indoor flush toilet – comforts the farm at Trepanier did not have.

Marlene, on the other hand, was used to more comfort – and staying dry. Every time it rained they put out a dozen old pots and buckets to catch the water that came through the roof. And it rained nearly every day throughout the winter. Worse, when they made the initial trip from Kelowna to Vancouver with all their wedding gifts to fill their "house," their vehicle was broken into during the night and stripped, leaving them with nothing. Every gift and all their clothing was stolen.

For Marlene, 20, with a infant child and a student husband, it was a difficult time. With last year's debts to repay, tuition, books and a year's cost of living to get through, they collected boxes to use as chairs and found an old door that they raised up off the floor for a couch. With another box for a table, the open window for a fridge, and an electric frying pan their only cooking appliance, conditions were cold, damp and grim.

After a couple of months at school, the summer supply of tinned food depleted, Chuck took what was left of their money and spent most of it on a pony for Carol, his sister. Marlene did not understand. There were things Mark, their own child, needed. It was a question of balance and priorities.

But Chuck was firm. He knew the conditions at the farm and the joy an animal could bring. Carol was eight, an age Chuck remembered from his own childhood, and the gift of a horse, he knew, could brighten her whole future.

That was reason enough. Carol got a horse, and Marlene and Chuck began looking for empty bottles. The few cents each bottle returned on the deposit added up every couple of days to a meal. At night they would unroll an old foam mattress and sleep together on the floor, rolling it back up again in the morning.

Encouraged by the success of his first year, Chuck worked harder now, devoting most of his time to his studies. To relax he worked out at the university's Olympic-sized pool. After 100 laps of the pool, he would do 250 push-ups or an equal number of sit-ups. If he was particularly stressed and had the time, he doubled the workout. It was a regimen he had begun when playing rugby and practised faithfully for the next 30 years.

His grades at the end of the year were an improvement over his first year. Chuck declined the summer job with Amax and took one offered by Atlas Exploration. Where other students, once they found openings, settled down, Chuck never wanted to repeat an experience. He said goodbye to Marlene and Mark and flew north in mid-April. It would be four and a half months before he returned.

He quickly discovered geology was a ticket to travel, not to tourist destinations but to the remotest corners of the world. Each chance he got, he would now go further and further into the field. The Atlas project was headed by the renowned geologist Aro Auho, who was credited for the discovery that became the Faro lead zinc mine in the Yukon. Besides meeting him, working with Atlas also offered Chuck the chance to see Canada's Far North.

Flying into Whitehorse, he then took the company's air charter to Ross River, a village on the river of the same name that drained the central Mackenzie Mountains into the Pelly, which then flowed into the Yukon River. Atlas had their main camp at Ross River, 200 kilometres northeast of Whitehorse. From there he flew another 100 kilometres east into the next drainage system and landed on Fortin Lake, where the company had set up a small outpost camp. For the rest of the summer, Fortin Lake would be his main base and he would explore out from it, for weeks at a time, into the surrounding wilderness, hiking on foot deep into the Selwyn Mountains where peaks reached up to 3,000 metres.

North and east of Fortin Lake, there was nothing to indicate that humans even lived on the planet. All the way to the Mackenzie River and up to the Beaufort Sea, the wilderness was unbroken and pristine. Although he was still within the boreal forest, the dwarfed trees were widely separated, the ground too barren of nutrients to support denser growth. Underfoot was muskeg, lichen-covered rock and permafrost. It was over the same ground that mammoths had roamed 10,000 years ago when Stone Age hunters brought them down with spears and arrows. Their ivory tusks, although rare, were still to be found lying about where the animals had fallen.

Atlas was exploring for lead and zinc deposits. With the approach of summer and near total light conditions, there was little else to do but work, and the field crews averaged 12-hour days. Geophysics and sampling around Fortin Lake had just begun, with the field crews stretched out over the countryside, when a tall, older man with an unusually refined bearing and a large pack on his back suddenly appeared, walking up the beach.

Chuck stared at him.

No plane had landed. The man had just walked in – 280 kilometres – from Whitehorse!

Gunther Lishy spent his winters trapping out of Atlin, British Columbia. Summers he wandered freely over hundreds of kilometres, prospecting for himself and sometimes working for other companies. Atlas had optioned one of Gunther's claims nearby and he had hiked in to see if they had any work for him.

They did. He was hired, paired up with Chuck, and when the work around Fortin Lake was completed a few days later, the two of them were flown by helicopter deeper still into the country and dropped off initially at MacCovy Lake, on the western edge of the Selwyn range of the Mackenzie Mountains.

For the next four months, the only contact the two men had with the outside was through the helicopter pilot, who flew in every couple of weeks to drop off food and collect their samples and, when they had finished their survey, to move them to the next watershed. From watershed to watershed through the Mackenzie Mountains, they climbed the peaks and sampled the valley streams.

Chuck and Gunther agreed on their first day that each man would be solely responsible for himself. That way there could be no arguments or bad feelings about the distribution of labour.

At the end of the day, after hauling 25-kilogram samples over a 40-kilometre traverse, Chuck was ready to eat. But their agreement meant he had to do his own cooking. They had no apple turnovers.

While Gunther meticulously began to set up his camp stove with his set of small pots and pans, Chuck went to their food cache, a small pit dug down into the permafrost, pulled out a steak and tossed it straight into the fire. Unprotected, the meat hissed and sputtered as Chuck poked it down into the coals under the flames. Gunther, looking on, said nothing.

Chuck next rooted out a couple of potatoes and threw them into the open fire. Opening a can of peas, with the lid peeled back for a handle, he placed the vegetables at the edge of the fire, to boil in the coals. His preparations for dinner done, he stretched out on the ground, his back to a stump, and waited for his food to cook.

It didn't take long. Before Gunther had even put a pan on the stove, Chuck was eating. Pulling the "charbroiled" steak out of the fire with a stick, Chuck picked it up with his hands, brushed off the ash and tore into it. There were no formal manners. Finished, he threw the bone back into the fire, then rolled out his potatoes, brushed them off and ate them – black skin, ash and all – like hot apples. The peas were harder to handle. Hot, the can needed a sock around it to keep it from burning his fingers. Spooning down the peas, Chuck tipped the can to his mouth and drained it, drinking the water with the peas until the can was empty.

Dinner was done. No dishes. No cleaning. Only one empty can for the garbage and a spoon, hardly dirtied, which was left out to make coffee in the morning.

They split the mapping and sampling work, as well. Each morning they got up early and headed off in different directions. At first Chuck found the life very lonely and the isolation intense.

Day after day he worked alone in the bush fighting bugs, with only the occasional squirrel or bird for company. The solitude was more oppressive than anything he had ever felt. Rather than being liberated, he felt trapped in the bush. A prisoner of his own mind, he thought constantly of quitting, of escape. He dealt with the isolation by staying focused on his tasks, his only relief to work hard.

He set company records, working nonstop, seven days a week. Yet the work was simple and the distance between samples sometimes hours long. He had a lot of time to be alone with his thoughts, with only Gunther Lishy for company in the evenings back at the camp.

He had been in the country for little more than a month – most of it spent thinking of Marlene and Kelowna, his past and the future, deeply lonely but too proud to quit – when he noticed one day that something had changed. The whole character of the North was different; it was subtle but very real.

Walking alone in the forest, the spruce and pine no more than seven metres high and spaced widely apart, he first became aware of a sense of deep calm. His step was lighter than usual. His senses, normally focused on his thoughts far away, were this day more attuned to his surroundings than they had been.

He stopped and took a good look around, breathing deeply of the scented air – the muskiness of moss and the pungency of forest saps. It was this new sensitivity to the life around him that was different. The change was internal. No longer preoccupied with thoughts that circled in his own head, he found himself relaxed, at peace with the green and brown and grey spaces.

It was as though he was returned to his childhood on the Prairies, lifetimes ago. Not since childhood had he felt so connected. Perhaps for the first time ever he felt he really belonged. It was wonderful. No longer a stranger. No longer lonely.

Now each morning he left camp with a light heart. Walking softly over the ground, moving quietly through the country, he saw a grizzly without being seen, watched caribou feeding and ate lunch on rocky shorelines while mink ran over his legs. And once he stood silently to one side as a pack of wolves ran by him, unaware of his presence.

Although the company had issued him a .44 magnum revolver for protection, he almost never carried it. It was simply extra weight, and there was nothing here to harm him.

Like Chuck, Gunther's background was German, but his was the other half of the old social equation. Aristocratic, his family had remained in Germany after the Fipkes left and so experienced the full terror of the new empire, of unrestrained power and submission to the national ethos. And the war. Captured as a young man on the Russian front, Gunther had been put in a Soviet prison camp and made to atone for the sins of his race and class. Released at last to return to his old life, he found that it had lost all its former lustre.

For Gunther, there was no other way to escape the bounds of history but to go – suddenly, completely and secretly. Quietly, under some dark clouds he would never discuss, he had slipped away one night from his former identity. While Interpol launched an unsuccessful search for the missing person he resurfaced, alone – anonymous but free – in frontier Canada. Giving up urban Germany, status and wealth for the remote wilderness of the New World, Gunther had come looking for something he could never have in Europe.

Gunther had a certain ascetic mastery over life that was rare to witness and extremely attractive to Chuck. Like Chuck's father, Gunther Lishy was an independent spirit, but more so. He spent his summers in the Yukon wandering its huge realms on foot as another might stroll the paths of a city park, comfortable in the wilderness, free to come and go. Gunther's life was entirely his own.

Toward the end of summer, with the retreat of the summer solstice, the hours of darkness were daily overtaking the daylight. More and more often the men were getting back to their camp after dark. Although it was harder to navigate in the night without benefit of visual landmarks, there was no real risk to it, and the land at night had a special beauty.

On this night, though, Gunther was worried about Chuck. Chuck had set himself a huge traverse for the day. Almost 70 kilometres long, it would take him over the top of a mountain chain to collect four soil samples. It was not the traverse that had Gunther concerned. It was the dead caribou, an old bull, that lay a few miles from camp on Chuck's return route. They could smell its rotten bloated carcass downwind nearly two kilometres away. Gunther knew the high flesh was an irresistible lure for any grizzly, and sitting on meat, a grizzly would go to extraordinary lengths to protect it. Gunther had seen the carcass. It was a big animal. A bear feeding off it would hang around for days. Anyone moving through the area was at risk.

On Gunther's insistence, Chuck had accepted his rifle. A .303, it was far more powerful than the .44 revolver. Chuck strapped it to the back of his Trapper Nelson pack. It was a brilliant day. He set out under a blue and cloudless sky, pushing himself harder than usual to make sure he would get through the traverse.

Crossing the mountain range, he felt so exhilarated, on top of the world, he decided to head up to the peak. The season was almost over. It had been a glorious summer. Climbing to the summit, towering over the land, he could almost feel the earth brushing against the sky. In the distance was another peak, and behind it another. And another. The Mackenzie Mountains marched on all the way to the Beaufort Sea, peak after peak, each one a new challenge, demanding effort but offering new vistas for those willing to scale them.

It was a revelation to look out and see all the valleys in shadow and all the peaks in sunshine, rippling across the land, from light to darkness to light. It was a vision Chuck would carry for years, knowing that peaks and valleys were but indivisible parts of the same landscape: one could not exist without the other.

Chuck laughed out loud, it had become so clear: Every dark side hid a brilliant truth; every success was but temporary, pointing the way to a new challenge. Life was wonderful. He laughed again, completely happy. And then he climbed down out of the sunlight.

The traverse had taken longer than he expected. Now, with only starlight to guide him through the blackness, he was moving even slower. He could see his hand in front of his face, even the shape of the trees near him and the outline of the mountains when he approached the carcass of the caribou.

Chuck knew right away the bear was there. He had tried to move well around the carcass, but the swamps had forced him to pass nearby. Too near. The bear heard him and came out after him.

Not expecting any trouble, Chuck had not unslung Gunther's gun, still tied to the back of his pack. Now he could not, if only to fire a warning shot into the air. The bear was much too close to stop. Instead, as he heard the bear behind him, he picked up his own pace, walking as quickly as he could. The bear was very close and moving fast.

All Chuck could do was keep going. The grizzly was following him, but it wasn't running – that at least was a good sign. It was close enough behind for him to hear its footsteps. Chuck was unnerved. He wanted to run but he didn't. The bear, he knew, might be provoked by his flight and start running after him. And Chuck knew how that race would end. All he could do was try to stay ahead of the grizzly, hoping that whatever it was that was keeping the bear at its own set distance would not change. The camp was still far away.

Every step of the way the bear forced his pace, as if breathing down his neck. It splashed through the muskeg behind him, followed him around thickets, over hills and scree slopes, one mile, then another mile. Oblivious to the branches that scratched at him from the sides and the low shrubbery that threatened constantly to bring him down, Chuck concentrated on his footing as he rushed at the pace set by the bear, on and on through the darkness. If he fell, maybe even slipped, the bear would be on him.

But he didn't fall. And the bear never attacked. When, in the distance, he could see the light flickering through the trees from Gunther's Coleman lantern, the bear finally broke off Chuck's trail, quitting its monitored chase, and scrambled back into the bush. Chuck did not know how much longer he could have kept up the pace, and he was immensely relieved to see Gunther's light and get back, finally, to the warm glow of the fire.

When it came time a couple of weeks later to say good-bye, Chuck could not. He had come to the North for a summer job, but Gunther's company and the country had changed him. The North had gradually seeped under his skin, into his soul, and claimed him. Now he did not want to leave. He belonged here.

He had experienced the late spring bloom into summer and summer fade away into the early northern fall. He wanted to stay and watch the rest of the year unfold, to witness the approach of winter, to experience the power of that season. He also wanted to trap through the snow with Gunther, to continue their partnership.

Chuck had not decided to quit school, not for good. But he wanted to take the year off and bring Marlene and the baby up to Atlin, where he could build a cabin for them to stay in while he learned the fundamentals of running a trapline. He knew he had only skirted the edge of the North's spaces. There was so much his partner could teach him.

Gunther didn't like the idea at all.

"No way!" Gunther said when Chuck revealed his plans to him. "I won't do it."

Dismayed and hurt, Chuck didn't understand Gunther's rejection of his offer. "Why not?" he asked. "I thought you liked me."

But Gunther knew his was not the way of the future. For his own sake, he would have preferred Chuck to stay.

"I do," replied Gunther. "That's why I can't allow it."

Gunther looked out at the blue depths beyond the snow-capped mountains. "Your education is more important than this. You finish your degree, and work for a year after that, and then, if you still want to come back and trap with me, you can. I'll be here. This will all wait."

CHAPTER TWENTY-EIGHT

TRILOBITES

THE next summer Chuck once more had a choice of jobs. Combining academia and hands-on work, he again picked the one that would take him farthest afield. For Chuck, exploration and discovery went hand in hand with learning. Life was becoming a grand adventure and it became his intention to see the world. To penetrate its last unknowns as deeply as a person could.

When Chuck had stood upon a mountain peak the previous summer looking out over the world, he had faced the north. Behind him, the Mackenzie Mountains drained to the west into the Yukon River. In front of him, in the far distance, over the divide, the streams ran down the eastern slopes into the Mackenzie River. One of the greatest rivers of the continent, over 4,000 kilometres long, it was also the least understood and the most inaccessible. Draining an area the size of Europe, it was fed by three huge bodies of water. Lake Athabasca, Great Slave and Great Bear Lakes all flowed into it as it wound north, crossed the Arctic Circle and disappeared into a myriad of channels at the delta wetlands on the Arctic Ocean, wetlands that in summer teemed with millions of waterfowl and supported tens of thousands of caribou.

Chuck longed to see it, and the Geological Survey of Canada offered him the chance. When Chuck joined the GSC for the summer of 1969, he joined a team of 17 scientists, all Ph.D.s. Their mandate, from the GSC's Calgary-based division known as the Institute of Sedimentary and Petroleum Geology, was to do geologic mapping and to study the rich hydrocarbon basins of the Arctic. They were searching for oil in the Barrens. Over the course of the summer, as they studied the conditions around Norman Wells, a small community on the Mackenzie River near the Arctic Circle, Chuck found the work particularly satisfying. Questions that could not be answered were pursued with total abandon. Creating an intellectually challenging space – one even university failed to match – his colleagues' company was both stimulating and liberating. As the early winter began to shake the wild geese out of their feeding grounds on the tidal flats of the Arctic islands, Chuck was beginning to think seriously of a career as an academic in order to satisfy his own strong need for discovery.

He was paired with Bill Fritz, Canada's leading expert on trilobites, the ancient segmented marine arthropods, probable ancestors of modern spiders and scorpions, long gone a hundred million years ago. It was no coincidence that a paleontologist was used to find oil. Unlike minerals, oil and gas had strictly organic origins. They were hydrocarbon compounds derived from bacterial action on the carcasses of ancient plants and animals such as the scavenging sea-bottom trilobites that littered the floor of the same ancient sea that had created the oil under Leduc.

The two men were camped alone, on a mountain peak far from Norman Wells where Bill had discovered a sedimentary sandstone layer in the exposed rock containing several different species of fossilized trilobites. On the Earth's surface, the decay of life produces methane – swamp gases – but in temperatures of 50 to 150 degrees Celsius and in subsurface depths of a few thousand metres, oil and gas are formed instead. Lighter than water, they rise through permeable rocks to dissipate at the surface – unless prevented from doing so by a structural trap of impermeable rock. As the presence of trilobites revealed the necessary conditions for oil – ancient organic masses in marine environments that were contained within porous rock – Bill recorded the frequency and type of the trilobites while Chuck mapped the stratigraphy, the rock strata.

Several days later, when their work was done, they packed up their gear, collapsed the tent and waited for the helicopter to come, as previously arranged, to take them away. And they waited. At nightfall they gave up trying to make contact by radio, their primitive set having no range beyond 20 kilometres, put their tent back up and crawled into their sleeping bags to weather the storm that had suddenly blown in off the Beaufort Sea and now raged around them, threatening to crush the tent. By morning so much snow had fallen they had to dig themselves out. Only the very tip of their peaked roof remained above the snow's surface.

Hiking up to the mountaintop with their radio, they stretched out the antenna wire there for better reception and stayed beside the set all day, calling out into the void and waiting for a reply, anything at all. None came. At night, deeply concerned, they crawled back into their sleeping bags. On the second day, they rationed what little food remained and considered their situation. It was desperate.

They were camped above 2,600 metres, far above the treeline in alpine tundra. They were on the eastern edge of the Mackenzie Mountains near Bonnet Plume Lake. Earlier in the summer, with the right gear and supplies, they could have hiked the 150 kilometres back to Norman Wells. But that was dreaming. The snow was already too deep to walk through. By nightfall, they decided to cut their rations in half. They had little to eat. Their supplies had been planned by an economical GSC and they were practically out of them the day they were set to leave.

The third day, bright and clear, produced no change: no aircraft, no replies to their radio signals for help. It was impossible that they had been left behind. The rest of the team all knew where they were. They had to know the two of them were still stranded in the mountains.

The two men shared some peanut butter and spent another night in the tent. In the morning they took turns keeping watch for any aircraft, conserving their own energy and what power was left of their radio battery for a sighting, as they stamped the snow down around the tent. If it snowed again, they would be completely buried. The weather, at least, was with them. Another clear and crisp day.

Perfect flying conditions – only no relief came. Nothing at all moved except some dry snow devils that blew up off the mountain like smoky tendrils twisting into the sky.

The fifth day began and ended the same way. That the GSC could have been so disorganized as to have lost them seemed incredible but increasingly likely. What the two men did not know was that on the day set for their departure, their pilot, in a Hiller helicopter, had set out to pick them up in the morning as arranged. Stu Blusson, one of the team's scientists who specialized in regional geology and was also a businessman with his own licence to operate a helicopter, went with him for the ride to get Chuck and Bill.

They had good altitude as they penetrated the mountains. Flying at 1,500 metres, they were still climbing when the entire collective column, the steering mechanism, suddenly disengaged. With no control there was no way to fly the helicopter. Immediately their machine began flipping through the air, somersaulting as it plummeted for a mile down to earth. With the chopper falling between two mountains into a steep ravine, the pilot managed to use the autorotation to right them and slow their descent just before they struck. The blades cut into the ravine's banks and further cushioned their fall before snapping off.

Then they hit. The transmission smashed through the frame to cut a clean space between the pilot and Blusson as the rest of the helicopter completely disintegrated around them, leaving them, amazingly, alive.

As Chuck and Bill slept relatively comfortably in their sleeping bags, Stu Blusson and the pilot suffered the same storm without shelter. Both parties were awaiting rescue.

Being a lean organization, the GSC had no backup for search and rescue. It took several days for a new helicopter to arrive from Yellowknife and, searching first through the vast mountainous region, to find the downed aircraft. Airlifted to safety at last, the pilot vowed never to take control of another aircraft, while the new helicopter went back in at last, after six days, to pick up the two men stranded on the mountaintop, who were down to their last spoonful of peanut butter.

CHAPTER TWENTY-NINE

KENNECOTT

CARRYING four extra first-year courses for interest and, by special leave, a graduate class in mineralogy taught by Jack Gower, Chuck graduated with a bachelor of science in honours geology in the spring of 1970, specializing in porphyry coppers. In five out of the six fourth-year subjects he was required to take, geophysics among them, he received first-class honours. He did even better in the graduate course, titled "The Theory of Ore Search." Scoring the highest mark, an almost perfect grade, earned him the respect, and later the friendship, of Jack Gower, his new mentor.

In the spring of 1970, beyond the doors of the university, opportunities waited that other generations had never dreamed of. His father was mistaken about one thing in suggesting geophysics as a future. There were not nine jobs being offered him on graduation – there were 50!

He didn't intend on taking any of them. For the time being he savoured the feeling and the view from his lofty position. His interest in geology had centred on porphyry coppers, the huge deposits of uniformly disseminated, low-grade copper minerals found in bodies of intrusive igneous porphyritic rock, the primary textural features of which were relatively large-grained crystals set into a fine-grained groundmass. Most of the world's copper came from the processing of porphyry copper ore.

Chuck had blossomed as an academic and had been accepted by Berkeley into its graduate school. There he would be studying under Charlie Meyer, a legend in the field. Although he still liked his steaks well-cooked, he was now a long way from his childhood days by the chicken pens of the University of Alberta. His new goal was a doctorate degree, to be a research scientist himself.

It didn't remain his direction for long. Jack Gower aimed him at another mountain. Gower had worked for the American multinational giant Kennecott Copper for 25 years and was the president of its Canadian subsidiary, Kennecott Canada, before becoming a professor at the University of British Columbia. He shared Chuck's interest in porphyry coppers and had been instrumental in the development of a new technology called "surficial leach-capping determination of primary and secondary ore grades at depth," which had helped make Kennecott a world leader. In its ability to find commercial copper deposits, Kennecott was unsurpassed.

In his graduate class one day near the end of the school year, Chuck asked Gower about the leach-capping research methodology, but the professor merely shook his head. He knew the answers to Chuck's questions, but he would not tell him.

"I can't," Jack Gower said. "It's classified information. It's the exclusive property of the company." And it was not taught at any university.

"The only way you'll ever learn it," Gower told him, "is to join Kennecott Copper."

That was the bait. There were things, then, that even Berkeley did not know and could not teach. To Chuck's surprise the leading edge of technology was not to be found in the universities at all, but out in the field. There, where private companies worked daily on their problems, they did their own research and made their own discoveries. The secrets they guarded were worth untold fortunes. Only when they had no more competitive value were they released to the public to be taught at the universities.

Like Chuck's father, the old professor did what he could to steer Chuck in the direction he wanted him to go. Graduating at the top of Gower's course, Chuck had qualities that Kennecott Copper could use. In the best possible position to scout out new recruits for the company, Jack Gower recommended they hire Chuck. Kennecott came for a look and put a brand-new offer on the table. Not just a job; all of Kennecott's secrets were also up for grab.

Chuck could not resist. Within days he, Marlene and Mark, now almost four, were flying first-class on Qantas to Australia. The new job was with Kennecott's Australasian subsidiary, and their new project was as far away as a person could go on Earth. Not just to the other side of the world but – time travelling into the distant past – to another reality entirely. Ok Tedi. And a whole new mountain range, back in the Stone Age.

A Generous Land

Australia, 1972

The most important thing is to own your own physical body.

—S. SUZUKI, *ENTERING THE STREAM*

CHAPTER THIRTY

QUEENSLAND, JULY 22, 1972

I T was Chuck's 26th birthday and he had never had a holiday like this. It was all pleasure, the pleasure of body and of light. The contrast with New Guinea over the past two years was immediate – and so bizarre as to verge on the hallucinogenic.

Following Salvador Allende's nationalization of its Chilean assets, Kennecott had flown the Fipkes out of the Vogelkop and back to Cairns, where they would be able to take connecting flights to Canada or, as the company hoped, agree to stay on working for them in Perth, Australia. Politely, Chuck had declined. There was unfinished business. Although he had left university two years earlier, his honours thesis, which was required to formally complete his degree, had still to be put together and submitted. And there was the reef.

The water was crystal. The light radiating through it bathed the Coral Sea in brilliant luminescent shades of blue and green. Drifting with the currents over the coral, diving down through schools of bright angelfish and silver drummers, or deeper, with a tank, following the light, penetrating down past blue starfish, poisonous marble cones and giant reef clams, the reef was dreamlike, visionary, blissful. There was nowhere to go, nothing to do, no one to report to, and he had an ace in the hole: one of his original conditions of hire with Kennecott was a first-class return ticket for the family to Canada. If things ever got really bad, he could bail out and log his father's land or trap furs with Gunther Lishy, but he was not ready to return to Canada, either. For now there was only the sea and the reef.

The weightlessness of the fish, like birds gliding through the water, could be matched, their element lived with them. Parrot fish, groupers and coral trout came in close for a curious look, nose-to-nose. Each a being with its own unfathomable intelligence.

Samedan Exploration came with a perfect offer for him. A subsidiary of Samedan Oil in the U.S.A., it had a porphyry copper prospect, a large volcano, 112 kilometres west of Cairns near Dimbula, which it was extremely excited about. Copper was a new field for the company, but it was convinced it was sitting on a major copper deposit and wanted Chuck to map it out. Even better, Samedan offered Marlene a job as well, to do some drafting and to cook for the field crews. The family moved to Dimbula, taking the ground floor of a fourplex apartment the company had rented for its employees, and Chuck went off to scout out the volcano.

It quickly became apparent to Chuck that the company had made a mistake. The deposit was not porphyry copper but simply a volcano with some pyrites.

The pyrites had been leached, giving it had the appearance of leach-capping caused by copper, but the effect was only caused by the pyrites. There was no copper in the ground.

To understand the chemistries involved required a technical proficiency Samedan was missing. More significantly, the company had trouble accepting bad news. Having convinced themselves they had hit upon a rich copper deposit, company brass did not want to read that they were wrong.

Chuck's reports on the property made it clear that the alteration Samedan was looking for in quantities was to be found in only rare trace amounts. Seizing on the existence of these trace values, the company continued to invest in the project and, to Chuck's increasing embarrassment, urged him to carry on with his mapping of the old volcano.

Regularly submitting his negative reports while he waited for Samedan to come to terms with the reality of its project, Chuck found the reef and the activities of his new friends more exciting than work.

Although he'd always been competitive, the Australian fondness for alcohol put Chuck at a distinct disadvantage. He drank, and sometimes heavily, but until he had arrived in New Guinea, his drinking had been casual.

To the Australians working in New Guinea, drinking had been a serious business. They would get down to it every night in the Ok Tedi canteen. Chuck would usually fall behind after a couple of hours and the beers would line up in front of him. In an environment where every drink was counted and the men took turns buying rounds, those who couldn't keep up were ridiculed. Wimps couldn't drink like real men! Try as he might, Chuck could not keep up. Night after night, he'd get blind with alcohol, and although he always made it back to his bed and pulled himself awake each morning before the others, he could not master the drink. In that hundred-man camp, he "practised".

Practised and practised.

He had a score to settle – to drink these Australian drillers under the table – and after two and a half years of heavy, hard drinking, he was ready. It was a different crew, but drillers were all the same.

They were working a drill project near the volcano and the crew was packing the gear away for the day when Chuck threw out the challenge.

"One thing about Aussie drillers," he said casually, as though commenting on the weather, "they're sure a bunch of wimps when it comes to drinking a few brew."

He took particular satisfaction in throwing the old insult back at them.

"*Wimps?*" It was enough reason for a fight. "Well, why don't we go and have a few stubbies!"

It mattered now, more than ever. He'd have to eat it if they "beat" him.

There were three drillers, their drill foreman and Chuck; the five of them settled into the pub for the evening. After three hours one of the drillers, dead drunk, fell over backwards and sprawled out on the floor. The publican, knowing the issues at stake, kept out of it, bringing the drinks. An hour later the second driller staggered off to the washroom, not to return. A short time after, the third, stone-faced and dull with drink, began to puke uncontrollably.

It was now down to Chuck and the drill boss. Chuck had so much in him he was not able to swallow another drop, and he was so dizzy he could hardly sit upright on his chair – but he would not concede defeat. Scrambling through his muddled mind, he tried to think of some way to get out of it honourably; he was finished and he knew it.

The drill foreman spoke first.

"How 'bout we pick up a couple of cases of stubbies and go to your place for a bit of kie?" Something to eat.

Chuck was elated.

"Well, I suppose, if you really want to," he said, trying hard to sound disappointed.

CHAPTER THIRTY-ONE

LIGHTNING RIDGE

SAMEDAN's continued positive feelings about its volcano ended when it brought out Charlie Park to look at the property. A world-renowned geologist who had written a classic in geological science titled *Ore Deposits*, Park confirmed what Chuck had known all along. There was no copper in the rock.

Samedan was disappointed but not entirely surprised to find its volcano was "worthless", and reassigned Chuck to do the work he loved the most – to search for new ore deposits. Now that he had a free hand to collect and analyze samples and, incidentally, to explore the country, Chuck's priorities shifted immediately, and work once again became the primary focus of his life.

It didn't matter to Samedan what kind of ore was found – as long as there was a market and money to be made. To identify target areas, Chuck spent his time researching the geological landscape from published material and, out in the field, collecting samples to fill the gaps in his information.

Besides copper and gold – both had been found in abundance in Queensland – there were other local minerals that Chuck was not familiar with but which seemed prudent to investigate. Nearby, a company mining molybdenum-tungsten allowed Chuck to drop down its shafts into the earth for a close-up look at the mineral formations. The molybdenite crystals he saw embedded in the host rock were as beautiful as the coral formations of the reef, and Chuck left with chunks of the ore sample and the knowledge of what to look for.

Chuck's investigation of the molybdenum-tungsten potential in the area and his physical survey of the landscape paid off when he found an area of altered mineralization that strongly suggested the presence of recoverable metals. Staking it on behalf of the company, Chuck moved it through all the preliminary exploration stages to percussion drilling – for a look at what lay underground.

Chuck was on-site directing the drill program when the percussion chips of rock suddenly started coming out as black as if they had hit oil.

But it was not oil; they had hit metal!

It was a solid mass of sulfide molybdenum-tungsten. An extremely rich deposit. Hopes soared with the excitement of the discovery. However, when they next drilled a diamond hole underneath it to prove the depth of the deposit, they missed it completely. There was no ore there. Still, the vein could have run off at some angle or another. More drilling was required to explore the ore body, and if it picked up somewhere else, it could still prove extensive enough to mine. But Chuck would never know the results of this last phase of exploration.

He had been with Samedan nearly a year. It was long enough. All he had left to do was finish his calculations and write up his reports on the molybdenum-tungsten find, and he was finished. A few more weeks.

Samedan asked him to come down to its head office in Canberra, the nation's capital, to finish his reports, and he agreed. The company saw it as an opportunity to convince him to stay. It wanted him to generate new exploration projects by doing literature research, to identify target minerals in areas with potential.

Chuck was flattered but he had told them he was not interested. Although the past year had been the most pleasant of his life, he was ready to move on. The security of a job and the comfort of a home – even one located only a few hours from paradise, a coral reef – was not enough. He had given his notice and would not change his mind. Still, his bosses wanted to try, and, for Chuck, the trip was an excuse to drive the coast highway into New South Wales, to investigate something there, away from the sea, that was of great interest to him.

Mount Capoompeta rose to 1,550 metres, one of the country's highest peaks. As Chuck drove around it, his vehicle climbed and then crested the Great Dividing Range into a new landscape. On the other side of the mountains were the arid interior lowlands. Chuck raced into them, across the flats, at full speed toward the Darling River watershed. Wet only when it rains, the landscape, dusty, barren and starkly pristine, was extremely stirring, especially as he neared Lightning Ridge, his destination.

Lightning Ridge was abuzz with activity.

Like well holes dug in search of groundwater, huge pits had been excavated everywhere, straight down through the surface. And everywhere, at the bottom of these pits, men toiled in the boiling heat.

A new strike in the old field had just been made, and a new rush was on. Hopefuls joined the established miners in poking about in the scrub, trying to divine where the land might be "hot," where fortunes could be made. Only half-understood by the local men, the strike was just being probed and claimed, and fever was running high.

Chuck parked his car, set up his tent and joined the rush.

Everywhere he went, his keen eye studied the lay of the land, absorbing the mood and information.

The rock underfoot was a soft sandstone. Formed by sedimentary deposits, it was composed principally of fine quartz sand compacted together with trace amounts of other minerals and elements, the most important of which, at Lightning Ridge, was hydrated silicon.

It was an ideal rock for small mining operations, easy to cut into and easily weathered. It was the latter quality that had been responsible for the formation of the silicon gemstones – the sole reason for the frenetic activity on the surface.

When the rains came, which they did seasonally, flooding the Darling River and washing effluents off the land which tilted south into the Indian Ocean, not all the water ran off the surface. Some of it managed to penetrate the ground. Over ages, as it percolated down through the sandstone, it dissolved the silicon and trickled it down to the groundwater table. There, over time, the silicon concentrated. Collecting together with free oxygen, it gradually built up into visible concentrations.

In the landscape of Lightning Ridge, these underground mineral clusters were known to be a compound of silicon and oxygen, but to the world at large, they were opals. And miners, each with their own small claims and private holes, were digging them up everywhere.

At night some men worked with lanterns, too impatient to quit their pits. Others got together in the cooler air to share their beer and stories. Their women, with them in the digs, were as ribald as the men. Describing in entertaining detail, their own sexual conquests, they had the men who were without women hanging on their every word before retiring to their own tents, alone with their fantasies.

Chuck studied the field from claim to claim, climbing down into the pits to examine the subsurface rock and the line of the old water table. The miners were pleased to show off their finds, and Chuck bought some opals from them. If they saw a stranger as one of them, they openly brought him into their circle and shared whatever information they had, harbouring no secrets.

Rarest among the opals were the black stones. Only the lucky miner ever found one. In one of the pits, Chuck was shown early on a beauty that he felt would make a wonderful gift for Marlene. A perfect black opal, it was valued at $3,000 a carat. Far more than Chuck could afford.

After a few days in their company, he met another miner who, like the rest, brought out his stones to show Chuck. Standing out from the others was a brilliant black opal. Almost a twin to the one he had looked at earlier. Chuck lifted it up, rolling it between his fingers, feeling its weight. Carefully he examined the stone, admiring its beauty, but said nothing about his desire to own one, knowing their value to be beyond his means.

The two men then talked of other things. Life in the diggings, of family and home and their experiences in the 'beyond'. As they were parting, the miner turned the conversation back to his black opal and casually mentioned that it was for sale for $15.

Chuck looked at the man intently. The man was either mad or it was a gift from the heart. In his face – red, glowing – shone the spirit of Australia. A land so hard and inhospitable that people could not have survived it without humour, strength and a hard-edged but deep generosity.

It was a gift.

Gradually, claim by claim, Chuck came to visualize where the opal deposits were and where they were not. With his experience in mapping invisible, underground deposits, he could see things the others could not – and what he saw was the hottest deposit in the field. To one side, along the leading edge of the richest deposits, the best opals lay, waiting to be unearthed, and there the land was unstaked. The claim was open.

In the exact area where he knew the strike would reach its glory, the field was there for the taking. For anyone. Here was the chance to make his own fortune. He could own his own claim, mine his own gems. Be his own man!

Quickly he resolved to stay. Beside himself now with the need for immediate action, he rushed to the mining recorder's office to register his claim before someone else grabbed it. He would stake the claim, carry on to Canberra to finish his reports, then return to Lightning Ridge with Marlene and Mark to work. It was the most exciting prospect of his life.

The mining rules for Lightning Ridge, however, contained some surprises. Written for the interests of free miners – in Australia, virtually anybody – the rules prescribed certain limits. The opal claims were only as large as a man could work himself and make a living – a rule that prevented anyone from claiming the whole region. Chuck was well aware of that rule – it allowed him to stake his own claim. It was the next one that caught him off guard. To prevent staking on speculation and the tying up of valuable property, the government required that all claims had to be worked, immediately and continuously.

Chuck was not allowed to register the claim and then leave it for even a few weeks. And any claim left unmined, even for a short period, was liable to be restaked by someone else.

It put him in a serious quandary. He desperately wanted to stake his claim and work it, but if he did, he would not be able to finish his reports for Samedan. The choice was to stay in Lightning Ridge and begin to mine his own opals, or continue on to Canberra to finish his job – as he had promised. He could not do both.

He paced slowly around the open claim he knew to be rich in opals. The air was as dry as the land was arid, but it was easy to breathe. There was a high energy to it, an electric charge that energized each step. The thrill of mining and finding opals across Lightning Ridge had stamped its own mood and character on the land, a reflection of the spirit of the hundreds of miners who worked here. An irresistible, contagious mood like the fever of a gold rush infused the air with the heady anticipation of discovery. More importantly, there was a future here for him, on this small baked piece of Australian outback. For as long as it lasted, it would be an adventure well-worth living, he knew.

Then, silently, he packed up his tent, climbed into his car and left. He could not quit Samedan without finishing his work. That was his first duty.

In Canberra he completed his reports, resisted Samedan's pressure to keep him on and walked out into the street jobless and alone. It was a condition he was becoming familiar with – and loved. Adrift, anything was possible. And some things were unavoidable.

For the past three years, the thesis he was required to turn in had preyed on his mind. It could not be put off any longer. For a month he worked on his paper, an original analysis explaining all the geochemical and geophysical processes of mineralogic zonation and alteration of porphyry copper.

Chuck was intensely proud of it when it was finished, and he had John Wilson, Kennecott's head of research, the man who had taught him the secrets of leach-capping at Ok Tedi, critique it before he sent it off to the University of British Columbia.

The feedback he got, that it was the equivalent of the master's thesis he had originally planned to do at Berkeley, confirmed for him that in the science of geology at least, the best graduate school was not found in academia but in the field – in the pits and shafts and ore faces of the mines around the world.

In Australia, one mine associated with the country's history, before all others, attracted him. Surviving the vicissitudes of the industry for more than a century, the ore deposits at Broken Hill – Chuck's new destination – continued, still, to form the foundation for the country's most powerful company

At the edge of the Barrier Ranges rising up out of the central basin, the company town of Broken Hill was on the site of the discovery of Australia's first real wealth. Broken Hill Proprietary Ltd. traced its origins back to an early discovery in 1844, when Charles Sturt, exploring up the Murray and Darling Rivers, far from the coast, in search of the great inland sea he believed would occupy the centre of Australia, walked over veins of lead and zinc protruding from the ground.

BHP's assets had grown since then. The company was now the largest and wealthiest in the nation, with annual revenues far exceeding those of most countries. As Chuck arrived in Broken Hill to explore the company's original claims, its shares were skyrocketing once again. Recent oil discoveries it had made in the Bass Strait between Victoria and Tasmania, breaking the country's total dependence on imported oil, had the value of its stock soaring to 600 percent of its pre-oil-discovery high. BHP would eventually take over the Ok Tedi project as well and turn that deposit into one of Australasia's most important gold and copper mines.

Chuck had nothing to offer the company when he arrived unannounced at the entrance to its mine in Broken Hill, yet it let him inside. Still mining the deep deposits of lead, zinc and silver after nearly 130 years, BHP had a complex underground operation that was a wonder of engineering science, and Chuck spent hours studying its operations as well as the ore it was following through the rock.

It was an experience Chuck would not forget. Not only did BHP open its doors for him, it gave him the grand tour. He had the run of the mine, its top people to answer all his questions, and a place at the table of its underground kitchen. That a giant would make time for an itinerant stranger, a young geologist simply curious, and treat him as an honoured guest was no less remarkable than the gift of a precious black opal by an Australian free miner. There was here, in Australia, a richness of spirit that, combined with the sun, the people, and the potential, made him question his decision to move on.

There was more than enough here to fill a lifetime.

Mineralogy had advanced since the 1800s, when the last great rushes swept the country. Then, exploration of the Earth's exposed rock surface in Australia, as elsewhere, was basic pick-and-shovel work. When the visible deposits were exhausted, when the ground was raked over, the prospectors and miners moved on, leaving the land. They had only scratched the surface – but it was the best their primitive technology allowed.

The new earth sciences of geophysics and geochemistry, however, could go where the old prospectors never dreamed of going. They created a whole new geological frontier.

The entire field was once again wide open. Australia – indeed the world – was on the brink of a new era in mineral exploration, brought on by these new technologies. Technologies in which Chuck was proficient. Geologists were in hot demand. Western Australia in particular was pushing like never before to unearth its treasures and had announced a need not for dozens but for hundreds of new geologists.

When Ed Fipke gently guided Chuck into the field of geophysics, he gave him the greatest gift a father could give his son – a limitless future.

Chuck was once again in the enviable position of having a dozen jobs for the asking. Except he had already made up his mind. It was time to move on. Australia was but an interlude.

Across the Indian Ocean, Africa was waiting.

Chuck upgraded their return tickets to Canada to allow them to fly through Africa, and their first stop was to be Johannesburg. He had no job prospects there. In fact, in the spring of 1973 South Africa was somewhat of a pariah in the world, and he had no idea what kind of reception a Canadian geologist looking for work there might receive. It did not trouble him.

He would find out soon enough.

PART THREE

In Pluto's Realm

South Africa, 1973–1974

Earth, is it not this that you want: to arise in us, invisible?

—RILKE, *THE NINTH ELEGY*

CHAPTER THIRTY-TWO

JOHANNESBURG

THE aerial view of Johannesburg was of an urban centre, a glittering jewel sur-rounded by a multi-hued aurora of red-roofed villas, spacious green gardens and blue swimming pools. Wealthier and more modern than Sydney or Perth, it was also more efficient. Chuck followed the signs through the airport directing him to the washrooms. HIERDIE GEBIED IS SLEGS VIR BLANKES

Down the corridor another sign over the entrance to the men's room pro-claimed BLANKE in bold Afrikaans in case some black or coloured person hap-pened to have wandered by mistake into the restricted "whites only" area. For non-whites, the more discreet sign indicating their permitted access was simply NIE BLANKE.

The Fipkes had arrived in South Africa.

After arranging the least expensive accommodation he could find, Chuck set about the purchase of an old "combie." Whether he found a job or not, he was determined to see Africa, and there was no better way to do it than from a Volks-wagen camper van – the family's new home and kitchen on wheels.

Leaving Johannesburg, they drove north in the combie, to Pretoria the capi-tal of the old Boer Republic of the Transvaal. He applied for a job with the Geo-logical Survey of South Africa, was told they would give him a decision in a few days, and then went off to explore. Everywhere the family went, whenever they paused at an intersection unsure of the way, sympathetic Afrikaners would offer them polite assistance and encouragement – a warm welcome.

Chuck had no need for concern about finding work – South Africa reserved a special place of honour for all whites. Blankes. Hedging its bets against an uncertain future – the country was already a nation under siege – it was actively recruiting European and North American immigration to bolster the ranks of its white population. Thousands of whites responded to the promises of citizenship and other privileges denied "the foreign Natives." Here, race, rather than an edu-cation in geology, determined the number of job prospects. In the burgeoning economy of South Africa, far more positions in management were being created than there were whites to fill them.

The privileges and inequities of exclusive power were difficult to see – even more difficult to condemn – when one was riding its crest or, like tourists, cruis-ing its highways, absolutely free from oppression.

Chuck was more interested in South Africa's wildlife than its politics, and after a short stopover in Pretoria, the family continued north into Transvaal.

Driving through the western acacia bushveld, they came to the boundaries of a wild island within the nation. Bordering Rhodesia to the north and Mozambique to the east, Kruger National Park enclosed an entire ecosystem that had been set aside as a game preserve. Larger than many countries, it had been saved from the ravages of encroaching white and black economies by the harshness of its own environment. Its arid climate was too dry and variable to support crops or cattle, and its infestations of tsetse fly, ticks and malarial mosquitoes made it too dangerous for human settlement. It remained as always, rich in a diversity of wild creatures, big and small. Classified as "parkland," it had rules for entry and use, but no other parklike quality at all.

In the cool air of the evening under a clear, starry sky, Chuck listened to the ground-feeding night plovers crying out in the darkness. Now and then, a deep-throated grunt or roar, or a nervous, higher-pitched cough would break the stillness and the illusion that the night was peaceful.

Leaving the compounds each day at dawn, Chuck roamed the park, exploring the land. While his family perched up on a ridge with a view, or parked in the shade of an ancient baobab where the ground moisture was just enough to sustain its enormously bloated trunk, he would wander over parched, dusty earth, seeping in its breathtaking beauty, as happy as he had ever been.

Creeping through the acacia bush of green and yellow-barked fever trees, he photographed magnificently-coloured hornbills, their presence revealed by a cacophony of raucous sounds. From nearer the van, he photographed lion, buffalo and giraffe, their large bodies completely dwarfing the wattled starlings, carnivorous strikes and oxpeckers which lived, symbiotically, among them. Believing implicitly in his own invincibility, he would sometimes wander far from the vehicle. Not covered by the same shield that protected him, Marlene was not prepared to take such risks, especially with Mark, and it led to occasional disagreements.

Struggling to scale hills in second gear, their old combie's small four-cylinder engine barely enough to power the boxy vehicle, was an exercise in enforced Zen. Chuck loved speed, and whenever he could, he would drive flat out – tires screaming – the rush of speed the most accessible of all thrills.

But if the combie did not respond to a heavy foot, the bushveld offered plenty of thrills to compensate. Even nature photography had its risks. To concentrate on the pictures he wanted, Chuck would have Marlene drive. During one excursion, they came upon a herd of elephants. Even with his 300-millimetre telephoto lens, the elephants were too far away for a good shot.

"C'mon! Let's get in closer!"

Marlene drove a little nearer. Chuck insisted Marlene move in closer yet. There was a large bull among the herd – a truly majestic beast of tremendous height. Chuck wanted to capture it in a perfect shot. Marlene was frightened.

"Closer!" Chuck demanded.

Several dozen metres at a time, they approached. Nearer and nearer, Chuck insisting that Marlene keep driving. She was extremely nervous, but Chuck ridiculed her fear. His own experience with animals in Canada had taught him they were not naturally aggressive towards people. He meant them no harm and expected none in return. However, the elephants too, were getting nervous.

Chuck urged Marlene to take them closer still. The elephants stopped feeding. Disturbed by the vehicle creeping up on them, they watched keenly. Chuck, his head out the window, studied them through his lens.

The large bull took more than a slight interest in their presence. Raising his head, his ears flared up and back. Then, moving toward them, slowly at first, he gathered momentum and broke into a charge. Rushing their van, towering over them, his bloodshot eyes completely filled the camera's viewfinder. Glaring malevolently down at them, he let out an immense roar that shook the vehicle.

EEEIIIAHHH.

Terrified, they froze. Adrenaline shot through Chuck, his heart racing so rapidly he felt it had stopped. With his tusks raised over the van, his huge bulk swaying, the elephant was poised, ready to crush them.

Chuck screamed at Marlene, "DRIVE! DRIVE! GET AWAY!"

As Marlene got the van into gear, increased their distance from the bull and made good their escape, Chuck began to breath easier.

"Holy shit, that was close!"

It was terrifying, but intensely thrilling. When he tried to discuss it with Marlene, however, to share the experience with her, she reacted less than exuberantly. As Marlene saw it, the risk was entirely of Chuck's making – not one they had happened on. Challenging life was not her way. The thrill was his alone.

After their encounter with the bull, one of the park rangers showed them a wrecked vehicle that had been rolled and crushed, two tusk holes in its side. The message was clear. Still, Chuck was not intimidated by Africa. He loved its power. No one could tell him what he could or could not do.

Catholic in her own sense of duty to her husband, Marlene, whether she agreed with Chuck or not, remained totally supportive of his interests and his needs, continuing to subordinate her judgement to his. Chuck was not sure why she did not make her own demands. He saw her as shy and he never probed her motivations, but it was not an expectation of his that she was fulfilling. He preferred having her by his side, joining him in all his ventures, but if she had chosen not to, if she had instead insisted on pursuing her own interests, he believed he would have accommodated her. How she chose to live her life was for her to decide. He only knew that he would live his own life as he felt it had to be lived, as he had always done.

From Durban, he telephoned the Geological Survey Office and learned they had decided to make a place for him. He could stay and work in South Africa for the government. It was an exciting prospect, but although the work was highly professional, the pay was extremely poor. He thanked them, asked for some time to consider their offer and continued on south, following the coast road to Port Elizabeth.

A landfall that the Portuguese had first made in 1488 under Captain Bartholomew Dias, Port Elizabeth gloried in white sand dunes at the edge of the surf, allowing Marlene and Mark to stretch their legs and explore without fear of attack by wild beasts. There were interesting things to look for in the sand. The trade winds blowing steadily off the Indian Ocean washed all sorts of strange treasures ashore, from bits of ancient shipwrecks to hand-blown fish floats and glass bottles.

The rains would not come until November, and each new day broke under cloudless blue skies. Africa taught that life was sweet and precious, and Chuck enjoyed each day to the utmost. He had two other job inquiries to make before calling the Geological Survey back. He was sure he could do better.

At Cape Agulhas, they hiked over rolling grasslands and stood before two oceans. Here the warm waters of the Indian Ocean mixed with the cooler currents of the Atlantic. It was a strategic spot, the Cape, and the Dutch had seized it first. Further west, along the coast, around the Cape of Good Hope, the Dutch had found a pleasant Mediterranean climate, rich soils and a safe harbour. Jan van Riebeeck saw its potential, signed a five-year employment contract with the Dutch East India Company and began Cape Colony in 1652 as a way station to reprovision Dutch ships travelling between Holland and its empire in the East and in the South Pacific.

It was the oldest white settlement in southern Africa. It was here Chuck had his second prospect, with a company whose roots were as old as the "modern" country.

By the time Cape Colony was seized from the Dutch by the English, it had become quite a valuable asset. In 1803, when the colony was forcibly appended to the British Empire, its Dutch Boer population had grown to several thousand. Increasing tensions between new English settlers and the Boers led to the "Great Trek," an exodus of Boers from the Cape. Between 1835 and 1840, 10,000 Boers crossed over the Orange River, which was the limit of British jurisdiction over Cape Colony and established the Orange Free State, an independent Boer republic. Others, continuing to move further north, entered the high veld country and established a second independent Boer state, the Transvaal. Britain recognized the independence of the two new Boer republics and they settled into a state of peaceful coexistence with the British empire. It was not to last long. The only reason for empire was wealth. Diamonds would be discovered in the Orange Free State and then gold in the Transvaal.

Forgotten in the quest for wealth were the Natives. Living around Cape Colony were two peoples: the San, known to the Europeans as "Bushmen," and the Khoikhoi, who were given the name "Hottentots" by the Dutch in the 17th century, which may have meant "Hot to touch."

Although believed to belong to the Khoisan Family, the Hottentots were possibly the mixed-blood offspring of San and Hamites. They had developed their own identity and were for long the preferred partners of single male colonizers, until mixed marriages were banned altogether. Further afield were the black Africans, the Bantus. Excluded from power, position and wealth – as had been the pagan Baltic tribes of northern Europe after their conquest by Christian armies of the Teutonic Knights – the Natives, in particular the more numerous Bantu, were seen primarily as a resource of the land, a muscular force and cheap energy to operate the new economy. That, too, would breed deep conflicts.

As Chuck drove his family into Cape Town, there was no evidence left of the old colony. The city that filled the valleys around Table Mountain and spread across the flatlands along the coast was completely modern. Once the capital of the British colony, it was now the legislative centre of the country. The old world had not left, however, it had only moved underground.

First they drove past the parliament buildings, where in 1890 Cecil Rhodes had ruled as prime minister and had crafted the laws that would become the foundation of South Africa. Since outright slavery had been abolished, he resorted to the classic European model of serfdom and class apartheid and imposed it on South Africa. Next, they drove by the walls of Pollsmoor Prison, where men who had opposed the regime but remained too powerful to kill were locked up. Nelson Mandela, an African lawyer from Johannesburg and a member of the African royal family of the Tembu, was inside, serving his 10th consecutive year of imprisonment.

Occupying plush quarters in the city and having enjoyed virtually unlimited wealth and authority since the early days of South African unification, Johannesburg Consolidated Investment Company, or JCI as it was more commonly known, remained one of the country's most powerful corporations. Chuck was planning to knock on their doors, offering his services as a geologist. The only company more powerful, more closely associated with South Africa's history, politics and character, was DeBeers, his third job prospect and, given the opportunity, his first choice.

There were, however, reasons to favour JCI as an employer. DeBeers, built upon old money and influence, had a company culture that remained difficult to penetrate. With humble beginnings, JCI was far more accessible, and its founder, Barney Issacs, was, after a century, still an inspiration to ambitious young geologists. Isaacs was an aggressive, crude Cockney who changed his name to the more fashionable Barney Barnato when he came to Cape Colony to make his fortune. Earlier, in 1871, the brothers Johannes and Diederik de Beer had discovered diamonds on their farm in the Orange Free State. The "DeBeers Diamond Rush" that followed resulted in 500 separately-owned claims, each one measuring the new, state imposed legal maximum of 31-feet by 31-feet, over the surface of the volcanic diamond-bearing pipe they named Kimberley. Virtually overnight it was surrounded by a new boom town.

The fabulous fortunes being made at Kimberley attracted Barney Barnato. And the British Empire. The diamond pipes were near the border between the Orange Free State and Cape Colony. To get them, Britain simply redrew the border, putting the new wealth within its control. The Boers were in no position to resist; the takeover was bitterly felt but achieved without war.

Barnato had his own plan for sharing in the fortune. He set up a company called Kimberley Central and waited for the free miners to exhaust themselves.

At the then-world-record depth of 365 feet, they could dig no deeper and the value of their claims crashed. As they sold out, he bought them up quickly. He was not alone. Cecil Rhodes was also standing on the sidelines and scheming. By the time Rhodes had secured the Rothschild family's backing for a buyout of the diamond interests, Barnato had acquired title to half the claims. He sold his interest to Rhodes for £5,338,650 sterling, securing one more consideration in the sale: membership in the exclusive British Kimberley Club. Since wealth and legitimacy went hand-in-hand, the acceptance was an item of significant personal satisfaction to him.

Not content with his fortune and club membership, Barnato continued to compete with the man who bought him out and with his moneyed European backers. When gold was discovered at the Witwatersrand, deep within the Transvaal, between Pretoria and Johannesburg, both men invested heavily, but beyond that, their interests diverged. Barnato became a philanthropist at the same time as he formed his new company, JCI. Rhodes was an imperialist. Not satisfied with the growth rate of his own fortune, he plotted with England to expand both their empires. Britain was then in economic competition with the emerging powers of the Prussian Second Reich and the United States. The gold reserves of the Bank of England were low and it needed the Transvaal's gold to underpin the sterling.

In return for promises of wealth and power, Rhodes undertook to engineer a war with the Boers. Moral pretence was required for soldiers to justify the sacrifice of their lives, however, and he was successful in creating it. By means of contrived provocations, British intervention became a cause and by 1900 half a million troops were brought to Britain's "defence" to crush the Boers. Loyal men from the colonies of Canada and Australia signed on by the thousands to fight the Boers for the honour of their king and God and Britain. Imperial regiments formed in Canada under British command, such as the South African Constabulary, were sent to fight alongside other irregular Canadian units like the Canadian Scouts. The Royal Canadian Dragoons, Royal Canadian Regiment and the Lord Strathcona Horse, Royal Canadians, all went as well.

The Boer campaign was commanded by Lord Kitchener, who, like Rhodes, fought for more than glory. His carrot was the coveted position of commander in Chief of India – if he concluded the campaign successfully for British interests. He set about to do so with a vengeance.

The Boers, fighting a guerrilla war, were resisting to a man, but their farms and families, left behind, were vulnerable. Burning their homes and their crops, Kitchener established a network of 50 concentration camps across the country and, driving Boer families off their land into the British camps, he saw the Boer spirit of resistance collapse. After 28,000 Boers, mainly children and women, wilted to death in the heat of the camps, the Boers gave up the struggle.

In 1910, Britain passed the Act of Union, formally uniting the two British colonies of Natal and the Cape with the two Boer republics of the Transvaal and Orange Free State. The *Act* did more than win the British the lasting enmity of the surviving Boers, it also betrayed the Native Africans by failing to give them the right to vote – perpetuating white minority rule for British South Africa. Two years later, in 1912, the South African Native National Congress was formed to advance black rights, politically and peacefully, if possible. Fifty years later, with no progress made, and violence and repression mounting, the leaders of its successor, the African National Congress party, were taken to court. Opposition to apartheid and the pass laws were treasonous.

While the Boer War transferred ownership of the Witwatersrand gold fields from the Boers to Britain, Kitchener moved on to his new post and Cecil Rhodes received his reward. Carving a strip off its British Trust Territories in the east, Britain turned Rhodes into a land baron with his personal empire. After the Boer War, Rhodes pushed farther north, adding the present-day lands of Botswana, Zimbabwe and Zambia to Britain's South African holdings. Zimbabwe, named Rhodesia in honour of Rhodes, became his personal fiefdom. His company, DeBeers Consolidated Mines Ltd., after buying out Barney Barnato, acquired all the other diamond properties in South Africa, and became the wealthiest in the world.

Chuck was unaware of the history or the current political situation in South Africa when he applied for a job with JCI. His own family's experience with imperialistic powers in Prussia and Russia had conditioned them into maintaining a distance from political events. Chuck was aware that nations did not operate under moral laws, but were governed by expedient self-interest. Morality, like the Church, wore different faces. All a man could do was his individual best.

Chuck, though, was not critical of power. It was part of the natural order and he was attracted to it, as he was by outstanding success. Weakness was no virtue. After all, if one had a choice, where better to be? In South Africa, in his own field of interest, there were three powerful and successful entities attracting him: the state, JCI and DeBeers. So far, he had applied to the state and had been accepted. Now it was JCI's turn.

The interview went well, he felt, and the written references he carried from all his previous employers revealed a dedicated geologist whose efforts were unstinting, one who mastered every task given him. It would take a few days to check out his background and confirm his references. Chuck was grateful for the delay. It would give him time to investigate the third, and most exciting prospect.

Leaving Cape Town, he drove up into the interior following the route of the Boer's Great Trek across the Orange River to Kimberley. Chuck knocked on the door of DeBeers. His philosophy had always been to go to the top and act like he belonged. Chuck presented his credentials and asked for a tour of their diamond mines. In South Africa, there were few people who showed up at mine doors, especially DeBeers's. The heart of white Africa, DeBeers had its own culture and was a private, exclusive club. Protective of its secrets, suspicious of outsiders, DeBeers saw everyone in one of two lights: with them or against them.

Chuck was not looking for any favours. He was offering his services. DeBeers looked him over carefully and gave him cautious, tentative approval.

"We might show you the mine," one of the men in the office told him.

It was a major concession – but then, what harm could come from showing a Canadian, a country geologist, the secrets of diamond formations?

"It'll take at least three days to get company clearance. You'll have to be checked through security."

They would, at the same time, tell him if they were prepared to interview him for a job. After they had investigated his background. DeBeers, like South Africa, did not want troublemakers in their midst.

Chuck had three days to prepare for the interview. And he did it in the most direct way imaginable. East of Kimberley was an open, high-veld game park roamed by white rhinos. Rather than stew in anticipation, building up tension, he had learned long ago the most effective mechanism for deep release was paradoxically the most intense stimulation he could find. Thrill-seeking calmed him. It also helped maintain a healthy perspective.

The entire region was crisscrossed with dirt road tracks and he drove the combie slowly, bouncing along the rutted trails as they kept a sharp lookout for rhinos. Spotting a group of rhinos in the distance, he stopped the combie and studied the terrain. After their experience with the elephants, Marlene refused to go any closer.

The van, in any event, was unable to negotiate the rocky slope that led off the road and down into the field of tall grasses where the animals were feeding. He'd have to sneak up on them.

Ignoring Marlene's protests, he left her with Mark in the vehicle and set off on foot. It was the only way he was going to get worthwhile close-ups. It was a dangerous game, but walking into his own fears put him on the edge where life was never more exciting, never more meaningful.

The rhinos were in a field of grass one-and-a-half metres high: perfect cover. Keeping low, Chuck crept in amongst them, stealthily, without being detected. He could hear them moving around him, their heavy steps on the hard earth, and he could smell them, but he couldn't find a good shot. They were busy eating, with their heads down; all he could see, peering over the top of the grass, was the irregular line of their spines. After several minutes, he gave up waiting for one to lift its head. Theirs was a rare confidence among herbivores. Placid, cow-like animals, they were not the least bit concerned, unlike the antelope who lifted their heads every few seconds to scan for enemies.

He conceived a plan: to make a sound that would force them to take notice. Chuck was a good mimic and he knew just the right noise – the night, hunting sound of the big carnivores. That would make them lift their heads!

He let out a rough, deep-throated snort.

NAAWGH!

It worked. The noise had hardly left his mouth before the rhinos went berserk. Instantly, the huge beasts were charging everywhere.

Galvanized into furious action by the sound of a predator, there were rhinos to the right of him, rhinos to the left, grunting loudly, rushing about, tearing the

Charles Fipke, on his twelfth Birthday, July 22, 1958, rural Alberta. In many ways, Chuck's upbringing was a typical Prairie boyhood, spent largely, when he had a choice, in the out of doors.

*Mount Ian, north of Ok Tedi, Papua New Guinea, 1970, where Chuck first
sought minerals on behalf of Kennecott. Travel was by helicopter over trackless
rainforests to nameless streams. Chuck and his crew would alight, take
a sample, then be picked up to move on to the next location.*

Chuck felt an immediate affinity for the local people, the first stirrings of what would become a life-long fascination with so-called primitive cultures.

On leave from Ok Tedi, Chuck tended his collection of exotic birds which he kept at the apartment where he, his wife Marlene and young son Mark lived. When Chuck and his family left Port Moresby for good, he set free his menagerie.

Warriors ancient and modern: In the early 1970s, parts of New Guinea were still rife with tribal warfare, little changed over centuries. More of a threat were Indonesian army "visitors" – heavily armed soldiers on border patrol who would pass through camp, demanding free access to food stores.

The Kimberley diamond "pipe," mined from 1871 until 1914, produced fourteen and a half million carats. Chuck's first exposure to diamond mining and mineralogy was during a 1973 tour of DeBeers mines while travelling in South Africa.

Chuck with son Mark and two trackers, in search of the San bushmen, South Africa. Chuck sought out members of this elusive culture and briefly lived in one of their camps.

More than any other aspect of their civilization, Chuck was attracted to the hypnotic rhythms of the dancing of traditional cultures he visited. In the Congo, the dances would often start after dark but continue past dawn.

Horseback was only one mode of transport utilized when collecting samples in back country Brazil, where Chuck (TOP, LEFT) explored for Cominco. The waters of the Amazon basin were also a lifeline along which modern civilization seeped into the roots of the rainforest.

"Norm's Camp" at Little Exeter Lake, Northwest Territories, home base for summer seasons of diamond exploration. "Club Norm" (the bunkhouse) and the "Taj Mahal" (cook shack) at Norm's Camp were rebuilt by Mark Fipke after they were destroyed by a grizzly and wolverine over the winter of 1990–91.

Chuck's method of collecting surface fine sand samples for diamond indicator minerals was deceptively simple. A sand sample was shoveled into a container with a fine-meshed screen bottom, where it was sieved, shaken vigorously until the finer particles all filtered through to the catch basin. The process was repeated several times, until the remaining fine sand sample weighed approximately 10 to 12 kilograms. The sample was bagged in plastic and marked with its location, then placed on the ground on a brightly coloured cloth where it could be easily spotted by a trailing helicopter crew. The sieve and basin were then cleaned carefully with a wire brush to remove every particle that might contaminate the next sample.

(ABOVE) *Chuck gives instructions to staking crew setting out to mark the Dia Met/BHP claim. All except Chuck wear protective clothing against the voracious insects.*

LOUIE PALU

Tension built as core samples – drilled at a 45-degree angle out under Lac de Gras – at first showed no trace of kimberlite. Then, just as hope was running out, the long sought-after diamond-bearing ore began to show.

Sometimes he is dubbed eccentric for his innovative mineral exploration methods. But Chuck's success has been as much the result of tireless, tedious interpretation of the exploration record as it is of inspired insight.

The Ekati mine, Lac de Gras, Northwest Territories: a fortune in diamonds – the fruit of one man's obsession and many others' hard work – lies just under the surface.

earth. Each one was thousands of pounds of muscle, scything deadly horns through the tall grass.

Chuck popped his head up, snapped off one unfocused picture, and quickly ducked back down into the cover of the grass. It offered little protection. Blowing air and making terrific noises, the rhinos shook the ground like locomotives. One thundered straight for him through the grass and for a moment Chuck believed it was all over. It ran right by him, missing him by a couple of metres.

Concerned almost as much with his own self-image as with Marlene's seeing him frightened, he held on for a moment longer out in the plains grass, then – image be damned – made a mad dash, running full blast through the grass towards the safety of the combie. With his head down he sprinted, trying to stay low, under cover, the rhinos continuing in unabated fury all around him at full speed.

He arrived breathless back at the van to find Marlene hysterical and crying. Convinced that when he left he was going to be killed, she could only watch with Mark in horror as Chuck had disappeared into the tall grass in the face of the rhinos' wild charges. The huge beasts had even surrounded the van, snorting aggressively while Mark and Marlene huddled inside, cowering.

When Chuck started the engine, it wouldn't turn over. Worse, he had parked it in a depression in the road and there was nowhere to push it but down, off the road, back towards the rhinos.

Marlene would not calm down and Chuck got angry. It was a weekday. There wasn't another soul in the whole region. She had to pull herself together and get out to help push. They got the van started and drove off, bumping and banging away, to the park's secure, fenced compound for a shower, and a beer. After some reflection, laughing heartily, Chuck confessed to Marlene, "I sure got the adrenaline going on that one!"

By comparison, dealing with DeBeers was like playing with antelope, especially after he called JCI back and was told they wanted him. Two-for-two, he was feeling confident when he rang back DeBeers. Not surprisingly, good news greeted him there, too. They were interested. Barry Hawthorne, they told him, would do the interview. Chuck was familiar with the name. One of the world's leading diamond geologists, Hawthorne was an important figure in DeBeers. There was more.

"You got the green light to see the mines. In fact, we're going to show you Finsch as well."

Chuck was pleased. Finsch was DeBeers's baby, the most profitable mine in the world. Very few people outside DeBeers had been allowed to see it. He had cleared security. They assigned him a Dutch geologist, from Holland, to show him around, and although Chuck's scheduled job interview was set for later in the afternoon, the geologist first took him to meet Hawthorne, to break the ice.

Chuck had his own way of dealing with people. There was one thing Chuck wanted from DeBeers and he knew Hawthorne could get it for him: a raw diamond still in its kimberlite host rock.

"Well, you know that's pretty rare to find," Hawthorne told him, not wanting to commit himself. Chuck's request was also against all of DeBeers' rules.

Chuck produced the opals he had collected from Lightning Ridge and made a gift of some of them to Hawthorne, who warmed visibly.

"I'll see what I can do," he promised.

After leaving Hawthorne, he and the geologist went off to visit South Africa's most famous site, the Kimberley mine. Closed for years, it had been left as a monument to South Africa's colonial beginning. It was here that Barney Barnato and Cecil Rhodes saw the future for South Africa. Now a great gaping hole in the earth was all that was left.

They next toured Finsch, stopping at several of the other mines DeBeers had in the area, diamond-bearing volcanic pipes appearing in clusters, relatively close to one another. Chuck was more than an idle spectator. He took extensive notes of everything he saw and heard. As was his practice when visiting mines, he climbed into the open pits, scoured the rock faces and went down into the shafts, absorbing everything and writing it all down.

The geologist who had been assigned to him was very knowledgeable and answered all Chuck's questions. For DeBeers such openness was a break with their usual practice, but geologists, one-on-one, are more often professionally curious than business-minded, sharing secrets that their business counterparts would shudder to know were being revealed.

The geologist even allowed him to take kimberlite samples from all the mines they visited and, more unorthodox still, gave him samples of all the indicator minerals for diamondiferous pipes that DeBeers had found in the streambeds around the region. These were minerals formed in the same conditions and coming from the same pipes that contained diamonds. The importance of discovering indicator minerals in a streambed – minerals which were far more common than diamonds in the host rock – lay in their revealing the likelihood of a diamond-bearing pipe being found upstream, not unlike the way Ok Tedi's copper field could be detected kilometers downstream by the presence there of indicator minerals for copper. The minerals which indicated the presence of diamonds were themselves unique: magnesium-rich picro-ilmenites, chromites, bright green chrome diopsides, and pyropes – dark mauve, magnesium-aluminum stones, also considered gems and more commonly known as a type of garnet.

For the questions the geologist could not answer, he suggested Chuck talk to Dr. John Gurney at the University of Cape Town. A comprehensive thesis filed there on indicator minerals contained the information he wanted. Dr. Gurney's own specialization, diamond geology, was new to Chuck, but he would, one day, become very familiar with the professor and his field.

By the time they finished the tour, Chuck knew almost enough to go diamond prospecting himself. It had taken longer than they expected and Barry Hawthorne, with whom he was to do the interview, had to fly out to Pretoria for a meeting. Promising to reschedule, Hawthorne left, without giving Chuck what he wanted – the diamond in the rough.

CHAPTER THIRTY-THREE

BARBERTON

THE Fipkes arrived back in Cape Town the same night that JCI put on its annual party. They were invited, but Chuck was in a dilemma. JCI wanted his answer on their job offer but he hadn't had his DeBeers interview yet. If he waited for DeBeers, he could lose JCI. Still unsure of what to do, he decided to go to the party.

Having checked out all his references before offering him the job, the management of JCI were pleased with what they read and Chuck received an exceedingly warm welcome when he arrived at the hotel, underdressed as usual. Three years had passed since he walked into Kennecott's welcoming party in Sydney, and Chuck had a lot more experience and confidence now.

Dr. Eckhart Buhlman, a brilliant German geologist who had conducted Chuck's job interview with JCI and for whom Chuck would be working if he took the job, greeted them as they came in and took Chuck and Marlene around, introducing them to the company's human faces. Except for the black serving staff, everyone in the crowded banquet hall was white, most of them Afrikaners.

Chuck liked Buhlman. A cultured, sophisticated man, he reminded him of Gunther Lishy. Although Buhlman spoke flawless English, the language of education and business in South Africa, and had lived there for five years, he would always be an outsider. The Afrikaans world was a closed society. Superficially polite, they were cold and detached. Full of contradictions, they were secretive and insular, yet international; modern and sophisticated, yet archaic and rigid.

Here and there, groups of Afrikaners were speaking Afrikaans. A mix of the Germanic languages of the 17th-century Dutch, English and German, it had evolved over the centuries into a language unique to South Africa. Some of the talk was of restricting instruction in black schools to Afrikaans, eliminating English altogether – a policy for the preservation of Afrikaans culture.

Most of the talk that was not political was of work: new contracts, new prospects, new ventures. The mood of the gathering was of polished frivolity, underscored with confidence and power.

For Chuck, the opulence was overwhelming. JCI was not a new company operating within a modern colony bursting with youthful vigor like Canada or Australia. It was a door into an old-world moneyed class that had ruled for millennia. It was a social order which had only recently been eroded by the advance of New World democracy, a process the Afrikaners seemed determined to resist.

There was no shortage of funds for an extravagant party. Having booked the ballroom of Cape Town's most exclusive hotel, JCI had a British rock band flown in from London just for the night. As in Sydney with Kennecott, JCI prepared a lavish banquet, a feast accompanied by cases of the finest South African wines and followed by liqueurs, pastries and tortes. After dinner, the band began to play and the bar was thrown open. Dr. Buhlman, seeing Chuck seated alone came across the room. Leaning confidentially close, he asked, "Well, are you going to join our little society?"

Chuck was caught off-guard. He hadn't, until now, committed himself. "Ah, yah, I guess so."

Chuck noted how the Afrikaners were more controlled and formal than Australians would have been. Their bow ties remained in place until late at night on the dance floor. But they made Chuck and Marlene feel at home and by early morning Chuck, who drank and danced all night, like only a Canadian could – and would – decided he would in fact stay.

The company moved him to Barberton to take over the exploration project, on a nearby antimony prospect they were working with a black field crew. He was thrilled with the location. On the northern border of Swaziland and near the western border of southern Mozambique, Barberton was in the eastern Transvaal right beside Kruger National Park.

There were certain privileges that went with white management positions in South Africa. Barberton was an Afrikaans town and minimum standards were expected to be maintained. JCI provided the family with a fully furnished house, a new four-by-four vehicle, an expense allowance to buy food, a complete benefit package and three black servants: a gardener to maintain the grounds, a houseboy, who lived on the property and did the cooking and cleaning, and Amos, the chauffeur.

Chuck had no complaints about the first two, but he wanted to drive his own car. It was a freedom, not a chore.

"But, then he'll be out of a job. And he needs the work to support his wife and children!" The case was argued with moral authority.

Chuck felt a sympathetic twinge but wasn't convinced. The company was ready with a compromise. They had been through it all before.

"Try him out for a month. Then, if it doesn't work, okay, we'll get rid of him ... but you'll find him very useful. Get him to do all your errands and your shopping. It'll free up a lot of valuable time for you."

It was an extremely comfortable existence, as intended by the company, one to which they hoped their employees would grow accustomed and find too seductive to leave. The privileges of the South African middle class made it difficult for those benefiting from them to see that they too were being manipulated in the same way, although more benevolently, than the blacks were.

The system of personnel management employed by JCI and the other large South African corporations for black labour and white lower management had been developed primarily in response to the historic Witwatersrand gold field problems.

Discovered in 1886 by George Harrison, a poor immigrant, the outcropping ridge of auriferous rock, miles long and known as the "Witwatersrand" was a deposit of low grade, gold-bearing ore, but one of the most extensive deposits in the world. With JCI and DeBeers claims securely in place and recognized by the Boer Republic of the Transvaal, the chief problem in mining the gold lay in attracting – and keeping – huge numbers of low-paid workers. In the first few years of the mines' operations, 50,000 black workers arrived annually and an equal number left. With gold pegged for years at $35 an ounce, the only variable in the profitability equation was the cost of this black labour.

After working on the problem for two years, Cecil Rhodes, both Prime Minister and Minister for Native Affairs, presented his solution to the Cape Legislative Assembly in July, 1894. The *Glen Gray Act* was proclaimed as the "ultimate solution" to the "Kaffir" labour problem – one which Rhodes would soon see applied to the Boer Republics after their annexation to the British properties of southern Africa. Brutally racist, it was a complex scheme of head taxes on unemployed "Kaffirs," restrictions on land ownership, inheritance laws – which prohibited all but one member of each family from acquiring land – and a pass system which was designed to throw huge numbers of Africans off their land and away from their traditional economy – and straight into the mines of JCI and DeBeers.

In the words of Rhodes the *Act*, which the legislature quickly approved, would take "these poor children out of their state of sloth and laziness and give them some gentle stimulants to go forth and find out something of the dignity of labour."

The measures were necessary. A free-market capitalist only when it suited him, Rhodes could not allow a free market to develop. For the wages being offered, labour would not come voluntarily. The Africans could not be dragged into the pits – Britain had abolished slavery. To offer fair wages would seriously impair the profitability of the mines. There was a middle ground.

By introducing a form of industrial serfdom to South Africa, Rhodes turned hundreds of thousands of Africans off the land, making them totally dependent for survival on what little they could make in the mines. Other sections of the new law provided that "breach of contract" and "escape" were made criminal offences. Africans who "deserted" their jobs were committed to prisons, where the conditions were decidedly worse than those in the mines.

To control their new labour force, a system for white overseers was also designed. With special privileges and perks, and a social status far above that of the black labourer, the creation of a white management class dedicated to its own survival was the key to the success of the whole scheme.

When Chuck was hired for extremely low pay but a generous benefits package, which included black servants, he was being bought into the system. Like the blacks who were unable to save enough to ever break away, life would become a treadmill. For the whites, at least, the benefits were designed to keep them comfortable while they remained dependent. As Chuck very quickly learned in Barberton, the Afrikaners had a vested interest in maintaining the status quo. No one would risk anything. And no one would go anywhere.

After the first month, Amos stayed. JCI was right. Having a servant run your errands did have its advantages. But it was a lonely life. Chuck loved to party. To let loose and have fun. Yet there were very few people he could party with. Socializing with the blacks was quite nearly a criminal act. Mixed marriages were illegal, as was all interracial sex. The blacks who worked for him maintained their distance. But surprisingly, the Afrikaners he came to know – the ones he worked with or who lived in Barberton – would not socialize with the Fipkes either. They even forbid their children to play with Mark, who attended the same white Afrikaner school. The philosophy of apartheid, existed within the strata of white society as well as outside of it.

Even more puzzling was the attitude of their next-door neighbours, a South African surveyor born of Italian immigrant parents and his Afrikaner wife. They were always very friendly over the fence, yet never once responded to the many invitations to cross over for a modest get-together. Helmar, an Afrikaner student working for Chuck who knew the surveyor, explained, candidly, that the family had only been in South Africa for 30 years. Although the surveyor, who was 29, was born in South Africa, his family was considered new to the country and he was only now receiving the first tentative signs of acceptance by his peers in the deeply insular Afrikaner society.

Just to be seen socializing with Chuck would jeopardize the surveyor's position.

Chuck had about 80 Africans, mostly Swazis, who worked directly under him; although he spent his days with them out in the field, they remained a shadowy people. *Apartheid*, an Afrikaans word meaning apartness and pronounced "*apart-hate*", was an omnipresent curtain between them.

Sometimes, out in the field during breaks, or after work back in the camp, the Swazis would add drums to their songs and cheer themselves with dance. The textures of sound they produced were far richer than anything Chuck had ever heard.

Curiously, a lot of the music they played had been developed or performed at the Witwatersrand gold fields. The thousands of Africans working there came from a dozen tribes, such as the Swazi, Zulu, Ngoni, Sotho and Xhosa, and would compete with each other for their own entertainment.

Where Stone Age New Guinea's monotonal drumbeats were meaningful only to the initiate, an expression of pure spirit with no musicality, Africa's drums were Iron Age, multi-textured and multi-dimensional. Its music was a joyous expression of life, simultaneously mystical, magical and celebratory.

It was so compelling that it blurred the lines that separated the races and it was capable of carrying Chuck away too, crossing over from Afrikaans to Africa.

But he was never invited to participate. Nor did he ever initiate a more meaningful contact. In South Africa that was not done. His own society was strictly limited to the other outsiders – the group of expats, who, like himself, had no long-term commitment to the country. Its problems were for the Africans and Afrikaners to sort out.

There was, however, one immediate problem that came with the job and resolving it fell squarely on his shoulders. The man he replaced was an Afrikaner who treated the Africans as chattel, not worth the pay they were getting. And as Chuck soon discovered, not only was the morale of the Africans low, his predecessor had actually seen to it that they received less than they were entitled to from the company.

After the *Glen Grey Act* became law, delivering hundreds of thousands of Africans to the Witwatersrand seeking employment there and in the diamond mines, the basic pay of the African was cut from a subsistence salary of 50 shillings a month to a starvation wage of 30. Recognising that the point of a starvation wage was to keep the labourers forever at their jobs but not actually to starve them, the "benevolent Christian" practice of giving out "free" food and clothing developed, to keep the labourers alive while the companies pretended to pay livable wages.

At Barberton, the argument for low wages was, as always, that the company benefits took care of all their actual needs. As had been company policy since its first mine started operations at the Witwatersrand, JCI promised weekly food rations of mealie-meal, nuts and fruit, free medical coverage, work trousers and boots, and most importantly, annual reviews of their salaries.

For the five years his predecessor had been at the job before being promoted, all the Africans had gotten from him was their basic low pay and none of the benefits. Nor had he ever reviewed their salaries.

Doing his Canadian best to be fair and reasonable, Chuck set out to improve their morale and knit them together as a team. Everybody got raises, new clothes and a bag of weekly food rations. Chuck climbed down into the trenches and rubbed shoulders with the Africans, showing them, by example, how to work. When the Africans got into fights with potentially lethal spades and pick-axes, he was between them in an instant, pushing them apart; when they were injured, he was there with the first-aid kit, stemming the blood loss. In every way he could, he tried to improve their lot and demonstrate that he was on their side, working together.

But they continued to treat him the way they treated all Afrikaners – distantly. He was "Boss." Or more commonly, "Bossy."

In spite of all his efforts, their morale, instead of improving, plummeted. The harder he worked at it, the worse it got. It was beyond his control. And completely frustrating.

After a few weeks, morose and sullen, they could hardly put any energy into their work. Chuck was beside himself, ready to give up. The situation reached crisis proportion when Marlene, who had also been hired by JCI to manage and track Chuck's exploration budget and to run the payroll, hit a snag and was not ready with the cheques on payday. Mistakes happen, but the reaction of the Swazis was a complete surprise.

They blew up. Extremely angry, they advanced on Chuck in an agitated mob, threatening rebellion. He apologized; the cheques were only one day late. The Swazis, however, were not interested in explanations, apologies or even solutions – they wanted, irrationally, to indulge their rage. Chuck felt their behaviour was inexcusable. It was no big deal. Their hostility put him over the edge. He was tired of trying to help them out and not getting anywhere. Now, he had had enough.

At first controlling his temper, he outlined everything he had done for them since he had arrived. Every man among them, he pointed out, had benefited from his efforts. He listed everything. As he finished and started describing the new position he would be taking from now on, his voice gave vent to his own anger.

"I've done my best for you guys! And now you're angry because we made a mistake? Because we're one day late paying?! Well, I want you to know that I'm not happy with you! I'm sick of your constant complaining and your negative attitude. From now on, don't come to me with your problems. Fix them yourselves! I'm not doing anything for you anymore! And furthermore, on every payday, I'm firing two men. Every payday, the ones I don't think are working hard enough are out of here!"

Then he walked off. The next day, he passed out their paycheques and fired two men. And the next payday two more, true to his word, he raised his voice and kept his own distance. Instead of showing them, patiently, how to perform new tasks, he would yell at them. He saw himself becoming more Afrikaner in his dealings with them; he saw no other alternative.

Partly, his behaviour was an expression of his true feelings: lingering resentment at their hostile confrontation. But mostly, after the first few days, he kept it up because it was so unbelievably productive! Their response to his anger, distance and discipline was dramatic.

Overnight, their mood and attitude towards work skyrocketed. No longer sullen, their morale soared. They shouted enthusiastic greetings at him each morning when he arrived and sang constantly while they worked out in the field. The sound of dozens of deep voices raised together, resonating in song was powerful and stirring. The men, challenged by their own joy, worked like never before.

Tribal, warrior people from Swaziland, their mood was wholly dependent upon his maintaining the role they expected of him. So long as he acted like a tribal leader, manifesting the qualities they respected – aggression, rigidity and power, even arbitrariness and unpredictability – they were happy to work for him and could never do enough.

Effective, but a Pyrrhic victory. Maintaining an angry, hostile attitude was trying, and false. As much as the men now respected Chuck, the gulf between them was absolutely uncrossable. South Africa was an exercise in isolation.

CHAPTER THIRTY-FOUR

RHODESIA AND NAMIBIA

IF Chuck had trouble seeing the future for southern Africa, JCI's vision was clear. Regardless of the political turmoil everywhere, it was business as usual. Confident that their assets would be protected by the South African government wherever they found wealth – the army was charged with the duty of safeguarding all South African interests – JCI continued to look for prospects beyond its own frontiers.

After Christmas, JCI sent Chuck north to Rhodesia. Three times the size of England, it had been run exclusively for the benefit of Rhodes's own British South Africa Company until 1923. Rhodes's company had the right to mine minerals, grant landholdings to white settlers and issue concessions to other companies to operate within Rhodesia. In return, the obligation of its directors to the country and its majority black population was, as always, to promote "good government" and "civilization."

But mining across southern Africa – the prospecting side of the operation, at least – had never been as difficult as JCI, DeBeers and the other companies formed by Rhodes and Barnato made it out to be.

The South African Department of Information maintained the party lie that black Africans – Bantu-speaking tribes – had entered southern Africa, and particularly South Africa, only recently – moving south over the Limpopo River at the same time that Europeans, colonizing the coast, moved into the interior.

The official line, printed in South African textbooks and told repeatedly to Chuck, had become part of conventional wisdom, providing some moral justification for apartheid. The country had been "vacant" land, and the few Africans who had arrived at the same time as the whites were neither Christian nor "civilized." The African, regardless of how low his position was with the superior Europeans, could only benefit from the contact. The party line had been deliberately crafted by the ruling upper-white industrial class for the benefit of the lower-white managerial class, who needed "special truths" to morally justify their superior position.

The sealed and secret records of the mining companies told another story.

Only a few miles from Barberton, buried in the town archives of Broederstroom and Phalaborwa, were records of Boer discoveries of large accumulations of slag from iron-smelting furnaces – operated by Africans! When the Boers arrived at Phalaborwa, the local Africans were still mining iron and copper deposits there, operating mines with shafts 70-feet deep, galleries and adits. The slag pile was 10,000 tons.

It was a site where mining had been carried on continuously for 1,000 years before the Boers arrived to take control. Similarly, at Rooiberg in the western Transvaal, the Africans had excavated 18,000 tons of ore since the fifth century before the Boers claimed it as their own. The Rooiberg Minerals Development Company commenced its operations early in the century simply by continuing the ancient workings.

A late iron-age people when the Europeans arrived, the Africans, in the Transvaal alone, were operating 60 mines: 31 for iron; 20 for copper; six for gold and three for tin. If mining and commerce in metals were the marks of a "civilized" people, the Africans were clearly civilized.

All the European prospectors had to do was look for the smelters. In Rhodesia, so effective were the Africans at prospecting, that of all the gold occurrences "found" there by the mining companies, only one surface deposit had been unknown to them.

By the 1970s, when Chuck arrived, all the old sites had been long since grabbed by the mining companies – and their African origins carefully concealed. Prospecting became more difficult after the mining companies seized the mines from the Africans. Only the occasional new ore body was discovered.

At the encouragement of Dr. Buhlman, Chuck completed heavy mineral orientation studies for copper and nickel on the Shangani deposit in Rhodesia. Once again Chuck was prospecting tsetse-infested savanna, digging down deeply into the dry stream channels to examine the sand deposits for mineral indicators that might reveal the presence of ore bodies upstream. In remote parts of the country, he met and worked with local villagers, but otherwise had minimal contact with the people and their politics.

He was lucky. Although he was no stranger to armed confrontations with hostile blacks, an encounter in the bush with ZAPU or ZANU guerrilla units would not have been so easily deflected. Like neighbouring Mozambique, Rhodesia's days were numbered. Although all political opposition had been banned and the various leaders of the African parties, Reverend Sithole, Robert Mugabe, Joshua Nkomo, Leopold Takawira summarily arrested – most held without public trial for years – the pressure of 5,000,000 Africans to be independent of the continuing control of 200,000 whites given exclusive power by Cecil Rhodes was building.

The most prevalent threat to Chuck, however, was not armed fighters, but parasites. The worst of these was bilharzia, a severe endemic disease caused by the trematode worm. Infesting all the waters, the worms were a particularly nasty problem, eating their way through the skin to occupy the bladder and intestines of their host. The medical advice, as in New Guinea, was to stay clear of all water. Chuck frequently found himself wading chest-deep through murky currents that even the locals would never go near. But he was fortunate. The wife of a German geologist he knew, who had never ventured into the bush, came down with a crippling case of the disease from the taps in her own home in Barberton. Yet he, forever in the field, never attracted any serious parasites.

From Rhodesia, he was sent to Windhoek, the capital of Namibia, another country in turmoil. SWAPO, the political organization resisting South African rule, had been recognized by the United Nations as the sole legitimate representative of Namibia's people. At the same time, the U.N. condemned South Africa's continued control over the country as "unlawful". In response, South Africa ignored the U.N., banned SWAPO, outlawed all opposition and in typical draconian fashion, enacted the *Terrorism Act*, which they made retroactive in order to criminalize formerly lawful association. Under the Act, Herman ja Toivo, SWAPO's most articulate and passionate spokesman was arrested, removed to the Afrikaner centre of Pretoria and sentenced there to 20 years imprisonment by the South African Supreme Court for his outspoken opposition to South African rule of his country.

Windhoek was a modern, white, South African-style city with residential neighbourhoods built in classic Cape Dutch and German designs. Beyond the city, the government's large rental quarters prevented the growth of the pervasive black slums that surrounded other African cities. Blacks in Namibia were not free to move or live as they pleased. The South African pass system imposed in Namibia required approval – which could always be revoked – to live in Katutura, the only officially sanctioned quarters for blacks. Like Johannesburg's Soweto, Katutura was Windhoek's solution to containing and controlling the local Africans.

In the heart of the commercial centre, all of South Africa's major corporations maintained regional offices in gleaming office towers. JCI was well represented. It had numerous interests in the country, and it was looking for more.

At Otjihasi, near Windhoek, Chuck first did a series of orientation studies for the company on a copper-zinc prospect. After that, he was sent deeper into the field to examine and report on a porphyry copper prospect that some earlier geophysical work indicated might exist.

There was no end to the work.

The country was a cornucopia of minerals. Little wonder South Africa was unwilling to give it up without a fight. Once launched on the quest for wealth and power, it was difficult for any company to quit, and impossible to turn back.

To Chuck, the alluvial diamond fields of the arid coastal regions around Oranjemund were one of Namibia's most interesting attractions. The "Restricted Diamond Area" known as "Sperrgebie," meaning "the forbidden region" covered more than 50,000 square kilometres, encompassing the entire southern one-third of the coastal Namib Desert. Fenced off with barbed wire, the huge concessions were carefully guarded. Trespass alone could be a capital offence and Africans who climbed the fence did so at the risk of their lives. The loose, gravelly material carried to the delta region over thousands of years by the Orange River was incredibly rich in diamonds. In 1920 Ernest Oppenheimer's company, Consolidated Diamond Mines, won an exclusive concession from South Africa to mine the diamonds, which travelled downriver along the Orange into the delta area and were spreading north along the coast by ocean currents.

Huge dredges were anchored offshore, which sucked up the sea bed and filtered out millions of tons of material, isolating the rare gemstones. Working day and night, the dredges were recovering one-fifth of the world's total diamond production: one-half of Namibia's revenues. The source of these diamonds, the pipes which brought them to the surface, were believed to lie in the original headwaters of the Orange River before it changed course over the ages. Some had been discovered. Others remained hidden.

Geology was a science, but luck and chance continued to play a major role.

Flying over Namibia's vast farms and plantations, driving through its desert lands and forests, wading up its tributaries with supporting teams of Africans from different parts of the country, Chuck was in a unique position. He had a foot planted deep in both worlds: a scout for the powers that kept the nation imprisoned, and a man committed to the quest for personal freedom. It did not cause him to suffer any guilt.

He was not responsible for South Africa nor, he believed, could he effect any change. His focus, like that of his father's, and his father's father before him, was utterly non-political. Life was entirely a personal experience.

There were arguments, too, that South Africa's dictatorship of Namibia was more benevolent than virtually all other African dictatorships. Certainly more benevolent than Namibia's former colonial masters, the Germans. Unlike the British, the Dutch and even the Portuguese, the Germans in Africa pursued a philosophy based wholly on brute force and royal absolutism.

In 1880 when Jakob Fipke was making his own break for freedom from Prussian captivity to a Ukrainian leasehold, the German Empire was landing forces between Portuguese Angola and British South Africa. The Imperial Commissioner responsible for German colonization and control over the African tribes was Dr. Heinrich Göring, whose son Hermann would later dedicate himself to the Nazi cause, surpassing even his father's infamous exploits.

Germany was, in 1904 in Namibia, already experimenting with concentration camps and methods of mass killing. Targeting the Herero African nation for extermination – a nation that had opposed them – General von Trotha simply marched thousands of people at a time into the parched Omaheke Desert, allowing the desert to kill them naturally, thus conserving precious ammunition. Not content to impose apartheid and serfdom, German rule put harsher controls in place, imprisoning thousands more Africans in concentration camps from which they were driven out to work the German mines and where they slowly died. Nazi Germany did not invent its system, it simply refined historic practices first developed in southern Africa.

More than anything, Chuck had come to Africa to meet the people. New Guinea had awakened a new interest: meeting natural people who were unencumbered by industrial economies and Christian ethics. These encounters could, he believed, teach him much about humankind, and about himself. He did not articulate this desire as a search for meaning, rather as a search for a place to fit in.

The most inhospitable region of Namibia, the northwest desert bordering the

Kalahari in neighbouring Botswana, had been designated as a homeland for the local San tribes – the !Kung Bushman. It was there that Chuck's deepest interest lay. A stone-age race, ancient among ancients, the San were reputed to be among the most capable of natural people left in the world.

What visions did they see? What insights could they offer?

Try as he did, he was unable to interest the company in investigating the region the San occupied, and Chuck left Namibia at the company's direction, without meeting them.

There would be other opportunities.

CHAPTER THIRTY-FIVE

BOTSWANA

Cʜᴜᴄᴋ had been in Africa for a year and out of Canada for four when he began to feel the desire to reacquaint himself with his own country. But he couldn't leave without at least trying to accomplish a meeting with the San.

Of the five distinct races that evolved in Africa the white Hamito-Semitics of the southern Mediterranean, the Nilo-Saharans of present-day Sudan, the Bantu Negroes of western Africa and the Forest Pygmies of the Congo-Zaïre River, it was the San, the Bushman, who had exclusively, controlled all Africa south of the Congo-Zaïre River for thousands of years. Half of occupied Africa had been their original homeland.

It was in the open country of eastern Africa and the high veld lands of southern Africa where all the species of the genus *Homo* evolved and mankind was born. As new races evolved or were driven out by more successful, more capable races, it was the San alone who in the end, held the entire field.

The most successful of all Paleolithic peoples, no other race could compete with the San. Although numerically few, they occupied the continent's most favourable territories. Of a combined continental African population that, in early Roman times, numbered less than a few million, the Bushman, living as nomadic hunters, never numbered more than a half-million.

Metal defeated them. The Iron Age ended their domination of southern Africa. With corn, cattle, and iron for spearheads and arrows, the Bantu Negro tribes multiplied rapidly, crossed equatorial Africa during the zenith of the Roman Empire and invaded southern Africa.

Although the Bushman mixed and traded with the Bantu, they never became an iron-age people. They took little from the culture of the black Africans. Rather than change, they chose to die and become extinct across most of Africa. Why? What could a people have that was more important than life itself? Chuck wanted to find out. If he was unable to go into the Kalahari with ᴊᴄɪ, he would go alone, with his wife and son.

He had a company-issued Toyota Land Cruiser with an open box, for his personal use. Packed with supplies, a 45-gallon drum of fuel and another of water, they left Barberton for Gaborone, the capital of Botswana. From there, he drove northwest into the heart of the Kalahari Desert.

At a dusty way station comprised of a few baked clay huts and a couple of bleached grey cement buildings, they picked up an African ranger as a guide. He was of mixed Bantu and Bushman parentage. Together the four went off into the desert, hunting for Bushmen. San.

There were roads through the country, dirt tracks that had been game trails for millennia, but the land was open, barren scrub and they were able to travel freely, making their own trails.

In the heat of the day the ground, almost too hot to walk on under a blistering sun, seemed devoid of life, but its creatures were only in hiding, waiting for the cooler currents of evening to stir their energies. The land undulated gently, its sandy surfaces held together with the roots of burnt grasses, prickly thorn scrub and acacia. Here and there, where water levels were accessible by deeply penetrating root systems, much larger trees dominated the scrub.

These were the "thirstlands," where annual rainfall was less than 26 centimetres. Blowing sands dominated the Kalahari only to the southwest. To the north lived the !Kung Bushman of Namibia, whose homeland on the border with Botswana allowed them to cross over into the Okavango Delta. An inland delta, the Okavango River never reached the sea, instead it flowed out of Angola and drained into a huge expanse of tsetse-fly infested swamplands during the rainy season.

Well to the south of the swamplands, their guide took them into the Central Kalahari Reserve and, towards evening, they found a young San woman alone in the scrub, kneeling on the earth with her hands clasped together as though in supplication. She rose to her feet on their arrival and watched them, her expression impassive.

Through the dust and waves of heat lifting off the plain, the sun, sitting low on the horizon, was a bloated fireball, shimmering like a mirage. In its warm glow, her body seemed to be a source of radiant energy itself. Her skin, exposed from birth to the sun, wind and dust storms, had a dry, worn look to it, but her eyes were clear and her body lean-muscled. Long-legged and golden, she was stunning.

The guide, advising them to keep their distance, approached alone and spoke to the girl in the strange click-language of the San. As she talked, she showed not the least anxiety over her situation, alone on the African savannah at the approach of night. Perhaps nineteen, she had an antelope hide tied over one shoulder, which swept down across her chest, leaving her shoulders and one breast bare. Apart from this simple garment she was without any clothing, shelter, or weapons.

After awhile, the guide walked back and reported that she had agreed to take them to her father's camp. Cautioning them again to be on their best behaviour, they were off. The San did not encourage contact with the outside world and would simply melt away into the desert if the meeting was not entirely to their liking.

The "camp" was a small structure made of sticks, barely a windbreak to lie under. Chuck approached with the gift of a water bottle and a knife, and communicating through their guide, asked the headman if they might camp nearby. The old Bushman pointed out a tall dead tree a half-mile away. Chuck was discouraged by the location but the old man was not comfortable with them any closer. After they had set up their own camp, Chuck invited the Bushman family to join them for dinner.

To Chuck's surprise the entire Bushman clan arrived later that evening to eat. The next morning, in the cool, misty-blue dawn, they were back again for breakfast. If it was only the food attracting them, that was enough. The Bushmen continued to make contact and after a few days, invited Chuck and his family to join them. Gradually, a comfort level developed in which each group felt at ease in the other's camp and they began to plan activities together.

Being accepted by the Bushmen, for Chuck, was the realization of a dream. Since childhood, he had loved the open country – the Alberta prairie, the British Columbia mountains, the Yukon alpine – but he had been usually alone in those spaces. His society, generally, saw natural landscapes in terms of recreation or, worse, wasteland.

Here, in Africa, among the Bushmen, was a different view. Although there were risks and dangers, so confident were the Bushmen in their own ability to deal effectively with their environment that Chuck was able to relax completely, and endeavour to see the world as they did.

A distinctive people, they were small in stature and narrow-headed, healthy, lithe, light-boned and leanly-muscled. Their hair, in tufts, was curled tightly. When they moved, barefoot over the ground, their steps were light; tireless, they preferred to squat while resting rather than to sit heavily.

Most unusual of all were their colouring and features. They were not Negroid, but Asiatic-looking. Their golden yellow skin, high cheekbones and Mongolian slanted eyes gave them a Nepalese appearance and early speculation was that this was the original Asian race. But it was not so; the striking similarities were coincidental. They were in fact the oldest race in Africa. It was from this common stock that subsequent groups emerged. The Bushman was nearest to the prototype of African man, and his connectedness to the natural world was a marvel.

Chuck loved being out in the open country with them. A creature of the earth, the whole of the Kalahari was as their skin. They had complete mastery over it. Spending their days on foot, wandering the thin acacia thornveld, they searched the desert for edible roots and tubers. Extremely capable hunters, it was from plants, however, that they received most of their sustenance and virtually all their water. Stopping at the least-likely-looking plant – a shrivelled-up little tentacle protruding from the parched ground – the Bushmen would gather around and with long, hardened, digging sticks follow the plant down for two feet to uncover a beet-like bulb called "bi" which they would then place carefully into an antelope-leather pouch. Later, back at the camp, they would crush the bi bulbs, filling ostrich eggshells with the extracted fluid. Aside from Chuck's water tank, it was their principal source of drinking water.

While Marlene remained nearer the camp with Mark, Chuck went out daily on the foraging expeditions, searching for berries from the brandybush plant, nuts, baobab seeds, leaves from the Transvaal Aloe, and Cucumis tubers. Everything was used. Dozens of plants were edible. Some were poisons, but even poisons had value.

Occasionally, in the distance, they spotted gemsbok, the antelope watching them as keenly as they watched the creatures, but the Bushmen hunters chose not to go after them. Chuck's own larder was enough for them all, and while he remained, their daily foraging expeditions were more out of routine than necessity. They were often followed by jackals. Small carnivores, with a similar size and appearance to coyotes, they would watch from a safe distance. When the men moved on, after a rest, they would scout the site looking for the remains of a kill or anything edible left behind.

For several days, the men tracked a leopard, just as Chuck had once tracked a mountain lion through the mountains behind his father's farm in British Columbia. By night, when the leopard hunted, they camped, sleeping together on the hard ground; by day, when it rested, they followed its tracks across the baking savannah, stepping in its steps, using the cover it used, hunting it in its own hunting grounds. Armed with bows and arrow tips poisoned with the juice of deadly beetle larvae, they moved sprightly over the land in an even, unhurried way, covering ground steadily. But the leopard, knowing it was being hunted, kept ahead of them. Eventually they broke off the chase and returned to the camp and their waiting families.

The Bushmen were only afraid of one animal: the lion. And they were only afraid at night. During the day, they could deal with the big cats; at night, the lions had the advantage.

Still, they went out sometimes into the darkness to hunt. Moving with them through the scrub, in the cool starlight was exhilarating – an experience of senses keenly-tuned and nerves alive to every sound and smell and movement.

In South Africa, visiting the game parks, he had been required to remain with his family inside large fenced compounds at night for security. There, one was forever a stranger, an alien, observing – no matter how close one got in fact – from a "distance". Here, beyond that frontier, Chuck hunted alongside the Bushmen. With their stone-age tools, they were the dominant life force. They knew it, and quietly revelled in their ability to command their world. Here, living off the land, sleeping on it, subject to its timeless rules was an intimate experience in being.

On the last night their small group was joined by another family. The younger women were standing off to one side of the fire, talking and laughing among themselves. Clad as the first San woman had been, with skin robes draped over one shoulder, they were lean and fit, confident and comfortable in the desert surroundings. In the light from the fire their partial nakedness, their provocative poses, their womanly features, all evoked responses in the young men, fuelling desire the way the sun's heat rakes thunder storms from the earth. The sheer physicalness of the body, an exquisite experience.

Playing his bow like a Jew's harp, striking the string with an arrow and fashioning sounds with his mouth, the old Bushman began to play for them. Respectfully, the women broke up their group and arranged themselves around the fire wherever space permitted. One, seating herself beside Chuck, brushed a smooth-skinned bare shoulder against him as a twanging, musical vibration, undulating like the land forms, gave wistful expression to the Bushman's spirit.

With the African ranger translating, the old man interspersed his bow playing with stories how the Great God left the land to live in the sky, how he transformed those left behind into the peoples and creatures of the world. The earth itself was alive. In the freshness of night, under the huge desert sky, Chuck watched the old Bushman as he recounted his clan's lore, the legends and the myths, in his ancient language. For countless ages, his people were masters of the world. It provided them still with all they needed. Everything within it had meaning and purpose, and a kinship with everything else. The San had achieved their place in the universe and resisted change. Already one with the wind, there was nowhere else to go. Theirs was the world that modern man, with mining and metals and a new religion, had left behind. As Chuck, reluctantly, had to do as well.

CHAPTER THIRTY-SIX

THE PEARL OF AFRICA

I myself consider myself the most important person in the world

—IDI AMIN, 1971

CHUCK had crated their belongings, shipped them off to Canada and left South Africa. While Marlene and Mark flew to Nairobi, Chuck had gone alone, to Zomba, the capital of Malawi, to see the famous Zambian copper belt – of particular interest to a geologist specializing in copper formations. After South Africa, it was a joy to be free again. Unemployed, footloose and uncommitted.

Chuck's unusual sleep patterns gave him an advantage over others. Falling asleep instantly anywhere, any time – and then waking after only a short period, he was refreshed and ready to carry on. Relying solely on "power naps," he could work for a couple of weeks without a single full-night's sleep.

He met up with Marlene and Mark in Nairobi. To save money they took a room in a hotel which rented by the hour. In the centre of Nairobi's prostitute district, it was seedy but cheap. A radical change from Barberton.

Having been away from Marlene a few days, he greeted her with the same thrill he had felt in her company when they were younger. His desire for his wife was not the least diminished by the years they had spent together, their intimate relationship remained exciting and passionate.

In the morning they rented a car, crossed into Tanzania and drove to the base of Mount Kilimanjaro. There, they passed into the security of the Longito Ruby Mine and then the Tanzanite Gem Mine, where Chuck spent hours examining the formations, taking notes and buying rubies and tanzanite gem stones.

Leaving the mines considerably lighter in cash resources, they travelled west into the Great Rift Valley, which was slowly breaking off east Africa from the continent as it had broken off Madagascar. The elation at being free again continued to buoy Chuck; released from the constraints of work and the repressive rule of South Africa, he flowed with unbounded enthusiasm. On top of the world, he was once more feeling invincible.

Arriving at dusk in the Serengeti plains, they began a futile search for a occupied campground, but they were empty. As it grew darker, he gave up looking and in a deserted spot began to set up the small pup tent he had bought to conserve their remaining funds.

Working under their car's headlights, driving in tent pegs, they noticed some movement at the edge of the light. There, framed in golden-tan against the blackness of the night, stood a couple of lions, watching them.

Instantly, Marlene was back inside the car with Mark. "I'm not sleeping outside with that!" she yelled, when Chuck called her to come back.

Ignoring the lions as their eyes gleamed in the reflection from the headlights, Chuck went on pounding in a couple more pegs. *Whack.* Movement from out of the night once again caught his attention: more lions. Fanned out, around the edge of the light, they were forming a circle – with him at its centre.

Still intent on camping out, Chuck continued to set up his tent. *Whack.* Keeping an eye on the majestic beasts. *Whack.* The earth was baked clay, unyielding. *Whack.* Another peg forced in. The lions were inching closer. Marlene yelled at him to get in the car. He held his ground. *Whack.* One of the lions crouched down, pressing itself flat against the earth. Then another went to ground. Their eyes fixed on him. They were huge animals. Wild, healthy and supremely muscled.

Marlene, from the car, continued yelling.

He wasn't going to leave. *Whack.* He wouldn't. *Whack.* He had something to prove. Marlene could sleep in the car if she wanted to, but he was staying in the tent. *Whack.*

All the lions were now pressed against the ground. Chuck knew they were not adverse to taking human flesh. George Harrison, the immigrant who had discovered the Witwatersrand gold field, had been caught by lions while hiking out into the eastern Transvaal. And eaten.

Chuck didn't want to give in. He hated to act out of fear. They were belly-crawling towards him.

Marlene was screaming.

"Am I going to run," he asked himself, "or be brave?" After all these years, he still wanted Marlene to see him as her hero: fearless.

The nearest lions were less than eight metres away, tightening the circle. They seemed ready to spring. Concluding that to remain on the plain any longer would probably be his last act, he ran. He ripped the tent from the ground with one motion, and darted with it into the car.

They drove until they found a hotel. No private toilet. No showers. Not even running water. A cement-block room with cots. Priced the same as at a five-star hotel in Johannesburg, one night's stay was the equivalent of an African's average yearly income. There were no options, they were too exhausted to argue. The exploitation of people in need had changed colour, but not philosophy.

To the east, near the town of Shinyanga, south of the swamplands of Lake Victoria, the Maduai diamond mine that had been developed in the 1930s was producing $10 million annually. Its production too low to interest him, Chuck decided to skip it; he had another mine to visit. After a few more days in the Serengeti, they returned to Nairobi to advise the Canadian Embassy of their travel plans – to the Kilembe Copper mines in Uganda.

"Absolutely not! It's strictly forbidden!" the Canadian staff officer insisted.

They had met him already before the trip to Tanzania. With South African stamps in their passports, there were several African nations that would never allow them entry. The Canadian Embassy issued them new "sanitized" passports. But the rules of travel to Uganda were clear: No Entry.

"Idi Amin's a killer. We can't allow Canadians into a country where their lives are at risk, and believe me, there's absolutely nothing we will do to protect you! You're not allowed to enter Uganda; it's that simple!"

Leaving Nairobi the next morning, their train was stopped at the Ugandan border by Amin's soldiers, who worked their way through the cars. Upon seeing Marlene, they announced she was not allowed to enter the country. It was one of Amin's new edicts. Just before their arrival, he had officially sanctioned polygamy in order to legitimize his marriages to four women, two of whom he later killed. To create a mask of official modesty, he had recently decreed that women should only wear long dresses. Marlene's dress was now too short for finely tuned Ugandan sensibilities! Marlene quickly changed into a longer dress and the train was allowed to continue, clanking and hammering its way around the swampy papyrus lowlands of Lake Victoria's north shore to Kampala, the capital of the "Pearl of Africa." Uganda was the blessed nation – the most favourable spot on earth.

By the time Chuck arrived, almost all foreign nationals had been quietly evacuated from Uganda and most of the embassies shut down. No one was safe. Even the American Embassy was leaving. Understanding the risks, only a few missionaries remained, together with a handful of expats who continued to work the mines. Near the Ugandan border with Zaire, the Kilembe Copper mine was still in production. Chuck was determined to see it, even though he had to cross all Uganda to get there.

They took a hotel in central Kampala. Tourists and business travellers having disappeared completely, they had their choice of rooms and the rates were extremely reasonable. It was now permanently off-season.

No more concerned for their safety than he was when exploring the bushveld of South Africa or the plains of Tanzania, Chuck took Marlene and Mark out for a stroll around the city. While the inner city was composed of modern office buildings, high-rise apartments and hotels, many of Kampala's side streets and market areas retained the character of another time. Red-tiled colonial buildings, rusting tin roofs, clay earth roads full of growing potholes which no one would repair. Electric power was sporadic and full of surges. Tap water potable under British rule was now unsafe. Large posters of Amin were pasted over building walls and raised on billboards. Everywhere they went, Amin's face followed them. Public executions were now a daily feature of life in Kampala, but their wanderings through the old town didn't lead them to any. They took pictures of colonial buildings like the British Kampala Club and the massive Imperial Hotel, its high, ornately decorated ceilings held up with Romanesque pillars and arches, reflecting a more stable and prosperous era. The white patrons and club members had since departed, but the stamp of the British Empire had been imprinted on the city and was still visible.

Previously, Kampala had had an international flavour. The Asian population had provided the city with its commercial life. Their business skills ran the plantations, marketed coffee, tea and sugar, and filled the shops with merchandise and trade goods. The streets, now almost empty, had once thronged with shoppers. The soldiers now in charge were incapable of plucking a tea leaf or picking a coffee bean, and the plantations they had seized were quickly going to ruin. Those stores not yet boarded up by their new owners were meagre and barren. Shelves, once emptied, could not be restocked. Where were new goods to be found?

A sense of gloom and fear pervaded the streets. The threat of death was in every soldier who eyed them suspiciously as they walked by. They were watched everywhere – a white family wandering Kampala taking photographs.

Behaving no differently than he had in the savannah, Chuck confronted the soldiers directly. In Africa, the possession of a spear or machete had long been a symbol of manhood. Once introduced, European rifles became the new symbol, and those who owned one had special status. Guns were the new law, and their owners cradled them lovingly. Chuck understood all that and was not intimidated. His year in Africa had bolstered his confidence. He felt comfortable dealing one-on-one with these soldiers, even those with machine guns. As in confrontations with the armed Natives in West Irian, as long as one did not demonstrate any fear, the reactions of the soldiers could be "controlled." They were no different from the Swazis he had worked with in Barberton, or the hundreds of other Africans he had hiked with through the bush in Rhodesia, Namibia and Botswana.

Ignoring them was dangerous; Chuck engaged them instead. Walking right up to them with Mark in tow, forcing a broad, practised smile, he pretended to demonstrate to his son the virtues these soldiers possessed, flattering them with questions about their units and weapons. Mark was genuinely interested in their guns, mostly modern automatic rifles. Over and over, as the soldiers showed off the guns, they relaxed, fell to boasting, and even became protective towards their admirers.

In the evening, as the sun slipped down and the air cooled, the heat rising in waves off the vast swampy grasslands of Lake Victoria's shoreline, full of moisture, turned to a mist which enveloped Kampala. Rolling in with a clammy embrace, obscuring detail, it changed the nature of the city completely. As elsewhere in ancient Africa, Kampala at night was a dangerous time. Instead of the sounds of shorebirds or night-flying insect eaters, sporadic gunfire punctuated the night. At dawn, the sunshine burned off the mists, and the city was the same. Edgy. Eerily calm.

From Kampala, they rode west on the old colonial steam-fired train, passing abandoned coffee and tea plantations as they travelled towards Zaire. Near the mountainous border, the train rattled through the Katonga Game Reserve, across the swamplands north of Lake George to the edge of the Ruwenzori Mountains and Queen Elizabeth National Park. Once, huge herds of wild game had been managed under British rule for the sport of wealthy big-game hunters, whose payment of hunting fees kept the parks healthy. The sport hunters were gone now, and the soldiers were loose on the plains. Having grown accustomed to killing people – for Amin, for their own sport, for wallets and rings – they turned easily to big game, using machine guns to slaughter wild beasts for ivory, hides and meat. Amin's armies were killing everything.

Dave Hadoto was a Ugandan African who had obtained a geology degree from the University of British Columbia along with a wife before returning home to work at Falconbridge's giant copper mine at Kilembe, nationalized by President Obote before Amin seized control. Chuck and Marlene had been guests at Dave's wedding in Vancouver and Chuck had maintained a correspondence with him since their university days.

They stayed with Dave, spending the days touring the mine and the nights with people who whispered about the horrors, risking their lives just to speak them aloud. Kilembe was entrenched in a bunker mentality. It held one of the last pockets of expatriates in the country, mostly Canadian and British employees of the previously Canadian-owned mine. The only topic of conversation after dinner was "politics." The politics of dictatorship. Even after everything they had witnessed, they were still in denial "How can one man and a small army of thugs be allowed to completely destroy a nation?" The very idea was anathema to them.

The killings however were real, and the fear widespread. There was only one solution they could see: remove the threat.

"Kill Amin," they whispered.

But who would do it? Nobody within Uganda had the means. And outside Uganda, who cared? Moreover, it was against international convention to 'interfere' in the private affairs of nations. Mass murderers, even ex-sergeants who seized control by mutinous means, were no less than Kings and Czars, sacrosanct once they reached the top echelon of power. Still, there was only one way to set the people free: "Kill Amin."

They repeated it like a mantra, no differently than revolutionaries elsewhere had dreamed the same heresies of freedom from oppression and an end to dictatorship.

The men, talking quietly in the night, voicing their hopes, were all afraid, nervously advocating rebellion, words which would have sent them to Makindye Prison if repeated outside. Worse than a bullet were the tortures which increasingly preceded death. Amin's killers were getting better at keeping their victims alive longer. The sexual tortures they had for women were even worse than those for men. But talking late into the night around the floor of the living room and smoking smuggled cigarettes from Zaire was their only resistance. They were too civilized to take action. Or too frightened.

It was a testament to their careers that these expats remained. Through nationalization, dictatorship and terror, they stayed with their jobs, prisoners of fear, clinging to what little security they had rather than leave with their lives.

After several days, Chuck decided against recrossing Uganda to return to Kenya. Instead, through Dave, he arranged to rent a four-wheel-drive jeep from the mine. He was not yet ready to leave. There was an entire race of people living here he had also come to meet, the Forest Pygmies. Chuck had few preconceived notions. He was attracted to cultures whose personal values and connectedness to the natural world struck a chord, but a "romantic" he was not – far from it. He was a hard pragmatist. Native pagan cultures had much he could not live with, yet they embodied unique wisdom gained over millennia and offered insights and compelling visions of the physical and spiritual realms. Chuck had fundamental doubts about his own place in society, and about "modern" values. Was society moving in the right direction? Or was it built on false foundations? Most importantly of all, was there another, better, way?

Chuck was not discouraged or intimidated by the politics of Uganda. He knew how to handle soldiers. He had a jeep and excellent maps of the region from Dave Hadoto. If he could get his family past the soldiers, he would find the pygmies. Following the border with Zaire, he drove the family north, into the primal heart of Uganda.

By nightfall he was on a track leading them deep into the equatorial rain forest. Beyond the soldiers, they were now on their own. No gas stations, stores or services. Barely a road. They were creeping slowly into the unknown. Chuck, advancing on the strength of his own instincts and faith was fully committed to following his own heart into the darkest corners of the world.

One of the men from the nights at Dave's, a prisoner of fear, had asked Chuck what he would do if he could do anything at all he wanted. Chuck, somewhat puzzled by the question, answered honestly, "I'm doing it."

They spent the night pitched on the soggy trail in their pup tent, and encountered no other persons. Following a series of rutted dirt tracks encroached by tendrils of vegetation, they came at last to their goal, a collection of beehive-shaped, leaf-covered, small huts in the rain forest – a pygmy village. As the jeep broke out of the forest cover into the little clearing, they were quickly encircled, the pygmies excitedly talking at them, brushing against them, as they climbed from the jeep. Dark as the Bantu Africans, the largest among them was no taller than four-and-a-half feet.

Chuck had prepared for contact loaded down with gifts for the villagers: pots, shirts, sandals and tobacco. The women, large-breasted and shorter than the men, jostled for position. Their noses were broad and their hair, an unnecessary cover in the jungle, was thin.

The gift giving over, the Fipkes were made welcome and shown to a hut.

One of the original five races of Africa, the Forest Pygmies remained in the grip of a stone-age culture of nomadic hunting and gathering. Their villages were easily dismantled and moved, or abandoned. Like the Bushman, they, too, traded with Bantu Africans for iron spears, arrowheads and metal ornaments, but their culture was entirely their own, with separate roots back into antiquity. Secure for thousands of years in the cover of the forest, they were now feeling the pressure of the world outside. The Bantu population, doubling every couple of decades, was encroaching on their forests, forcing the pygmies to retreat deeper and deeper into the diminishing equatorial jungles.

There were few old people among them. The forest was bountiful and starvation rare, but when disease set in, as it did regularly, debilitating whole villages and preventing them from collecting food, they quickly succumbed.

Marlene stayed behind in the village in the morning when Chuck went out and kept her eye on Mark, who spent his time with the pygmy children practising their spear throwing. For Marlene, living in a grass hut at the edge of the jungle and pounding strange roots to prepare meals with the pygmy women was challenge enough.

Under the jungle canopy, the air was heavy with moisture but not unpleasant. Moving in single file along a faint trail, their small frames worked rapidly through tangles of creepers and stalks that stopped Chuck. He had to work to stay with them, concentrating on his footing. Stinging ants, snakes, poisonous beetles and dangerous plants were sidestepped by barefooted pygmies who sometimes forgot to point them out to Chuck. But he kept up, refusing to be outdone. Out of the sun's searing rays, the darkened forest floor was spongy wet and, with a temperature in the mid-eighties, relatively cool.

The men, hunting for monkey, fowl, bushbucks and bongos – anything they could kill with their poisoned arrows, but the bigger the better – moved silently, aware of every movement in the forest around them, no matter how slight. Some of the village women followed with baskets, collecting plants and roots that were unknown in the modern world but having properties valued by the pygmies. Nothing killed, but their baskets filled, they returned to the village. This was the daily round, men and women emptying out of the village most mornings to forage for food, returning in the early afternoons to prepare evening meals, and afterwards, free to dance all night. All night and into the next day, if they wished, sometimes sleeping past noon.

They worked little. The forest gave them food, shelter and medicine – even an assortment of drugs, which they used both recreationally and religiously. Marijuana, harvested from the wild, was smoked constantly. Emotional and spontaneous, pygmy life had an easy rhythm and time spent with them passed quickly. Unlike the Bushmen, who were almost serene, the pygmies were volatile, daily demonstrating a whole range of human passions. Exploding with emotional energy when they were entertained, they laughed with their whole bodies, giving themselves completely to their mirth. Angry, their hostility was equally unrestrained. They fought viciously with one another in the camp over the slightest provocation.

Chuck enjoyed their company. Communication, although they spoke no common language, flowed easily; they shared jokes and laughed frequently. The days were adventures on the hunt. Stalking through the forest beneath giant African mahoganies and an understory of oil palms, the pygmies were masters of the forest. And of the night. It was in the dark, after the reality of the forest faded, that the inner world of the pygmy emerged.

It began with the preparation of dinner. *Thump*. Manioc was ground down in large wooden bowls. *Thump*. The steady pounding of wood-on-wood provided a background for song. *Thump.* As the women worked around their smoky fires, the music would begin. *Thump.* Voices floated from the darkness, haunting melodies and high, pure sounds, as though the forest spirits themselves were singing.

The music gathered momentum. Drums joined in, laying down complex cross-rhythms with the voices. Then, harplike string instruments took their turn, as the men and children, carried away, added their voices. Pausing to eat, they continued again, bamboo pan-flutes taking up the song where it had been left. The pygmies lived with spirits and magic and sorcery. Ever-present, the spirits could cause death, but they also gave life. The music played to both worlds, integrating the ethereal with the physical. Songs to appease the forest spirits, songs to solicit their guidance. Songs for the hunt, women's songs and men's songs. Songs for birth and death, and love. A young woman rose up to dance and the others, encouraging her, crowded around, giving voice to her physical expressions. The movement of her body, sensual and erotic, had its own language, communicating motherhood and uninhibited sexual passion.

Enticing their guests to join in, the pygmies danced with them in the night, through the shadows of flickering firelight. There were no limits to imagination, no boundaries or controls. Intoxicated by the mysteries of the night and by marijuana, the music and the dance lifted them all higher and higher, until the energy they reached enveloped everything, connecting each to the other as the depths of their souls were turned inside out and flowed into the night, personal and infinite.

Chuck danced in a sweat-soaked frenzy with the pygmies in the heat of the jungle. He danced until nothing else mattered, until past and future ceased to exist and the intensity of being became so strong that there was only one reality: this moment, this movement, this night which seemed to last forever, pounding out a physical rhythm, liberating pure feeling. They danced until exhausted, rested, made love, and then danced again as more drums were added. Gleaming like polished ebony, black skin wet with sweat, the villagers seethed with forces unknown outside the forest as the drumming went on, hour after hour.

They danced until the first rays of dawn's light cracked the darkness of the eastern sky to reveal a misty morning. With the towering ghostlike forms of trees looming over them, they fell asleep, nearly delirious, on grass mats to a screaming chorus of daytime insects playing out their own song.

Wilder still were the spirit dances that took place before the elephant hunt – three days and three nights of ritual dancing and spirit appeasement.

Smaller than the savannah elephants, with rounded ears and shorter tusks, the forest elephant was still a large and formidable creature. Hunting them with primitive weapons was dangerous. Sometimes men were killed. When a herd was encountered, a lone hunter would sneak right up alongside the animals and slash the hamstrings of an elephant's back leg. His job done, the hunter would dash back for safety while the rest of the party would burst out of hiding, yelling and screaming to frighten the herd away from the wounded animal. Alone and crippled, the elephant would slowly be toppled with spears and arrows.

The ceremonies for the elephant hunt began as on other occasions. During the day, the harps played as the village rested from the heat, only the flies displaying any vigorous energy. But towards evening, when the drums started, the reality of the barefoot, earthen village was transformed as if by magic. Animal spirits in the vaguely human forms of pygmy dancers, emerged from the forest around them. Great, lumbering creatures, they rushed through the darkness on four legs, circling the fires and the huts, as the children drew near the adults for protection. Powerful and agile, bodies pale with clay, draped in skins, beating the earth, the spirits spun about the village in time to the drums, moving frenetically between the people, drawing them deeper into their rituals, uniting the world of spirit, man, and beast in a ceremony that had survived from the dawn of human history.

They ate, smoked, slept and danced for three days, then they set off, in single file, their small dark bodies moving rapidly through the forest along ancient trails. There was honour to be gained from the hunt. The prize, hundreds of pounds of meat and fat, was the greatest in their world. The pygmies had no use for the tusks. The Bantu Africans, however, were keen to acquire them and the ivory was easily traded for almost anything the pygmies desired.

Chuck desperately hoped they would not encounter any elephants. He had nothing but respect for these gentle giants and to see one killed, even by pygmies with arrows and spears, was not an event he wanted to participate in.

The men were in a festive mood. Moving around immense trees and through groves of flowering plants saturated with sweet fragrances and birdsong, the jungle had a delightful accessibility and beauty, revealed solely by the pygmies' intimacy with its secrets.

As they searched for elephant spoor, they allowed themselves to be diverted by choice edibles, constantly gathering and eating food as they travelled – small sour fruits, nuts, grubs which, to Chuck, had a pasty starchy flavour, bitter leaves and certain sweet flowers. A flight of bees always stopped them – honey, like elephant meat, being a treasure of the highest order. There were several species of honeybees in the forest, some viciously aggressive, others passive and without stingers. Honey, when it was found, was devoured immediately, uncontrollably, the men seemingly oblivious to the stings they suffered. For water, they would stoop and drink from the surface of the numerous streams they crossed or from shallow pools filled with quicksilver fingerling fish.

The hunters moved steadily westward and crossed the border without pausing, entering Zaire. For the pygmies, the Uganda-Zaire border meant nothing. For a white man hunting elephant with them, the border had an altogether different significance. To be caught within Zaire without documents would present a problem. Chuck kept the problem to himself. He could never, in any event, have found his way back alone. That they knew where they were, navigating without obvious physical features to guide them, was as remarkable a feat as the Bushmen navigating the Kalahari. Without the pygmies, Chuck would have quickly perished. To see any distance through the forest, the pygmies did not rise up but lay down on the ground instead. Visibility was best from the ground, although generally, fifty yards was the outside limit, so dense was the growth.

The forest elephant was an elusive creature. The hunters stopped often to examine feeding sites to determine how long it had been since their quarry had passed. Heavy with the breath of the forest, the rich air sharpened the senses and they were all vigilant. Not only the men but the whole forest seemed to Chuck to be listening. And watching. As they passed, the shrill of insect life around them ceased, the insects sensitive to the tiniest of vibrations in the still space. Both man and creature were alert to the life around them.

It was easy to see where the elephants had been. Eating several hundred pounds of bark and foliage each day, a feeding elephant in a herd cleared large openings in the forest. But the hunters never got nearer to the animals than their spoor.

After several days on the trail the men turned back. Chuck was lucky. They had killed some shy and clear-eyed Colbus and Vervet monkeys with poisoned arrows and surprised several small duiker and bushpig, which the men chased into their nets and speared, but to Chuck's relief, they didn't kill any elephants.

They hadn't found any.

CHAPTER THIRTY-SEVEN

BUJUMBURA

Marlene and Chuck parted company with the pygmies after a month, Chuck with a bundle of pygmy artifacts. Retracing their steps to the Kilembe mine, Chuck returned the jeep to Dave, and then with his family, crossed the nearby western border of Uganda into Zaire.

Formerly the Democratic Republic of the Congo, formerly Congo-Kinshasa, formerly the Belgian Congo, formerly Congo-Leopoldville, Zaire had a tortured colonial history and was, now, firmly under the military dictatorship of General and President Mobutu Sese Seke. Another "President-for-Life," his ruthless exercising of power to further his own personal interests set the standard for his troops who, loyal followers, found it expedient to do the same. As almost everywhere in Africa, it was the soldiers the people feared most – the men with the guns.

Chuck, Marlene and Mark spent the night in Beni. They were now in the Congo River watershed, the Zaïre. Draining a region almost the size of western Europe, the river basin was one of the most inhospitable areas of the world, a vast land of river, swamp and jungle.

Due west of Beni, connected by road, was the old town of Stanleyville, rechristened, like the Congo River, with a new African name, Kisangi. South of Beni, they passed an old Belgium road marker indicating the exact location of the equator. Riding in the open box of a truck until dark, Chuck and Marlene were dropped off at the edge of the road near a small settlement, where they were directed for shelter to the only "hotel" in the region. A mud hut, it was without water, electricity or even windows. A single door opened into a darkened earth interior with a small supply of candles for light. During the night, with Mark sleeping between them, rats scurried over them in search of food; futilely they tried to keep them out. Worse than the rodents themselves were the fleas they carried. Vectors for crippling disease, flea bites were as common in the towns as mosquito bites.

In the morning, another open truck carried them further south. Standing to the wind, watching the world rush by, feeling the splash of warm air across their faces like a cleansing shower was an elixir after their miserable night confined with rats.

Chuck loved travelling; Marlene – nearly as much – was getting used to it. And Mark, old enough now to make his own friends, was becoming more able to take care of himself.

Jammed into local buses, riding the backs of open trucks and jungle taxis, they passed through Butembo, Luofu, Rutshuru, Goma and Kalehe on the way to Bukavu, a Zaire town at the south end of Lake Kivu on the border with Rwanda.

Although the names were all new, many of the towns had been built during Belgian colonial rule and still retained an old-world European elegance, set incongruously against a third-world African background. Others had been sacked and burned during the Congo revolt, leaving empty ruined shells of buildings flanking the streets. They would never be rebuilt.

At Bukavu, they took a room, hired a local guide and went off in search of mountain gorillas. Their first day, mostly on foot, they searched the slopes of the mountains draining into the Ulindi River, a tributary of the Lualaba which flowed, like all the rivers, into the Congo-Zaïre.

On their second day, they found fresh spoor. Following a trail of excrement up a mountainside, their guide quietly signalled that they were close. The droppings were still warm to the touch.

The gorillas were up in the trees, feeding. Huge animals, they did not swing from tree to tree like monkeys, but climbed down to the ground and travelled overland from tree to tree, moving slowly. Generally peaceful, the gorillas occasionally did attack and were quite capable of inflicting serious injury or death.

Chuck moved in as close as he could. Standing right in their midst as they came down a tree, he was photographing them as he would friends, when a large male descended the trunk hidden from view. Stepping out from behind the tree, the gorilla rushed towards Chuck, stopping no more than two metres away, and let out a mighty roar.

"Auughhhhwww!"

Glaring malevolently at Chuck, the gorilla, easily two or three times Chuck's size, rapidly beat on his chest in a fierce display of power. Chuck's heart started racing. He got the message. His adrenaline soaring, Chuck quickly stepped backwards, putting more distance between them.

Chuck spent as much time as he could with the gorillas. As long as he kept his distance the gorillas tolerated his presence, man and beast studying each other with equanimity.

They were preparing to leave Bukavu when Mark got sick, showing symptoms of dysentery, a dangerous illness for a child in Africa. Arrangements were made to catch the once-weekly Air Zaire flight from Bukavu to Bujumbura, the capital of neighbouring Burundi. There they hoped to be able to secure a proper diagnosis and treatment for Mark.

At the airport, they had cleared customs and were waiting to board when, just before the plane was scheduled to depart, President Mobutu Sese Seke, had all the passengers' tickets cancelled and commandeered the plane to fly his private party to a secret destination.

Desperately concerned with their son's illness, Chuck and Marlene looked for other routes out, but there were none. Back to Uganda overland would take days, and the horrific inside-stories detailed by Dave Hadoto had convinced Chuck not to risk a second crossing through Amin's realm. Overland from Bukavu to Kinshasa would be even more torturous, and in the wrong direction. With only one flight leaving Bukavu each week, they had no choice but to wait.

It was a difficult week. Losing their son in Africa became a real possibility. Mark was seriously ill, yet all they could do was to keep him hydrated. With African children, as with adults, death was a constant presence. Among the pygmies, half of all children died, and for the adults 40 years was a long life. The Bantu fared a little better.

The next week, they arrived again at the airport and went to customs. This time the Zaire officials took umbrage at their haste to leave and tore into their bags. Chuck's rock samples and pouches of chalcopyrites poured out. Although brittle and lighter than gold, the chalcopyrite had a brilliant metallic lustre. Spilled over the hard counter the heavy golden-yellow mineral sands looked enough like gold to convince the soldiers that it was. Their reaction was immediate. Chuck was roughly arrested; he was a smuggler!

Two soldiers grabbed him. He resisted. More soldiers, yelling in French, rushed to control him, jabbing his ribs with their machine guns, threatening to shoot. Chuck tried to explain the misunderstanding – the samples were from his friend, Dave Hadoto, from the copper mine in Uganda, not gold from Zaire. They were even wrapped in newspaper from Kilembe in Uganda.

But he had the pygmy artifacts with him as well. And the pygmy areas of Zaire were all restricted zones. He had obviously been in the jungle a long time. Why? What was he doing there? The soldiers, understanding no English, refused to listen to him. Chuck became desperate. He couldn't allow them to drag him off, leaving Marlene with Mark, alone and sick in central Africa. The solders were unsympathetic. Mark's survival meant nothing to them. Dying children were a fact of life.

Chuck was well aware of the treatment other geologists had received in Zaire. While he was in Barberton, two Falconbridge geologists, sampling in Zaire, had been arrested crossing the border with ordinary sand samples. They were dragged off to spend three hard months in a Zaire prison, while their company tried in vain to have them released. Chuck had no company behind him and the Canadian government was notorious for offering little real assistance to its nationals. He was on his own.

The soldiers were not about to be bought off. Reflecting their government's hostility towards Americans, they were not looking for cash. Whatever money he had they would get anyway.

The blank passports, newly issued out of Nairobi, were also suspicious. Why did they have new passports? There were no tourists in eastern Zaire. Or in Uganda! White travellers had no legitimate business in Zaire, especially English-speaking "Americans"! What was his real business?

Everything looked bad. The plane was loading. The passengers who had cleared were leaving the airport. The soldiers kept their guns trained on Chuck, as they discussed what to do, waving the passports and examining his artifacts and the golden sands. He tried to interject, but they ignored him. He was a prisoner.

It suddenly got worse. They had been discussing the prisoner's wife and child and had now reached a new decision. Surrounding Marlene and Mark, the soldiers grabbed them as well. They, too, were now under arrest. The whole family was to be taken!

Chuck's protests could be heard throughout the airport. An elderly Belgian woman of obvious status, even in post-colonial Zaire, came to their rescue. She translated Chuck's protest and his explanations into French, which the customs officials understood, adding the weight of her own opinion in support of Chuck's innocence. The men with the machine guns were not impressed, however. The white woman had no rank with them. If anything, her intervention made them more aggressive. They began dragging the resisting Chuck towards the outside doors. The woman ran off, shouting a promise to Chuck that she'd try to locate a senior officer.

While the soldiers struggled with Chuck, Marlene looked on helplessly with Mark. A Zaire jail would finish him. Pleading, Chuck delayed them. The plane finished loading and readied for takeoff.

The woman returned finally with a general from the Zaire Army. Explaining quickly to Chuck that she had done all she could and could not miss the plane, she hurried off. The general spoke some English.

Chuck appealed to the officer, explaining his interest in geological samples and the soldiers' reasonable misunderstanding in believing the samples were gold. He had a wife and a sick child. They were tourists, not prospectors or smugglers, a family travelling together from Nairobi to see Uganda and Zaire.

Relenting, the general agreed at last to let them go. Smugglers, the officer reasoned aloud, did not travel with their families, or collect souvenirs. Overruling his men was the prerogative of rank, indeed it proved his position. Chuck and his family were set free, however, all their possessions except his camera, clothing and papers would stay.

Chuck didn't look back. Carrying Mark and running through the doors, he raced out on to the tarmac, where the plane had taxied for take-off. Its engines were already running up; the brakes on. It was an old DC-3 and he stood directly in front of it on the runway, waving his arm back and forth to get the pilot's attention. The pilot saw him and angrily gestured at him to get out of the way.

Chuck refused to move. A French pilot working with Air Zaire, the man was as hostile as the soldiers; Chuck couldn't care less. He wasn't leaving unless he could get on the plane. The pilot, cursing him through the glass, pulled the throttles back to idle the engines and then opened the doors, allowing them to climb aboard. Within a few minutes, they were airbound and flying over the Zaire border into Burundi.

They landed at Bujumbura, its capital, a slum city no better, except for its larger size, than Bukavu. Medical services in Burundi were virtually nonexistent. The Fipkes went instead to the Catholic Mission for help. The presence of a white family at the gate was cause enough for immediate admission to the large residence and seminary. The gatekeeper took them directly to meet the head of the mission, who was in the dining room eating lunch.

The doors opened. Marlene and Chuck, carrying Mark, stepped into the room and stopped, astonished at seeing a lavish banquet spread out across the table. With numerous meat dishes, breads, an assortment of vegetables, overflowing fruit bowls, wine bottles, expensive crystal glasses, china and cutlery, it was a feast. Opulence of this kind one expected to see in the dining room of JCI's head office, not in a Catholic mission in starving Burundi.

The priests and seminarians, all Africans, were even more shocked by the sudden penetration of their private inner sanctum. Caught in the sin of indulgence, they froze in their places, like deer in the night immobilised by the glare of headlights.

Deeply embarrassed, a couple of the men rushed to the door and ushered the family back out of sight. Marlene's Catholicism a ticket, the Fipkes were allowed to stay in a room for two days – upon payment of first-class hotel rates – until the next flight to Nairobi.

Chuck was looking forward to finally putting Africa behind them but, leaving Nairobi, presented yet another problem. Their original Nairobi-to-Rome tickets, arranged by Chuck while he was still in Australia, were now "stale-dated." Air Kenya, the carrier he had booked, refused to honour the tickets. The airline personnel, officious and typically African in sticking to the rules, gave Chuck no latitude and turned to the next customer in line, ignoring his protests.

The Italians rescued them. Alitalia had flights on the same route. With grace and no concern at all for the irregularity, they transferred the tickets, boarded them and flew the Fipkes to Rome.

Mark, on medication, was rapidly recovering.

Exhausted and robbed of their belongings they were, nevertheless, thrilled to be out of Africa.

PART FOUR

The Fire
Down Below

South America, 1975–1977

Won't you, sir, also try your hand at some contest?

—HOMER, *THE ODYSSEY*

CHAPTER THIRTY-EIGHT

THE CANADIAN PACIFIC RAILWAY

NEARLY broke, Chuck and his family landed in Montreal. Chuck flew on alone to Vancouver to begin looking for a job and Marlene and Mark purchased tickets from the Canadian Pacific Railway. A rail trip meant a long and tiresome journey across the huge country, but it was much cheaper than airfare. JCI had never paid well and after leaving South Africa, they'd spent nearly all their money.

The Canadian economy had worsened considerably since Chuck had been in the country four years earlier. The mining industry was in a state of paroxysmal withdrawal and new graduates were not finding jobs. Some of the geologists Chuck had gone to school with were now unemployed; some driving taxi-cabs and selling cars – on straight commission. But with the work experience he had accumulated, Chuck had no trouble securing a new job.

Like JCI, Cominco was a mining company with roots stretching back to the birth of the nation. Its history, like that of so many other giant companies, was inseparable from the lives of the men who had once ruled the young country and who for a time even shared the field in Africa with Cecil Rhodes.

When the British Pacific Colony of British Columbia agreed, in 1871, to join the Confederation of Canada, it did so on condition that the central government build a rail link across the vast prairie of central Canada – from sea to sea. It was a business opportunity with potential. Anxious to secure the contract Hugh Allen, knighted that year by Queen Victoria and owner of the Montreal Ocean Steamship Company and several Nova Scotia coal mines, resorted to bribery.

It worked. Secretly financed by American railroad money, Allen put up $360,000 and his men were in on the rail link – but it didn't last. When Sir John A. Macdonald's Conservative government, sensitive to the political issue of foreign ownership of the "national railway," discovered the American connection, Macdonald insisted Allen dump his southern friends. Angry, the Americans rushed to the opposition-party Liberals, confessed their sins – and Prime Minister Macdonald's – and the ensuing scandal brought down the government.

Next in power, the Liberals began construction of the railroad on a cost-effective, self-financing basis. However, with his crimes completely forgiven in a press controlled by his friends, an unrepentant Macdonald won the next election and quickly scrapped the Liberals' railway program. This time, keeping the details under better control, he awarded the "national railroad" to a new group of friends led by Donald Smith.

These new men were well-connected. Donald Smith had been a fur trader with the Hudson's Bay Company, which still owned nearly half the territory of Canada. A director of the company and its largest shareholder, he was also a Conservative Member of Parliament in Macdonald's government as well as President of the Bank of Montreal.

The gift of the railroad was one of unimaginable largesse. Macdonald emptied the public purse for them. On February 15, 1881 Smith incorporated the Canadian Pacific Railway (CPR)and the government made good its promise, giving the group $25 million in public funds to build the railroad and 10 million hectares of land to develop as an ancillary benefit. Moreover, Macdonald committed the Canadian government to pay for all the survey work the company required – a bill which amounted to $37 million, an astronomical figure for the times.

The well-connected Donald Smith, born a Scot, acknowledged later for his "contribution" to the new country by being returned to Britain as Canada's High Commissioner, was elevated to the peerage in 1897 as the first Baron of Strathcona and Mount Royal. Two years later when Britain, acting through the agency of Cecil Rhodes, forced a war on the hapless Boers in southern Africa, the new Lord Strathcona, Canadian banker and railroad builder, raised his own Canadian regiment for the cause. The Lord Strathcona Horse, a mounted regiment, was fielded entirely from Donald Smith's own purse and shipped off to Cape Town to fight under Rhodes for the British banking interests. Made heroes in Canada by the Conservative press, the men who broke the Dutch farmers for the gold of Witwatersrand were reviled only by the Quebec French who, seeing the exercise as a classic case of conquest and oppression by British imperialism, sympathized with the Boers and rioted in Montreal when the troop ships returned.

The CPR grew quickly. Expanding into real estate by selling off its landholdings around new settlements, the CPR sold one of its many acreages, a farm lot in Leduc, Alberta to a German immigrant family, the Fipkes. The land would, ultimately, be inherited and then sold by Ed Fipke.

The company's mining interests were less extensive but extremely lucrative. In 1898, the CPR bought up a small railway charter serving the Kootenay mining area of southwest British Columbia. They were after the railroad, but it came with a lead and zinc smelter at Trail, a small town located between the Monashees and the Purcell mountains near the Washington border. This smelter and its associated mines became the nucleus of CPR's mining operations. In 1906 the company created Cominco Ltd., a wholly-owned subsidiary, to operate the smelter and its lead and zinc mines.

With a parent like CPR, Cominco soon became an empire unto itself. Adding to its gold and silver mines in the Kootenays in 1910, it purchased the Sullivan Mine in nearby Kimberley, the richest deposit of lead and zinc in the country.

The smelting of lead ore and the separation of its metals is a high energy technology. With favourable business rules and generous government support, Cominco created West Kootenay Power, a wholly-owned subsidiary, to provide the smelter with electrical power from a series of dams on the Kootenay River.

So successful was the electrical subsidiary that Cominco's capital costs were paid off quickly and the huge surplus power they generated was sold to the government for public consumption at a handsome profit. Cominco had free power, cheap transport of ore over its own rail lines and virtually no competition.

The company's healthy profits in the years since the Second World War, when demand peaked for lead and zinc, had done little to improve the efficiency of its operations. What had changed was the size of management. It had burgeoned since the early days and, as with its parent the CPR, a job in Cominco was considered a sinecure.

By the time Marlene arrived in Kelowna, having crossed the country on CPR's original trans-Canada line, Chuck had secured a position with the company. Cominco was drilling a molybdenum prospect in northern British Columbia called the Moly-Atlin Property. Work was already in progress and the geologist running the program was needed elsewhere.

Before he flew north to take over the project, Chuck studied the geological reports for the project and the drilling plans that had been filed. It was immediately apparent that the project had some serious and fundamental problems. The drill sites had all been "spotted" on the basis of molybdenum in rock geochemistry. They had targeted an area to be drilled on the basis of only two rock samples that had created a high moly reading. Worse, they were drilling in a rock zone which, in porphyry copper terms, was known as the propylitic zone, a region of alteration in granitic rock which is "cold". Sometimes visible molybdenite mineralization occurred in it, but as far as Chuck knew, ore grades had never, ever, been found in it.

The man who had interviewed and hired Chuck was Dunc Heddle. Nearing retirement age, very senior in the company and a kind man, he was approachable. That the company had approved the drill plans as submitted by the project geologist made Chuck somewhat circumspect in his approach.

"Dunc, I've never seen a paper, hey, which validated the method we're using here – analysing rock geo-chem grab samples and then using the results to spot drill holes ... Like, have you seen, hey, any research indicating that that's a way to spot holes and drill?"

The older man thought about it for a moment and then conceded that, no, he hadn't. He then waited for Chuck to finish his point.

"Well," started Chuck. "I think every hole that's been planned here will be a dud! Like, it's all wasted money, hey. All the drilling is in the wrong place!"

"It's your call, Chuck," Heddle replied, unperturbed. "You've got the budget – spend it the way you think it should be done. That's what you've been hired for."

But Chuck did not exactly have a free hand. The budget had been written up by his predecessor, and he had laid all the wrong foundations. The company standard, fairly common in the industry, was "budget plus 10-per cent." Chuck had to get the work done without exceeding the budget by more than 10 per cent. If he could not do it, if he went over, he would be fired.

He rushed to get up to Atlin to stop the work before any more money was wasted. Built during the Klondike gold rush at the same time that the Witwatersrand gold was attracting attention outside of Africa, Atlin was snuggled up behind the rugged coastal mountains of the Alaskan panhandle, near the Yukon border. The airplane touched down on Atlin's dirt strip, which, wide and dusty, ran alongside Atlin's cemetery. An overgrown forest of poplar and pine held rotting crosses and old stone grave markers, the final resting place of some of the men who had come from distant lands to experience the thrills and dreams of the Klondike gold rush. Weather and whiskey had killed most of them.

His last thoughts of Atlin, years before, had been of living here with his family in a small cabin and trapping with Gunther Lishy. Now he was back, but the reunion with Gunther would have to wait. A helicopter was already warming up to carry him to the camp, set up on the Moly-Atlin property several miles south of Atlin on a mountain slope above the lake.

Chuck had been expecting as his first priority to stop the drilling and move the holes, but actually seeing the site from his vantage point in the helicopter gave him something new to worry about. The camp was a series of platforms built on cribs and stilts anchored into the side of a steep mountain rock face. It had obviously taken herculean effort and expense to perch the camp, suspended, from the nearby cliff face. The logic was easy to see. Rather than locate at the lakeshore 500 metres below, and fly the men up and down to the drill site, the original project manager had decided it would be more expedient and ultimately less expensive to locate the camp right beside the site they were drilling. There the men could sleep and work in shifts, within walking distance of the site. And there was no denying they had done a tremendous construction job – except for one thing: it was right on an old avalanche run.

Chuck had the pilot take him up the side of the mountain, hovering slowly, while he carefully studied every face, slope and rock crevasse above the camp. Near the top, balancing precipitously and overhanging the slope which led to the camp, were broken and cracked rock cornices, ready to fall.

"Jesus, this is bloody dangerous!"

Higher still, the mountain was buried under a mass of snow and ice that had weathered through each short summer. Subject to winds tearing around the peaks and wide daily fluctuations in temperature, the snow was unstable and hanging out along the edges. When it came down it would bring tons of loose rock and cornices with it.

The easiest thing for him to do would be to simply move in and complete the project exactly as it had been laid out. The drill program, he knew, would produce no results, and the property, good or bad, would be abandoned, but nobody would be any wiser, or even care much. So long as he did it under budget, and he could, the company would be pleased.

He didn't give that option much consideration, however. Instead, he began to move the camp off the avalanche run one small helicopter load at a time. Chuck was discouraged. He hadn't even started yet, and already his budget was disappearing. He was moving backwards, beginning from scratch at the bottom of the valley. At least he had the personal satisfaction of soon knowing he had made the right decision. Three days after they had relocated the camp at the lakeshore, the drillers, setting up new drill targets, noticed movement far above them.

"AVALANCHE!"

The cry brought Chuck to his feet instantly. Rushing from his operations tent, he looked up the mountain to see what was coming. It was nearly 5:00 AM. In the summer, just south of the 60th parallel, the sun was already well into the sky. Everyone watched, immobilised, as a wall of snow mixed with broken rock slid down the mountain towards them, far too quickly to outrun. The avalanche wall, 12 metres high, swung away from them with the contours of the mountain. Following the avalanche run, it slid overtop the campsite they had just abandoned and roared off down the mountain into the valley. Stunned, the men walked over to where their base camp had been only days earlier, but there was nothing left. Every trace of the old camp had been wiped off the mountain.

Whenever they could, the men would go into Atlin for a break. With the camp now situated on the lakeshore, it was an easy trip by boat. In accordance with company policy, the camp was "dry" and the men had to leave for a drink. Chuck was glad of that. Drinking had been a routine in the canteen at Ok Tedi, and alcohol marathons had become the norm afterwards in Australia. Even in conservative and repressed South Africa, alcohol remained one of the few permitted releases. In the camps, especially among the Africans cut off from families, alone in the evenings, drinking helped numb the senses. Still, it took its toll. On his arrival in Atlin, Chuck had dried out, and quickly: three days of hiking over the big slopes had sweated it out. It was a new feeling and he liked it.

Relocating the holes took days of new work. Each target hole required a drill platform and Chuck, after identifying new targets, put all the men to work building new platforms and moving the drills. Flying the crews back and forth every shift change from the lake to the drill site was quickly: eating up his remaining budget. He tried to compensate by restricting the drill program and focusing energy on what he saw as their best prospects. It worked.

In one hole the bit sunk its teeth into a massive molybdenum deposit – one of the highest grade sections he had ever seen. Chuck had another hole set to attack the deposit from another angle, but after hitting an unexpectedly thick layer of overburden, the rods cutting into the mountain at an angle started to stick at one hundred and sixty feet. He was now approaching his "10 percent over budget" limit. He told the drillers to pull out and shut it down. If he lost the rods and casings their replacement cost of $25,000 would have put him over the line.

He was unable to explore the deposit, but he had proved it was there – and he had done it "under budget." With the hit on molybdenum, his bosses were more than pleased. The company decided to keep the claims. And Chuck.

Chuck had worked all summer on the site, and although he had been allowed one paid leave to go home for a week, he had not taken it. Too close to budget and too conscientious to leave when daily decisions affected the outcome of the whole project, he had stayed in without a break. Impressed at first with the quality of his work and now with the results, the company lifted him rapidly through several salary levels. Far from the centre of the company and its political machinations, he began to see a future with Cominco.

It was now late fall, and before Chuck left Atlin he stopped for the last time at Gunther Lishy's cabin to say goodbye. The two men had met several times during the summer, the first time talking all night, Gunther wanting Chuck to recount the details of his overseas adventures. Although they both remembered their last discussion well, neither of them spoke of it directly. There was no need. The man who had come north to Atlin working for Cominco was a different person than the one who had left years before. Then, Lishy's life had offered an alternative to life on a company treadmill. Chuck no longer needed to live apart, or wanted to.

The appeal of the forest was its simple life, avoiding material ambition, being close to nature and listening to the sound of falling snow. But his education had given him a skill and with that, a window on the world. His experiences had changed him. He still felt compelled to explore the frontiers, to seek there the last wild refuges, the ancient forests and cultures, but new desires had been awakened with the possibility of "success." A huge ambition was now beginning to assert itself within him.

While working in the north, Chuck had, on his own, done some heavy mineral sampling for Cominco. His work was something the company had not seen before. Dr. Geoff Harris, Cominco's head of research, called Chuck in to see him when he got back to Vancouver. Harris asked him what he was doing with the heavy minerals. The company's exploration technique had remained the classic one, practiced for generations: to look for interesting rocks and then analyze them. Chuck explained his heavy mineral philosophy and the practical successes he had experienced in New Guinea, Australia and southern Africa. Harris immediately recognized the potential of the new techniques. Excited by the research Chuck had done, Harris asked if he would present a paper on it for the company. Moreover, he wanted Chuck to set up a lab for Cominco to allow them to do their own heavy mineral separations and analysis.

Believing he had a future with Cominco, Chuck agreed. He began, at once, to collect orientation samples downstream from known deposits of mineralization types Cominco was interested in, to build a database. Chuck was assigned assistants for the project and each night they all stayed on past midnight, building the lab in Vancouver and conducting concentration experiments on bulk orientation samples. Chuck was happy to work late. When he left, it was only to a dingy room in a Hastings Street hotel. Marlene and Mark were living with her parents in Kelowna, at the end of a 55-minute plane flight each weekend.

The work interested Chuck. Each new sample expanded his knowledge and he constantly improved his own methodology. As Jack Gower had told him when he was still a geology student, there were things university could not teach. The research he had been doing was one of them. He now took orientation samples from a volcanogenic copper-lead-zinc deposit near Harrison Lake, B.C., another from a deposit of lead-zinc in carbonate rocks at Sheep Creek being mined in the Kootenays, and another from the porphyry copper deposit at Brenda Mines near

Kelowna. To those, he added the information from his own work on porphyry copper orientation studies.

The results were excellent. The company organized a meeting of all its geologists in the province and Chuck delivered the speech on heavy minerals to them. Harris was more than pleased. "Anything you want, whatever you need, just ask and it's yours."

Following the presentation, Harris's boss, Hugh Morrison, also congratulated Chuck on the quality of the research he had done. The lab and the heavy mineral analyzes would give new direction to the company. And they would publish his paper – the most gratifying reward for Chuck.

It was a good moment for Chuck – one of several in Cominco – as future horizons broadened. Cominco had an opening, in Rome. The job was Chuck's if he wanted it. He did. He added studying Italian to his late nights and raced to finish the lab. Then an entirely different offer came in. A geologist was required to sample the Brazilian outback. He could move to Rome and practice his Italian, or live in Rio and explore the jungle. It was no contest. He had already been to Rome. But the Amazon – the largest jungle on earth – dwarfed the Congo and still had undiscovered stone-age cultures.

Cominco wanted him to look for lead-zinc deposits in carbonate host rocks in the limestones and dolomites of Minas Gerais and Bahia, Brazil's eastern provinces, but he had no experience in the field. He turned to the company's experts for help.

Ken Carter had been a classmate. After several years with Cominco specializing in the mineralization of lead-zinc deposits, he had become quite proficient. He indicated to Chuck that using the measurement of geologic sections to reconstruct paleogeologic environments was the key to finding environments which would host new lead-zinc mines. Chuck then went to Bruce Moyer, who gave him a large bag of sphalerite-zinc ore samples: hands-on study. Ted Mareiro next explained the deposits in terms of optimum structural settings. He suggested Chuck look for fault-bounded, high-uplift areas, covered by marine carbonate and capped by shale sequences.

"What I think's happened," Mareiro explained, "Is that rainwater has leached the lead-zinc from the shales in the adjacent fault zones and redeposited it in the underlying porous carbonates."

Chuck thanked them. Their information was all valuable in its own right, but it was piecemeal. The company had no central unified theory he could access. He was on his own. That the world's major zinc producer did not have its own strategy for finding lead-zinc deposits surprised him.

Every other company he had worked for had research files on the type of mineralization they specialized in and a structured approach to their exploration methods. Kennecott even had a secret file of technology available only to their own geologists. Cominco had the appearance of a modern mining company, but Chuck had to remind himself of its genesis. It was the accidental offspring of a railroad company.

He had to build up his own file and there was little time to do it. Brazil waited. Chuck still had to finish writing up his presentation of the heavy mineral system as a complete technical report to guide Cominco's future operations. The evening before his scheduled departure his paper was still incomplete. He worked throughout the night, finishing just under the wire in the early morning. Leaving it on his boss's desk, he raced to the street with his bags.

He was late. Offering cabbies incentives to run lights and being the last to board planes was becoming a Fipke trademark. He promised this driver a $20 tip if he could get Chuck there before the plane took off.

"Where you going?" the cabbie asked.

"Rio de Janeiro," Chuck replied, and then added, "Brazil," in case the man didn't know where it was.

"Well, that's interesting," the driver said. "I've just come from there."

"A holiday?" Chuck asked, surprised.

"No, not exactly," the cabbie replied as he raced up the ramps to a bridge over a channel of the Fraser River. He headed out to the airport, which was perched at the edge of the delta beside the sea.

"I went down years ago for a look and just stayed," he explained. "I was there for 25 years."

"No shit?!" Chuck's interest was aroused. "That's a long time. Why?"

"I don't really know if I can even explain it," he said, "But you'll understand when you get there."

It was tantalizing. Driving like a madman, the cabbie raced along the wet, winter roads. Chuck enjoyed the recklessness of it all.

"So why did you decide to return after 25 years?"

"Biggest mistake of my life," he answered. "I just thought since I was Canadian, it was time to come back. To get on with my life. To stop having fun. You know, the old 'guilt' thing? The voice of my father: 'Make something of your life.' "

Chuck understood that sentiment. "And now?"

"Driving a cab. Hardly a life, eh? You know … sometimes we burn ourselves up completely, following the wrong roads! All I'm doing now is trying to get enough money together to get out of here … I'm going back."

CHAPTER THIRTY-NINE

BRAZIL

Chuck's Cominco contract in Brazil was for two years with a living allowance of $1,000 a month. Tourists and expatriates had their favourite haunts in Rio, usually in the districts of Ipanema and Leblon. Rio's nightlife there was the clubs and the Samba. Downtown there was another kind of nightlife: knives and guns.

He was quickly pressured to take an apartment in one of the English-speaking enclaves, but Chuck was not interested in the English neighborhoods or in spending his free days lying on the beach at Copacabana or socializing at Canadian barbecues. He wanted to live in "Rio."

Jardim Botanico was a quarter in old Rio named after the area's magnificent botanical gardens. Chuck took an apartment there, was joined by Marlene and Mark, and they set out to explore. A short walk led them to the base of Corcovado Mountain, 709 metres high. At its peak the 30-metre statue of Jesus with outstretched arms embraced the city.

Their landlord, who lived in the building, was a relatively wealthy Brazilian military arms dealer. His passion was designing better machine guns and he immediately engaged Chuck in a discourse in broken English, on the merits of his own slide ejection mechanisms.

The apartment was laid out in grand old-world style, with high, ornately plastered ceilings. Wide-shuttered windows opening onto balconies ushered in the warm breezes of sea and jungle. It was easy to forget they were in a city of teeming millions. The apartment even had its own maid's quarters with a separate balcony. At $400 a month, the rent was less than half paid for cramped quarters in Leblon or Ipanema.

Marlene and Chuck were both pleased with it. Strolling the new neighbourhood at night, people greeted them warmly in Portuguese. The feel of the streets permeated with moist, heady tropical air was like the return of an old and good friend. The edge of the jungle was only minutes away.

Interested in exercising their own limited English, the neighbors befriended them. Dinner with the landlord became a regular event. If Chuck was interested, the landlord said, the door was now open for arms trading. Politely, Chuck declined.

With Mark, now eight years old, he hiked to the top of Corcovado, cooled off with cold soft drinks at one of the cafés near the summit, and then raced down along steep trails, flying through the thick, lush forest, leaping obstacles and swinging around trees back to the city below. The outing became a kind of ritual, to see who could race the fastest down through the jungle. Lagoa Rodrigo de

Freitas, the lake, was also within walking distance and they explored it on foot, poking along the edge of the water with Snoopy, Mark's Doberman – a gift from Ed Fipke to his grandson. A large male purebred, it was gentle and protective of Mark; the boy and his dog were constant companions.

Chuck was out walking Snoopy late one night when he noticed candlelight flickering through the thick foliage of the Floresta da Tijuca. He approached the edge of the jungle, and peered into ancient Africa.

The large slave populations that had been brought from Mozambique and Angola to Portugal's South American colony had not been completely Christianized. After being liberated, many had even reestablished up the coast north of Rio, the life they had before being dragged from Africa. African villages now flourished along the coast of a jungle an ocean away from Africa. In Rio, at the base of the statue of Christ, African macumba rituals now took place under cover of night.

Africa had teased him, but Brazil seduced Chuck completely. A mix of old-world colonial European, black African and native American, the Brazilians were sophisticated yet passionate, a product of history and climate. The evening heat, silky and humid, brought out the women, who moved along the promenades in slow graceful groups of threes and fours. Clad in short, tight-fitting dresses, they did not look away from passersby but rather matched their interest, each group appraising the other intently.

Brazil was not warm; it was hot. The kind of heat that drove people out into the night seeking release. Sunset came early, and perfumed nights were saturated with mystery.

Even driving in Rio was a passionate affair. There were no speed limits and everyone drove as fast as their cars would allow. If a car wanted to change lanes and a smaller one was in the way, it would simply force the smaller one over. Nobody stopped for lights or accidents. Driving was always thrilling, a reckless headlong rush into madness. In only a few months, Chuck's car was a mass of scar tissue, each scrape and dent, like the landscape of a boxer's face, memorializing an encounter with a road opponent for space, power or right-of-way.

Cominco's offices were in a tower on Avenida Copacabana, a block from the beach. In a neighborhood of cafés, clubs and excellent restaurants the attractions were too difficult for Chuck's boss, an Austrian, to resist. As Chuck soon learned, George spent more time in the clubs chasing skirts than at work. Not that Chuck would have seen anything wrong with that if George had had some other redeeming qualities, but Chuck couldn't find any. Beneath a mask of false jocularity lay another, baser personality.

The office opened up into a hall, which connected to some other businesses and an elevator. Chuck was surprised to learn that neither the size of the building nor the need to use an elevator discouraged thieves. Cominco, with one secretary-receptionist, did not cater to the public and few visitors entered. A Brazilian branch office whose sole purpose was to explore for lead, zinc and other economic minerals, they saw no need for more office staff or even an locked hallway door.

Their secretary, a petite Brazilian woman, had already suffered several robberies by the time a man walked in from the hallway with a knife and left with her purse. She was grateful that was all he had taken.

Nerves frayed, she asked Chuck to install a lock on the door. Chuck thought it a reasonable request. He knew that George didn't believe she needed the door locked, but George was not the one being robbed. Chuck immediately installed a lock she could use when alone in the office.

A middle-aged man with grown children and a wife, George returned after his customary liquid lunch to find the door locked. Too furious to knock, he kicked the door in, breaking it down. It was his decision: no locks.

The more Chuck had to deal with him, the more he hated him. A geologist educated in Europe, George was poorly trained and cared very little. Overweight and constantly perspiring, his body gave off a sharp, sour odour – a product of inner turmoil and bad diet. Always the last to arrive at work, George spent most of each morning reading English-language newspapers and retiring early for "lunch" at a neighborhood club. He had been drunk when he kicked in the door.

Basic, rude and self-absorbed, his transformation when one of the bigger bosses flew down to Rio for a look was something to witness.

Chuck hardly had a chance to say hello when they arrived. George would have them out of the office at every opportunity. Attentive to their slightest needs, he was fatuously obsequious, doing everything he could to ingratiate himself. As soon as they left, George would revert to his old self, reading the *Latin American Daily Post* in the mornings and hunting women in the afternoons.

The worst of it for Chuck was that George did not know the basics of exploration. For George, position and promotion within Cominco had come not from skill but from social networking, from being a "team player" – playing the right games with the right teammates.

Chuck agreed with George on only one point: the women of Rio were beautiful. Unlike North American women, they aggressively encouraged male contact. A man had only to wait for a woman to approach him. It was a siren call difficult to ignore, and the beach down the street was filled with sirens.

Chuck, resisting George's example and failing to join his team, incurred his boss's wrath. George, who preferred people less capable than himself, soon began searching for ways to defeat Chuck.

The moribund atmosphere of the office poisoned Rio itself for Chuck. He was grateful for every chance to get away into the field. At least in the Brazilian bush, he could master his own life and work unimpeded. There he worked off his frustrations by becoming a production powerhouse. He considered his employment a trust which required he do his best – even if no one cared, or worse, hated him for it. The more sloth he saw in the office the harder he worked, determined to break every record Cominco had.

He went out for six to eight weeks at a time with Carlos Bertoni, the Brazilian geologist who worked as his assistant. Covering huge areas, collecting record numbers of samples and ignoring personal risk, he and Carlos covered every major system in eastern Brazil. The "method" had its own dangers – wading into swamps and up rivers to get the best possible samples exposed them to parasites, which, if left untreated, could considerably shorten one's life.

The test for the environmental health of an area is the proportion of older people to the general population. Brazil, especially in the outback, was full of young people. That made it more exciting, but the hidden message was clear. Life here was brief.

Possibly the worst risk, among many, was the *barberos*. An aggressive nocturnal insect attracted to the scent of flesh and more bloodthirsty than any mosquito, it hunted human prey in the dark. Almost unheard of by tourists, its bite was believed nearly always fatal. The barberos hosted the parasite *trypanosoma cruzi*, which, upon entering the human bloodstream, attacked the heart muscle. Death came sometimes in a matter of weeks, more often, in a couple of years, as the heart muscle became slowly crippled. The infection was known locally as *chagas* and was endemic to Latin America. Tropical disease experts prayed chagas would stay there. If the parasite spread to other vectors, such as mosquitoes and ticks entering North America, it would wreak more havoc. There was no cure and it was already killing thousands each year in the jungle.

Chuck was sleeping in a cot on a thin rubbery mattress in a rough hotel in an outback hamlet when he was bitten. The pain woke him instantly. In the grey moonlight from the curtainless window, he saw a grotesque batlike little beetle fly off his arm. Recognizing it immediately as the creature the Brazilians called the barberos, it was impossible not to react. Despite having been told not to disturb the wound if bitten, he instinctively shook his arm vigorously as he leapt off the bed to turn on the light. The bare, low-watt bulb, dangling from a raw wire cast a gloomy glow in the miserable space. He raised his arm to the light to examine the wound. At the edge of the bite he could see the creature's deposited excrement, its signature. The barberos always defecated as it gorged itself with blood; it was in its feces that the parasites lived.

Carefully, he wiped the feces away from the bite. Chuck was lucky. Tests conducted back in Rio confirmed he was free of the disease. Not all barberos were hosts, but the parasite could only penetrate his body if the feces of the barberos came into contact with the wound. If he had slapped at the pain, or rubbed the wound, he might have wiped excrement over the bite and become infected.

Carlos Bertoni was not so lucky. Several months after Chuck's encounter, Carlos was bitten. Unlike Chuck, Bertoni tested positive for chagas. The news crushed him. It was a death sentence. After getting the report, he could hardly find the strength to leave the clinic. Chuck stayed with him. The clinic quickly followed up the results with two more tests. Both were positive. Bertoni was devastated. As a Brazilian, he knew only too well what to expect as he waited to die: an internal rotting away. Desperately he continued to hope that the tests were wrong. They were not perfect, but after three, the chance of a mistake was extremely remote. The country's foremost specialist on chagas was a British doctor doing research who maintained a clinic in Rio. He was expensive, but Cominco covered employees' medical costs. The doctor conducted the only test known to be certain. It required Bertoni to be bitten again by a laboratory-bred barberos.

After the blood test, the doctor pronounced the results: Carlos did not have chagas. It had been a false alarm. With his life restored to him, Carlos became the happiest man in Cominco's employ.

After their chagas fright, the two geologists were not alarmed much by the jungle's other parasites. Even a large festering boil on Chuck's calf was let go for several days until he finally broke it open to find it filled with the larvae of some form of blowfly. Having hatched under the skin, the worms were feeding off his flesh. As they grew in size, so did the "boil."

Cominco had retained the services of a specialist in Brazilian parasites, Dr. Meyer. Trained in the U.S., he too, was expensive. Chuck and Carlos were regular patients. Every time they emerged from the field, they hosted a zoological garden of tiny creatures that eked out their lives inside human bodies. Meyer looked forward to their visits, joking that they were an entomologist's dream. Parasites of every type and description occupied niches within the men's bodies. Meyer put them on drug programs that took one to two weeks to work, during which time they wrote up their field reports. As soon as he pronounced them bug-free, they would return to the jungle and plunge once more into the forest's secret depths. The parasites were only dangerous if allowed to live. For the local Brazilians from the country-side the company sometimes hired to help collect samples – men who had no access to Meyer's expensive bug-purging drugs – the jungle was a harsher reality.

The Brazilian backcountry in which the two men worked was a strange world. Sometimes modern, sometimes 17th century, yet always unique, Brazil had for long been a world left hanging somewhere between its hazy frontier and the old-world colonial creation the Portuguese had made of it.

By the time Portugal began exercising imperial control over Brazil and impos-ing its state religion over the new colony, Catholicism had become an ideology of extreme conservatism, rigidly preserving the status quo. Earlier, the Church had direct rule – for a millennium its own armies and its own courts enjoyed absolute power, sharing it only when expedient to do so.

After the 15th century, however, it lost much of its former power, as well as its moral authority, in the climate of the Renaissance. During the late 15th and early 16th centuries, as Spain and Portugal first stepped ashore in the Americas and Africa, treaty negotiations between the Popes and the Kings laid down new rules of conduct that would govern their relationships for the next couple of cen-turies. Civil control, including nominations to ecclesiastical offices and positions in church finances, was established over many church activities.

The Church arrived in Latin America as it had spread across Europe – under the protection and power of the ruling political elites. Likewise, in Brazil, it remained a main tool of conquest and of "pacification," and an essential feature of subsequent social control. However, once the Brazilian empire was consolidated and Portuguese rule firmly established, the Church assumed that its Christianization process was complete.

It was not. In many quarters throughout Brazil, Christianity was but a thin veil thrown over a different face. The native religions it attempted to supplant merely hid themselves beneath Christian rituals. While churches proliferated, indigenous pagan beliefs did too.

The religio-magical world of "modern" Brazil was more pagan than Christian. To many Brazilians the vengeful Catholic God and the entire panoply of saints – the lesser gods – were merely another layer, and more evidence, of the spirit-world and the supernatural that infused life everywhere.

With the limits of civilization extending only a short distance into the forest from Brazil's seashores and major rivers, *bandeirantes*, soldier-citizens of imperial Portugal and the more recent *seringueiros*, fortune hunters who invaded for rubber and gems, had not been interested in settling down. They were after wealth that could be carried away. Distant from law and free from ethical boundaries, their influence in the backcountry was still strong. A legacy of blood and easy morality governed when they were gone.

Brazil stood out as unique in other ways, too. Unlike that of the puritan British-American settlers and the Spanish conquistadors, the Portuguese sense of humanity that was generally practised, perhaps only of necessity, was kinder and more universal in Brazil than anywhere else. In Brazil the native populations and the freed slaves were embraced in a working relationship unseen elsewhere.

Out of this mix of Indian, African and Christian European emerged the Brazilian *mestizo*. In all the time he spent in the forest, over all the ground he covered, Chuck encountered very few Native people. They had virtually disappeared from much of the country, but not by imperial design or racial conflict. More casual and intimate forms of human contact had been their demise. The mixed blood of intermarriage had transformed a large Native and slave population and a small European one into a new mulatto-mestizo people: the Brazilians.

Romance was at the heart of Brazil, a way of life more than a diversion or occasional need. For a time, when Carlos Bertoni was sent to work on another project, Chuck was assigned two young Brazilian geologists, who, typically, considered their personal lives separate from and far more important than their work, and who shared a passion for women.

Tracking his men down was typically the first chore of Chuck's day. They were rarely in their rooms. He would start looking where they had left off the night before, usually among some girls. Although the men all felt anonymous, their presence in most towns, and their activities, did not go unnoticed. There were always people Chuck could find who would help collect them. Rousing them and pushing them through breakfast took the first three hours of the day. Exhausted from a night of lovemaking and still inebriated, they would insist on stopping at 11:00 a.m. for a mid-morning coffee break, laughing at Chuck's eagerness to work.

"In Brazil, my friend, a man does not live to work as in America. Here, he works to live!" Luis would argue persuasively. Othon, seeing Chuck weakening, would agree, "And how a man lives is more important that what he does for a living."

Chuck had tried to resist. "Look, you guys. We've only been on the road for an hour! C'mon, we gotta keep going. We've got a lot of work to do, hey!"

"Aw, Chuck," they sighed. "This is Brazil, not Canada. The work's not going to get away. Besides, how can we live without coffee?"

This day they pulled over to a little roadside café where the two men began chatting up the girls working there, their hangovers and previous exhaustion purged instantly. Their waitress leaned low over the table to wipe it. Her long legs beneath a short wraparound skirt were finely muscled and smooth-skinned. When her shirt fell open from her neck, exposing her bare breasts and her large, dark nipples, Othon responded. He put his hand on her leg beneath her skirt and slowly began sliding it up. It had almost disappeared before she slapped it away. Othon had been here before. They knew each other.

Twenty minutes later, their coffee finished, Chuck went to the toilet. When he returned, Othon and their waitress were gone. So was Luis.

"Now where the hell did they disappear to?"

An old Brazilian man sitting near their table grinned and made an obscene gesture, pointing out the direction they had taken. It didn't require any pounding on doors to find them. A high-pitched, breathless, musical staccato filled Chuck's ears as soon as he walked around the corner of the building. They were already having sex with the women they had met in the cafe.

It was one of the few excuses Chuck would tolerate for tardiness; in Brazil it was the norm. He ordered another coffee, and finished it. Still the notes of rhapsody had not reached their crescendo. Chuck, cursing under his breath, couldn't wait any longer. It was getting really late!

Luis would not get up to answer the door and yelled at Chuck to enter the room. Othon was engaged with their long-legged waitress who, oblivious to the world, continued to sing the rhythm of rapture. Luis, watching from another bed beside them, had the young woman's sister peering over his shoulder. More modest, she covered herself with the bed sheet when Chuck entered. Othon didn't mind the intrusion. He was rapidly exchanging comments in Portuguese with Luis as he continued making love, the two men enjoying themselves.

"Every time he touches her, goes inside, she has an ecstasy," Luis explained unnecessarily. "Othon says this woman is the best to please he's ever known."

Chuck decided to give him some more time. It was a special occasion.

It was now after noon. They had only a little while left on the road before lunch. Enjoying a meal which, in classic Latin style, refused to be rushed, his colleagues were quickly exhausted again. After a bottle of wine to ease their meal, they dragged their feet into the stifling afternoon heat, incapable of more exertion.

At 5:00 p.m., they were begging to call it a day, to get a room, shower and settle down for a late supper. Afterwards they were off in search of another open-air club to meet more women, to laugh, and to dance, and to live the romance. And so it went. Day after day.

Occasionally Chuck gave up on them entirely and went out alone to catch up on the goals he had set. Doing the work of three men, Chuck was driven. His own internal standards set the pace and the tone of his life. He didn't seriously question it. It was simply who he was, and he could be no different.

But Chuck believed in more than hard work; he believed in hard living, in giving everything his all. Sometimes, especially after he had worked hard through the day, he would join Othon and Luis for the evening. Partying wildly until dawn, he would then show them up by putting in a full, hard day's work.

Every little town had at least 15 to 20 girls in it. In the backcountry, Brazil was peopled with the young. For women in a traditional society, salvation lay in being desirable to men, and their greatest efforts were reserved for young professionals.

His own trips into the outback with Carlos Bertoni met with some success. A few of the samples they had recovered came back as hits and returning to explore them, they worked their way back to the area of mineralization. Chuck found several prospects which, like the Moly-Atlin property, were left for the company to decide whether or not to explore in depth. Drilling in Brazil was a problem. There were no rigs in the country, at least none for hire. If Cominco wanted to drill, they would have to fly in their own equipment and crews. The company was not ready for that, so Chuck carried on with the broad survey of the land, looking for prospects, and finding them here and there, to add to the company's inventory.

Every two months he called Vancouver to inquire about the publication status of the report he had finished the day he departed. Cominco's response was always the same "Soon." They were moving ahead on it. And, they added, they were pleased with his work.

Chuck's relationship with his boss continued to deteriorate. Every time Chuck came in out of the bush to ask for something, George was there to assert himself, usually by denying Chuck the equipment he required to do the job.

Cominco's little four-wheel-drive wagon was not up to the challenges Chuck put to it. The backroads of Brazil were difficult to navigate, especially in the rains. Greasy mud strips hacked from the forest, ruts in them were often so deep that a car's wheels would slide into them leaving the chassis to support the vehicle. Special Brazilian four-wheel-drive trucks with enormous wheels were used to traverse highways, but even these were not used to attempt the oxcart trails Chuck drove.

After one particularly hazardous field trip Chuck ordered a winch. The trip had been made during a tropical downpour, and he had buried the vehicle in a swamp after dark. He and Carlos had worked through the night in the water and deep mud, tormented by mosquitoes, digging it out a few inches at a time by building a bed under the wheels. It was the rainy season and they were working far back in the jungle, kilometres from any settlement. They needed a winch. But when George saw the order he quickly tore it up. He would not allow them to have one.

For Chuck, who had personally managed dozens of men while he ran his own programs and who had operated big budgets on major projects worldwide, being stuck under George's thumb was intolerable. When Chuck next put in an order for a series of duplicate aerial photos in order to map stratigraphy, George changed the order, allowing him only one photograph per site.

"I need to have two photographs side by side to make it stereoscopic," Chuck explained. George was a little unclear on the concept, and was as usual, unbending.

"You always need stereo pairs," Chuck insisted. "It's the only way to get proper measurements. Without the other set, I can't do the calculations."

George refused to budge. It was his prerogative to determine how the company's Brazil office was to be run, to exercise his discretion over all expenditures. Brazil was his fiefdom.

Chuck lost control finally over an expense account. In the bush, expenses were hard to keep track of and receipts more difficult to obtain. No matter how careful, one always ended up subsidizing the work out of one's own pocket. He and Carlos had been camped near an artesian spring they had discovered smoking in the jungle. The water was sulphurous and nearly hot. They made it their bush base. After work each night, they would bathe in the pool before crawling to sleep in their tents. Hot springs in British Columbia were always a delight and always safe. Brazilian springs were another matter. This hot spring came with its own species of parasites. By the time the two men became aware of them, the skin over their entire bodies was horribly infected. Dr. Meyer found it fascinating, but even he was careful not to joke about it. The disease was awful. Chuck continued working, and turned in his expense account as usual, to be approved by his boss but this time George scanned it quickly and thrust it right back.

"Redo it properly!" he ordered.

With his skin burning, even his testicles dried out and cracked, Chuck was on a painfully short fuse. In the past, he had avoided arguments with George. Not now.

"Why?" asked Chuck.

"Because the figures on your expense claim don't line up overtop each other." Chuck couldn't believe it.

"You mean, *that the line isn't straight?*" Chuck asked, incredulously. This was a new low.

"That's right," George said, glaring at him, all pretence of civility now gone.

"Can't you read it, George? Can't you figure it out?" Chuck said insultingly, now angry as well.

"That's not the point."

"*Well, what the fuck is it George? What's your point?*" Chuck was shouting.

"I want it done right," was the hostile reply.

Chuck stared at him, wondering how it was possible the man had survived so long. George was trembling in anger. Lines of sweat from his brow were running down the sides of his face. This loathsome vision, to Chuck, was beginning to personify Cominco.

"Shit," Chuck said, shaking his head, his voice back under control. He had done his best to be civil. This was it. "I've been in the bloody bush for the past two months working my ass off! I've found new lead-zinc mineral deposits! ...

I've staked them!... The whole Brazilian project is working because of my efforts and you're hassling me because my fucking numbers aren't in straight columns! What the fuck is the matter with you?!"

They glared at each other for another moment before Chuck continued.

"You know what I think? I think you should take a break from the beach. I think you should try hauling your ass into the bush and do some work yourself! You don't like the way I do things, get someone else!"

That shut George up. They both knew he was incapable of doing the work. Seething, he backed off, and walked away. The battle was Chuck's, but George wasn't defeated. Rather than attack Chuck directly, he changed his strategy. He would attack Chuck's reputation with the company instead. Secretly, George opened a file on Chuck. Documenting Chuck's "attitude problems" became George's new project. He had nothing else to do.

Upon entering the outback, Chuck often encountered *garimparos*. Living on rafts on the rivers, their diesel generators pumping air to divers wearing primitive bell helmets, the garimparos were a class of Brazilian free miners. Guiding suction tubes 15 centimeters in diameter, they vacuumed sediment off the river bottoms. The sediment was mechanically panned or jigged over corduroy-like wilfley tables on the rafts. Running gold operations mostly, with their crude machinery, the garimparos appeared to have stepped right out of the 19th century. Some of them carried arms for self-defence and for hunting as they moved up and down the waterways – the highways – of Brazil. The government had little presence in the outback and the people working in it had created their own society. Dark, rough-shaven and fierce-looking, groups of garimparos in from the bush drunk and made their own law.

Walking down the rough streets of their jungle river towns was like being transported to the gold rush towns of the American West, the Yukon or Australia of the past century. The streets were muddy when it rained, and dry and dusty under the heat of the sun. Skinny male dogs roamed free everywhere, prowling about for food and the rare bitch, tail between her legs, that ventured out. Darkening meat hung blanketed with flies in slabs under the shade of a wooden awning at the butcher's store. Boardwalks and grey weathered buildings, many no more than three metres wide and pressed tightly together, often fronted both sides of the street. Those along the river, built to overhang the water, dripped their sewage into the stream, to be taken up downriver by the next family, who washed dishes or brewed tea in it. Most of the buildings were poor one-room bars, with rough-cut benches, a couple of bottles of whiskey or rum and several cases of beer. Glass, like paint, was too expensive to afford, and wooden shutters covered open windows, coal oil lanterns dimly lighting dark interiors. Frightful-looking prostitutes, thickly made up, one or two to a bar, provided the visiting garimparos with some release. Squeezed between the bars were gold buyers, their small scales on counters in front of their own tiny smelters.

Those garimparos who knew what to look for were dredging for diamonds as well as gold. Heavy, diamonds sometimes panned out in the Brazilian-style jigs, left behind with the gold when the lighter sands were washed away. Nor were the garimparos alone in their search.

DeBeers was also in Brazil, moving quietly through the forest searching for the source of Brazil's greatest "stone" – a giant, 700-carat gem-quality diamond which had emerged from one of its streams. Another 3000-carat industrial, found tumbling down the jig blanket by a garimparo, came from another alluvial deposit somewhere in the jungle.

DeBeers had so far discovered a dozen pipes but none of them were diamond bearing. Like the source of the alluvial diamonds panned from the delta sands of the Orange River in Africa, the field here was wide open. The prospect of shifting his exploration efforts from lead to diamonds began to stir Chuck. Somewhere out in the Brazilian jungle were ancient diamondiferous volcanic pipes so rich they carried gem-quality diamonds as large as 700 carats from the depths of the Earth to its surface.

The more he felt the excitement of the garimparo towns and the more he learned about DeBeers's jungle hunt, the more he wanted to become involved. Researching all the literature he could access in Rio on Brazilian diamond geology, he visited the garimparos's river-dredging alluvial operations at every opportunity and examined their gems. The more he learned, the more the attraction diamonds took on.

Far more precious than gold, some diamonds were nearly as old as the Earth itself. Peridotitic diamonds, derived from diamondiferous peridotite rock, were formed in the lithospheric upper mantle between 2.6 and 3.3 billion years ago. A gem that had survived for billions of years was truly a rare and precious thing. Ecologitic diamonds, formed between 900 million and 1.6 billion years ago, were by comparison, young.

In those very distant times, buried deep within a young, hot Earth, at a time before life began to crawl from the sea, diamonds were being formed, growing at the edge of the fires near the core of the earth. Buried in the deep keels of land masses that floated slowly across the surface, the diamonds that were created would, when this age ended, not be created again. By the time dinosaurs evolved, the continents had drifted together to form a single land mass, Pangaea, the whole Earth, and under it, the diamonds. Pangaea began to break apart 200 million years ago. First, two supercontinents, Gondwanaland and Laurasia, formed; later, the seven continents. Molten rock flowed to the surface along fault lines caused by the breakup of the continents drifting over the hot convection currents of the Earth's core. Volcanoes spewing magma brought the diamonds to the surface. But not all volcanoes, and not everywhere: only those where the geotectonic evolution of the depths beneath an eruption were favourable to diamond formation and only when the movement of lava to the surface had the right vortex of speed, temperature and host rock chemical composition. Otherwise the diamonds were destroyed.

Rare indeed.

Under Brazil, when it was part of some unknown configuration of continents but likely connected to southwest Africa, the kimberlite host rock, flowing as magma towards the surface, tapped the ancient diamond zones located almost 200 kilometres beneath the earth and brought the gems up to the light. With a lot of traffic and changes on the surface since then, free diamonds had been incorporated repeatedly into new rock, then eroded and reconstituted, over and over again. The diamonds in Brazil had been recovered in host rocks and materials from numerous different ages. They had been found in Proterozoic Precambrian conglomerates, one billion years old; in Paleozoic conglomerates, 300 million years old, then in the Cretaceous-period conglomerates of the Mesozoic era – after the Jurassic age – approximately 120 million years old and in the Tertiary period of the Cenozoic era. Always in conglomerates.

Against that background a geologist could say with some certainty that the eruptions that brought Brazil's diamonds to the surface took place over a billion years ago. Once intruded over the surface, the rock was broken down by weather and the freed diamonds were then scattered by the elements. Mixed with other sands and stones, the diamonds were imprisoned again in the new rocks that formed the conglomerates of the Precambrian period. When those, too, eroded after millions of years, the diamonds were set free again only to become part of the next age of conglomerate rocks. And so it went from age to age, from the Paleozoic to the Cretaceous to the Tertiary. But heavy at birth, the diamonds stayed heavy, and never moved far from their original channel – the pipes which brought them to the surface of the earth.

The place where the garimparos had panned the diamonds from the river's bottom would have been relatively near their original source. But in a billion years the Earth itself had changed radically. The core of a volcanic pipe, still rich in diamonds but weathered down, eroded and buried, had been a mere pinprick on the land originally. If any of it remained now, it would be even more obscure.

There was another possible source for diamonds. The deep keel that had created them in that very distant age was still believed to exist, and within it the diamonds. More recent volcanoes, if they intersected that keel, could be as diamondiferous as those ancient pipes. It was in this hope that DeBeers, which had followed the source of their African gems across the sea to Brazil, was examining the newer pipes, even as they continued to search for the ancient ones.

Chuck wrote to Cominco's Vancouver office, proposing that they allow him to expand their Brazilian exploration efforts by including the hunt for diamonds. It was a thick report and in it he strongly recommended they take on DeBeers. He volunteered to lead the effort. Cominco was not interested.

Disappointed but not surprised, Chuck stored what he had learned in his own head. It would not go to waste. Sooner or later, he knew, everything came around, like the diamonds themselves. Somehow, somewhere, he would make use of it.

Chuck continued to experiment with heavy mineral samples, developing and refining his techniques for the separation and concentration of various target minerals found in large samples. The maid's quarters in their apartment became his lab and the open air of the balcony took the place of a fume hood where the toxic heavy liquids he worked with, like methylene iodide, dissipated less harmfully than in a closed room.

He bought a centrifuge and taught Marlene to do mineral separations based on the specific gravities of the different minerals. Later, when he made friends in the geology department at Rio's university, he was given space to locate his lab there. Whenever he returned to Rio from his long stints in the jungle, he would bring back heavy mineral samples for himself, sometimes from the known, commercially-worked mineralizations of other mines, to study and refine the techniques of target mineral isolation.

During the day, he worked in the office, writing up his reports and studies for the company. At night he worked at the university exploring new aspects of heavy mineral research. He was nearly ready to do another paper, an update of the research he had done for the first one, but he still had no word on what Cominco had done with that first paper. He continued to call Vancouver every couple of months to check on its status. When would it be published? And always he received the same answer: "Soon."

The frustration he expressed to his South American friends evoked a typically Brazilian response: Be patient. Enjoy living.

Chuck listened. And gradually, as the months blended into years, he felt himself changing, seeing things he had not seen before, feeling things he had not felt before. Brazil awakened the senses. Deep, complex and inviting, Brazil, he knew now, could hold him for a lifetime, and still have more to give. There was a kind of magic here that seeped slowly under his skin, that was gradually transforming him from an outsider to a native. Marlene had just given birth to their second child, a baby girl, Cristina Anne, born September 26, 1976. Under the law, Cristina was Brazilian, permanently entitled to a Brazilian passport. Chuck was pleased to have roots of his own in Brazil.

Chuck finally got word, after two years, that his paper on heavy mineral work had been published at last. Every Cominco office in the world was going to receive a copy and a direction that it was a "must read." Heavy mineral methods were the new approach the company was taking in exploration. In fact, soon after adopting the methodology, Cominco had a major hit in Alaska. The Red Dog Mine north of Fairbanks would become their most valuable lead-zinc asset worldwide.

But the sight of his published paper, so eagerly anticipated, profoundly shocked Chuck. For whatever reason – perhaps only that a change in exploration policy was too fundamental to credit a new contract employee with – Chuck was given no credit for the paper or for his research. Authorship had been appropriated by one of the senior bosses. His name, not Chuck's, appeared in the title. There was a second person named – a young woman Chuck had met – as co-author. Reading over the material, Chuck spotted her contribution. It added little.

Chuck felt cheated and defeated, but the worst was yet to come. His two-year contract was up for renewal. When George brought him the news the man was smiling. The company had decided not to extend it. Chuck was floored. He'd been fired.

Chuck called his friends in the company, but they were unable to help. The decision not to renew his contract was made "at the highest levels." Even an internal transfer within the company, back to Canada, was out of the question. The Fipkes would have to find their own way back home. Cominco would do nothing for him. It was over. Unemployed in Rio.

Although he tried to put on a good show, he was devastated. He couldn't even imagine looking for another job. Completely and utterly discouraged he wanted never to have another boss.

Knowing what the future was to be for Cominco would have made his demise a little less traumatic, but Chuck had no way of knowing that the knife would turn in the company. Within a few years, a major purge would decimate the ranks. George himself would be fired and, after his wife left him, would die in Rio of a heart attack on the beach. The man who had usurped authorship of Chuck's paper would also be fired. Others would end up promoting dubious mining claims with questionable penny stock companies. Some would retire, while a few of the less fortunate would be forced onto the dole. In a curious twist of fate, the man who had been ultimately responsible for firing Chuck would himself come looking to Chuck for a job several years later – and would be turned down.

Cominco would survive its crisis and under new, vigorous management emerge ultimately as a trim, healthy mining company, but in 1976 it was a beached whale, and Chuck's feelings for it were at an all-time low. Chuck had worked hard to prove himself, out-producing everyone. He had risked his life repeatedly for Cominco in the jungle. He had found the company new mineral prospects. He had done his best. And it was not good enough.

Walking the streets of Jardim Botanico, Chuck struggled to rally his emotions. All was not lost, he told himself. He had saved $16,000. He was free and uncommitted. He could now do exactly as he pleased. It was a rare opportunity.

He had wanted, when he first came to Brazil, more than anything to see the Amazon and to live with unacculturated native Indians. Unfortunately, as he had learned, there were very few pure Indians left, and in his present circumstances, access to those that remained was virtually impossible.

Brazilian contact with the aboriginal peoples had not been particularly benevolent. Integration had been the rule, but as with colonial conquest everywhere, European diseases, bullets and battles also took their toll. Nor were the excesses all historical. Until discredited in 1967, the military government operated the Indian Protection Service (IPS). Publicly aiming to safeguard the few remaining native cultures and protect Indian lands, the agency was, instead, covertly pursuing a policy of wholesale slaughter. Relief supplies flown into the villages were heavily laced with arsenic. When the Indians learned to avoid the "aid", the IPS campaign became more overt, replacing poison with machine guns.

The Brazilians, mulatto and mestizo had much natural sympathy for the plight of once-free native Indians like the Xingu, who occupied a remote region in northern Mato Grosso and Goiás. After the secret mission of the IPS was revealed, public support for the Indians grew. In the end, legal walls were put up around the Indians, strictly controlling access to the Xingu and other native cultures. Contact was deliberately being minimized to allow them to live their lives uninterrupted, in the old ways. Chuck couldn't get in to see them.

They stayed for Rio's Catholic Christmas and the wild New Year's celebrations, but there was no reason to remain any longer. Shipping their things back to Canada and carrying what they needed on their backs, they left a few days later. Mark was 10, and Chuck knew that after their regular hikes up Corcovado and their races back down through the jungle Mark could handle himself. Cristina, just over three months old, would travel on his back.

His life with Cominco already far behind him, they set off, free again.

Chuck was not giving up on meeting Amazon Indians, he was only changing direction. Peru had ancient Indian cultures he could slip into. They would enter the Amazon from the west.

CHAPTER FORTY

REVELATION

AT Pucallpa, a large village on Peru's Ucayali River, Chuck rented a couple of rooms for Marlene, Mark and the baby and went off alone down the river.

Cut from the jungle on the east side of the Peruvian Andes, Pucallpa was a series of small, roughly hewn, weather-bleached wooden houses with covered verandas where one could sit and watch the river drift by. Beneath the buildings which were raised on stilts over the muddy earth, chickens scratched for food and chased each other, while small, thick-bristled pigs kept the snakes away and rooted endlessly in the garbage dumps. Open to the night air, tiger mosquitoes carrying dengue fever – the painful arbovirus infecting hundreds of thousands throughout the region – blew through their rooms. Marlene kept the children carefully under nets at night and creamed with insect repellents by day. She did not know how many weeks Chuck would be gone, only that the trip was important to him and that Pucallpa was safer for the children.

It was village life familiar to Marlene. With some changes it could have been the Congo or their base back in the Vogelkop. Now it was the Amazon. It was not unpleasant. There was a small dry-goods shop by the riverbank with some tables and chairs, where one could spend the afternoons sipping soft drinks and watching the children play soccer in the field beside the Catholic-run school.

The Ucayali River was one of the major tributaries of the upper Amazon. It opened up, towards Iquitos, into a wide lakelike body of water that flowed gently for thousands of miles across the entire continent to the Atlantic. Water traffic moved continuously past the village. Diesel engines, chugging noisily, pushed crafts upriver from Iquitos with freight, and, more quietly, back down with fresh produce. Small, native dugouts, laden until they were almost on a level with the surface, were paddled silently by Indians. Some were only small children, taking garden crops or wild jungle cuttings to or from some market along the river. The river was the heart of the country, its blood and soul.

Chuck had considered taking Marlene and the children with him beyond Pucallpa but he knew, from his experience in eastern Brazil, the jungle was too dangerous. One could not stand still for more than a few minutes without being bitten by something. Life had a more voracious appetite in the Amazon than in the Congo. Bites, not serious in themselves, quickly became septic. Parasites were endemic. He had never once returned to Rio from the bush without at least two different parasite infections – usually more.

His passion for exploration had not diminished, although the focus was subtly changing. There was still the question of whether or not the ancient, pre-Christian cultures, most of which were still being destroyed and were now only to be found scattered in far pockets of the world, had insights to offer, and whether or not their spiritual values were healthier than the culture which had replaced them all.

But where once, Chuck had loved the quiet serenity of the forest, he was now addicted to change. He loved the barrage of information that cascaded upon his senses when he moved through foreign worlds: it was life on a sustained peak. The constant stream of information stimulation was its own reward.

Chuck made his way to the village of Cetipo and there, leaving the river, got a ride through the bush on a track that ended at a mission with a jungle airstrip. The missionaries had their own plane, one of the few in the region, to access the more remote Indian villages in their crusade against the last remnants of the poorest pagan cultures. For a fee, they agreed to take Chuck.

The plane was already out, however and not scheduled to return for another five days. He would have to wait. The delay was worthwhile.

Blue macaws came out of the forest and filled the clearing with colour and raucous banter. In the evening, he watched the forest manufacture its own weather. Heat from the jungle sent streams of moisture into the cooling sky; flashes of lightning lit the night. Curiously, there was no accompanying rumble of thunder or rain – nothing to disturb the night's shrill insect chorus. At sundown the earth sighed and expelled its pent-up energy. The warm, thick air breaking free of the canopy condensed immediately, cloaking the forest in grey, ghostly mists.

The mission had several books written in English. To pass the time Chuck read them all, as he mused about the past and wondered how to deal with the future. He wasn't expecting any answers at the mission, or even in the Amazon. But an answer came to him anyway, not from the country, or the missionaries, but from one of their books. It was titled *How to be Successful in Business* and it changed his life.

At a moment when Chuck was receptive, the book spoke to him with the force of revelation. As an employee, limited to a working wage and subject to being ruled by the management philosophy of others, one could never be free, never grow. Only individuals with courage enough to go out on their own could define their own limits. And, as the book said, those limits were only the ones we make for ourselves. Beyond them, anything was possible. There are no limits.

It was a philosophy of optimism that Chuck recognized immediately. It was the expression of a youthful soul before it had been assaulted by life.

Sharing office space with George and working with Cominco had been so traumatic that Chuck had determined never to subject himself to anything like it again. And here, in his hands, was a philosophy which spoke directly to him: do not go back to work. Be your own boss – never again an employee. There was a choice. Quickly, he made it. He would go into business for himself.

The problem was, no geologist with seven year's field experience could hold himself out as a consultant. The industry would laugh at him. He didn't even have a master's degree. But he did have something: his heavy mineral theories. Rather than give them away to companies like Cominco, he could sell the new heavy mineral prospecting methodology. He could change the nature of exploration worldwide.

The more he thought about it, sitting in that jungle hut, the more excited he became. He could build his own lab in Canada and continue to refine the technology. By the time the plane came in, Chuck had reevaluated his experience with Cominco. It had given him the incentive to get out on his own, and he would. His future was waiting.

CHAPTER FORTY-ONE

COCKROACHES

THE plane dropped him off at another jungle dirt strip, the kind used by guerrillas and drug couriers. The strip was deserted and when the plane took off again he was alone, in the quiet of the jungle. After a few minutes, some people appeared from out of a trail to lead him back to their village beside the river. An Indian village with an airstrip, it was too altered by the modern world to interest him. It was not his final destination. Going straight to the dugout canoes that were sunk in the water and mud at the edge of the river to keep them from drying out and cracking, he engaged a man to take him deeper yet into the forest.

Sitting in the mud which filled the bottom of the canoe, riding low in the water the two men set off, paddling up the river, Chuck in front. He was in a jungle where diesel motors did not venture and to which chainsaws had not been introduced. The water, only a fingertip away, was dark and full of sediment.

"Piranya?" Chuck pointed into the water, using the Spanish pronunciation.

"Si! Si!" His guide nodded vigorously.

"Mujeres?" Chuck asked, sweeping his hand around them to indicate the jungle.

The other man didn't understand. Chuck laughed and outlined the curves of a woman in the air and again indicated the forest.

"Muchas mujeres?"

The Indian smiled but answered him seriously, "No Senor, solo jungla."

No women. Only jungle.

Chuck laughed again and they paddled on, their small craft cutting cleanly through the water, leaving a low wake rippling through the vegetation hanging down from the edge of the forest in a green wall beside them. The exercise stretched muscles that were rarely worked and Chuck put his back into it, enjoying the workout as they wound their way through mirror-surfaced channels. They moved deeper into the forest until they came to the Asavo Indian village. Bumping up gently against a muddy bank, they climbed out.

Chopped from the bush along the edge of the river, the Asavos' village was a collection of huts made of saplings, grass fibres and palm leaves, raised up off the ground on stilts. The hut nearest the forest was barren but well-maintained, and the villiagers led him there, to settle in among them.

The first night, sleeping in a hammock inside his hut, he was swarmed with biting creatures. He groped for his flashlight and clicked it on. In the beam he saw hordes of tiny black bugs all over his body scurrying from the light. Springing quickly out of his hammock, he shook the bugs off, retied his mosquito net tightly around the hammock, and crawled back in to sleep. Within minutes, they were again swarming him, eating him alive!

Again, he retied his net and again they got through. No matter what he did, every half hour another dozen bugs penetrated the net. They resembled tiny cockroaches and after the first sleepless night in the hut, he understood why it had been abandoned.

The Asavos, sleeping on hammocks woven from fibres of jungle plants did without mosquito netting and lived mostly naked. Chuck had at least some protection. At dawn, his body was covered in welts. In the morning, when he went foraging for food with the Indians, he tried to remain interested in what they were showing him, but he couldn't.

Something had changed in him since last he had lived with ancient cultures. He was now absolutely committed to life in the mainstream. Even if he was in the backcountry of Brazil or Peru, he was still an agent of modern technology and commerce. His future, he now knew, lay in competing within his own culture for a place at the top. If there were rewards, he would find them. If there were not, if the values were hollow and the system a fraud, he would keep looking. But his own culture was the only direction open to him. Everything else, he realized now, was a diversion; it only postponed the inevitable. Already he could feel the need rising in him to get started, anxious to begin his next journey. Yet he resisted the call. There was no telling when he would be this free again, drifting between worlds, days to himself.

As well, his unexpected disinterest in the life of the village partly lay in the nature of the Indians themselves. Lacking the vitality of the Africans, they were subdued, as though defeated. Their lives were easy, but they went about their daily chores with little enthusiasm and spent the better part of each day in quiet contemplation.

Chuck would have preferred to have gone into the jungle's remotest corners, to live with its least-impacted Indian inhabitants. There were still some natural Indian cultures left – deep in the forest where the missionaries had not reached them. But their remoteness put them beyond his means. He would need to mount an expedition of the kind Kennecott ran in West Irian. Alone, he could do no more, so he determined to make the best of the situation and concentrate instead on the physical spaces.

In the Amazon, the best was being out on the water. From the perspective of the river, viewed from a distance, even the jungle looked inviting. The old jungle pilots who spent years cruising its canopy, lifting in and out of its little bush strips, had one word to describe it: *magico*. With twice the life-diversity of the Congo, the Amazon was richer in colour, in sound and in energy than any place on earth. On the river, the days were serene, the interaction between mangrove-like forest and water always pleasant to the eye. It was a heady experience to drift along the waterways, to paddle up tiny tributaries through narrow channels in the weeds into oxbow lakes, like crater floors surrounded by jungle walls. Floating motionlessly, waiting for fish to rise while watching dragonflies hunt for prey and white egrets and herons stalk the weeds, he found the water a place of dreams.

Chuck's reveries took him constantly to Canada, devising business plans and making mental lists of inventory and prospective clients. The more he thought of his relationship with Cominco, the more he was prepared to admit to himself that he was like his father. Ed could not tolerate working for others either and, in spite of the hardships it caused, Ed had never changed to fit someone else's mould. Ed had lived his own life. Chuck considered it likely that human character was a matter of genetics just as it was for other animals; whatever the reason, he and his father were cut from the same cloth. Chuck, too, wanted to be totally independent. He, too, would pursue his own dreams.

After 11 years in geology, including the earliest days at UBC, it was now impossible to see the wild land they drifted through without looking at everything he saw for signs of mineralization.

Paddling up a narrow channel of clear water in a tributary creek he spotted something familiar in the water. Stopping the canoe and stripping down naked, he slipped over the side and dove to the bottom. It was a "float," a rock fragment displaced from some nearby outcropping vein. Through the water, it had looked promising – and it was. In his hand he held a chunk of massive sulfide. It would have greatly excited Kennecott or Samedan or even Cominco. Without analyzing it, he couldn't say whether it was from a deposit of copper-zinc or copper-lead-zinc, or if it contained associated gold and silver or other metals, but even without the analysis, he knew it had the potential to lead to a mineable deposit upstream. Chuck made a mental note of the location and, now in business for himself, decided to disclose it to no one. If money was to be made from its discovery, it would be his.

That was the way of the modern world. That was his own path now.

In the evening, after a meal of roasted fish and roots baked in coals prepared by one of the women, Chuck was reluctant to return to his own hut to feed his flesh to its inhabitants. He encouraged the villagers to play their music. It was the first real joy they had demonstrated. A lighthearted sense of delight and discovery absent from their daily activities appeared in their music. Indian flutes sending pure, birdlike notes dancing into the night redeemed the entire village experience for him.

Back in the fast track, the family flew on to Leticia, Colombia, further down river. Running along the edge of the central square, sloping down towards the river, was Leticia's open air market. Perched like gargoyles along the rooftops were hundreds of large Black Vultures. As comfortable on the ground as the dogs who kept their distance, the vultures ruled the garbage piles, covering them so thickly the mounds themselves seemed to heave with a dreadful lifeforce of their own. Lice-ridden and filthy, the carrioneaters took the place of pigeons underfoot although people gave them a wide berth rather than risk contact.

Poised strategically on the banks of the Amazon, with Peru across the river and Brazil at the south end of town, Leticia was one of Colombia's main ports of departure for the cocaine produced in the country's southeastern jungles. Carried by high-speed boats into Brazil, it was flown through a maze of jungle strips into Venezuela, Guyana and Surinam, and then north again into the great consumer markets of America. Drugs to create the illusion of excitement. Chuck had no interest in them at all.

His thrills were real.

CHAPTER FORTY-TWO

BOGOTÁ, COLOMBIA

In Bogotá, the Fipkes checked into a respectable hotel, something they did every couple of weeks for a break from the street living Chuck preferred, and when the hotel staff cautioned them about straying too near a particularly dangerous neighbourhood, he immediately got a cab to drop them off in its very heart. Chuck loved challenges. After Rio, Bogotá was the second most dangerous city in the world. Its murder rate alone was ten times that of the United States.

Like Rio, Bogotá was Catholic to its core. Old-world values ruled. It was a system that took care of its own and left everyone else to fend for themselves. Money, power and position were everything. Off-duty policemen freelanced at night as "guns-for-hire" and would do "street cleanings" of undesirables for the price of a few dollars a body. There was lots of work. Hundreds of thousands of people lived on the streets or in shanties no better than windbreaks. Some lived underground in the sewer systems. An entire sewer subculture had existed for generations in Bogotá. Yet, like Rio, it was a city of fabulous wealth, magnificent churches, European-style mansions and private estates. Although less than five degrees north of the equator, it was located high in the Andes and its misty, temperate climate, tree-lined boulevards and old-world character with manicured gardens and stone walls draped in flowering bougainvillea, were reminiscent of the moneyed British Properties of Vancouver or the more exclusive neighbourhoods of Oak Bay in Victoria. Apart from such superficial similarities, Bogotá was at once one of the richest cities in the world and one of the most desperate.

Chuck was not intimidated by poverty. Indeed, he could draw strength from it. He knew well its hunger and the driving ambition it could create. Poverty, as he could attest, was not altogether bad, as long as one could transcend it. Chuck, carrying Cristina, with Marlene and Mark by his side, wandered the streets, absorbed in the tension and conflict of the area. Alive to subtleties of behaviour among the children, he looked for that spark of ambition which he knew would carry them through life.

Chuck had nothing to fear from the people. In his heart, he was one of them and they had no cause to resent or attack him. He had not come to provoke them but to see how bad Bogotá could be. He had seen worse. He could survive this, too, if he had to.

Finding a neighbourhood bar, they all went in for a cold drink and something to eat. As was the custom in South America, children accompanied their parents, and although they attracted looks and the bar was rough, nobody bothered them. Back in their hotel, Mark became desperately ill. They waited for it to pass, hoping his condition would improve, but during the night, his condition deteriorated. Doubled over in pain and incontinent, he began crying out for help. Alarmed, Chuck turned to the hotel staff for assistance. Immediately, they drove him and the boy to the hospital. As they pulled up, Chuck's heart sank. There was a huge lineup. It was the middle of the night and the queue began inside the lobby, stretched out its doors, led down the stairs to the long paved entranceway and turning, continued on down the street for a block.

Critically ill people, some crippled and dying, sat huddled with their families on the cement, or stood stoically, hour after hour, perhaps day after day, moving slowly along, waiting in line for their chance to be seen. The hotel staff took the Fipkes to the front of the line, and as they negotiated with the hospital administration in Spanish, Chuck stood next to the people who had waited so long that they were past the doors, in the lobby. The first in line was a woman carrying her ailing, big-eyed young daughter. There were many sick children behind her.

When the doctor arrived, he took Mark first, and leaving the staring faces and the crowd behind, they were ushered into a private examining room.

"It's appendicitis," the doctor pronounced shortly. "We have to operate immediately." The operating room was open and the doctor, ready. Chuck didn't know what to do. Money was not an issue. He had been told the cost, and although it was high, he could pay the bill. If the doctor's diagnosis was correct, his son could die without the operation. Still, Chuck didn't know if he should believe the doctor or what he should do.

"Look," he told the doctor who was becoming impatient. "I have to call the Canadian Embassy."

He was able to get through and after some insistence was given the home phone number of the Canadian ambassador.

"Don't let anyone operate without first consulting our doctor," the ambassador advised him. He gave Chuck another number to call. Again, luck was with him and he got through. The doctor, a Colombian, was of the same opinion.

"Under no circumstances do you allow anyone to operate on your son. Go back to your hotel and if he gets worse, call me and I'll come to see him. Otherwise, come to my clinic in the morning." He gave Chuck the address.

It had taken nearly two hours and as they left the hospital, he passed the woman, still waiting first in line with her daughter. The large-eyed child was now dead and the woman was weeping miserably. She wasn't alone. Another child near the front of the queue had died on the steps.

Chuck followed the trail of suffering back out into the night. It was surprisingly cold, and in the dim light, people huddled together as much for comfort as warmth. For many, it was all they had.

PART FIVE

Pangaea's Children

Canada's Northwest Territories, 1977–1997

Only of this I am sure: I am singing, and therefore existing.

—B. ANTONICH, *HOME BEYOND THE STAR*

CHAPTER FORTY-THREE

KELOWNA, 1977

"**N**ow what?" Marlene asked.

It was a reasonable question. Chuck didn't have a lab, the banks had refused to lend him any money, and with no salary coming in, they had barely enough for their own needs.

"I go to the top!" he replied, his philosophy unchanged over the years.

Chuck adapted a company legal structure from Pat McBride, his old mentor, to his own purposes and incorporated C. F. Mineral Research Ltd. on the 13th day of June, 1977. It cost him $250. For another $200 he bought a 1967 Chevy station wagon with a 327-cubic-inch, v8 engine. He now had his own company and transport.

He also had a pregnant wife and two children, and they were back living with Marlene's parents.

After 10 years on the trail with Chuck, Marlene now wanted her own home and some security. Every time he had left, she wondered if he would return. He had been lucky, almost charmed. But it couldn't last forever. Sooner or later, the plane would not be found, the helicopter would slide into the mountain, the river current would be too strong, the mud too deep, the avalanche too wide, the poison too toxic, the disease too virulent. If "it" ever happened, she would be alone with the children. It was a frightening prospect. Over the years her own natural caution had grown stronger in reaction to his headlong, and sometimes reckless, rush into life. The children were her primary responsibility.

Chuck agreed to a major compromise. He had $12,000 left from his savings from Brazil. Although his new business needed everything he had and more, he agreed to split the money. Marlene took $6,000, made a down payment on a house at 263 Lake Avenue in Kelowna and moved in. Chuck spent the rest on legal fees, patenting the processes he had developed over the years.

Borrowing money from Mark's paper route, he drove to Vancouver, moved in with Marlene's sister Fay and her husband Ron, and called Earl Dodson. In spite of his painstaking preparation, he was nervous and his stutter, increasingly under control as an adult and often undetectable, was this day pronounced. It was not a stutter that stuck on words. It split at thoughts, on phrasing, as though his mind, cluttered with information, switched tracks in mid-sentence, requiring him to concentrate to keep the focus on a single subject. For Chuck, relaxation lay in speeding up the external experience. At slower speeds he sputtered, like a high performance race engine at idle.

"Yea ... Hi, Earl! ... It's, ah, me ... Chuck. Just got back from South America."

"Chuck! Well, how are you?" Earl seemed genuinely pleased to hear from him. A good start. Earl was a senior geologist with Chevron Oil's mineral division.

"Oh, good. Real good, hey. South America was just tremendous!"

"Still with Cominco?" Earl gave him the opening.

"Well, no … hey. Like, I'm on my own now. I've started my own business … and, well actually Earl, that's why I'm calling … I'd like to get together and talk about it."

"You haven't quit geology?" Earl asked.

"Oh, no … I … I'm still into it.… What I've got is a new heavy-mineral technique for detecting mineral deposits."

Earl Dodson had worked with Falconbridge before he took the job with Chevron. Chuck was aware that he already had some experience with heavy minerals there. Chuck moved quickly to dispel any notion Earl might have that the ideas he was promoting were trivial.

"I've just patented the technologies … like, it's really different, hey … I mean it's fantastic.… What can I say? You almost gotta see it work to believe it. But really, it's the best method of exploration I've ever heard of, hey. And, like, I've really been out in the field these last few years, hey, and there's nothing that compares with it anywhere!"

Earl's interest was piqued. Chuck had never been one to indulge in exaggeration. In geology, especially in exploration, excessive optimism was dangerous. Chuck had always been known for understatement. Chevron's geologist got right down to it.

"What exactly is it you're selling, Chuck?"

Chuck liked business that way. Straight ahead.

"Chevron still using the classic exploration techniques?" Chuck asked. The classic method was simply to spot a promising-looking formation, take a "grab sample" from the ground, and analyze it. If it contained metal, one looked further. If not, one moved on. That was conventional geochemistry. And it was Chevron's approach. With it, exploration was hit-and-miss. Mostly miss. And very costly. In a search for gold, the likelihood of picking up free gold in a grab sample, even one taken from relatively near the source of a major deposit, was extremely remote. Earl Dodson was among those who knew the inadequacies of the system.

"I've got a new method you won't believe," Chuck said.

"What's the downside?" Dodson asked.

"There isn't any," Chuck replied. Except of course the cost of his own fees. And the use of his lab. "It'll save you more money than you'd believe." A safe answer.

Earl met him for lunch, Chuck paid – one had to appear successful – and Chevron was signed up as his first client. Chuck's timing was fortuitous. Chevron had just targeted some areas of Vancouver Island to explore for massive sulfides and the company was presently laying out the exploration program. Chuck could help.

They agreed on a price of $40,000. Chuck was keeping it under control, but his heart was singing. The contract price, however, included lab work, and he didn't have a lab – they were expensive. As soon as he left Earl Dodson, Chuck contracted a glassblower to make the glassware he needed, designed and ordered the construction of a special fumehood, designed a wet-shaking, wet-sieving unit and put in an order for a Frantz Separator to be delivered to his house, all cash-on-delivery. The separator alone was worth $6,000. With his materials on order, Chuck went to Vancouver Island with Chevron's geologists and trained them in his methods of sampling. Rather than have the geologists take just a handful of sand from each location, Chuck had them begin with 90 to 135 kilometres of the same material, filtering it first through a screen of minus-20 mesh to remove all the larger pieces and then washing it down in a pan to leave the heaviest fine-grained materials remaining, enough to fill a 12-kilogram bag. From the geological terrain Chevron wanted sampled, Chuck instructed their geologists to take not merely a few dozen small grab samples, but over two hundred of the 12-kilogram bag samples.

Now, with over two tonnes of fine sands to analyze in his lab, Chuck had to face the fact his lab, although on order, was still more dream than reality. Almost as an afterthought as they were leaving the island, Chuck turned to Earl, "Oh, Earl ... I'll need an advance on the contract, hey ... like, to cover some of my expenses."

"Sure," Earl agreed. "What do you need?"

"Well ... ," Chuck knew exactly what he needed, but he quickly decided to aim higher, "Say ... half now ... and half when the work's done."

The check for $20,000 arrived just in time to pay for the equipment which landed cash-on-delivery on his doorstep.

The "lab" included Marlene's kitchen, the analysis beginning with Marlene drying out the sand samples in the oven before moving them into the backyard. It was like the operation he had experimented with on the balcony of their apartment in Rio on a grander scale. The system worked perfectly – for two days. The bearings of the wet-sieving unit burned out. They couldn't take the pressure of heavy use. Harley Pyett, Marlene's father, a retired heavy-duty mechanic, came over to help and as often as the units burned out he repacked them – every two days. Gradually they began to work their way through the tons of sand.

Separating materials according to their specific gravities, each 12-kilogram sample was slowly reduced to a five-to 10-gram concentrate – a reduction of 1,200 to one – which was then shipped off to be assayed. Chevron was impressed. Chuck had not exaggerated the value of the system. If there was a deposit upstream, his sampling and concentration techniques were exponentially better able to detect it than any other method currently in use.

From an original, unscreened field mass of loose gravel and sand, equivalent to several tons, the total concentrated weight for assaying when Chuck finished was two kilos. Chevron became a regular customer, and C. F. Minerals took off.

Marlene was glad of it. Chuck hardly noticed, but there were days when there was no food in the house. By the time C. F. Minerals was able to repay Mark the loans on his paper route, Mark was out $500 on his "accounting" to the Kelowna *Courier*, and running out of excuses.

CHAPTER FORTY-FOUR

SUPERIOR

Superior Oil, a company based in the U.S., was, like Chevron Oil, in the hunt for gold.

"Hi, Mike! Chuck here! How you doing?"

"Chuck! How are you? How's the family? … "

"Oh, real good! … Good, good … They're fine."

"How's Cominco?" Mike asked.

"I'm out," Chuck replied. The tone of his voice conveyed some of the feelings he still had about the company. Mike picked up on it right away.

"Oh? … What happened, Chuck?"

"I'll tell you, but some other time, hey. It's a long story. It's history now anyway."

Over a decade ago, in the early sixties, Mike Wolfhard had worked for Cominco too. When he quit to return to university, he shared some classes and common interests with Chuck – porphyry copper under Jack Gower in particular. Several years older than Chuck and a year ahead of him at UBC, he was, like Chuck, a married student with a family, and they had socialized frequently. It had been some time since they had last spoken to one another, but the world of mining was a small one and it was easy to follow each other's career.

After graduating at the top of his class, Wolfhard had gone to Quintana, a company exploring for porphyry coppers in British Columbia. When Quintana's money began to run out and the company started to wind down, Wolfhard moved to Superior Oil which, like Chevron, had recently decided to create a minerals division: Superior Minerals. Nor were they alone. Oil companies, flush with cash, were everywhere expanding from fossil fuels into earth minerals, a field, they would soon discover, that only superficially resembled their own. Standard Oil, to get a jump on the others, bought Kennecott itself, still with its Ok Tedi assets, only to find it had jumped in over its head.

Based in Reno, Nevada, Wolfhard was one of Superior Oil's new mineral managers. He was in Vancouver only for a few days.

"What about you?" Chuck asked. "What's Superior like to work for?"

"Pretty demanding – result-oriented – but they're dynamic," Wolfhard replied. "Our mineral division is new. We're just putting it together, so it's exciting. There's no baggage yet, if you know what I mean?"

"I know *exactly* what you mean!" Chuck laughed. Politics ruled companies as much as governments.

"Hey, you looking for work?" Wolfhard asked suddenly, the reason for Chuck's call not yet apparent. If he were, he'd have a place with Superior.

"No, actually … I'm on my own now. I've started my own business."

Briefly Chuck described the processes he had patented and was promoting. His sales pitch had improved. He now had a track record and a functioning lab behind him. When he finished his outline, he threw out the hook.

"I was kinda hoping you might be able to give me some leads."

Wolfhard had taken it all in. If what Chuck said was true, and he didn't doubt Chuck, it could prove a real advantage to the company – like Jack Gower's leach-capping system was to Kennecott – and to him, for bringing it to them.

"Chuck, let me see what I can do … Superior likes new ideas. You know the history of Superior Oil?" Chuck didn't. Wolfhard kept it short. "Howard Keck is principal shareholder. His father was an oil-well driller and founded the company. He built it up with new technology for locating oil into one of the most successful independent oil companies in the world. The point is new technologies, that's what gave it the edge. Creative approaches made it world-class. I think Superior might just want to hear your ideas as well. I'll buy lunch."

Wolfhard was right. Superior was interested. The company flew Chuck down to Nevada to address their geologists at a departmental planning meeting for their upcoming exploration project. The specific targets they had worked out were confidential and he was not given access to the field, but he had done his research and could speak in general terms. He knew what Superior was looking for – a commercial-sized deposit of micron gold. They sought not a small, rich vein with a short mining future but a massive, low-grade deposit they could mine for years, returning a steady profit over their operating costs: a "heap-leach deposit." In heap-leaching, the gold ore is bathed with a cyanide solution on a heap pad and the gold leached out. The company's plan was to conventionally sample a huge region. Chuck had something to say about their proposal and his new analysis.

"The first problem with prospecting, is that even downstream from a known commercial deposit, regular geochemical methods often fail to detect the deposit. As the gold is heterogeneously distributed and can be present in such minute quantities, it's unlikely you'd find even a trace in a sample as small as a cupful of sand. It's like throwing a hook into the ocean and hoping to pull out a fish. The fisherman at least knows there's fish in the water, so he won't quit. But the geologist only knows his sample of sand assayed with no gold, so he moves on – and misses the strike!"

The limitations of the system were well-known to everyone in the room. Chuck then asked the question every prospector had been asking for 5,000 years.

"So, how can we improve the odds?"

There were no good answers. To put his ultimate point in perspective, Chuck continued working through the problem.

"Instead, of scooping up the usual little cupful of fine sand and geochemically analyzing it for gold, or some other, even rarer, trace element, we could shovel up hundreds of pounds of material from each spot we wanted to sample and analyze it all."

The idea was absurd. One might as well geochemically analyze the Earth, grain by grain. It was theoretically possible, but practically impossible. The limitations had been accepted by the industry long ago. But not by Chuck. To him, the possibilities for growth, like reality, were infinite. It was simply a matter of keeping an open mind – and staying at the edge of new technologies.

"There is, in fact, a way to do it, to analyze hundreds of pounds of field material for those elusive grains of gold – and to do it economically!"

They sat up. He had their attention now.

"You begin with several hundred pounds of gravel and then screen it down through a fine mesh to a sample size of 10 to 12 kilograms of fine sand. Instead of taking one conventional grab sample from each target area, you take several of these larger samples. In fact, it's better if you collect tons of material – remember hey, that the larger the sample, the better the odds. Back in my lab, I concentrate the samples down by washing them, then wet-sieving them, jigging them and then, using tetrabiomethene and methene iodide, I separate the material, first with the heavy liquids, and finally electromagnetically, removing all the waste, step by step, until the elements I've been targeting – like gold – are left concentrated in the five-to-10 grain sample that's left behind, ready to be geochemically analyzed or assayed."

Superior was suitably impressed, but Chuck had still more.

"Statistically, we can probably expect to pick up 100 to 150 anomalies – trace amounts of gold – in the 500 to 600 samples taken across a whole region containing favourable formations. So, what's that going to tell you?"

He paused for effect. He wasn't looking for any answers. He had them. "Gold is fairly common, and widely distributed in trace amounts throughout any favourable geological landscape … So let's assume the geology you've targeted is favourable for gold. The anomalies won't tell you much more than you already know. One hundred to 150 gold anomalies are one hell of a lot of targets to follow up on. Each one is extremely expensive to explore and, ultimately, could lead nowhere at all – just free gold in the sand."

Chuck was enjoying himself. With a professional audience it was as close as he'd get to a critique of his work, but he was on solid ground. Like his father's painted farm pictures, he had something worthwhile to sell. Prospecting was gambling with high stakes and nobody liked losing. He could improve the odds, dramatically.

"But if one of those anomalies leads back to a deposit, you've got a new mine, you with me? So what do you do, hey?" he asked them. "Follow them all up? Go for broke?"

There was no other way. It was the soft midriff of the industry, their Achilles' heel. Only free trappers like Gunther Lishy or big companies with deep pockets could afford to prospect for long. Without a strike, the resources of everyone in between soon withered away. Chuck dropped his second bomb.

"You don't have to follow them all up! All you have to do is collect the initial samples. My lab can determine, hey, whether each anomaly is simply common background gold and worthless, you with me? or has *potential* – whether in fact it eroded down from a micron deposit."

The stir in the group was satisfying. To be recognized by one's peers as making a contribution was, it seemed, one of life's purposes. Everybody had only one question: How?

It was a technical issue, but the practical translation meant a significant improvement to the cost-benefit equation. What Chuck offered was a more efficient route to success.

"Gold in heap-leach deposits are, as you know, associated with other minerals like antimony, arsenic and lead – the pathfinder elements. At the same time I'm concentrating the gold from the samples in the lab, I'm concentrating these pathfinders. By isolating them magnetically and concentrating them – they have specific gravities greater than 2.9 – I can also separate these target minerals from the same field samples I'm screening for gold, you with me? If a sample contains not just gold, but also the pathfinders, then you're downstream from a deposit. All without leaving the lab!"

The room was silent, his audience absorbing the import of his lecture. It was simple yet revolutionary. Chuck was as fully engaged as he could ever be.

"I don't know, hey, where your samples are actually coming from – you take the field samples – so you're never compromised. If I get only one or two of the pathfinders in the sample, or their relative concentrations don't match the chemical profile of a commercial gold deposit, I can tell you just how hot your sample is – whether it's worth following up or forgetting."

The lab costs weren't cheap, but they were a small fraction of what it would cost to follow up the same samples in the field. Chuck's techniques were so refined he could isolate a few grams of targeted elements from a huge mass of material. It was a revelation.

Superior bought in.

While Chevron got C. F. Minerals off the ground, Superior Oil gave it a direction and a license to pursue its own dreams. Like all sciences, geology was a world that was only dimly understood – there was far more to be learned than was already known – and Chuck loved exploring its dimensions as much as he loved following jungle trails to ancient cultures. The mysteries of the history of Earth and its features were no less exciting and challenging than those of the human and animal world: even more so. The scientific frontier he was exploring was like a virgin land. No one had ever penetrated it before.

Largely it was a frontier of the mind, a creative release that required new thinking to solve old problems. He could probe the unknown while at home with his family at the table. The lab now replaced the land as his favoured plane of experience, and it was here he would spent endless hours, for years. Above all else, the lab was his private world, and always accessible. Whenever he felt the need, he could use it to plunge into the mysteries of life.

While Superior's geologists were collecting the field samples from their secret locations in Nevada, Chuck collected orientation samples – uncontaminated, downstream samples from all the known gold deposits in Nevada. Back at his lab he analyzed them to establish what new compounds the pathfinder minerals were now in, after the oxidizing and magnetic changes of the tertiary period – as long as sixty-five million years ago – had taken place. He adjusted the system accordingly, specifically designing a method of concentration, taking advantage of the natural properties of the minerals to ensure the highest geochemical contrast to background waste material for the mineral separations.

It involved meticulous, detailed work that kept him at the lab, occupied for days. Determined to prove himself, Chuck had more than his reputation at stake. Less dramatic and immediate, but no less challenging than confronting African rhinos and his own fear in New Guinea swamps, this swim in the mainstream of geology and science was a competition for his own place on the leading edge.

The results were extraordinary. He turned up nearly 20 gold anomalies that had associated pathfinder elements. It was a major hit! Chuck didn't know whether the anomalies were all from the same watershed, downstream from one large deposit, or from several, but he had no doubt each one represented a heap-leach gold deposit.

Excited, Chuck was anxious to follow up the results, but he couldn't – it wasn't his play. He had run exploration programs and been privy to inside information for so long, it felt odd to be excluded. But he was; it was strictly Superior's game.

It was not just the dream of being self-employed that Chuck was after; he wanted to explore, too. His greatest hope, unspoken, was that his own company would one day take him out into the field, where he could compete at the same level field with the big players in the great treasure hunt itself.

With the positive samples plotted out on a map, Superior's field crew worked up the hot watersheds, collecting samples along the way, closing in on the gold-field. When Superior's geologists finished, another large load of sample bags arrived on Chuck's doorstep for processing. In one of them he found a perfect chemical match to the profile he had developed in his orientation study of samples taken downstream from Nevada's operating gold mines. It was a beautiful, heavy-mineral anomaly of gold, arsenic, antimony and lead: a near-source sample.

Somewhere upstream, nearby, was a major primary deposit – a mine – waiting to be uncovered. Superior was on the edge of the discovery and Chuck knew it, but it was some time before he heard the final outcome.

"We lost it," Mike told him at last. "Our geologist, not being astute in the field, walked upstream from the hot sample, scrambled right overtop the gold deposit without recognizing it, and took a sample higher up. Needless to say, that one was negative. We should have followed it up more quickly, but we put it on the back burner too long. Another geologist hiking the same creek spotted the deposit and staked it. It's gone!"

It was a major find. That deposit became Nevada's Goldbar Mine. Chuck was as disappointed as Superior.

It wasn't the only one missed. Another hot anomaly the company took too long to close in on was also staked under their noses by a stranger. That deposit became the Paradise Peak Mine. The discoveries, although made by others, proved conclusively that Chuck's methods were reliable. From now on, matching chemical signatures to chemical profiles was the new approach to prospecting for Superior. "Hot samples" took on a whole new meaning.

Not only large companies became his clients, but small ones, too. Size was no longer a prerequisite for success. Anyone with the time and resources to explore could play the field. Ken Daughtry, the owner of Discovery Consultants and a member of the Kelowna Prospectors' Club, employed Chuck's methods and lab to develop his own discovery into a gold mine. So successful was he that within 10 years he discovered four commercial gold mines that were put into production.

But Superior didn't lose them all. Using Chuck's lab and the sampling techniques that they had followed in Nevada, they later moved into Idaho and hit another hot gold anomaly. This time they quickly staked it. Further exploration proved it out, and Superior Oil's minerals division now had its own gold mine.

With his new business Chuck was now at the centre of the treasure hunt, excitement sometimes running at a fever pitch. The frustration of staying on the sidelines, however, was unbearable. Fortunes were lost and won in his microscopes, and he was itching to get into the play.

He knew he could do better.

CHAPTER FORTY-FIVE

DIAMONDS

THAT first summer the lab rumbled all day and throughout the night in Chuck's backyard. As he worked over toxic heavy chemicals in the open air, Marlene took care of the financial records, maintained the books and, even after the new baby, Charlane Rosemarie, was born on the 18th of September, 1977, eight days short of one year after Cristina's birth, continued to dry the samples in the kitchen and operate the magnetic separator. Mark, now aged eleven, ran the wet-sieving unit after school.

By midwinter, when the temperature in Kelowna dropped below freezing and stayed there and the chemicals seized up and wouldn't thaw, it was time to move. Chuck relocated the lab indoors to Powick Street at the edge of town. Business was steady, he now had a permanent staff, and he could, after a fashion, afford the rent. His first employee was Carol, Chuck's sister, who for the next three years would only draw expenses for room and board, allowing Chuck to put her salary to use in building his business. Once she was paid her back wages, she invested it again in Chuck's ventures, and stayed to work with him for seven more years. It was an investment that would, ultimately, pay off.

During the spring of 1978, Mike Wolfhard had secretly completed a market research study for Superior Minerals. Calculating world reserves, production and future demand, he identified two minerals which were declining in supply and would peak in value in a few years: platinum and diamonds. Quietly, Superior Minerals decided to target diamonds and called Chuck.

"Can you do concentrations for diamond indicator minerals?"

For Chuck it was as if a door which he had found in Africa and tried to pry open in Brazil suddenly swung free on its hinges. Chuck had kept all his notes from his research in Brazil and the actual samples from his tour of Finsch and the other diamond mines DeBeers had let him see in South Africa. It was not much to go on, but then, the published literature on the subject was almost non-existent. If DeBeers knew more about diamond geology, about the chemistries involved in diamond formations and diamond exploration, they were guarding their secrets carefully. As DeBeers had long known, and as the Russians were quickly learning, a good gold mine was worth millions. But a diamond mine was worth billions. Finding one was the greatest treasure of all time.

"I can." Chuck replied confidently. He'd learn. He would have to. This was his chance. The diamond hunt had begun.

Superior had bagged thirty samples, which they shipped to him, and he designed a separation and concentration process specifically for diamond indicator minerals. Once concentrated, a careful examination of each individual grain in the concentrated sample under a microscope – the indicator minerals associated with diamonds being visually identifiable – would determine if any diamond indicator minerals were present.

Concentrating each sample bag down to several grams each, he did the final microscope work himself. The samples were from an undisclosed American location, but one after another, they proved to have no indicator minerals. None at all.

He was doing the microscopic work at home, and was picking through the last sample when Marlene called him – for the second time – from the kitchen.

"Supper's getting cold!"

"In a minute!" He had only a small group of grains left to examine when he flipped over one of the last remaining particles. Attached to it on one side was a green chrome diopside – the only indicator mineral found in the entire program. By itself it was insignificant and Superior quickly moved on to survey new prospects, but this contact with Superior had a profound and lasting influence on Chuck. The green chrome diopside he had found proved his methods would work as well for diamonds as it did for gold, and Superior carried him along into their new play, the hunt for diamonds.

In their search for a North American diamond pipe Superior quickly had results. Twenty-five miles northwest of Fort Collins, Colorado, in the Front Range of the Rocky Mountains, there was an insignificant rock quarry. Some of the stone which had been cut from it was used on the floor of the Fort Collins airport. The company quarrying it found that it crushed easily and were supplying it for roadbed construction when a geologist with the Geological Survey of Wyoming arrived at the gates. He had followed a geological formation south of Wyoming's southern border right to the quarry. The unusual nature of the soft quarry rock, which bore no resemblance to any of the surrounding rock, struck him instantly. When they began sawing into it to cut him a sample piece, their saw broke. A fluke, but they had hit a diamond! The rock was a kimberlite pipe that had intruded, ages ago, into the regional rock. And it was loaded with diamond indicator minerals!

Superior rushed in, bought it from the operators, named the pipe "Sloan 1" – in the DeBeers' tradition – after the name of the farmer on whose land it had been located, and, after the construction of an expensive plant on the site, began processing the kimberlite.

Evaluation of the commercial potential of diamond-bearing volcanic pipes was, however, a new science, and the company was overly optimistic. They soon discovered that diamonds alone do not justify a mine. The pipe was not of commercial grade. Their recovery rate was only eight or nine carats per 100 tons of kimberlite, and even those were diamonds of poor quality.

After Superior contracted Chuck and a field crew to sample the entire area and process the collected samples at Chuck's lab, many more diamond-bearing kimberlites were found and evaluated. However, when no economically viable diamond pipes were discovered among them, Superior closed the recovery plant, put the whole property up for sale and left. For Superior, Sloan was extremely disappointing. Still, for the industry, it was important in geological, if not economic terms; when Chuck studied it, it provided new clues.

Vladimir Sobolev was a world leader in diamond geology. A Russian genius, he had sampled the South African diamond fields and advanced several theories for diamond formations. Chuck found Sobolev's papers fascinating reading – especially in light of the Sloan area pipes. It had long been known that diamonds were not formed within the Earth's crust, but beneath it – in the zone of the upper mantle in rare rock formations known as peridotite and eclogite. Formed at depths of 180 kilometres and more, the diamonds were floated to the surface in a rare volcanic rock type known as kimberlite magma. In his studies of the Earth's mantle – the zone below the crust and above the core – Sobolev postulated his theory that it was only in the deepest layers of the crust where the Earth's pressures were the greatest that diamonds could have been formed without burning off. Therefore, according to Sobolev, it would only be in those magmas that passed up through the deepest layers of the crust that diamonds could be collected and brought to the surface.

It was a difficult theory to prove. South Africa had never studied the thickness of the crust around its diamond formations and there was little data available worldwide to support Sobolev's theory. Only oil geologists plumbed the depths of the Earth with seismic blasts, in areas of geology unsuitable for diamonds. But there was some deep crust information available.

Chuck found that a seismic line had been mapped across the United States and coincidentally, it went right through the Fort Collins area. Right where the Colorado diamonds were found, the crust was at its thickest point in the country, 50 to 55 kilometres wide. As far as the Sloan pipes were concerned, Sobolev was dead on.

Then Chuck came upon some unpublished work of the Geological Survey of Canada. A geologist, Dr. Ray Price, had done some seismic work around Fernie, in the southeastern corner of British Columbia. On the eastern edge of the Canadian Rocky Mountains near the border with the United States, the geology was similar to that of the Fort Collins area. Utilizing blasts from the deep underground shafts of the coal mines in the area, Price had seismic-mapped the Mohorovicic discontinuity, the boundary surface separating the Earth's crust from the subjacent mantle. Named in honour of its discoverer, Andrija Mohorovicic, it was estimated to range between 5 to 10 kilometres beneath the ocean floor and 35 kilometres beneath the continents – although the existence of deep keels reaching down 60 kilometres or more under some mountain ranges had been confirmed.

Chuck obtained unpublished copies of Ray Price's maps. There, just outside the town of Golden in the mountains along the edge of Banff National Park, was a bull's-eye! A deep keel zone. If Sobolev's theories were correct – and Chuck was betting on them – there were diamonds there, waiting to be found. It was a mountain range that had been combed for a century by prospectors looking for gold, silver and lead. But no one had ever searched the range for diamonds. It was a whole new field.

Chuck put together a proposal to explore the region for diamonds and went out to market it, approaching first Placer, then Bethlehem and finally all the major Canadian mining companies. His enthusiasm soured rapidly however as, repeatedly, their reactions were negative. He was unable to find a partner. "Disinterest" was expressing it mildly. Dave Snyder, an executive officer of one of the companies Chuck approached was quite candid in expressing the general sentiment of the local mining industry.

"Chuck, don't take this personally, but British Columbia is notorious for having fraud artists running exploration companies. The last 'diamond project' I heard about was a few years ago ... A couple of crooks out of Vancouver salted a creek near Whistler with a few stones and then dragged some investors out to prove to them how they'd been panning diamonds from the creek bottom. One of the fellas scooped up the sand and when he panned it down to three diamonds turned to his partner and said, 'Hey, where the hell's the fourth diamond?' "

Chuck was aware of far more sophisticated, but no less deceitful, schemes that had been perpetrated through the Vancouver Stock Exchange. Most commonly, those companies raised capital to acquire or develop absolutely worthless properties from silent partners who later secretly shared the wealth with the company's executive. After going bankrupt, the same group would resurface later with another company – and another "promising property" to develop. But there was no basis for any comparison with those companies, Chuck insisted. "You know as well as I do, hey, that they're almost always run by promoters – not geologists!"

"Still, there are a lot of rogues in the business," Dave argued, refusing to budge from his position. "One learns to be suspicious."

Chuck could not agree. Generally, the insiders knew who was reliable and who was not. In his view, it wasn't negative experiences that had informed their attitudes, rather, there was a kind of blind intransigence that defined the working paradigm of the industry. Most mining companies, in spite of the flexible and progressive requirements for exploration, were obstinate and reactionary, basing their future plans on past successes and – the narrowest thinking of all – the belief that if nobody else was doing it, it couldn't be worth doing. The very idea of prospecting for diamonds in Canada was, simply, ludicrous.

"If we didn't have the courage to fly, hey, or to cross the oceans to explore ... to grow ... then where would we be, Dave? We wouldn't even be keeping warm around a fire. I mean, that's how we advance, eh ... with new ideas."

"Chuck, I don't disagree ... I'm not defending the decision. I'm just saying it's difficult to know who to trust and what to believe. All I can say is we're going to stick to what we know. That's the safe money. There's nobody in this country with exposure to diamonds. It's all foreign turf. Diamonds, like lions and tigers, belong to far more exotic climes than Canada!"

Lack of imagination was a human condition, Chuck knew. Even if their present circumstances were killing them, as they were killing those Canadians still working the Kilembe copper mine in Amin's blood-soaked Uganda, "better the Devil you know" than risk change.

In the end Chuck modified his sales pitch to target precious metals, burying the diamond prospects in the body of the report, and returned to the market, still hoping to pair up with a Canadian company. He still had no luck. Worse, the modified proposal had its own serious drawback: targeting precious metals in the Rockies was an old story. The mountains had already been thoroughly prospected. Chuck knew that he could do much more with the same field in his lab, but to everyone he approached, it remained old ground which had been already picked over for a century.

Most of the companies that looked at the proposal thought it was too bare-bones. When they reached the clauses in the proposal that dealt with Chuck's belief that the Rockies might also hold the potential for diamonds, their eyes glazed over and their lips grew thin. Any talk of diamonds operated like a knockout punch.

It was not the first time Chuck had been disappointed in trying to interest a major company in diamond exploration. Cominco had reacted the same way when he proposed they expand their Brazilian search to include diamonds. It was more than a resistance to new thinking; there was a certain snobbery among Canadian companies. To take direction from a stranger, especially a stranger like Chuck, was to suggest they were incapable of planning their own future. A first impression, indeed even a deeper understanding, of Chuck was of an individual who was not particularly concerned with appearances or social rules. His shoelaces were often undone, documents frequently misplaced and luggage lost or forgotten. Like the quintessential absent-minded professor, so deeply focused was he that he rarely saw himself. Marlene packed his things and took care of details, while Chuck worked and dreamed.

Americans were more accessible. There, foreign birth, stutters and dress codes were much less important. They were far more ready to do business with strangers, and new ventures – even risky ones – had a welcome reception with companies south of the border. Too, it helped to deal with companies that knew something of the technologies on which he was basing his proposals. With Americans, and with those who were already familiar with his work, he did much better.

He had two bites. Ben Baldwin of Shell Oil, another client, had collaborated with Chuck on an exploration project for uranium in the Okanagan Valley, knew his capabilities and was interested. Even more encouraging, it was not metals they were interested in, they liked the idea of exploring for diamonds. Shell offered to put up 51 percent of the exploration budget. Chuck needed only to raise the difference.

He flew at last to Nevada, where his friend Mike Wolfhard had managed to raise Superior's interest: his second bite. Jack Langton was a short Texan who sported a wide-brimmed cowboy hat, cowboy boots and big cigars. As the man in charge of Superior's mineral division, all the projects were Langton's call.

"Okay Chuck, it's your show!" Langton boomed out from his seat at the back of the room. "You got 20 minutes!"

He sat back and listened carefully as Chuck began his presentation, reviewing the literature, his survey plans and the technology as he made his arguments to prospect the Rockies. Beside Langton sat Mike Wolfhard and Hugo Dummett.

As Chuck spoke he noticed Wolfhard leaning over every few moments to whisper something to Langton. Before being transferred to the mineral division where he was put in charge of minerals research, Wolfhard had the satisfaction of seeing Superior's stock soar in value beyond $1,000 a share, the highest-priced stock on the New York exchange. Then, six months after a 10-to-one split, it rose back up to $600 a share. Superior wholly owned Canadian Superior Oil, a major company in its own right, 60 percent of Falconbridge, and had a controlling interest in MacIntyre, which in turn controlled Noranda. The company was expecting Wolfhard and Dummett to perform the same magic with its mineral division.

Dummett seemed keen. Langton maintained a poker face. Chuck concentrated his attention on Mike Wolfhard and Dummett, the company's newest employee. Professionally distinguished, Dummett was a big man, gentle and sophisticated. A South African with a master's degree in geology, like Chuck and Wolfhard he had specialized in porphyry coppers before moving to northern Queensland, where he became a naturalized Australian. Prior to moving to Australia, he had explored for diamonds for DeBeers in Angola. Superior approached him after a worldwide search for a geologist to head their diamond exploration program.

Chuck liked him immediately. In fact, he liked everyone associated with Superior. The company lived up to its name. Unlike some of its competitors, managed by less secure people who dissipated their companies' energies by exploiting the weaknesses of their employees in an interminable pursuit of internal power, Superior's management philosophy was to exploit the strengths of its members, creating a self-supporting team with a positive vision. Efforts and ability in locating commercial deposits, rather than loyalty to company bosses, was the principal criterion for promotion. As obvious as it seemed, it was a rare philosophy to find practised, and a major reason for Superior's success.

Chuck was only a few minutes into his presentation when Jack Langton interrupted him. Waving a two-page handout summary Chuck had given them at the start, Langton said, "I see you're proposing this here exploration venture as a joint venture?"

"Yea, that's right," Chuck said. "This way if we can get two or three companies financing the exploration costs, we can spread the risk out a little."

The offer by Shell to take up to 51 percent of the cost and the majority interest in any commercial deposit found was spelled out in the pamphlet. Chuck was only looking for a contribution by Superior.

"Could one company take a hundred percent of the project?" Langton asked, his intent not entirely clear to Chuck.

"Well, although the project was envisioned as a joint venture I suppose if a single company really wanted a hundred percent, we could make those arrangements."

"Fine!" Langton announced. "We'll take a hundred percent!".

Superior put up the full US$200,000 for the budget and brought Falconbridge in on the project, splitting their hundred percent between the two companies, 51 percent Superior, 49 Falconbridge. Chuck, under the agreement, maintained management control of the field and all the lab work.

Chuck was elated. He had ambitiously undertaken to sample over 50,000 square kilometres of the southern Rockies. His personal interest in the value of any commercial deposit he found would be a 10 percent net profit royalty. It was more than he had dreamed of when he decided, in the Amazon, to go independent.

It was the summer of 1978. His business was booming, he was back in the field exploring, he was looking for diamonds and he was now in it for himself. And he had Superior Oil and Falconbridge backing him!

He put his heart and soul into the project and worked like never before. As a field leader he was relentless. The crews were up before dawn and out until dark, and Chuck set a pace through the day he expected them all to keep up with. By the fall, as snow was beginning to bury the mountains, making the work treacherous, they were getting the first lab results back from the samples they had taken around Golden.

The whole crew was bunked together in a single motel room in Cranbrook. Chuck demanded a tight budget program and the men were sleeping in a row on the floor when the phone rang. It was 4:00 in the morning. With two babies only a year apart, Marlene was busy during the day with the family. The only time left to her to do lab work was the night, when the children were asleep. Familiar with the principles and the mechanical operation of the lab, Marlene had kept pace with all the changes since Chuck built his first experimental lab on the balcony of their apartment in Rio.

She was doing the final microscope work, picking through the concentrates looking for diamond indicators, when she put a new dish of grains from a concentrated sample under the scope. Bright green, the indicators stood out like neon in a desert night. Excited, she phoned Chuck immediately while she continued to pick through the sample.

"Are you sure?" Chuck asked. He knew Marlene wouldn't be mistaken, but he'd been asleep. She could identify a chrome diopside almost as well as he could.

"I'm positive," she replied. "It's just loaded with them!"

He was wide awake now and, roused the crew. With the usual braying chorus of complaints, made even more vocal by the early hour, they paused only to pick up take-out breakfasts at a 24-hour restaurant and were off, driving north in the night into the mountains to the town of Golden.

Chuck was keeping it well under control, but he was very excited. They had a hit! He knew in which sample Marlene had found the chrome diopsides. It was one of only a hundred samples they used a helicopter to collect, high up in the Rockies near Mount Freshfield. Chuck had taken it himself.

When they arrived in Golden, he and Paul Tomlin, one of the men from the crew, chartered a helicopter and were off. It was still early in the morning, but they had a lot to do: find and stake an ancient volcanic pipe, one that might be worth more than all the gold ever produced in the region.

Chuck had the helicopter put them down at the site where he had taken the sample. He wanted to walk to it. Moving slowly upstream, his head to the ground examining everything, he spotted a small piece of foreign rock that did not match the surrounding stone. The "float" could only have been washed down from a higher outcrop. It looked like kimberlite! He kept on. They were near the top of the mountain when he climbed over a ridge of harder rock and looked down into a snow-filled bowl, a cirque, carved out of the side of the peak by the erosive action of a glacier. Under the cirque, Chuck knew, would be the top of a volcanic pipe. Buried beneath snow and ice, it couldn't be seen, but it had to be there. Kimberlites were soft rock. Almost always eroded down from the surface like craters, or mountain cirques, they were commonly in-filled with sedimentary rock and buried, or formed the beds of lakes.

Chuck and Tomlin quickly took several more samples and began to stake the area, working furiously until the pilot pulled them off the mountain at the edge of darkness. Chuck spent a restless night in Golden while a winter storm gathered over the Rockies and closed in around them. In spite of the snow which continued to fall heavily all day, they flew back up at first light with Eric Birkland and Tomlin's son Dan to finish staking the pipe. Then, after collecting hundreds of samples from the edge of the cirque northward to the Columbia Icefield, while the entire mountain range disappeared rapidly under snow, they flew off, the program over for the year. It would be spring before they could return.

It had been a good summer. Their sampling program had taken them from near the American border in the south, to beyond the Columbia Ice Fields in the north – everything he had promised Superior he would do. And he was within his budget. Best of all, he had found a pipe. Just as he had predicted.

Back in his Kelowna lab for the winter, Chuck spent all his time concentrating the samples they had collected, examining the concentrates, and researching new technologies to probe deeper into the formations of diamond kimberlite. There were some other heavy mineral anomalies among the samples. One in particular, taken from the Albert River near Radium Hot Springs, looked promising for gold and tungsten, and they staked it together with a lead-zinc prospect they called "Paul Mike." But it was the diamond indicator minerals that caught everyone's attention. Excitement was running high. In addition to the chrome-diopside-rich pipe – the cirque – they had staked, they found several pyrope anomalies in some of the other samples from the region. Pyropes were magnesium-aluminum members of the garnet group. Usually a deep, fiery red, these indicators were a brownish colour. Still, all pyropes were associated with basic igneous rock, like kimberlite, and were an indicator mineral for diamonds. Finding them was a good sign.

It was hard to sit still that winter. Pipes always occurred in clusters. With both pyropes and chrome diopsides in the samples, Chuck and his partners all knew there had to be at least a dozen more kimberlite pipes, besides the one Chuck felt sure he had found, scattered through the mountains. With the information available to them at the time, the project literally glittered.

CHAPTER FORTY-SIX

GOLDEN, 1979

Hugo Dummett and Chuck had much in common: porphyry coppers, Africa and northern Queensland, as well as an interest in diamonds. They spent the winter speaking frequently by phone, planning the program for the next summer season, waiting for the snow to melt. Hugo, as anxious as Chuck, arrived in early June of 1979. Renting a Jet Ranger helicopter, they took off into the Rockies to see what they could spot from the air.

Above the tree line, among the glaciated rock faces of the mountains, now that they were looking for them, they almost expected to see the pipes themselves from the air. Instead, all they saw were sheets of ice and fields of snow, snow so deep that whole trees stood buried under its smooth, unbroken surface. They had come too early. Disappointed, Hugo returned to Nevada, and Chuck waited alone for warmer weather.

Over the winter, Superior had been building their knowledge and expanding their capabilities in the economic assessment of kimberlites. Kimberlites were extremely rare worldwide, but not every kimberlite pipe carried diamonds. And of those that did, only one percent was sufficiently diamondiferous to be economic. There were, in fact, less than 30 commercial pipes in production around the world and, of those, only about 10 were major producers.

That was one of the reasons why diamonds were the most valuable gemstones in the world. Diamonds were extremely rare – and so incredibly old. To hold one was to touch time before life. The creation-time of diamonds predated the ancient age of the phylum *Arthropoda*, the invertebrate trilobites which first began to move on the ocean floors 550 million years ago. Beyond the Cambrian and deep into the Precambrian, diamonds reached back nearly to the time of the earth's own boiling creation.

Wolfhard was cautiously optimistic. Unbounded optimism in the mining business was dangerous to the health of a company. Despite its scientific approach, mining was more an adventure in the unknown, of informed intuition at best and desperate guesswork at worst. It was gambling with risks that would break most men, and often did, but with stakes that kept them trying. All the players had their own systems, some better than others, but one needed an attitude, as well as skill, to stay in the game. There were so many pitfalls that the overeager tended to crash before they even knew they were falling down.

Wolfhard knew it was expensive to assemble a good team, but in the long run he knew it paid off. To protect Superior from making the same mistake it had in its Sloan investment, Wolfhard needed the best. Now was the time to bring in the experts. John Gurney was the man whose research on the chemical compositions of diamond bearing kimberlites in South Africa was so highly recommended by the DeBeers' geologist, during Chuck's tour of the Finsch mine. If the compositions of the Golden pipes they hoped to find under the snow indicated not just diamonds but good commercial grades, the professor from Cape Town would know.

Chuck, too, had spent the winter productively. When he first started his company, he had approached the Federal Business Development Bank (FBDB)for assistance and the bank turned him down. Unlike American investment banks, new technologies were anathema to Canadian banks. The FBDB did, however, offer another program – one that was more of a social service than a banking function. The bank could assist new businesses by matching their needs to the expertise of retired professionals. Chuck had been losing nights trying to keep his wet-sieving units running when the FBDB sent him Frank Moore, a retired mechanical engineer.

Frank moved into the lab, studied the processes and began redesigning the system. Together with Chuck and Stan Emerson, a gold miner from Yellowknife hired initially to help prospect and to machine new parts, the three men rebuilt everything. From fume hoods to shakers and separators, every piece was uniquely engineered and integrated. When they finished, Moore and Emerson were so pleased they stayed, joining Chuck's team.

Eventually the snow melted. Stu Blusson was a geologist with the Geological Survey of Canada when Chuck worked the Mackenzie Mountains as a student. It was Blusson who had travelled as a passenger in the helicopter that crashed on its way to pick up Chuck and Dr. Fritz, the trilobite expert. Unlike the pilot, who never flew again, Blusson remained undaunted. In spite of his success on the Vancouver Stock Exchange, he continued to hire himself out as a consultant with his own helicopter.

They spent the night in a motel off the Trans Canada Highway just outside the community of Golden, tucked in the Rockies between Glacier and Yoho National Parks. It was a beautiful morning, early August, and the mountains were backlit by a pure blue sapphire sky.

Blusson's little piston-engine helicopter was parked behind the Imperial Oil service station on the highway. They wiped the dew off the bubble, unscrewed the doors for better visibility, strapped themselves in, and then cranked over the engine. *Plup ...plup ...*

Nothing happened. Blusson tried again, and cursed. The batteries were dead. A Hughes 300, the helicopter had been on lease to a company in Niagara Falls, and had been flown back to Calgary where Blusson had picked it up the night before. It had worked fine yesterday.

"Let's go see the garage!" Blusson suggested. He needed a 24-volt battery. Three eight-volt batteries rigged in series would do, but the garage didn't have any.

"What about the ones out back?" Blusson asked. He'd seen batteries with a pile of other parts near the helicopter.

"You mean the ones on the dump?" the attendant asked.

"Yea."

"Go ahead and take them!"

They hooked them in series to his own battery. Chuck by now was hoping the engine wouldn't start. Blusson tried again. This time it turned over and with a great rattling noise kept running. Chuck cursed. Blusson yelled at him over the noise to get in. There was a narrow bench seat in the front which could accommodate three people. As Blusson was warming it up for take-off, Chuck's doubts began to grow. The engine sounded awful.

"Stu, your engine sounds really rough!" Chuck had to yell to be heard. It was rattling like a blender filled with rocks. Blusson listened to it for a moment, nodded his head in agreement, offering by way of explanation that it hadn't been overhauled in some time, then took off.

Flying northeast into the Rockies, they followed the highway for several miles, then turned at the mouth of the Blaeberry River where it emptied into the Columbia and followed the narrow valley as it wound its way climbing between high peaks and glaciers, brilliant in reflected sunlight, towards Banff National Park. Ahead of them the valley floor narrowed and then rose into mountain divides. The more altitude, the thinner the air, and the less lift the tiny helicopter had. Ahead of them were craggy peaks and rock spines at 2,700 and 2,900 metres – peaks they had to fly over. Only they didn't have the power to climb to those altitudes.

Blusson wasn't deterred. The sun was out and the air currents were moving. Snuggling up against a towering rock wall, Blusson flew alongside it until they hit an updraft. It was easy to feel – they immediately began to rise as though riding in an invisible elevator. Blusson rode it into the sky and when it ran out, hopped to the next updraft.

From updraft to updraft they climbed like a raptor with the rising air until they were soaring, thousands of metres up, above rocky spires and summer ice, wide open to the blue beyond. They had their first alpine creek in sight now. Chuck's lab had identified chrome diopside anomalies in it. They no sooner were above it when Blusson yelled, pointing excitedly. "*THERE'S THE PIPE!*"

Dead ahead, a round green patch of rock was intruding the paleozoic limestones. It was small, only 40 metres in diameter, but it was a pipe. A kimberlite diatreme. And it was beautiful! Having been "recently" exposed by the retreating Campbell Glacier, it hadn't been weathered long enough to oxidize – and the kimberlite was raw and fresh.

Blusson took them down and they landed right on top of it, breathed deeply, bagged some samples, named it the H.P. pipe, after Hugo Dummett – the "Hugo Pipe" – and took off again. It was exhilarating. Chuck was almost able to put the condition of their aircraft out of his mind.

They flew next along the ridge to the upper edge of the Campbell Icefield, which marked the western boundary of Banff National Park at Mount Fresh-field, the peak rising over the ice to 3,336 metres. There, right at the upper edge of the ice, was a reddish patch of rock, like an old, faded bull's eye.

"*THERE'S ANOTHER PIPE!*" Blusson yelled.

Chuck liked him. Blusson was a hard player but he was capable, and he had an eye for spotting pipes.

"*AND ANOTHER ONE!*" Blusson yelled again. The two pipes were near each other, both red ochre splashes on the grey background.

"*AND ANOTHER!*"

There were three together. Above the ice, these raw kimberlites had been exposed for years and the olivines in the rock, magnesium-rich iron silicate minerals, had metamorphosed on the surface to green serpentines, deep red hematite, rich in iron, and limonite, a yellowish hydrous ferric oxide. There they were, splashed with colour, each one as different as an original work of ancient art.

By noon their aerial reconnaissance had been so successful that by flying the anomalous creeks they found 16 pipes. They were nearly delirious with excitement. After gassing the Hughes, Chuck placed a quick call to Hugo Dummett to tell him the news, and then they went back out for the afternoon. They weren't stopping to eat or worry about the tuning of the engine now. As Stu Blusson pointed out to Chuck, what one had to look for were disruptions of the stratigraphy. Pipes bore up through the rock strata in carrot-shaped columns before cooling and solidifying into rock themselves.

The disruptions they were looking for were not recent events in geological time. Most of the volcanic pipes found around the world that carried the ancient gemstones to the surface dated back to eruptions in Pangaea, the "whole earth." The subsequent upheavals of the continents raised the pipes, bent them and sometimes opened them up, exposing them along their sides. One had to scan the rock faces and walls to get a sense of the rock formations, the stratigraphy, and then look for the intrusions – the pipes cutting up through host rock. Every rock had its genesis and, ultimately, a mystical nature. The chemistry of its elements led one into subatomic physics and there, at its most basic, rock was revealed as a composition of unknown particles, pure energies moving at lightning speeds: anything but static.

By the time they returned to the mountains, still riding the air currents for their elevation, Chuck's eye had become almost as keen as Blusson's in spotting the ancient disturbances. Only when the light was fading and flying had become tricky did they return to Golden. They had 10 more pipes on their maps. Their total for the day was 26.

The news that night rocked Superior and Falconbridge with the force of an earth tremor. Absolute security was necessary, but the excitement was hard to contain. It was a major discovery. Hugo Dummett and John Gurney both knew that when eruptions of kimberlites occurred they usually resulted in clusters of pipes. Sometimes as many as 50 had been found with a separation of 50 kilometres between the farthest extant pipes. However, the probability of finding pipes with diamonds among them was still low, and lower yet that any diamonds found would be of sufficient quality and quantity to make their mining profitable. Still, as professionally cautious as they tried to remain, a high tide of intoxicating elation swept their ranks like a contagious fever.

Generally it was the largest pipes in every cluster that had proven worldwide to be the best, so Dummett instructed Chuck to begin sampling and staking them first, as quickly and quietly as he could.

The great Canadian diamond rush had begun!

CHAPTER FORTY-SEVEN

THE JACK PIPE

"JACK" was the biggest. Named for Jack Langton, the CEO of Superior's mineral division, and utterly rugged, Chuck insisted they stake it, and the men set to work. A huge red block that cut the stratigraphy, the Jack pipe looked more like a brecciated sandstone than kimberlite or one of the less common but closely related lamprophyric rocks.

A close visual examination revealed the course of its life. Blasting up through the earth's surface in some disturbing, distant past movement, the upward force of the volcanic material, gas-charged and venting at the surface, created a crater with a diameter many times greater than that of the pipe. Immediately after the explosion, as the pressure in the shaft released itself and the flow stopped, the matter of the surrounding rim collapsed back in to fill the crater, layering the upper levels of the pipe with eroded rocks mixed with the solidifying magmas. Pushed up into a mountain peak that had later been ripped away along one side, the exposed edge of the pipe ran along the face of the mountain from 2,650 to 2,960 metres. A series of steep, jagged cliffs and columns under a ceiling of blue glacial ice, the Jack pipe was a formidable-looking formation. They sampled it, staked it, and moved on.

As they worked, they discovered several more pipes in the area and, adding them to their inventory, sampled and staked each of them as well. At the end of the day they were back on the H.P. pipe, the very first pipe they had found, just under the wall of the Campbell Icefield Glacier. Eric Birkland had been brought up to help sample and stake. The three of them squeezed into Stu's tiny helicopter as it flitted weakly from pipe to pipe.

They were up around 2,400 metres but in the summer daylight the rock faces they scrambled over were warm to the touch and they were working in light clothes. Above them, a field of ice perhaps dating back to the last Ice Age stretched for miles across the top of the mountain range. It created a climate of its own – quite different from that of the summer slopes of grey rock screes across which the men scrambled.

They collected three samples from the H.P. pipe. Big ones, each of them weighed 35 kilograms and the weight of all the rock, together with the three geologists, was pushing the load limits for the little aircraft.

"Maybe we should do this in two trips, hey? … Like, take the samples out first, and come back for us?"

"Well," Blusson reasoned, "We're pretty low on fuel … so I figure our carrying capacity is improved. I think it'll balance out." He wanted to try it. If he could lift them off the ground, they could get down the mountain in one trip. Older and more experienced, Stu Blusson was both pilot and professional consultant. Chuck respected education and experience. He deferred to Blusson's judgment, and the three men squeezed back inside.

Blusson cranked up the engine. The rotor blade, pushing air down against the ground, formed its own cushion to lift up off and they were hovering. Airborne. Everything was fine. Blusson turned the helicopter around, faced down the mountain, and, shadowing the creek that took the meltwater from the ice over the pipe, they began their descent.

Dropping into the valley, 300 metres away, they hit an airstream flowing off the icefield. Compacted over millennia, the ice of the glacier was denser than that of any frozen lake. Deep blue and extremely hard, it was also very cold. On the still, summer day, the air over the ice had become chilled. The very molecules themselves lost energy, slowed their vibrations and fell together. Thick and heavy, a river of frozen air was flowing off the ice, cascading down like a water-fall 300 metres away – an invisible raging current falling through the warmer, lighter air of the rocky slopes. As the helicopter flew into the chilled airstream, the machine was powerless to resist its flow. Driving them down, they smashed into the creek. The skids spread apart, the tail assembly disintegrated on the rocks and Eric Birkland flew out the door. Miraculously, nobody was hurt.

Climbing out of the wreckage and away from the creekbed they quickly took stock of their situation. They were above the tree line. It was rapidly getting dark, and cold. They had no supplies or cold-weather gear and no way to call for help. The battery was dead and, without it, the radio was useless. Blusson wouldn't abandon it. Stripping the radio from his helicopter, he carried it with the dead battery while they hiked down the mountain to the relative shelter of the trees. There they stripped their pockets of possessions, pooling their resources. The men were fortunate that Marlene, who always packed for Chuck, had thought to put some survival matches into his sampling vest. Just in case. The fire was a godsend.

During the night, as the temperature dropped below freezing and the air remained clear, they saw a light blinking among the stars against the blackness of the sky: an Air Canada jet flying from Vancouver to some eastern destination. Blusson grabbed the battery, and thrust it into the fire, heating it on the coals, right next to the flames. He jerked it out, quickly connected the radio and had enough power to call out a Mayday to the jetliner passing far overhead.

The pilot heard him and managed a response before the radio fell completely dead. Then, they waited. Huddled at the edge of the fire, their backs, turned away from the heat into the night, froze.

The Air Canada pilot was not the only one to relay a message for help. Mar-lene had called the motel at night to speak with Chuck. It was a routine they had established years earlier. Whenever Chuck was away, if he was near a phone, they spoke to each other every day. Told he hadn't come back, she became alarmed and phoned Hugo Dummett, who was then working another project near the Mexican border in Tucson, Arizona. Dummett quickly put into motion a search-and-rescue operation to go out at first light. There was nothing anyone else could do until then. It was a sleepless night for everyone.

Chuck spotted the rescue helicopter while it was still deep in the valley, minutes away. He rushed to put a torch to their brush pile, a mound of green spruce boughs they had gathered the night before and placed in a wide, dry creekbed. The smoke rose up into the sky in a thick black column. It was early dawn, but the daylight was well established and their signal smoke could be seen from kilometres away. Waving from the ground, the three men watched the pilot come straight towards them. Rising up the mountain, maintaining an elevation which would allow him to recognize the individual features of a man on the ground, he was no more than a hundred metres over the ground as he first approached and then flew directly overhead – right through the smoke plume from their signal fire – and kept going! Chuck cursed. The pilot hadn't even seen them.

At 11:00 o'clock, no other aircraft having been spotted, Eric elected to try to walkout. It would be a hard hike. They were far up in the headwaters of the Blaeberry River, and it was nearly 48 kilometres zigzagging down cliff faces and through rough country to get out. But he didn't want to spend another night shivering at the top of the mountain. Chuck gave him their matches and Eric left. He and Blusson gathered more firewood, ripped off more spruce boughs for a new and bigger signal fire, and waited.

Seven hours later another chopper appeared on the horizon, at the edge of that pilot's own search sector. They lit their signal fire, sending another cloud of black smoke into the sky, and they were rescued.

With their precious samples intact, they picked up Eric, still hiking but growing very tired and grateful to fly the rest of the way down the mountain, and enjoyed a big dinner. The pilot who saved them was hired for the rest of the program and, early the next morning, they were back among the peaks, working even harder, to make up for the time they had lost.

CHAPTER FORTY-EIGHT

MARK FIPKE

THE ice field abutting the Jack pipe was a dangerous place. Filled with crevasses more than a hundred metres deep, the breaks at the surface were blown over with crusted snow. The holes were impossible to see, like a minefield. Chuck was making his way around the edge of the field over the ice when the ground beneath him broke away and he crashed through. He was lucky. It was shallow and he hit soft snow at the bottom. Uninjured, he crawled out and continued across the glacier.

Mark had just turned 13 and Chuck had him assisting with rock sampling along the glacier's edge. The only way he believed he could spend time with his son was to bring him out to the project – but it was not a playground. Mark was expected to do the work of a man. It put a serious strain on their relationship. Even though Mark was only a boy, no one could ever complain that Chuck showed his son any favoritism in the field. Although Chuck was running the project it was a joint venture with Superior and Falconbridge and the work had to be professional. Mark had to be above reproach. If anything, he had to work harder, for less, than the others.

Chuck was ambitious for his son. He wanted Mark to excel, but he rarely communicated his feelings. His being more at ease with technical problems than emotional ones was partly a reflection of the cultural norms he grew up with, partly personal comfort. He didn't praise good work from his son, he expected it. He wanted his son to be more than one of the crew; he wanted Mark to follow in his own steps as a geologist. But it was Chuck's dream. As they continued to work together in the field, Mark felt increasingly emotionally distanced from Chuck. The classic irony was that Chuck loved him deeply. He simply demonstrated it the only way he could, doing his best to give Mark valuable experiences and set the highest possible standards.

More carefully now, Chuck tried to step lightly over the ice, but gravity defied his will to lightness – and he broke through again. Again he was lucky. The crevasse was another shallow one. He dropped three metres and stopped, bones jarred.

Twice was enough. To help sample the "Jack" and "Mark" pipes – the latter named in honour of his son and, like the Jack, a vertical, cliff-hanging terror – Chuck hired a professional mountaineer, Rudy Gersch. Even for the experts the risks were real. In the previous six months, Rudy's brother and wife had both been killed in separate avalanches while helicopter skiing. In spite of his losses the rewards of working in high altitude spaces kept Rudy enthused.

Rudy's passion for cliff-hanging sparked Chuck's interest, and Rudy set him up for the experience. With a secure line to the top, Chuck rappelled down over a vertical face to take a sample off the cliff. Hanging from a rope with a 50-metre drop beneath him, chipping rocks into his sample bag, with his adrenal glands firing, was as heart-stopping as anything he had ever done before.

Chuck was too heavy to climb back up now, so Rudy had to lower him down toward the surface of the ice sheet far below. Descending out of sight of the men above him, Chuck was being lowered blind to the ice. Beneath him, the ice edge had separated from the vertical rock face, leaving a gap, a crevasse between ice and rock, into which Chuck was now descending. The crevasse was deeper than the ones he had fallen into, and as the rope slackened he bounced his way from side to side into the darkness until he was able at last to find firm footing and secure himself against the wall to await rescue. The hole was a trap from which escape, on one's own, was impossible. After being pulled out, he decided once was enough. He would leave the cliff-hanging to Rudy.

Still, it was red-hot work in cold-blue spaces. Even Tom McCandless, a doctor of geology who had specialized in kimberlites and was sent by Superior to assess the pipes, could hardly contain his enthusiasm. Confined to a wheelchair, he hovered right at the faces in a helicopter, as close as the pilot dared.

Still, it wasn't near enough for McCandless. He wanted to examine the Jack more closely, to actually touch it. But how? Hugo Dummett, with him in the helicopter, offered a solution. With no weight at all to his legs, McCandless was very light. And Hugo, a bear of a man, was very strong. Having the pilot land them nearby, Hugo carried his friend to the mountain.

Tom McCandless and John Gurney were both on contract with Superior to construct a chemical profile of a diamond-bearing kimberlite. As they had discovered, the presence of indicator minerals alone did not translate into the presence of diamonds – especially gem-quality ones. Garnets were of many different but subtle chemical compositions, as were the chromites, ilmenites and bright green chrome diopsides. One needed to know the exact elemental composition of all the indicators to know whether their combined chemical signatures indicated the presence of diamonds. Simply identifying the minerals was not enough.

John Gurney had been sent by Superior back to Africa to do secret orientation studies of the kind Chuck had done for copper and gold. Travelling across all of southern Africa, Gurney collected rock samples from all the known diamond pipes. Then Gurney analyzed them with a microprobe at Cape Town University. Knowing the published diamond grades for each commercial pipe, Gurney and McCandless were then able to correlate the results of the analyzes with the presence and grade of diamonds. When they finished their study they had produced a fairly accurate chemical profile of a quality diamondiferous pipe.

This was information Chuck did not have. Sitting now with McCandless in the helicopter – fellow geologists, working on the same project – Chuck asked him about the study. McCandless was professionally tight-lipped. Superior had strictly instructed their geologists of the necessity to keep company secrets.

Everything about the project was confidential. Superior was building up a solid base of technical expertise, but they were not sharing it with Chuck. It was not a matter of discourtesy. One simply did not give away secrets, especially to a potential competitor.

Later, one of Superior's geologists did volunteer one piece of critical inside information to Chuck. The purple pyropes were only indicative of diamonds, he said, if they had high concentrations of titanium: an important revelation. Superior had much more but Chuck didn't push the geologist. He wasn't especially concerned. So long as Superior had the right information and he and Superior remained partners, he could rely on their expertise. It was a team effort. And they were as committed to finding a diamond mine as he was – so he believed.

He had no reason at all to suspect that the information Superior's geologist gave him about high titanium in the pyropes was deliberately false, or that Superior's owners had another agenda.

Meanwhile, the exploration continued. Cliff faces, too steep to climb and too rugged and difficult to tackle by rope, were sampled by helicopter jumps. It was dangerous work. Balancing on a landing skid while the helicopter hovered beside the cliff ledge, Chuck instructed Mark to move from the narrow skid to the near-vertical cliff face. Mark was scared, but he did what he was told. From the narrow ledge, Mark gave Chuck a quick wave as the helicopter fell away from the mountainside, leaving him standing alone on the outcrop. Sitting beside the pilot, Chuck navigated, moving his ground crew of seven men, and his son, from site to site, leapfrogging them to each new location he wanted sampled. Everything had been subordinated to his standard of perfection, obedience and cost-efficiency. It was his reputation the crew was working for, and his promise to Superior, to be cost-effective, was sacred.

This day Mark looked down the steep talus slope below him and shuddered. Nearly vertical, it dropped 80 metres before continuing in a more gradual decline to a creek far below. Having to move from the helicopter to the ledge had been bad enough, but the thought of stepping back out, from the ledge into the air, to grab the thin skid of the helicopter when it returned, terrified him. He put it out of his mind and went to work.

He had no time to waste. If he was not ready when his father returned there would be hell to pay. Quickly he collected the rock sample he had been directed to take from the cliff face above him, stowed it into his pack, and then returned to stand at the edge of the ledge, loaded down with approximately 35 kilograms of new weight on his back. He knew he could do it, step from the ledge out to the rail of the helicopter and then swing back aboard – he was capable of more than most 13-year-old boys – but he was also careful.

On the helicopter's return, the plan was for his father to reach out from the helicopter skid to take the sample first, then assist him to climb aboard. Looking down again, Mark quickly decided he could not do it. It was not a matter of being disobedient, it was simply against his better judgment.

Chuck did not consider the site too difficult or dangerous to pick up Mark.

Had Chuck an easier landing site, Mark would have been directed to make his way there, with the sample. But Chuck was gone, and Mark, alone on the ledge, began to see things differently. It was a long way down. If he slipped when he stepped out to the helicopter skid, he believed he would die. Fear set in.

It was cold and raining, the rock was wet, and the helicopter skid, a thin strip of metal railing, was a frail-looking life-support system. With the wind gusting through the valley, Mark feared the helicopter would not remain completely still. At 13 he was light and had not yet grown out of his boyhood frame, but even with his weight, he knew that stepping on, or off, a hovering helicopter – even one that kept still – was dangerous. If the pilot failed to compensate for the weight shift, at that exact instant the helicopter could swing like a pendulum, while he dangled like a bell over space. The very thought made him queasy.

There was another option. Four hundred metres below he could see a wide sandbar beside the creek where a helicopter could land. Flat ground.

He made his decision. Down he went, scrambling so fast he very nearly flew down the mountain. He raced with all the speed and skill he used in Rio when he ran with his father down Corcovado under the statue of Jesus. He was quick then and sometimes beat his father to the bottom. Those were good memories.

He was in the alder bush beside the creek, moving as fast as he could when he heard the helicopter returning. The sound of its steady chop quickened his already racing heart. The rule with helicopters – which Mark well knew – had never changed over the years: Always return to your drop-off site. Knowing what his father's reaction would be if he caused them to waste even two minutes he ran as though his life depended upon it. He had less than 50 metres to go.

Mark expected them to come down the mountain looking for him once they had seen he was no longer on the ledge. They should know he wouldn't go up, he reasoned. There was only one direction left. When he broke through to the sandbar he saw, to his dismay, the helicopter, far above him, still hovering at the cliff's ledge at his drop-off.

Loading his flare gun, he fired it straight at the helicopter. The flare fell short and they didn't see it. His panic rising with each wasted moment he loaded another flare and fired it up, higher, to arc through the air beside the helicopter. But the men inside were searching for him over the rock faces beside them, looking the other way.

Chuck had become alarmed to return and find Mark gone. He could see the entire talus slope below the ledge and Mark was not there. Mark knew better than to play games. Chuck knew he wouldn't deliberately hide or break the rules. Desperately Mark fired another flare. And another. Five precious minutes passed before they saw him. A week's wages for Mark in helicopter time. Mark scrambled aboard and faced his father. Chuck was furious.

It was an experience Mark would never forget. Listening quietly, he swore to himself he would never be like Chuck – as Chuck too had once promised he would be different from his own father.

A boy in men's company, Mark was naturally ostracized. Nights were especially difficult. In the evenings when the men went out, he was left alone in the motel room a summer of emptiness. For Mark the bush camps were like a return to South Africa. He hated South Africa and the Afrikaners – as he now hated working for his father and living with the field crew. A Canadian boy attending an Afrikaans school, he was treated as though he were a leper by the Dutch Afrikaner children. Aware, too, of the role Canadians performed in the Boer War, they never spoke to him. Even eye contact was rare. Completely isolated, he had played alone for years, his best friend his mother. He dreamed now of being sent home, back to Kelowna, of being with his own friends, of freedom.

Chuck would not let him go. It was the first time Chuck had ever brought Mark into the field, but he intended it to become a regular routine. There would be work to fill Mark's summers for years, for a lifetime. Now was the time to teach his son the standards he'd be expected to live up to. Mark learned quickly – a good student, but sometimes he made mistakes.

Chuck had the pilot put them down beside a streambed and instructed Mark and another man to take one sample each while they waited. Mark rushed out. His sample was further away but he wanted to beat the other man. The clock was ticking. He had his sample bagged and was running as fast as he could back to the helicopter, the main rotor spinning through the air ready to lift them off the instant they were back aboard. All that counted to Mark was speed. The other man was also finished, and running back, ahead of him.

Mark understood his father wanted him to be perfect, that mistakes were not tolerated. The only way was to be above reproach. He ran as fast as he could. There was a log between them and the open door of the helicopter. The other runner went around it. Three metres behind, Mark saw his chance to catch up – and to beat him.

Running straight for the helicopter's open door, he hit the log with his knees bent, springing off the top. As he lifted off the log, he looked ahead into the horrified faces of his father and the pilot watching from inside. Under the roar of the spinning rotor Mark couldn't hear them, but he could see their mouths working frantically. Screaming. Too late, he was already in the air, sailing up into the rotor's scything path. In reaction, he cringed. Just beneath the blade there is a calm space. His head entered it, rose to within centimetres of death and then dropped away.

He'd beaten the other man back to the aircraft.

The cliff samples taken off the Jack pipe proved to be the best. Falconbridge had a metallurgical lab and they were sent there to be processed. The first sample Falconbridge looked at had one beautiful, blue-white, gem-quality octahedron. A crystal with eight triangular faces, it measured .53 millimetres – just crossing the threshold of .50 millimetres, which classified it as a macrodiamond.

The level of excitement soared with its discovery. It was the first diamond ever recovered in British Columbia. Hugo Dummett and John Gurney came to comb the claims, deciding on behalf of Superior what to do next.

One of the first questions Chuck wanted John Gurney to answer was whether the Jack pipe was actually a kimberlite or a closely related lamproite. Lamproites were less understood than kimberlites. Their indicator minerals were to some extent different, and the economic assessment of the pipe was less certain if the rock was a lamproite. Both types were potentially diamond-bearing and the distinction was more of an academic and technical issue exciting Gurney's interest than an answer to big business's one question: Was the pipe economic?

They had in fact found two diamondiferous pipes. The Mark pipe had yielded a diamond too, and had, like Jack, yielded samples with good compositions of indicator minerals. The recovery from the samples they had taken however, strongly suggested low diamond grades. In a 450-kilogram surface creek sample taken downstream from Jack, only one small, yellow diamond was found.

Still, Chuck was hopeful – the samples were not consistent, and there was an explanation for the disparity which kept interest high. The surface samples from Jack were barren, yet the cliff sample which contained the diamond was also rich in chromites and contained another microdiamond of industrial quality. It was quite possible that when the pipe erupted, the crater infill rock that mixed with the diamond bearing rock diluted it to some considerable depth below the surface. The only way to determine whether or not the grade improved at depth, below the infill, was to take the project to the second stage of exploration: drilling.

That decision belonged entirely to Superior and Falconbridge. It was their money. Chris Jennings, another South African with diamond experience, was working with Falconbridge and toured the claims together with Hugo Dummett and John Gurney. Each of them, independently, made their own assessments and then reported back to their bosses.

Armed with the cost analysis, risk assessment, geochemical results and expert opinions, Hugo Dummett pitched for the joint venture to drill. He had Superior on his side until he flashed a slide of the Jack on the big screen. The very sight of it killed the project. It was so high, so rugged and so steep that its physical characteristics alone scared them off. Under a wall of ice and with the short Canadian alpine summers to contend with, it looked too formidable. The decision Superior made was final. They shelved it.

There were other anomalies left to explore. To the south of Golden a series of kimberlite pipes Chuck had found there, near Crossing Creek, also had good concentrations of chrome diopsides, but it was the Jack that showed the best promise among them all – and Jack was dead. Superior needed easier projects.

Chuck had known the odds were against finding a pipe with an economic grade sufficient to return the investment on the cost of a mine, nevertheless, it was a depressing conclusion to a wildly exciting adventure. Great expectations were often a prelude to bitter defeat.

Chuck was not about to give up, however. He had never been inclined to harbour regrets. All one could do was keep looking. Their huge effort was not wasted. From a technical point of view, it was a great success. He had found the first diamond pipes in British Columbia. The more he considered the experience, the more he found to be grateful for: C. F. Minerals was booming; he had new important contacts; the base metal claims – the Albert River tungsten claims and the Paul Mike lead-zinc claims – still would be followed up. For Chuck, though, it was the sweeping exploration project and the discovery of the diamond pipes that had completely captured his imagination. That was treasure hunting of the grandest sort.

He was hooked. Next time he'd do better. Next time was being determined hundreds of kilometres away, in a completely serendipitous way.

As the snow fell heavily over the Rocky Mountains, smothering the claims under another winter, and as Superior and Falconbridge were determining not to expend any more resources on the Golden pipes, a geology student at UBC, 560 kilometres to the west, in the coastal rainforest city of Vancouver, was making plans to head into the Northwest Territories in the spring.

Another mining company, looking for base and precious minerals, had stumbled on an old volcanic pipe in the northern Mackenzie Mountains near the Arctic Circle. It meant nothing to the company and they ignored it, but the student thought it would make a good study for a thesis. He guessed there might be some interest in ancient Arctic volcanoes.

He was right.

CHAPTER FORTY-NINE

THE MOUNTAIN DIATREME

INFORMATION in geology, as in espionage, is prized but volatile; its flow, beyond the laws of physics, is unpredictable. Yet its power is such that a mere whisper spoken in the right ear can change the course of lives. Like the news of the first gold strike in the Klondike, information can blow with the force of a windstorm across the land and inspire a whole nation to dream. Fortunes can be made – and lost – on rumours, and huge resources can be staked on the slightest chance of discovery. The thrill is in the adventure. To quest is human nature.

Welcome North Mines had done a broad reconnaissance through the Mackenzie Mountains along the border of the Yukon and the Northwest Territories. They had been looking for the Canadian mining mainstays, the heavy metals, and when one of their geologists stumbled on a diatreme, a volcanic pipe, he simply noted its existence and its location, named it the Mountain Diatreme and moved on. The information had no value to the company and there was no need to protect it, so word of the Mountain Diatreme, spread slowly through the industry.

Colin Godwin was a classmate of Chuck Fipke's who remained in academia when Chuck left with Kennecott. Godwin developed his reputation in research, and when Jack Gower died, he took his place as a professor of geology at UBC. In the summer of 1979, Godwin was free and Chuck hired him as a consultant. Godwin experienced for himself the excitement of the project at Golden and Crossing Creek. The new professor also developed some hands-on experience with kimberlite and a new interest in old volcanic pipes. When one of his students picked the Mountain Diatreme to study, Godwin, who was his thesis advisor, was only too pleased to offer his encouragement. In the spring of 1980, the student went north, bound for the Mountain Diatreme. It was a classic breccia-filled volcanic pipe. Carrot-shaped, the upper crater zone had eroded away over aeons to expose the underlying diatreme rock.

In the fall, the student returned, bearing rock samples and field notes. As Godwin suspected, the rock he brought back looked like the very kimberlite he had worked on with Chuck. Godwin showed a piece to Jimmy McDougal, who had been working for Falconbridge for years and had access to their metallurgical lab.

McDougal was a good geologist who later received the prospector-of-the-year award in Canada for discovering a major copper deposit at Windy Craggy in the Tatshenshini watershed of northwestern British Columbia. When the results of the analysis from the Mountain Diatreme came back, McDougal took them personally to Godwin. Not only was the rock sample kimberlite, it also had several indicator minerals in it, and three microdiamonds. It was hot – and it was wide open! Godwin immediately passed the information on to another friend who rushed north and staked it before the Arctic winter sealed the land off for the next eight months. Godwin then approached Chuck.

Chuck's life was now as settled as it ever had been. The years since his return to Canada from Brazil had been exceptionally good. Two years after Charlane's birth, Marlene had her fourth child, a boy, Ryan Augustus, born the 30th of November, 1979. With three small children to raise and the lab to help run when Chuck was in the field, Marlene's life at home was thoroughly committed and exhausting. But, to her, work and family were not burdens from which to escape. Instead they were a personal challenge that gave her life meaning. Like Chuck, she worked for the family and their business for years without a break, never taking a day off. With rarely a harsh word, she was an anchor for the family – to Mark, she was a saint. Their relationship, forged in Australia and South Africa, Brazil and Peru, when for weeks at a time they only had each other to rely on, was special.

In the spring of 1981, Chuck was making plans to fly north to examine the Mountain Diatreme before offering its new owner an option. C. F. Minerals had now grown to employ 36 people full-time and was running flat-out, 24 hours a day, seven days a week. Its revenues, too, were better than Chuck had ever dreamed of when he first conceived of the business in the mission in the Amazon. They were enough that he allowed himself the purchase of the first luxury item he had ever bought – a real racehorse, a champion thoroughbred.

Chuck's knowledge of racehorses had improved considerably since his Princeton racing days, years ago. In the British and American breeder's magazines, there was one horse which stood out from all the rest: Secretariat. He not only won virtually every race he entered, he set track records, creating new standards for racing like no other horse in history.

Secretariat's bloodlines were impeccable. Secretariat had been sired by another Triple Crown winner, Bold Ruler. Bold Ruler had also sired Irish Ruler, who sired a mare which produced a perfectly proportioned foal, Boldest Spirit.

In horses, breeding was everything.

Boldest Spirit was as close as Chuck could afford to get to the mythic horse himself. He had high hopes for her. Unlike the tired racehorse of his youth which disgraced him at the country track in Princeton years ago, Boldest Spirit was capable of taking that field. Chuck's horizons had changed over the years. No longer content with setting his sights on winning races in British Columbia, he wanted to breed a horse that could compete with Secretariat. Secret dreams placed him at the winner's circle of the Queen's Plate, the Kentucky Derby and the New York Belmont Stakes. For those whose horses were merely good, it was an expensive hobby, but for those whose horses were exceptional, the game paid handsomely. A real winner was worth as much as a gold mine.

Chuck flew up to the Mountain Diatreme, hiked the country, examined the pipe and signed an option agreement. He then went to Superior and proposed a new joint venture in which, as before, Superior would fund the work, Chuck would run the field, and they would share in the final results, if any. Superior called in Falconbridge again to share in the new project, and Falconbridge sent out Jim McDougal to personally investigate the property before either of the companies would commit themselves.

Just as Colin Godwin's student had done the previous summer, McDougal cut out some samples from the centre of the pipe and then shipped them off to the same lab to which he had previously sent Colin Godwin's sample. Again, after the lab concentrated the rock and analyzed it, the results were identical: the sample contained not only diamond indicator minerals but several microdiamonds. The picture it created was of a pipe that showed promise.

The lab's processes were confidential and Chuck was excluded from participating in the analysis, but he was shown the concentrates, beautiful to a diamond geologist. Superior and Falconbridge immediately signed the new joint venture agreement, and Chuck was once again planning to spend a summer in the Northwest Territories – exploring now not for trilobites and evidence of oil in the Mackenzie Mountains but for ancient volcanoes and diamonds. Knowing that pipes occurred in clusters and that the Mountain Diatreme would not be alone, Chuck proposed another broad sampling survey of the country: of the kind they had undertaken through the southern Rockies. Superior agreed, and the joint venture now moved north.

Chuck hired Stu Blusson as a consultant but retained the services of another pilot, Brian Robson, and a Hughes 500D helicopter from Trans North to do their flying. On the first weekend of July 1981, they set up camp at Palmer Lake in the Mackenzie Mountains. Frank Moore, the mechanical engineer, had signed on as cook, just for the excitement of the trip, and Chuck again brought his son, Mark.

With nearly 24-hour daylight and two ground crews, Brian Robson began flying long days and the crews worked from 7:00 AM to 11:00 PM. Chuck now had "budget" sampling down to a science. While most exploration companies used small ground crews with a helicopter that would wait for each sample, Chuck used a large crew and a single helicopter that never stopped flying. It was the high cost of exploration that kept the players in the field lean and crushed most of those who tried to enter the game. Chuck's efforts to work harder for less were appreciated by Superior, and his crew's daily average of 80 samples set another record.

Hugo Dummett flew up when Chuck and Stu were still at Palmer Lake, to inspect the Mountain Diatreme, 22 kilometres south of the lake, and take new samples for Superior. A few days later, he was on his way out, flying back to Norman Wells. The plane, a charter from Nahanni Air, was empty and he took a seat in the cockpit beside the pilot. Hugo asked him about his summer, and on hearing Hugo's accent, the pilot commented that he had flown some other South African geologists on a charter out of Norman Wells just a few weeks ago.

The pilot could not have dropped the news into a more interested ear.

"Who was that charter for?" Hugo asked.

"Monopros," the pilot told him.

Hugo knew that Monopros was a subsidiary of DeBeers and immediately guessed at the import of this news. DeBeers, the South African giant, was here, in the Northwest Territories. And they only hunted for one thing – diamonds.

"Where did you fly them to?" Hugo asked.

"I took them into the country around Blackwater Lake."

As soon as they landed, Hugo obtained a map of the region around Blackwater Lake and then contacted Chuck, relaying what he had learned from the pilot. The map didn't give them much to go on. "If you get a chance," Hugo stressed, "you really should take out a plane and find out what they're up to."

Chuck had every intention of doing that. In 10 days, their work around Palmer Lake finished, and Chuck moved the camp to Mile 222 on the Old Canol Road. Built during the war to supply oil from Norman Wells to Whitehorse and to the American troops stationed along the West Coast waiting to repulse an expected Japanese invasion, Mile 222 was a bustling little summer community, a transportation centre for high-tech exploration of the region's minerals.

Mile 222 stood in stark contrast to the other communities of the region: Fort Good Hope, the oldest furtrading post of the lower Mackenzie River, located nearer the Mackenzie delta, and Fort Franklin, to the south, were more typical. There, the smell of curing meat mixed with wood smoke to hang like ground fog on cold, still days. These were quiet communities in which the children played freely while half-wild dogs, sometimes in packs, followed strangers suspiciously and sniffed at drying caribou skins, nailed to the outside walls of low log houses chinked with moss and rags. The more valuable skins of red fox in their silver and cross-colour phases, and mink, wolverine and marten were inverted, stretched out on boards and kept safely indoors, to cure slowly. With glass windows, generators, oil tanks and skidoos, the villages presented a strange mix of old and new, of traditional Indian ways and better technology, but they remained essentially foreign cultures, quite unlike those of the white communities in the north.

Poking around the corners of the white community at Mile 222, Chuck took stock of the competition. There was no air strip at Mile 222, so the companies had all chartered helicopters, which sat among the barrels of their own fuel dumps and mountains of supplies. Tents, plywood radio shacks, command centres and warehouses dominated the space. Sophisticated communications and transportation systems were everywhere, with geophysical instruments and the latest earth-probing sensors.

Pan Ocean Oil was here, prospecting along an axis adjacent to the one the Fipke-Superior joint venture had just finished sampling. Chuck traded information with their crews. They planned on recovering 800 samples, they told him, and had budgeted for 600 hours of helicopter time. They were hoping to finish their sampling program in two and a half months. Chuck didn't tell them that he had completed his survey in only 10 days, or that he had used only 120 hours of helicopter time.

Another company's gear caught his attention: Hudson Bay Mining. They were conducting underground testing of a lead-zinc property they had near Mile 222. More importantly, the company, like Monopros, was controlled by DeBeers. Chuck wanted to move in for a closer look but, not wanting to alert them to his own interest, he passed them by. He knew they'd be under instructions to keep their operations strictly confidential – he had something better in mind.

Chuck and Stu quietly asked around for DeBeers's helicopter pilot and then casually approached him, as if by chance, to see what they could find out. He was happy to talk. Bubbling over with information. DeBeers had given him one of the best contracts of his career a 1,000-hour charter! And the budget they had for their survey, he told them, was one of the highest he had ever seen: two million dollars!

"Oh really?" Chuck asked, pretending surprise and sharing the pilot's point of view. "What kind of people are they?" Apartheid and all. "Like, how are they to work with?"

"Unreal!" the pilot answered. "One time they had me fly all the way from their camp on Blackwater Lake to Fort Franklin just to pick up a load of ice for their scotch!"

"Really?" Chuck said, grinning. Blackwater Lake was due south of Fort Franklin, and east of the Mackenzie River – Chuck's next destination.

Chuck ordered in a helio-courier plane for this reconnaissance job. The highly specialized, large-winged aircraft was equipped with great soft balloon tires. It could land almost anywhere on the tundra and take off again in as little as a hundred metres.

"They're really suspicious, hey! I mean these guys don't like anybody near them! Don't look down! Stare straight ahead!" Chuck ordered the pilot. They were 300 metres over DeBeers's camp at Blackwater Lake. Chuck could see the men below, looking up at them as they passed over. He did not want to alert DeBeers to the fact anyone was even aware they were there. But he took everything in. The DeBeers crew had done a tremendous amount of work, cutting parallel geophysical lines and conducting heavy mineral bulk sampling systematically across huge expanses of the country below.

One of the men on the ground was studying them with binoculars. Chuck had his pilot continue to fly, bearing straight ahead, until they were out of sight, then instructed him to turn around and, flying wide around DeBeers' camp, they returned to Mile 222. As soon as they landed, Chuck paid off the pilot and sent him directly back to his own distant base. Even if DeBeers asked around, nobody would know anything.

Chuck waited a couple more days to let things cool down and then took off with Stu Blusson on a new helicopter charter at 2:00 AM. It was daylight, but all the camps worked on southern schedules. At 2:00 AM, he knew, the camps would be asleep.

Now, Chuck was moving in for a closer look. DeBeers had secured two "concession" blocks from the territorial government – each one a huge block of land, many times greater than a mining claim – within that they held exclusive mineral rights. That, and the work they had been doing, suggested DeBeers was sitting on something that had the South Africans very excited.

Navigating, Chuck kept his pilot in the dark and talked about gold as he set a course which kept them out of sight of DeBeers's camp until they landed on the ground immediately to the west of DeBeers's concessions. High, mountainous country moderated by the Mackenzie River basin, it was forested and totally unlike the flat, barren lands of the tundra to the east. It was easy to slip in unseen. Quickly, he and Stu collected eight bulk sand samples from the streams and left.

Overnighting in Norman Wells, they were on the tarmac early for their flight south the next morning when they discovered DeBeers's supply dump. Casually they walked by. Forty-five gallon drums, which had been slung out to Norman Wells from Blackwater Lake, were lined up along the runway ready to be loaded and flown away. The rows of barrels were all labelled for delivery to DeBeers in South Africa: tons of rock samples, tightly sealed.

Hugo Dummett didn't like the Mountain Diatreme. Although Chuck had found and staked several other pipes adjacent to the original claim and the analysis Falconbridge had done revealed the potential for an economically viable diamond deposit, Hugo found the compositions of their indicator minerals unusual.

When he had passed to Chuck the information he had learned about DeBeers's operation in the north, Hugo collected six more samples off the joint venture claims, three of these from the centre of the Mountain Diatreme. Hugo sent them on to Falconbridge for processing. As before, the results were more than promising. Microdiamonds were once again found among the indicator minerals in the kimberlite. Still, Hugo's misgivings about the pipes continued.

The samples Chuck had spent 10 days collecting and then processing in his own lab to concentrate the indicator minerals produced completely different results. No indicators turned up at all: not downstream from the Mountain Diatreme, not downstream from the other pipes, nowhere throughout their whole survey. Not one of the 800 samples Chuck's team had collected contained any indicator minerals. They were all barren. Yet the samples Hugo had taken directly off the centre of the Mountain Diatreme – all samples which Falconbridge had processed in its lab – were rich in indicators and diamonds. Puzzling.

It was so unusual that Hugo Dummett and Chuck presented a joint paper on the analyzes to an international geochemical conference at UBC. There were oddities in nature, it seemed, that could not be accounted for in science and geochemistry. Chuck knew the fault, if there was one, did not lie in the processes his lab utilized. If proof was needed, the samples he had collected at the edge of DeBeers's concessions at Blackwater Lake provided it. Chuck concentrated them himself and then bent over the microscope. Contained within a small plastic dish, the grains that were left after the concentration process jumped out at him under the intense magnification. Indicators of all kinds were lighting up in the dish!

Taken from a different watershed than the one their joint venture had been sampling, these new hot samples pointed to the existence of a totally different source than the pipe cluster to which the Mountain Diatreme belonged. There was another trail here to follow – a trail on which DeBeers was already camped.

Chuck called Hugo for instructions. His own lab could concentrate the indicators and identify them, but he could not go the next step and chemically analyze them. Rather than send these indicators through Falconbridge to the lab they had been using, Hugo now had Chuck fly them to Superior's own lab in Austin, Texas.

Pipes were difficult enough to find, but pipes with commercial grades of diamonds were extremely rare. One could spend years bankrupting budgets on pipes which had all the right indicator minerals but contained no diamonds at all, or on exploring pipes that did contain diamonds but of grades too poor to be of commercial value. Knowing the indicator minerals was simply not good enough. There were other chemical clues which, when understood, could be used to predict accurately everything but the color of diamonds in a pipe.

Ever since his transfer from Superior Oil to Superior Minerals, Fred Meister had been carefully building up a world-class lab capable of handling all of Superior's geochemical needs. The lab was now ready. It could take a diamond indicator mineral, break it down into its elemental composition and then compare the composition to the chemical profile of a "hot" indicator, which Meister had previously researched with John Gurney and Tom McCandless – research which continued to give Superior a major advantage over its other competitors. Superior didn't know all the secrets, but they knew a lot more than Chuck did, and they were not sharing their information. Worse, Superior was not merely guarding their new information; they had also engaged in disinformation. When one of their geologists revealed to Chuck that high titanium values in the pyrope garnet indicator minerals meant quality diamonds in the pipe, he had been acting under instructions – but the information was false. Like Kennecott, which protected its leach-capping technology, or Chuck, who had patented his concentration processes, Superior was simply guarding its edge from all competitors.

Superior's false information leaks neither benefitted Superior nor hindered Chuck. To apply the detailed chemical profiles to the indicators in question from a pipe of unknown value, one had to use highly sophisticated tools. Equipment like a scanning electron microscope and its associated probes were necessary, to break into the atomic compositions of the indicator minerals. Chuck had neither the information nor the instruments. He had to rely on Superior, and on Hugo.

Chuck knew when he shipped the new concentrates to Fred Meister in Austin that there were garnets, chromites, ilmenites and chrome diopsides in them and he still believed that high titanium in the pyrope garnets was a positive value. Some of the pyrope garnets from the DeBeers's Blackwater samples which Meister analyzed did contain high titanium values – but they were not, in fact, desirable. The same samples, however, also contained garnets of a type classified as "G10s", which, Meister and Hugo knew, had pyrope profiles that were a perfect match for the garnets from the diamond-bearing kimberlites from the South African pipes.

Not only the G10s – garnets that were higher in chrome and lower in calcium than other garnets – but, one after the other, the other indicator minerals, when analyzed under Meister's scanning electron microscope, proved to be chemically identical to those found in the best commercial diamond deposits.

Fred Meister rushed the results in to Hugo Dummett, who studied them for a moment and then phoned Chuck, extremely excited. The samples Chuck had collected with Stu Blusson near Blackwater Lake at the edge of DeBeers's concession had kicked – big time.

CHAPTER FIFTY

THE SLAVE CRATON

CANADA was still a great unknown. Superior liked Chuck's work on the Mountain Diatreme, which continued to intrigue them all with its apparently conflicting chemistries, and they were especially excited by the new prospect around Blackwater Lake. But the familiar trails for diamond hunters were in Africa, and it was there that Superior was concentrating its major efforts.

As the kimberlite samples from the Mountain Diatreme were sent through Falconbridge to their lab, Falconbridge was also sending the lab other kimberlite samples from Africa. Unknown to everyone, by not cleaning the processing equipment – the screens and ball mills – effectively, the lab was accidentally contaminating the samples from the Mountain Diatreme with samples from Botswana. The very first sample that came off the Mountain Diatreme, collected by the student from UBC, was contaminated with another sample in the lab. The Mountain Diatreme, as Chuck's downstream heavy mineral samples had established, was barren. However, the sample it was mixed with was not. Diamond indicators, and even diamonds themselves, were left behind in the processing equipment and came out with the next sample analyzed from the Mountain Diatreme.

The lab error might have been discovered had the lab not somehow repeated it with the second sample taken by Falconbridge's own geologist. Incredibly, the mixing of samples produced an identical result, the same chemical properties and content of microdiamonds, confirming the "correct" analysis of the first sample. And still the results might have been questioned, if not for the third set of samples, taken personally by Hugo Dummett and processed by the same lab. It was "impossible" that the results – still unchanged – did not reflect the true nature of the Mountain Diatreme. The coincidental contamination of the samples for the third time with other samples with exactly the same properties as the previously substituted samples was beyond belief.

Yet it happened.

The Mountain Diatreme had no future, although none of the joint-venture partners knew that then. It continued to present itself as a unique chemical puzzle, potentially economic. More importantly, without the lab's contamination of samples, Chuck would never have been surveying the Mountain Diatreme, Dummett would not have gotten wind of DeBeers's presence, and Chuck would not have collected the Blackwater samples that Fred Meister, in Superior's lab, accurately reported were hot.

It was a false start but, incredibly, these errors combined to put Chuck on the right trail.

Africa, too, was producing results. Chris Jennings of Falconbridge, engaged in a separate joint venture with Superior, was working with airborne magnetics in Botswana. The technology worked and they found a new cluster of African pipes. Too anxious to follow the procedures that Superior had developed – of first sampling the pipes to identify their chemical signatures – the ground crews moved rapidly to drill them. Predictably, the holes were mostly barren, but the work in DeBeers's backyard aroused the sleeping giant. Whether Superior had anything to sell or not, DeBeers did not like the competition. Superior had not yet completed its exploration work with Falconbridge on the Botswana pipes when they opened a confidential line of communication with DeBeers to sell the whole Botswana field. More significant changes were to come for the joint venture.

In their Reno offices in the Nevada desert, Hugo Dummett was plotting Superior's next move in the Northwest Territories, to follow the hot chemical trail they had found at the edge of DeBeers's claims, when the order came down from the top to pull out. The joint venture had just been killed.

At a joint meeting of the Boards of Superior and Falconbridge, the directors had decided that the two companies would no longer compete in each other's backyards. Rather, the two companies would split the continent between them, Falconbridge taking Canada and Superior, America. What it meant for the joint venture, for Chuck, was that Superior could no longer work in Canada. The instructions to Hugo were clear: Quit all your Canadian projects. Immediately!

Under the new rules, Falconbridge had the right to have assigned to it all of Superior's interest in the Mountain Diatreme and the Northwest Territories. If the company wished to remain involved, if they saw any future in it, the project could continue with Falconbridge replacing Superior as Chuck's boss. Falconbridge wasn't interested.

Dismayed, Hugo called Chuck with the new development. Hugo was out of the play, but Chuck did not work for Superior or Falconbridge. And it was only the Mountain Diatreme project that was locked into the joint venture and under Superior's control. The rest of the country was wide open.

"If you can't continue, do you mind if I do?" Chuck asked. Maintaining good relations with Superior and particularly with Hugo was important to him.

"Look, as long as you don't use any of Superior's money or our name, and you stay completely independent, you do as you please, Chuck. And I'd do it soon, if I were you. You're on the trail of something real hot!"

Hugo was a good friend.

It was early winter and the ground was already buried under snow when Chuck landed back in Norman Wells, and went on the offensive. DeBeers had secured the mineral rights to two large "concessions" near Blackwater Lake. Many times larger than a standard claim, a concession block could only be registered when there were no other competing claims within the concession block territory. Chuck now intended to box in DeBeers. In order for DeBeers to

expand, to secure the abutting concessions, the land within them had to be completely free of any foreign claims. Leading a field crew of six, Chuck immediately
staked small claims at the corners of each of the four abutting quadrants, thereby
preventing DeBeers from taking the adjoining concessions. Then he made an
application for the concessions themselves.

With winter falling, the land had been emptied of its southern fortune
hunters, the equipment had been tied down or flown away, and nearly all the
planes and helicopters had left. The skies were quiet. Even the geese and the
cranes were long gone. So, too, was DeBeers. Only the Métis remained behind,
with the ravens, and the Déné, racing over the land with skidoos, getting their
winter traplines ready.

Without Superior's resources behind him, Chuck was hard-pressed. Exploration was expensive, and diamond exploration in the far north very expensive.
He had little money and only limited knowledge of the technology.

His goal was clear. He had to follow the trail of indicators back to the source.
If all the pipes were not already within the boundaries of DeBeers's concessions,
there was a good chance some of them would be within his.

His strategy for achieving it, however, was not clear. He needed $36,000 and
an irrevocable letter of credit to secure those concessions. Chuck gathered his
friends – the people who had helped him build C. F. Minerals – and offered them
new partnerships. Stan Emerson, the man who had constructed the wet-seiving
unit in the lab, went to his bank, borrowed $25,000 and bought in. So did the
others. Stu Blusson's friends from a Toronto-based company, Quinteko, also
bought in for $25,000. Blusson himself contributed his experience, and Chuck
contributed his lab and field skills. The "Blackwater Group" as they called themselves, was born. It was a partnership none of them would regret.

Stu Blusson recognized the rock formation which hosted the Mountain Diatreme and knew that it also outcropped along the MacDonnel Range east of the
DeBeers concessions. As a result Chuck surrounded DeBeers to the north, east
and south with eight huge concessions. He ignored the west. The indicators he
had found there with Blusson and Hugo's lab had been carried downstream
from the east, from the direction of DeBeers' concessions.

It was the most they could do: a gamble, but the risk was well worth the
potential reward. In nervous anticipation they passed the winter, waiting for the
spring of 1982. As soon as the ice cleared the creeks they were back. Running on
the tightest shoestring budget he could devise, Chuck continued to look for any
way to cut costs. Chuck squeezed them all for everything they had. They slept
only in tents, ate canned food, walked long distances, worked long hours and
Mark, when he came up to join the program after school, was paid half-wages.

It was the leanest operation Chuck had ever run and they had a few casualties,
people who broke after only a couple of weeks and fled. But he did it. They not
only sampled all their concessions, they went beyond them. When Mark
returned to school in the fall, having turned 16 in the field, and when the Arctic
winds were once again blowing down from the Beaufort Sea, Chuck finally left

for Kelowna. There, he didn't see daylight for months, for now he went on another offensive – in the lab.

Typically returning home at 2:00 in the morning, he found a warm dinner always waiting. After the birth of their fifth child, Laura Amanda on the first day of October 1982, Marlene found the demands of family enormous, but she continued to do what she could to assist.

Life at the Fipke home on Lake Avenue was chaotic. Two adults, a teenager, four young children, a multitude of pets, friends and toys were cramped into the small space, which was filled with furniture and cases and crates that had never been unpacked from their travels abroad. In the century-old heritage house, left in nearly original condition, they ate in the ancient kitchen and competed for use of the single bathroom with a constant stream of guests, visitors, employees and clients, who stayed in semi-permanent encampments on the floor. It was a hectic, daily rush of meals, dirty dishes, equipment, samples, maps, plans and lists, excitement and stress, packing, sorting and storing a thousand items and details.

Chuck confided everything to his wife. What he forgot, she remembered. Marlene assisted his organizing, arranged his tickets, paid his bills, packed his socks and matches, inspected his gear for damage and got him to the airport gates on time. Theirs was a true partnership.

Tons of samples had to be processed before the results came in, slowly but steadily. Over the winter, Chuck concentrated the samples himself and identified what indicator minerals he could. Superior had cut themselves out, but Hugo Dummett had never stopped believing in Chuck's mission. Secretly, he kept his hand in. Chuck continued to send him small packages of potential indicator minerals he had extracted from the concentrates using a microscope, and Hugo continued to have Fred Meister analyze them.

Most of the samples were hot. The chemistries pointed to a field of rich diamond pipes. Chuck and Stu Blusson were thrilled but, after plotting them on a map, they were completely perplexed. The distribution of the indicators didn't make any sense. How far could the indicator minerals have gone from the original pipes? Try as they might, they could not find any evidence of pipes. Yet the samples were hot across a huge area.

Around Golden, in southern British Columbia, the evidence of magma intrusions was everywhere. Kimberlite dykes, as well as pipes themselves were present throughout the claims. But in the North, despite a whole summer they had spent collecting hot samples around Blackwater Lake, prospecting everything, walking and flying over the land in Blusson's rebuilt helicopter, and finding everywhere all sorts of indicator minerals that could only have come from pipes, there was absolutely no evidence of a local source.

The pipes? Chuck and Stu looked at each other. Where were the pipes?

Chuck and his associates were not alone in struggling with this question. DeBeers was spending millions searching for the answer. Convinced the pipes were near their own hot samples, perhaps having been buried over time, they were digging deep to locate them. In their conviction lay Chuck's only advantage over DeBeers. In competing with Chuck's team in the Canadian Arctic, DeBeers had revealed its handicap.

DeBeers played its exploration projects close to the chest, relying on company geologists to do the work. The men they had in the Canadian field were mostly South Africans. In southern Africa, as in Brazil, indicator minerals might flow down to the sea, but only along major rivers that tore down kimberlite pipes. Everywhere else they were never far from their sources.

When DeBeers found strong evidence of kimberlite pipes around Blackwater Lake they looked no further. Expecting the pipes to be nearby, blinded by their own paradigm, they took out their concessions and began to dig.

The wide distribution of indicator minerals told Chuck and Stu a far different story. Born in a land of ice and snow, they had spent summers hiking among the glaciers that still covered most of the northern mountain peaks – the remnants of huge ice caps that once covered the entire land. There were indicator minerals in the creeks that drained the eastern slopes of the MacDonnel Range of the Mackenzie Mountains. That suggested they ought to look west, upstream, into the mountains. But there were also indicator minerals to the north and south of DeBeers' concessions, and to the east of them, far from the MacDonnel Range on the east side of the Mackenzie River.

There couldn't be pipes everywhere! But where was the source of these minerals? As soon as the land thawed enough to permit it in the early spring of 1983, the two men were back in the North, looking.

The answer, Chuck discovered, was lying innocuously on the ground. The cold water of a stream was splashing over it, keeping it clean. He was sampling the stream east of the Mackenzie River when he saw it through the water. He picked it up and turned it in his hands, studying it. It was an ordinary enough boulder, grapefruit sized, and few geologists would even have given it a second look – exposed boulders in creek beds were what one expected to see – but Chuck knew this stone did not belong. He was familiar with the sedimentary geology of the MacDonnel Range and recognized that this rock was not part of it. Only one other body had its characteristics – the Slave Craton. A unique section of the earth's crust, the Slave Craton was an ancient rock body, which, most significantly, was almost 500 kilometres away – to the east!

Chuck showed the rock to Blusson and together the two men searched the surface, finding several more boulders scattered about. Digging through a deposit of glacial till confirmed Chuck's conclusion. Among the rock debris left thousands of years ago by the melting glacier were numerous pieces of the Slave Craton.

The hot samples of indicator minerals, plotted on a map, crossed watersheds and mountain ranges. No creeks or rivers had spread them over these great expanses. Nor had all these small boulders from the Slave Craton rolled 500 kilometres to the west by themselves. That was the key. Fields of ice 3,000 metres thick once covered this land. As it spread out, the tremendous force and weight of the ice cut deeply into the rock, grinding down the surface layers and spreading them for hundreds of kilometres.

Chuck and Blusson assembled all the glacial maps they could. The samples from their concession to the east of DeBeers's had hot indicator minerals, and the samples they had taken further east of their concessions, in the unstaked tundra, revealed that the ground there was littered with them, too.

The maps confirmed what they had guessed and what DeBeers had so far missed. There were numerous directions to the ice flow and its movements were never constant, but the major drift had been from east to west. The Slave Craton was to the east. That was the direction they had to go. It was a huge area. Almost the entire Canadian Arctic to Hudson Bay. Somewhere a cluster of diamond pipes was hidden out there, had been waiting for millions of years, fire under the ice.

CHAPTER FIFTY-ONE

EAST OF MACKENZIE

By the summer of 1983 a new financing arrangement with the partners in the Blackwater Group had been concluded and Chuck was once again ready to burst. He now knew there were no pipes in his concessions – or in DeBeers's – and he let them go. DeBeers had nothing: the field was wide open.

When the Earth's axis tilted beyond the equinox towards the sun, he got on his way. The South African monolith remained locked in its search of the Mackenzie river basin, and Chuck was flying with Stu Blusson alone across the tundra, to the east. Sweeping in a grid pattern back and forth across the Arctic Circle, they left the mountains and the scrub forest of the Mackenzie basin and nudged slowly eastward into the tundra flatlands, north almost to Great Bear Lake, and back down, southeast of Blackwater Lake to the northern edge of Lac la Martre. They sampled all the watersheds, the major rivers and the eskers until their money and the season ran out. They had pushed their frontier 400 kilometres to the east and had returned to Kelowna with hundreds of bags, tons of sample material.

Chuck again used his own lab to concentrate the samples and quietly sent the best of them on to Hugo, who continued to have Fred Meister analyze them as a favour. The samples that kicked, kicked like the best. They were all coming from the same hot source – or sources. Chuck could now follow the flow of ice as he plotted the hot samples on his map. The ice did not deposit the indicators along a straight line pointing to the source. Instead, it smeared them, first in one direction, and then another, and another.

Indeed, there had been different ice ages. The pipes that burst the surface here 50 million years ago had the indicator minerals ripped from the surface of the kimberlite and spread around not only by the last ice age, but by all of them, over millions of years. But Chuck and his crew were on the right track, and getting closer. As the samples approached the Slave Craton, Hugo Dummett reported an increase in the number of G10 garnets in their samples.

John Gurney's was not the only study done on diamond pipes that revealed the significance of G10s. The Russian diamond expert Vladimir Sobolev had also identified their importance in his research. But neither Gurney's work nor Sobolev's were available to Chuck, and he had to rely exclusively on Hugo's word that the samples were heating up.

The short Arctic season was frustrating. The only consolation he could find was that it enforced a period of calm, and nobody else could prospect through an Arctic winter. But another event, far more disruptive, broke the seasonal rhythm of the search and seriously threatened his chances.

In a move that caught them all by surprise, Howard Keck sold out his interest in Superior to Mobil Oil. The new owners could have maintained Superior's mineral technology and its staff if they wanted to; however, they didn't. Oil companies everywhere were ending their brief flirtation with minerals. Even Fred Meister, who had developed the oil-locating technology, found himself unemployed. Mobil's philosophy was simple: oil and gas. They were not interested in minerals. Overnight, Superior's entire mineral division was shut down!

Chuck was on his own. He needed Superior. Apart from DeBeers and a lab John Gurney had in South Africa, there were no other labs in the world that analyzed diamond indicator minerals or even knew what to look for. He cursed. It was rotten luck. Bad timing.

The demise of Superior Minerals changed everything. He had neither the instruments nor the scientific expertise to conduct his own analysis. At the very least he needed a scanning electron microscope, but that instrument cost nearly a quarter-million dollars, and even if he had one, he wouldn't know what to look for.

Hugo Dummett found work with Westmont, a new American company backed by European money. Unflagging in his support of diamond exploration in the Northwest Territories, he tried, without success, to interest his new employers in joining Chuck's search. Their focus was fixed firmly on gold, and he could not budge them.

Dummett was, however, able to correct one piece of misinformation Chuck had. Released at last from Superior's cloak of secrecy, Hugo was finally able to tell Chuck that high titanium in the pyropes was the opposite of what to look for. Pyropes from diamond-rich pipes were usually characterized by low titanium.

Chuck thanked him for the information. It had not mattered while he had Superior's technology to rely on, but now that he was on his own, it could have hurt. He wasn't naive enough to blame anyone – he understood competition better than most – and his experience with Superior had been entirely positive. It was one of the finest companies he had ever worked with. He was sorry only that it was over.

His life would now become more difficult. Even when he had access to Superior's lab, he had challenges enough – he was working flat out. The best rest he could get was on aircraft, where there was nothing else to do except sleep. He had not taken a break since returning to Canada from Brazil years ago, and even alcohol, once a familiar companion, had dropped out of his life. He didn't have time to drink.

His research, his heavy-mineral surveys for clients, his own exploration programs and the headaches of a large staff at the lab cost more than his free time. His family was growing distant. As much as he wanted to bring them together, it was impossible; they were in different worlds. His four younger children hardly knew him. He was almost a total stranger to them. Mark especially continued to drift away. Their perspectives were different, and they argued constantly.

Mark, now seventeen, was in his final year at Kelowna Senior Secondary.

Rather than apply himself to studies, Mark had taken to staying out nights and partying hard. To Chuck, school grades were important. Chuck wanted Mark to study maths and sciences, prerequisites for university geology. They argued over that as well. Mark wanted to stay with woodwork, metalwork and electronics. He was skipping classes, and his grades continued to decline. The more Chuck pushed, the more Mark resented him.

Two weeks before Christmas they had a major argument. Chuck laid down the law: Under his roof, eating his food, Mark would have to live according to his rules. Mark would not. Chuck told him to leave, and Mark was glad to go. He moved in with Frank Moore's grandson. It was an awful Christmas for the family.

Numbed by innumerable details, Chuck's exuberance for life had no room left to express itself. His hair, once thick and blond, had over the years turned dark and was now thinning. Even in the free spaces of the North, the wind that blew across the tundra was only wind. It had lost its magic. Chuck was in deep. The challenge he had taken on was enormous, and his only salvation was to beat it. Escape lay in one direction only – through the top.

Chuck knew enough to keep going for the time being, but sooner or later he knew he had to face reality. He did not have the detailed chemical profile of a diamond kimberlite. Without the resources of a company like Superior, how could he hope to compete with DeBeers? The immediate concern again was money, always money. Chuck pushed the doubts aside. Once he got nearer the diamond field, he could worry about the technology to assess it.

The Blackwater Group had already exhausted their funds. A new source of capital was necessary; there were no other options: he had to start his own public exploration company. It was not a pleasant prospect. The Vancouver Stock Exchange, not alone among stock exchanges worldwide, had its share of listed companies with sophisticated – and utterly worthless – schemes to raise money. A new exploration company announcing it would search for diamonds in the Arctic would immediately be panned as another crooked and artlessly simple attempt to feed at the trough. Even the mining companies that should have known better ridiculed the very idea of Canadian diamonds.

Worse, Chuck could not very well advertise the strengths of his case. There were some educated ears out there, DeBeers among them, that would race ahead on the trail if Chuck let it be known where it was leading.

Superior was trying to shop its claims before they shut down and had the French consortium BRGM interested. Chuck took the French geologist Jean-Claude Serre on a tour of the projects, and when they flew up to the Mountain Diatreme he used the opportunity to collect his own 200 pound sample for future analysis. When BRGM turned Superior down, Chuck made his own offer to Superior.

The original "British Columbia Joint Venture" partnership agreement Superior had signed with Chuck, and then brought Falconbridge into, required that Superior fulfill certain obligations in maintaining whatever claims the joint venture staked and in safeguarding Chuck's interest in them. With Superior's withdrawal from the project, ownership of all the existing claims had to be resolved. As much as Hugo wanted to keep them, and to carry on, Superior would not allow it. Falconbridge, completely uninterested, wanted nothing further to do with the project. When Chuck suggested that Superior assign the claims to him in final settlement of their joint venture agreement, he found a sympathetic ear with Hugo.

Hugo called Fred Ackerman, the CEO of Superior and pushed Chuck's cause. "Look, these guys have worked damn hard on these claims, if anybody deserves to have them, Chuck does!" It was a moral argument in a business world, but Hugo and Fred believed in fair play. Fred agreed, and Superior assigned to Chuck all the rights in every mineral claim the joint venture had staked. Chuck was now sole owner of all the claims.

Meeting with the Kelowna businessmen who had become his partners in the Blackwater Group, Chuck made plans for a new company, Dia Met Minerals. Steve Dimbicki, a mining engineer who had worked with the United Nations, was chosen to become its first president. Bill Mitchell, an accountant, and John McKenzie, a retired former vice-president of Alcan, would both be directors. So, too, would Frank Moore, the mechanical engineer and their field cook, Stu Blusson and Chuck. Chuck's contribution to the new company was use of his lab, his own expertise and the claims from the joint venture. In return for 960,000 shares, all the claims were transferred to Dia Met. Each of the others contributed $10,000 in return for 10,000 shares. Chuck, too, put in $10,000 to give the company some quick working capital. Blusson alone argued he was a special case. He claimed a superior right than the others to the company by reason of his past performance with Chuck in the exploration work he had done with Superior and later in the North on their own. Although he had been paid for his work on a consulting basis and was still a partner in the Blackwater Group which continued to retain an interest in the Northwest Territories, his arguments found a sympathetic ear in Chuck. He liked Blusson and wanted him in on the new company. Blusson was familiar with the Vancouver Stock Exchange, knew how to prospect and could squeeze energy out of a dead battery. Blusson received 150,000 shares. Although that unequal treatment caused some serious dissention initially, the group stayed together and moved ahead with its plans.

Ken Northcott, a respected mining engineer, wrote up the engineering reports, and Keith Christofferson, a Vancouver securities lawyer with a master's degree in geology – who liked what he saw, and would later buy in and join them as a director – was retained to draft the prospectus.

They hoped to have the company listed by the spring of 1984, or at the latest by the start of the Arctic season in July. It was not to be. Lawyers and paper trails went on interminably. By the time the documentation was approved by the British Columbia Securities Commission for listing on the Vancouver Stock Exchange it was October – they had lost the entire season – and the most difficult part of the whole process was still ahead. They had not yet raised any money, and they had incurred considerable expenses.

With the approval of the Securities Commission, they were now entitled to sell shares. The plan was to release 500,000 shares at 50 cents a share to raise a quarter of a million dollars to continue the exploration program. The reality was different. Not a single brokerage firm in Kelowna would touch them. The brokerage houses in Vancouver shunned them as well. The big ones would not even make time to talk to them. In a world of high finance and international business, Dia Met was a country player with nothing to sell. No broker was prepared to recommend the stock to his or her clients. Instead, odds were given that Dia Met would not survive two years.

That was too optimistic. Dia Met was struggling to survive the first month! When Chuck returned to Kelowna, Dia Met was already a company on the verge of collapse. Then the carrion-eaters moved in. With "perfectly legal" backroom deals, they offered Chuck over $200,000 for his shares and promised to return all the claims to him personally. Once the company was listed on the Vancouver Stock Exchange, its shell would be all they wanted. Others came in with assorted plans to remove all the directors and turn over the company for a quick profit, or to transfer all the claims into another shell, part of an acquisition scheme to raise cash for that company and enrich Chuck at the same time. Sweet deals, only Chuck would have to cut out his friends. That he refused to do.

And then there were the schemes that didn't even pretend to be within the law. Overtly criminal, the scams to make money were complex and virtually fail-safe. Ever since Parliament, under pressure from certain lobby groups passed the *Protection of Privacy Act* in the early 1970s, prohibiting the police from resorting to wiretapping for criminal intelligence activity – the only investigative tool they had – organized crime in Canada had operated unhindered. Even the robbery gangs that had once regularly hit banks and Brink's trucks moved into the safer and more lucrative rackets of high finance and money markets, while the police shifted their focus almost entirely to chasing down the lowest level of visible street criminal.

For Chuck it was an eye-opener.

Finally a real offer arrived in the form of two brokers from Vancouver who put together a proposal Dia Met's board felt they should take. The brokers wanted Dia Met to issue two classes of share warrants, "A" warrants and "B" warrants with different rights attaching to each class. They wanted not 500,000 shares but a total of one-and-half million, with attached warrants to sell. Their commission would be 20 percent, plus the immediate transfer of 200,000 seed stock shares for themselves, as a bonus.

Chuck didn't like it. Other companies that had followed the same course had "papered-out". There were simply too many shares for the value of their claims. Every time the share value promised to rise on good news, the investors would unload them with the demand at the bid prices, and the value never went up. It was a one-shot deal which usually precipitated the end of the company – a sell-out. But he was outvoted. Without the deal, they were finished anyway.

Despondent, Chuck drove out to the country to work with Boldest Spirit. He was boarding his mare at a farm and stables in Westbank, just outside of Kelowna on the north shore of Okanagan Lake. It was a pleasant drive. The last few kilometres along the waterfront were especially peaceful. The lake was flat, its water absolutely calm. Even from the road he could see through to the lakebed in the shallows. The remarkable clarity of the water invited contact. But its summer colours were deceptive. The Okanagan had the only desert in the country and the warmest temperatures, but the October nights were cold and the only people who ventured into the lake were wearing wetsuits and riding windsurfers. Still, the sunshine was warm and golden, and the big cottonwoods and willows that lined the road were green and full of life. It was Sunday afternoon, the only free time he ever allowed himself in a week.

On the far side of white board fences some of the best horses in British Columbia grazed. As individual as people, several of the horses were recognized by Chuck and he slowed to look at them before turning at the entrance to Russ Bennett's farm, where his own horse was boarded. The smell of earth and straw and horses was strong. He liked it: another world. Walking over muddy ground he passed the exercise yard and a barn on his way to the stalls where Boldest Spirit was kept. A couple of young girls rode up quickly, trotting their horses, posting smoothly. Bennett's daughter and a friend, they stopped to chat with Chuck, shared a joke with him and rode on. Another world.

Chuck had brought some treats for Boldest Spirit, a bag of carrots which he fed the mare one at a time while he talked to her, offering tender endearments. She was a beautiful thoroughbred and he was hopeful she would produce an even more successful foal, perhaps a stallion.

Chuck was still brushing her down when Russ Bennett came over. Bennett was one of the most successful horse breeders in western Canada, his horses consistently taking top awards in the province each year. A businessmen, he was also interested in new ventures with potential.

"Well Chuck, how's your little company coming along?" he asked.

"To tell you the truth, Russ, it's the shits!" Chuck replied honestly. He told him about the problems they'd been having, and the latest deal they were about to make. Bennett agreed it would kill the company. He thought about it for a moment and then offered Chuck a gift. "I know a broker in Vancouver who might be able to help you out. If you like, I can give him a call and see if he'll meet with you."

Chuck jumped on it. He had nothing to lose.

"All right," Bennett added, "I'll give him a call tomorrow and see if I can set up an appointment. Are you free?"

To save Dia Met, Chuck would have walked to Vancouver and camped there for a month. He laughed. "Oh, I'll fit it in!"

True to his word Bennett called him the next day. The broker was Tony Hepburn, and he had agreed to meet Chuck in Vancouver at 10 o'clock the coming Wednesday morning.

Hepburn's office was on the top floor of the Stock Exchange tower on Granville. A senior member of Odlum, Brown, one of Vancouver's most powerful brokerage firms, Hepburn was also the chairman of the board of governors of the Vancouver Stock Exchange. Hepburn's wall was covered with photographs of horses. One was of Misty Morn. Chuck recognised the name.

"Is the mare Brandy Morn?" He asked. She was. The two of them then launched into a half-hour discourse about horse breeding. Brandy Morn was one of Russ Bennett's mares and he'd sold her foal, Misty Morn, to Tony Hepburn. By the time Hepburn brought the subject back to business, they had already established a common ground. Finally he asked, "Why did you come to see me, Chuck?"

Chuck told him about the claims they had from Superior which he believed warranted further development. When he finished Hepburn shook his head.

"I'd love to help you, but we only deal with blue chip stock. You're talking about a risky vse venture. Strictly gambling. We don't do those kind of deals."

Chuck did not respond. It was the same story he had heard all along. All they could do was give Dia Met away. Tony Hepburn was not finished, though. It was not their practice, he said, but he could do Chuck a favor. In order to list its shares, Dia Met needed a sponsoring broker to do the initial placement. Hepburn would not sponsor them, but he promised that if they could find a broker who would, he would take 70,000 of their 500,000 shares to sell.

It was a start.

When Chuck left the office, he immediately called Channing Buckland. Like Hepburn, Buckland was one of Vancouver's top brokers. He was a friend of Stu Blusson and had earlier given them some advice on business and stock promotion: "Whatever else you do, don't go off exploring for diamonds! You start talking about diamonds and everybody will think you're nuts! No one will touch you!"

He had been right. The advice had been given early on before they began their broker search. Since then Chuck had not been able to get through to him, and Buckland was not returning his calls. This time he picked up the phone. Briefly, Chuck outlined the deal he wanted for Dia Met and then asked Buckland if he could come to see him. Buckland tried to put him off.

"Chuck, the market's saturated. There's just too much speculative mining stock out there already."

Chuck was ready for it. "Oh really?" he said. "Well, I've just come from Tony's, hey, … you know, Tony Hepburn? … and he's taking 70,000 to sell."

That got him.

"Tony Hepburn's doing that?" Buckland was surprised. "Well, okay. Come on over. We'll work something out."

Buckland agreed to match Hepburn's 70,000 shares and, more importantly, to sponsor them.

Chuck was on a roll. He asked Buckland to come to Kelowna to address the Prospectors' Club, and Buckland agreed to that as well. The directors put on a banquet at the Capri Hotel and invited all the Kelowna brokers. Buckland arrived in a private jet and gave a little speech about Dia Met. They sold out: 500,000 shares. No special bonuses, no warrants, no new share classes and no dumping of shares. It was October 1984, and their shares were finally trading on the vse. Except for the loss of the season, they had everything they wanted.

Dia Met was now a reality.

CHAPTER FIFTY-TWO

THE GLACIAL DIVIDE

IN the spring of 1985 before the Arctic summer season began, Chuck finally gained access to the secrets that Superior Minerals had guarded so carefully. John Gurney's diamond report, prepared initially for Superior and, coincidentally, Sobolev's study of diamond-bearing kimberlites, were both published. Together, the two papers contained precisely the information Chuck needed – the particular elemental composition of the indicator minerals which were associated with diamond-rich pipes.

The complex formulas were multipurposed. An analysis of the relationship between chrome and calcium in the pyropes identified whether the pyropes were formed with barren, weak, moderate or high grades of diamonds. Simply by analyzing the character of downstream indicator minerals, without ever recovering a diamond, without even finding the pipe itself, one could predict with fair accuracy what the diamond grades would be within the kimberlite pipe from which those indicators had come.

Stu Blusson had promised to work the 1985 season with Chuck, but now was setting up a mine project at Puffy Lake which had his full attention. Their plan had been to fly north on the first of July. Stu called and asked Chuck to wait until the 15th, then, until the first of August. When he called again, to tell Chuck to hold off until mid-August, Chuck told Blusson to meet him in the Arctic, and left alone. He was lucky he did. Blusson never got away.

The ice flow wasn't even. Like currents and eddies in a windstorm, it had several centres and the thick sheets which once covered the Arctic had spread the ground-down surface material out in different directions. More complicating was the fact that each ice age had its own unique characteristics and flows. As was later determined by Stu Blusson, a strong east-to-west flow was followed by a northeast-to-southwest-trending ice flow, which itself was subsequently obscured by the last ice age with its dominant flow of ice trending from the southeast to the northwest.

Even in that old world of ice, all was not frozen. Rivers ran through and under the huge ice sheets, forming their own deep beds of gravel and rock and sands that, when the ice finally melted, were left exposed as eskers, long sinuous ridges that snaked unevenly across the country. The till they contained had been scraped off the rock surface by the movements of the ice over the distance it had travelled. Between Coronation Gulf and Great Slave Lake, the eskers, which generally followed the flow of the ice, were roughly laid down along an east-west axis.

At the eastern edge of the Arctic, inland from Chesterfield Inlet, on the northwest coast of Hudson Bay, following a line that runs north-south, 50 to 100 kilometres west of Baker Lake, was a glacial divide. It was a high point of land. There the ice split. East of it, the ice flowed towards Hudson Bay; west of the divide, the ice spread out, flowing north over the Arctic Islands, south down into central Canada and due west to the Mackenzie River – all the way to Blackwater Lake where DeBeers was digging for diamonds.

Chuck began where he and Blusson had left off two years earlier. He planned to work his way right across the Arctic to the Glacial Divide. Using assumed names and billing everything to "Norm's Manufacturing," a fictitious company named after Norm Oftedal, a steady and unassuming employee of C. F. Minerals who had never been north, Chuck chartered various float planes, regularly changing his pilots so that no one of them could piece together his true purpose. As his pilots flew him back and forth across the Arctic Circle, moving steadily eastward from Coronation Gulf to Queen Maud Gulf in the north and Lac la Martre and Great Slave Lake in the south, he talked only of gold. Wherever the ice and tundra allowed them to land, he sampled the streams, eskers and lake beaches – anywhere the minerals would have concentrated and the sampling looked good.

Flying single-engine Cessna 172 and 185 float planes, carrying maximum loads of fuel, it was necessary to tie up to shore at night and sleep on the open tundra, as he worked slowly towards the coast of Hudson Bay, to the edge of the ice flow at the Glacial Divide. Somewhere between Lac la Martre and the Glacial divide was his diamond field.

Sampling quickly and alone, he had flown thousands of miles, but they were now losing light daily. Already great flocks of Snow, Brant, and Canada geese that fed on the tidal flats and nested on the islands of the Arctic Ocean were moving south in broad arc formations. Thousands of birds were vacating the land, fleeing the approach of another long killing night. Only a few birds would remain. The snowy owl, with its feathered legs would stay to hunt the ptarmigan which burrowed into the snow to escape the winter storms. The white gyrfalcon, too, would remain. For centuries a favorite of the Mongol horseman who used them in falconry across the steppes from Siberia to the Chinese plains, they knew no national boundaries. Circumpolar creatures, like many Arctic denizens, they were as common in the Russian tundra as they were in Canada.

Chuck watched a single gyrfalcon soaring low over the land as though enjoying its mastery of the open countryside. There were plenty of small creatures for it to eat: voles, lemmings and ground squirrels. Winter was another matter. That any bird could survive temperatures that dropped to 60 degrees below zero Fahrenheit always struck him as remarkable. The pilot had tied their aircraft up to shore and was heating some canned chili for supper over a Coleman stove, giving Chuck a peaceful moment alone. A couple of ravens flew over, studying the two men intently, and then landed about a hundred metres off. Scavengers, the raven followed the predators – grizzly, wolf and man. A lonely trapper or prospector was always cheered by the seeming desire ravens showed for human company, and they could be brought right into the camp routine. But it was opportunistic behavior only. The lure of easy food attracted them. Like other creatures they did what they could to survive.

With a breeze blowing off the lake there were no bugs, and one could watch the night take over the country in quiet solitude. Almost as soon as darkness settled, the sky around and above them was filled with the dancing lights of the aurora borealis spilling over them. Magnificent displays of colour swept the heavens from the horizon to a height of almost 1,000 kilometres over the Earth, into space, enveloping the tundra in curtains of shimmering greens and yellows and purple. They were strange, unearthly forms, once thought by some to be the spirits of long-dead races moving over the earth – bright lights even in the blackest hour.

In the morning, after beans, eggs and coffee brewed in classic northern style, boiled with the grinds and then strained, they flew off and the ravens moved in, hopping over the site of the abandoned camp, hoping to find some leftovers, if only a spoonful of cold beans scraped off a plate onto the moss.

When the fuel ran low, they flew into Baker Lake or Yellowknife, but stayed only long enough to store the samples, load up gas and go again. Chuck never allowed his pilots to stop long enough to attract much attention, to answer too many questions. In prospecting, flight plans were never too exact. When they took off, it was Chuck who navigated. The pilots were merely a taxi service, cooks – if they knew how – and company. If their plane ever went down, blowing over in a storm or flipping at the edge of a lake in gale winds, rescue would be problematic. To find a plane down in the Arctic was nearly an impossible task. Some had been lost without a trace for years.

Some locations Chuck liked better than others. One in particular among the hundreds and thousands he eventually walked over he would never forget, although it was only afterwards, when he was again alone in his lab peering into the concentrates, that the features of the spot burned themselves indelibly into his memory.

After he collected his last samples – as far east as the ice had come – along the top of the glacial divide, he was relieved. It was snowing and the North was freezing up, but the broad survey was at last over. He had done it. From their first concessions around Blackwater Lake across the tundra to the Glacial divide was a distance of nearly 1,200 kilometres. Somewhere within it – an area of 520,000 square kilometres which he had sampled – was his diamond mine.

Chuck flew back with his samples to Kelowna and once again buried himself in his lab for the winter. Sample by sample, using large, detailed maps he spread out in a windowless, double-locked planning room, he plotted the results. Like pieces of a puzzle, one by one the greater picture began to emerge.

The trail of indicator minerals, so minute that only the concentration techniques he had patented – and no one else was using – could have detected them, began at Blackwater Lake, spread east in a wide band across the country and then suddenly came to a focus halfway to Baker Lake and the Glacial Divide. Three hundred and twenty kilometres northeast of Yellowknife, in the region of the big lake known as Lac de Gras, the trail abruptly ended.

That was it!

Chuck remembered the place well. A few miles north of Lac de Gras across the barren lands was another large body of water. A wide shallow lake that never completely freed itself from ice in the summer, Exeter Lake was bordered on the south by the long line of an esker which, 12 metres high, dammed its southern shoreline, separating it from a much smaller, unnamed lake on the other side. Protected under the wall of the esker and running perpendicular to it, a coarse sandy beach led from the esker along the shoreline of the unnamed lake for a couple of hundred metres. It was a protected spot, sheltered from the wind and easily accessible.

Only a few weeks earlier the plane had glided in to the beach and Chuck waded the last few steps to shore. From the top of the esker, he could see for dozens of kilometres in all directions. Wolf droppings and ancient caribou trails rutted into the earth, following the path of the esker between the two lakes. It was an advantageous route. The breeze across the top kept the mosquitoes down, close to the ground. One could breath deeply of the air without inhaling the bugs and feel the curve of the Earth, the horizon dropping off like the sea all around. The immensity of the space was a profound experience. A wonderful spot.

The sample taken there, at the base of the esker at the edge of the beach told him he had arrived. It alone contained over 1,500 chrome diopsides and 6,000 pyrope garnets. It was smoking! Two other samples taken nearby bore it out. It was the end of the trail.

He was among the pipes!

CHAPTER FIFTY-THREE

CHRISTMAS, 1985

WHEN Mark left before Christmas in 1983, he lived with friends for a short time and then returned home. The respite had changed little. He maintained both his distance from his father and his own late-night interests, and did not make his grade 12 year.

In the summer of 1984, as Chuck was preoccupied with the lab and starting Dia Met, Mark had a new girlfriend, Leslie Leydier, and a job at Malibu Grand Prix, an entertainment centre with scaled-down racing cars, a track, electronically timed lights and a clock. Like his father, he loved speed. By the fall, his girlfriend pregnant, Mark was enrolled by Marlene and Chuck in Immaculata High School, a private Catholic school. Chuck was still hopeful his son would finish high school and go on to study geology at university. It was not to be. Mark left Immaculata before Christmas. With Leslie expecting in April, Chuck and Marlene offered their full support. She was accepted as one of the family and the marriage took place on the eighth of March, 1985. Their daughter, Alexis Paige Fipke, was born the following month on the 24th of April.

Chuck knew well that neither an early marriage nor a baby required a couple to bury their own dreams. On the contrary, one could pursue an education and a career beyond the furthest reaches of civilization with a family. Whatever his relationship with Mark, it could always be turned around, he believed. Sooner or later Mark would realize he loved him and was only doing what he thought best. If Mark wished to return to school, Chuck would support them. If Mark needed a job, the lab was ready to take him in or, if projects were being run in the field, he had his choice of positions. At full pay. Whatever skills Chuck could offer Mark, he did.

Mark enjoyed married life. Although he still loved speed and was sometimes recklessly wild, he was now, as his grandfather Ed described him, "his own man." When the government opened a prospector's school on Vancouver Island, Mark enrolled, the youngest student in the program. It was a two-month intensive course in basic geology, structural geology, mining law, rock identification and blasting. Mark did well. He graduated and became a licensed prospector.

Christmas of 1985 was more promising than ever. Mark, Leslie and Alexis were living in a small rented bungalow on Patterson Street in Kelowna. After briefly trying his hand at other jobs, Mark returned to work with his father.

Chuck was sitting on a field of diamonds. If Chuck could somehow make them his, the future was theirs.

CHAPTER FIFTY-FOUR

THE DEPARTMENT OF REVENUE

Chuck had to face reality: he needed a better-equipped lab. He needed, too, to know more about the field – where exactly the pipes lay – before he could begin staking, but, more important still, he had to confirm the field was worth staking. Although diamondiferous, the pipe clusters at Golden had proved uneconomic. So, too, had those at Fort Collins, Colorado. The Mountain Diatreme and its related pipes had no diamonds at all. With the resources he had, he could not afford to make any mistakes.

C. F. Minerals had concentrated the samples he had collected over the summer of 1985 and isolated the indicators, but he could not go the extra step necessary and analyze them. Even to determine whether the garnets in his samples were G10s, he needed probes or a quarter-million-dollar scanning electron microscope (SEM) to identify them. Chuck was stuck. He could go no further.

A country expresses its economic philosophy and its social policies no more clearly than in its tax regime. Regardless of the values it publicly espouses, it is the tax system that ultimately defines favorites. In the 1970s, it was culture. For every dollar invested in Canadian film productions, the investor could write off nearly a dollar and a half. The nascent industry exploded, although few of the films produced ever made it to a public screening. The government hoped to do better with the mining industry when it introduced the Scientific Research Tax Credit, a tax incentive for research and development. For Chuck the timing could not have been better, although the new rules soon proved to be a mixed blessing.

Putting up $25,000 himself and collecting most of the rest from an SRTC contract with Dave Mackenzie, who had bought into Dia Met to become the company's newest director, the program allowed him to purchase the SEM at no cost, after tax. It was a gift; a tool for "research."

Chuck and Stan Emerson took a course from Dr. Mike Whitehead in New Jersey to learn how to operate it. When they finished, their skills were still crude but sufficient for their purposes. Then, with the instrument and their new knowledge of what to look for, Chuck set to work after Christmas, delving first into the chemistries of the indicator minerals he had concentrated from the three samples collected along the esker north of Lac de Gras.

As he broke down their molecular structures, he was able to compare their elemental compositions with those obtained from the commercial diamond pipes of Russia and Africa. They worked late at night, under the strictest security. By spring the results were unequivocal and unbelievable. Some samples contained indicators that, when analyzed, revealed they had emanated from pipes unlikely to be especially rich; others, however, and as he had expected, the three "smoking" samples, revealed a pipe or pipes with an altogether different potential. To be certain, he reworked the indicators again, comparing their signature with the industry's best profile.

There was no question about the results. That ancient raised riverbed, the hard-packed gravel esker he had stood upon, which meandered like a drunken rampart across the tundra, ran past a diamond pipe rivalling South Africa's best mine. The indicator minerals in the sand samples taken from the edge of the esker and from the beach at Exeter Lake north of Lac de Gras had come from a nearby source – a kimberlite pipe – which had all the characteristics of the best diamond mines in the world.

Pipes always occurred in clusters, and he knew that with diamond pipes the clusters usually numbered 25 to 35 pipes. Of those, two or three would be sufficiently rich to be mined. At an estimated value of $70 a ton and 400 million tons, the pipes were worth $28 billion. It was one of the richest prizes in history, but the pipes were not his until he staked them, and he couldn't do that. He had no money left to finance the necessary next step – to locate the pipes and stake them. And now he had no way to get new financing.

Paradoxically, the government's tax rules, designed to attract investors' money to the development of Canadian mining projects, killed any chance he had of finding investors for his project. To qualify for the tax shelter, investment money had to go into the ground, to develop existing properties – not fund exploration. Chuck did not have the ground to develop. And with no money to stake the claims, he was not eligible for the financing.

Unable to complete the intensive sampling and staking program that was now required, the ground was left open. More than ever, secrecy was critical. No one could breath a word of what they had found or it would be lost overnight. DeBeers had enough resources to fly in helicopters and crews and stake the whole region under his nose. All Chuck could do was stay tight-lipped and wait for an opening. Until then it was anyone's game.

CHAPTER FIFTY-FIVE

GOLDEN BEAR, 1986–87

THE Scientific Research Tax Credits opened a Niagara of money. As long as a company could stake a claim or option one, they could find cash to play with it. Money was flowing freely and no one cared how it was spent. Crooks swarmed the field. With guaranteed tax returns, investors did not care where their money went.

Dia Met could not compete for this lucre. Investments in exploration projects did not qualify, and nobody who had security in this new tax game was touching the open share market. The Northwest Territories was effectively shut out.

Chuck discussed the problems he was having with Hugo Dummett, who over the years had become a friend, and advisor. Hugo had kept his hand in the play for as long as he could, and even after the demise of Superior, he remained committed, in spirit at least, to their effort, assisting in any way he could.

The two of them now went out, canvassing the majors as well as the minors, in search of a business partner for Chuck that could fund the project. Hugo contacted Western Mines of Australia, and then CRA, which operated the huge Argyle diamond mine in Western Australia's Kimberley Province, sharing with them some of the new data. Neither company was interested. Chuck tried to sell the project to Cambrian Resources, with no success. Together, the two men approached every company they could think of that might be interested. None was. The companies were cold to the proposal – the very reason Chuck had formed Dia Met in the first place. Try as they did, they could not raise the money needed to stake the pipes. It was discouraging.

Chuck was confident they were out there, waiting under the tundra; but he could not get to them. After millions of years they would keep a little while longer, he told himself. Sooner or later, the opportunity to go back would present itself. Until then, there were always the traditional mining mainstays to hunt for: lead, zinc and copper. In geology one had to be flexible. Exploration was a roller-coaster ride.

There was plenty to do to keep himself and Dia Met busy. If not diamonds, then gold; if not gold, then platinum …

In his own lab, the more proficient he became with the new SEM probe technology, the more he realized there were large gaps in his understanding of the petrology of kimberlites and lamproites and the genesis of diamonds. Turning to the government for a grant to research and develop the field of diamond exploration in Canada, he was given $350,000 and three years to prepare an "open file" report for the Geological Survey of Canada. Like the SEM, this grant was another gift. Although the research he generated would have to be made public, it would be his entry into the exclusive club of diamond geologists.

C. F. Minerals, too, continued to run around the clock with new clients and new projects. Petro-Canada was exploring for lead-zinc on Ellesmere Island and flew Chuck to within 350 kilometres of the North Pole to examine its project. After that trip, he went to Peru on behalf of the United Nations.

Once again Chuck found himself on the shores of Lago de Titicaca, but he was on business now and the altitude made him ill. At 5,100 metres he scrambled over the rock and talus to the site of an ancient gold mine, developed during the Inca empire and continued by the Spaniards after their conquest. Downslope, mixed with the tailings, there were extensive fluvial and glacial sediments that contained large resources of low-grade placer gold. Peru desperately needed the investment and returns the mine would provide. The question was whether it could be mined economically. It could not.

In Canada, on behalf of Dia Met, Chuck raised some money on the Jack claims. Hopeful in spite of the poor surface chemistries, they drilled down through the crater's infill to see if the pipe improved at depth. It did not. Only two microdiamonds were recovered in the drill core. The diamond grades, as had been predicted by the chemistries, were too low to be commercial.

And still, the hot pipes in the Barrens waited …

Next they looked at gold in northern Ontario. North of Kenora, Ontario, the towns of Red Lake, Balmerton and Madsen were still, after decades, operating gold mines. Further out, Pickle Crow, a boomtown based on gold, was now a ghost town, but its companion community, Pickle Lake, perched on the shore of an arsenic-rich lake and thrusting up into the northern limits of the boreal forest, was still alive, and still booming.

Chuck flew to Pickle Lake to look at a property. South of Hudson Bay, it was all Canadian Shield, a glaciated landscape of smoothed granites, crystal waters, pike and pickerel, moose, black spruce and blackflies. Chuck liked what he saw and optioned the claim. Upstrike from the large Pickle Lake gold mine and with the same geology, the property had potential. But all he could say was that there was gold at the surface. The extent of the deposit, its economic potential, needed to be proved out. Chuck had already completed expensive geophysical and geo-chemical work on it when he received a provincial government notice that he was required to pay a hefty assessment fee – to keep the claim. Dues.

To Dia Met the fees were an additional cost without gain that tipped the risk-benefit equation in favor of abandonment. Reluctantly, Chuck let it go and returned to British Columbia, where new gold discoveries and a better business environment had the markets trading furiously.

Chevron, in partnership with Homestake, had struck it rich north of the wild Stikine River. Relying in part on the heavy-mineral prospecting techniques taught them by Chuck and on C. F. Minerals's lab for the concentrations, Earl Dodson, Chuck's first client whose contract with Chuck had financed the pur-chase of the lab equipment, had staked the claims and Chevron was now in the process of mapping out the deposit. Just south of Tatsamenie Lake and east of the glacier-capped coastal mountains that separated the lake from Juneau, Alaska, the rich gold deposits that Chevron had named Golden Bear were in the mountains of the Taku River watershed – Gunther Lishy's old haunt. His trapline was the next watershed, to the north.

Only Lishy was dead now. His skeletal remains, rising to the surface of Hutsigola Lake after years in a watery grave, had been found washed ashore in the late summer of 1985 – with a bullet hole in them. He had been murdered. Four years earlier he had been dropped off at Hutsigola Lake by a float plane and had failed to appear, weeks later, at a rendezvous for the return trip to Atlin. Instead of Lishy, a long-haired stranger, dressed partially in animal skins and roughly sewn cloth, paddled out to warn the frightened pilot that death stalked the bush. With only a pack of dogs for company and a diary that chronicled his desperate battle with "sneak-arounds" and "torture-druggers" – spirits of the night – Michael Oros, known throughout the wilderness region as "Sheslay Free Mike," had lived alone for years in the northern wilderness, hunting his nightmares.

The search for Lishy had quickly developed into a manhunt for Oros who, as capable as Lishy of surviving alone in the bush, but armed and wrestling with phantoms, became a living nightmare for the RCMP. When they attempted to arrest him, he disappeared into the forest and then attacked them, hunting the hunters. A winter shoot-out in the deep snow of Teslin Lake resulted in the murder of a young officer by Oros before Oros's own gun strangely misfired and he was shot.

Chevron had drilled the claims with good results and was sinking a shaft and starting the second phase of their drill program when Dia Met applied to buy in. Raising a million dollars through the sale of its shares to First Exploration Fund, an investor fund set up to take advantage of the investor tax relief, and joining up with Island Star, another minor player, Dia Met's bid for an option to earn 49 percent of the claims upstrike from Golden Bear was approved by Chevron. Dia Met stock soared and the board celebrated, riding the roller coaster to the top.

They had hit the big time. Golden Bear was hot – one of British Columbia's richest gold deposits. Then the environmentalists organized against it. Focusing on the fear that a road from the village of Telegraph Creek on the Stikine River to the mine site, the first in the region, would hamper the movements of the resident woodland caribou, the voices grew more strident. The provincial government agreed to reconsider its road permit. In the meantime, perhaps even for the duration of the mine's life, all transportation into the remote area would remain by helicopter.

Chuck found it difficult to stand by, but Chevron was the project operator and, as a minor player, Dia Met had no control over the program or the budget. Chuck went off to conduct his own exploration instead. Poking around the perimeter of Chevron's claims, just south of the Golden Bear Mine property, he discovered some promising gold targets. Calling them the Bandit Claims, Dia Met staked them on behalf of the Chevron joint venture, raised another $200,000 – the budget for the program – through the sale of more shares to First

Exploration and brought in a crew to explore them. Fresh from his prospector's course and with a blasting license under his belt, Mark was made camp manager. At the age of 20 he already had eight seasons in the field.

The Bandit outcrop hung over a rock face above a loose talus slope at 2,700 metres. Cold and incredibly steep, it faced a permanent ice cap across the valley on the facing slope. Summer weather consisted of low dense cloud with rain, sleet and snow. It was a rough location, but the gold concentrations at the surface were spectacular. It had to be drilled.

A drill camp was a real place: a physical plane where problems could be solved with geochemistry and geophysics. Each perosn brought his own skills to focus on a single purpose. Chuck was happy to be back into it. He was running a crew of 12 to 15 men. Some, like himself, were always coming and going. Mark spent the summer on the face of the rock at the Bandit claims, setting off blasts and ensuring that their satellite communication systems continued to function – and doing whatever needed to be done.

Access to the Bandit camp remained an intractable problem. The camp's altitude and physical position presented a real challenge to the pilot they had chartered. Even in the bloom of summer, blizzards blew down from across the ice fields, heavy with Pacific moisture and frozen rain, blinding them for days. And still the chopper would come in.

Mark would wait outside the camp, his hood off, listening through the sounds of a storm for the chop of the main rotor. The pilot, Mark Andreij, flying almost totally blind, would come in from Atlin hugging the rivers and staying low in the valleys until he reached the base of their mountain. A narrow rock ridge, a spine, ran from the edge of the camp down to the foot of the mountain, and the pilot, recognizing the landform when he reached it, would hug it, riding the ridge up the mountain. Hovering dangerously close to the rock, sometimes no more than three metres off the ground – all the visibility he had in the snow and cloud – he would crawl up the steep mountain face, fighting buffeting winds, towards the camp.

One day, during a storm, Mark heard the helicopter without seeing it. He lit a flare and drew the helicopter to him, to the narrow ledge, the landing pad he had blasted out of the cliff face. Lying flat on the wet ground, the flare in his hand, Mark brought the machine down right overtop him. As its skids touched, he was already strapping it down to keep it from being blown off the mountain.

It was the most dangerous flying Mark had ever seen. For the passengers coming in, the flights were a living hell. For Andreij there was a special kind of challenge in them that he liked.

A geologist with a doctorate, Ed Schiller was a new director of Dia Met when he flew up to the Golden Bear claims on behalf of Dia Met for a progress report from Chevron's project manager and a personal look around. He didn't like what he saw.

"What have you spent so far?" Schiller asked the project manager. It was a fair question. On tight operations, budget expenditures were calculated daily. The fact that it was Dia Met money the project manager was spending should have made him even more careful. It was not his money to blow. The manager didn't have a clue; he guessed $400,000. Schiller told him to get what records he had and then began to add up the figures himself. A few hours later, Schiller's rough calculation was that the drilling had cost at least $800,000!

Schiller immediately shut down the project down. Although the field was entirely under Chevron's control, Dia Met's money was financing the drilling and their agreement with Chevron gave Dia Met that option. It was an extremely unpopular thing to do. The project manager resisted. The budget was for a million dollars, he argued. He was still under budget. Schiller stuck to his guns and forced the camp to close. He suspected the project manager had spent even more than $800,000. He was right.

When all the bills were collected and totalled, they found that the project manager had spent $1.6 million. Dia Met only had a million, and the drill program had been a near-disaster. Rather than proving out the claim and defining its boundaries, the drill results were poor – much worse than they should have been. They had hit too many barren holes. It had been bad drill placement on top of poor management by the project manager. And now Dia Met owed $600,000 to the kitty.

Earl Dodson's job as well as Dia Met's future was on the line. It was not his fault, but it was his department. Dodson reviewed all the expenditures and managed to find $200,000 in management fees and other expenses Chevron could absorb. It helped, but it left Dia Met still owing $400,000 – money they needed to stake the diamond claims in the Northwest Territories. The pipes seemed to be getting further and further away ...

Once again Dia Met returned to the investment-fund market. Selling more shares on the gold claims, they raised $400,000 and settled their debts with Chevron. They had not hit bottom yet. Their contract with Chevron was only an option agreement. To stay in, they had to make their next payment, and they could not do it. Unable to renew, they sold their rights back to Chevron for a one percent net smelter royalty interest. The value of their stock plummeted.

Dia Met was lucky to get out when they did. Chevron, like Superior before it, decided in the end to quit minerals completely. It shut down its entire mining division. Homestake took over the property and assumed Chevron's obligation to pay Dia Met its smelter royalties. The feasibility studies on Golden Bear, which had initially excited the whole industry and decided Dia Met's commitment, continued to read like a dream. The gold deposits were so rich that it was anticipated that all capital costs would be paid off within the first two years. The profit potential was tremendous. Realizing it was another matter.

The project continued to suffer setbacks. The ground conditions were unstable. In a fault zone, the shafts were susceptible to cave-ins, and the underground work was more complicated than had been expected. Metallurgical problems followed. The equipment designed to process the ore was not capable of doing the job. The problems were not unique, but the anticipated start-up date kept getting pushed further and further into the future.

Dia Met fared no better on the Bandit Claims. Winter came early. Working under threatened avalanches in heavy snow conditions, Chuck finished the project for $225,000 – $25,000 over budget. The directors had to pay the difference themselves. The drill results were even worse than at Golden Bear; Bandit turned out to be a surface deposit with no depth to it. Dia Met rolled it into the claims Chevron had, took its one percent smelter royalty agreement and left, absolutely devastated.

CHAPTER FIFTY-SIX

NEW ZEALAND, JANUARY, 1988

An offer awaited Chuck in Kelowna which promised to put a little distance between him and the disaster of the Golden Bear and Bandit claims. Trace amounts of platinum had been found around Riverton on the bottom end of New Zealand's South Island, and the geologists on the project had read a paper Chuck had written on platinum exploration. The offer to come to New Zealand to run their heavy-mineral survey was just the holiday he needed. The budget was someone else's headache, Canada was locked in winter, and New Zealand was a new country in the bloom of summer.

Chuck took a room in a small hotel named The Riverton. In the morning he was alone in the dining room having breakfast when the most ragged, unshaven and rough-looking man stumbled out of one of the rooms and sat down heavily at the table next to him.

"Holy Christ! What a grub!" Chuck thought. He himself had showered and dressed to meet his new clients. The other man sized him up slowly with bleary eyes and shook his head, obviously displeased by what he, too, saw.

"Going dancing are we?" he asked Chuck. He looked like he'd been sleeping on the ground in the bush for months without changing his clothes.

"Little early for you?" Chuck replied. It was not quite 7:00 AM. The man was in no mood to argue. "Partying late with the Maori," he explained. Chuck looked at him more carefully. The idea of Maori parties evoked memories of other bush parties he had known. A Polynesian people, the Maori were lords of their islands when the *Pakeha* – the white men – arrived, and they fought long and hard to avoid submission. In the end, British sovereignty was proclaimed over New Zealand in 1840 and the Maori were disarmed and integrated. However, preserved beneath jackets and ties was the Maori spiritual and cultural identity, and they kept their get-togethers in the country, practiced solely for fun. Bush parties.

The stranger leaned across and held out his hand, "Ray Dawson!" Chuck accepted his offer and pulled out a chair at his own table, "Chuck Fipke."

Ray told Chuck he made his living foraging for rare seashells along the rugged, nearly inaccessible southwestern coast. He hiked in over long distances, spent weeks living alone at the edge of the seashore, and when he came out, he wanted to party nonstop. "Not much different from the life of a prospector," Chuck commented.

Platinum had been discovered a century earlier in New Zealand, but all the deposits were too poor to be commercial. Riverton was a new discovery, and the company that had brought Chuck in was hopeful it would prove to be different. Chuck spent the day training the New Zealand crews and plotting an attack on the drainage systems to achieve the most efficient survey of the region.

Ray was waiting for him at the hotel when he finished for the day and was in no mood to waste any more time. Chuck would have to skip dinner. The party was waiting. There had been few such offers over the past 12 years. Chuck's life since South America had been consumed by work. He needed the release. Ray wasn't Maori, but he was accepted by them, and they were his preferred company.

Chuck loved the night, when the darkness narrowed his focus like a laser beam to the instant being lived – to a single point of time in a space where nothing existed beyond the shadows of the light except the great unknown. The alcohol carried Chuck away, and the dancing returned him to a time and space that was his alone, far from the lab, Dia Met and his own ambitions.

The New Zealand nights with Ray Dawson, the Maori and alcohol, were another world, where one could play like the gods – or demons – uninhibited, powerful, eternal. With Ray, it was back to drinking in classic Ok Tedi style. Chuck was out each night until 3:00 and up each morning at 6:30, hiking the drainage systems with the field crews. Then it was back to the never-ending Maori party. The exercise, tramping over the country, worked off the alcohol, but the effort took its toll and Chuck began to look more like Ray as the days went by.

There was platinum in the creeks and they found the sources – another technical success – but, like all the other platinum deposits unearthed in the country, these, too, were uneconomic. The New Zealand geological environment simply didn't lend itself to commercial deposits of platinum. Still, the hopeful would keep looking. For Chuck, it was time to go home; he needed the break.

"Hey, Ray! If you ever get to Canada, remember you got a place to stay, you know!" Although he never expected to see Ray again, Chuck liked him.

After three weeks of working hard and drinking heavily, Chuck felt close to collapse, yet somehow restored. It was only his body that was tired. Like a morning plunge into the cold sea, New Zealand had been invigorating. Once in the aircraft he slept all the way back to Canada.

CHAPTER FIFTY-SEVEN

NORTH OF YELLOWKNIFE

In the spring of 1988, the government announced an end to the investor tax shelter in mining stock. The flow-through tax benefits were scrapped and the funds which took investor money and spread it around the industry all started to shut down. One of the managers from Equity Preservation Fund, whom Chuck had dealt with on several occasions and who was also associated with First Exploration Fund, called to tell him they still had some money left, cash they were looking to invest. He suggested to Chuck that if Dia Met had any new claims they wanted to develop, anything, the final money was theirs.

Chuck decided to push the Northwest Territories. Even though the caller had reiterated that they were only looking to fund advanced projects, Chuck thought he had more to go on than before, in particular the "open file report" he had been commissioned to do for the GSC. With the assistance of John Gurney and Rory Moore, it had been completed and was scheduled for publication: an 1,183-page, comprehensive study on diamond exploration. Because of it, his new proficiency in the field of diamond exploration was becoming widely recognized.

Having a confidentiality agreement in place, Chuck met with the fund managers and their geologist-advisors and presented his arguments for the existence of an Arctic diamond field. As soon as he finished his presentation, Dr. Jerry Carlsen, chief geologist of First Exploration, jumped on it. His enthusiasm quickly carried over to the other managers, who suggested that if he could stake something – any ground at all – in the vicinity of the pipes, he would get himself a claim to develop, one he could then use as a base for exploration. He did, and they traded him $125,000 for another piece of Dia Met.

Two long years of distress and digression had passed, but now, finally, he was back on track. Norm's Manufacturing was returning to the North!

Chuck was deep into planning a sampling program centred on the esker at Exeter Lake when the doorbell rang. Fresh off the plane and ready to party, Ray Dawson stood on the doorstep, grinning broadly. He took the living room. Whatever stories Chuck had told him in New Zealand, the reality was that with three shifts running around the clock at the C.F. Minerals lab, his other projects and Dia Met's new operation in the Northwest Territories to plan, Chuck was totally occupied fighting fires. Ray's arrival created new demands. Following Chuck to the lab each morning, he waited impatiently for the work to end. It began casually enough, a few drinks after work in a club called the Willow to watch the strippers before going home. Chuck felt he owed it to Ray to take him out. By the time they finished touring the other clubs and finally settled into the discos, it had turned into a nightly ritual.

Marlene wasn't especially enthused. Ray's occupation of her living room was invasion enough. The two men out exploring Kelowna's hot spots was worse. It took its toll on Chuck as well, although he attempted to minimize it by moving Ray out and bunking him with another geologist friend. As he had discovered in New Zealand, the effects of late nights lasted longer than they used to, but the dance floors here were smooth and the music had familiar roots. The temptation of delirious release offered by the nights was again irresistible. It was a lifestyle with its own routines and rewards and, once into it, difficult to shake.

At last, they all boarded a plane to Calgary, the first leg of the trip back to the Arctic. The flight was a welcome respite from the nightly bar scene. And the Arctic was dry. Where they were going there was no pub they could walk to in days.

Their last stop in civilization was Yellowknife. Ray warmed at once to the frontier mood of the northern city and its possibilities for adventure. They booked two rooms at the Explorer Hotel under assumed names and headed out to enjoy their last night.

It was summer in the North, another short reprieve from the prevailing frozen darkness, and some of the locals, suffering from "summer madness," were completely frenzied. Chuck and his party could hear the Golden Range bar, vibrating a block away. Inside, they mixed easily, exchanging jokes and avoiding the fights that broke out every hour. With no bouncers, the brawls were allowed to run their own course and only the losers were forced to leave. For Chuck, the rough scenes were hardly worth any attention, but Ray took it all in and kept his back firmly to the wall. The motion was fluid. Strangers greeted each other like lost brothers, swapping stories, leads on hot jobs and gripes about the high cost of northern living. When Chuck and Ray finally made it back to the Explorer Hotel, there was little night left. The sun was down but the sky had the quality of a summer's dawn just before sunrise, shimmering expectantly. Two hours later they met again for an early breakfast. Chuck was anxious to get going.

With only $125,000 to spend, it was a lean operation, as tight as any Chuck had run. Security was also an issue. Besides Ray Dawson, Chuck was relying on only two other trusted men: his son Mark, and Dave Mackenzie, who would fly up in his own Piper Super Cub and meet them at the camp.

Yellowknife was a port on Great Slave Lake, a body of water large enough to support its own freshwater fishing industry. The city was also the staging centre for the Arctic. Bob Jensen was waiting for them at the docks, his plane floating between a couple of old wooden gillnetters. As far as he knew, the men he was contracted to fly for were prospecting for gold. No mention of diamonds would ever be made in his presence. Swinging their gear over the pontoons, the heaviest items a three-metre inflatable Zodiac in a duffel bag and a 15-horsepower motor and gas can in a packing crate, Bob nosed them out toward the mouth of the harbour, opened the throttle to a deafening roar, rocked the floats up to skate the surface, spraying water in broad fantails behind them, and lifted off: airborne and on the start of their last leg north.

Chuck sat in the front beside the pilot. The whole of the Arctic lay spread out before him through the windshield. Behind him sat Ray and Mark, each quiet.

Chuck was glad to be back. It had been too long, and the struggle relentless. This time it would be different: he was sure of it. They were riding to the crest once more. He put his head back and immediately fell asleep. Behind him, Mark also dozed.

Ray could not. It was the strange new landscape. Yellowknife, from the air, sat at the edge of a black, boreal forest. Poor soils and harsh weather had limited the growth of the conifers, mostly black spruce and tamarack, and the forest was sparse, its trees spindly and stunted. From 1,200 metres the trees were bristly spines on the gently contoured rock faces of the northern plain.

As they flew north the trees thinned rapidly and the forest levelled out until, more and more tortured, hugging the ground like rock garden shrubbery, the trees stopped sprouting altogether. The treeline was clearly visible to them from the air; it corresponded with the southern limits of the continuous permafrost zone. Looking along its edge, it was a straggling line that stretched off out of sight beyond the horizon.

Beneath the surface, unseen, was frozen ground which would permit no penetration. The active layer – the thin surface zone which thawed each summer – was, in places, no more than a few centimetres thick. In areas of exposed bedrock, it extended down several metres into the rock. Beneath the active layer, the earth was forever frozen. With a mean annual air temperature of around minus nine degrees Celsius, the ground below was frozen to depths of 275 metres and more.

They crossed the treeline into the tundra. Ray had never seen anything like it. An immense, treeless plain of grey rock, muskeg, glacial tills and water. To the New Zealander, whose life had been lived among the verdant mountains and teeming seashores of the South Pacific, the tundra was aptly named the Barren Lands: an empty, lifeless, featureless plain. It was a landscape of the mind, more like a black-and-white photograph than a three-dimensional space. To the early Europeans who first saw it, it was a world devoid of life and value. To the Inuit who roamed the Arctic for millennia, the North had its own magic.

Winter had not blown off the land over which Chuck and the others now flew. Protected in the lee of the wind, and from the warming rays of the summer sun, snowfields in late June still blanketed slopes, while ice floes filled the bays. Some of the smaller lakes were still completely ice-bound. Desteffany, a large lake, was open. The waves breaking across the surface and crashing along a grey rocky shoreline gave them the direction of the wind. Jensen put the plane's nose into the wind, dropped the flaps and let his craft slip back to earth, bouncing over the surface until it settled heavily into the water, rocking with the waves.

They were 50 kilometres southwest of the hot samples from the esker at Exeter Lake and an equal distance west of Lac de Gras – far enough, Chuck felt, from their real search area not to draw attention to it. Desteffany would be their base.

As Jensen cut the engine, gliding them toward the rocky shore, the men jumped from the pontoons and splashed through the frigid water, saving the metal from rubbing over the sharp fractured rocks that lined the bottom. Their exposed skin went numb in the water almost instantly. Standing on feet they could not feel, they formed a chain and unloaded the plane, then pushed it back out to the open water, where Jensen once again turned it into the wind. Roaring away under full power, he took off – he would return later with a load of aviation gas and motor fuel – leaving the three of them standing alone on the shoreline.

Before their feet dried, the smell of their bodies, the concentrations of expelled carbon dioxide, drifted off across the tundra and brought in the mosquitoes. The clouds that gathered around them continued to grow larger until the sound of hundreds of tiny, buzzing furies, hungry for their blood, broke the absolute stillness of the space.

CHAPTER FIFTY-EIGHT

DESTEFFANY LAKE

CAMP consisted of two tents, a large Coleman stove, some food coolers, a pit dug into the permafrost to keep the perishables and several drums of gas and fuel for the plane and the outboard motor. Mark, Ray and Bob Jensen shared one tent while Chuck and Dave Mackenzie occupied the other with the Coleman. Unless the wind was blowing hard enough to keep the bugs on the ground, all the cooking was done inside, behind the protection of canvas walls. Outside, the mosquito populations continued to grow until the sound they made was like the distant roar of highway traffic.

The bugs were a plague. There was no escaping them. In the open, one had to keep constantly on the move, always running, as did the caribou, to avoid them. Worse than the mosquitoes were the blackflies. More tenacious, they worked their way up pant cuffs over the tops of one's boots, crawled down collars and wormed through every opening they could find, rooting in one's hair to get through to the flesh. Toxic, their bites could make a person delirious.

Chuck assigned tasks for the crew. Mark, dropped off each morning with the Zodiac raft, spent his days alone on Exeter, Ursula, Providence, Yamba and several of the other big lakes collecting samples from the beaches and sandbars and from the streams and creeks that emptied into them. If the distances were not too great, he hiked inland for several kilometres to sample eskers or other locations where Chuck believed indicator minerals may have been concentrated. They were searching for the pipes.

The advantage of the Zodiac was the freedom it gave Mark to speed around over the water ahead of the bugs, but it was a lonely life, working long days with never another human in sight, and sometimes it was dangerous. Once, when he was slowly crossing a large body of water attempting to reach the shore to make the planned evening rendezvous with the aircraft, a windstorm blew in across the tundra without warning. In the wide, shallow lake the surface quickly rolled up into huge swells. Within minutes, waves of freezing water were breaking overtop the Zodiac. Only the tarp, which Mark had hastily tied from the bow around himself and to the stern kept the craft from being swamped.

As the craft bounced off a wave, the wind slipped in under it and instantly lifted the bow on end, standing the entire craft up, like a sail to the wind. If the Zodiac were to flip over, the freezing temperatures would kill him in minutes. Desperately, Mark kicked up off the transom and threw himself over the bow, trying with the weight of his own body to force it back down to the water. For a long moment it hovered there, between life and death, the wind holding it up against his entire weight, before it gave and came crashing down.

In July at the height of summer the sun was setting at midnight and rising again at 3:00 a.m. In the short time it hovered below the horizon it remained light enough to fly a plane, read or fish. They caught some grayling and a couple of trout, which Jensen grilled over the Coleman. Most meals were prepared by Mark or Dave. Chuck's contribution to their country cuisine was his morning coffee – strong enough to eat holes through a person's stomach. In the evenings, huddled together for supper in Chuck's tent, they would recount past life experiences and swap stories of their daily adventures.

The weather was not the only threat. The wildlife were unpredictable, too. The barren ground grizzly lived in the open tundra and hunted the caribou herds. The largest subspecies of the grizzly family, they were incredibly powerful and, for all their bulk, could chase down a running caribou in a short distance and kill it with a single blow. Neither were all grizzlies afraid of people. Some saw them as food.

Mark's first encounter came after he had left the Zodiac on shore and was hiking inland for a sample. Cresting the rise of an esker he almost stumbled over a grizzly that was engaged in stalking a caribou. He quickly dropped to the ground before either animal saw him. The grizzly had its back to him and was likewise pressed low to the ground like a cat, taking advantage of the terrain to keep under cover as it crept towards the caribou, attempting to get close enough to run it down before the caribou spotted it and fled. The grizzly had the wind in its favor. So did Mark. Quietly he crawled back out of sight and retreated to the safety of the Zodiac, without the sample.

Even witnessing the aftereffects of an unsuccessful attack set the crew's hearts racing and their adrenaline soaring. Mark was skirting the edge of a wet bog when some movement low in the water caught his attention. He went to investigate. It was a wounded caribou. As Mark came into its sight, the creature panicked, tried to lift itself to its feet, shook horribly and sagged back down, exhausted, watching Mark with deep sorrowful eyes. Across its hindquarters were the crippling claw marks of the grizzly which had raked it. The wounds were fresh. The dying animal had not yet attracted any ravens or wolves. But the bugs were there: a cloud of insects was feeding on the open wounds.

Unarmed, there was nothing Mark could do to ease the creature's suffering and he hastily withdrew, abandoning it to its own fate. But the horrific vision stayed with him and when he described the encounter to the others, Ray, who had the least experience with Canadian wildlife, was especially concerned and grateful for having been assigned to work with Dave. There was, Ray believed, security in numbers.

Landing on eskers which sometimes were as smooth and hard as gravel strips, Dave and Ray would each collect samples and then fly on to the next site. The combined weight of the two men and their samples, however, took its toll on the Super Cub. The uneven ground created enormous pressures for the frame of the landing gear to absorb, even with its ballooned tundra tires. They had been sampling for a couple of weeks when their routine ended abruptly. Rolling into a dip on the ground soon after landing, the plane's wheels went down and then did not rise fast enough as the land came up on the other side. Instead, the structural supports of the landing gear split apart, the wheels spread-eagled, and the aircraft ground to a halt.

Dave cursed. They were 60 kilometres from Desteffany. They were also far from any lakeshore the float plane could land on to meet them. Dave cursed again, as Ray nervously took stock of their surroundings. Gingerly Dave climbed out, careful not to cause any further damage to his plane, and inspected the break. It was repairable, after a fashion. He jury-rigged the wheel-posts together with rope and managed to lift the plane back up onto its wheels. He could take off.

But not with Ray. Promising to come back with the float plane when he could, Dave instructed Ray to stay put until the others decided how and where to pick him up. Then, racing across the top of the esker, blowing back sand and ancient surface dust, Dave lifted off and flew away, a receding speck against the sky that, smaller and smaller, disappeared, leaving Ray behind.

The New Zealander was alone on the tundra, in the barren lands, with the mosquitoes. In the north lay the blue haze of the Arctic; in the south, the small, bright little sun of cold comfort. In the middle of nothing, him – and a million mosquitoes. The realization of his own vulnerability cut like a knife through all his defences. A dimensionless infinity dwarfed the simple form of a man. That one lived or died meant nothing here.

A big man nearing 60, but with tremendous reserves of physical energy, Ray paced nervously up and down along the top of the esker to stay ahead of the bugs, while he kept a wary eye open for the larger carnivores. He had seen them from the air, and although they often ran from aircraft he knew that a man on the ground was a lot less intimidating.

All a person could do, alone and unarmed on the tundra if he were to see a bear, was hide. On the tundra? Where?

Ray waited anxiously for rescue, and waited. It had been early in the day when Dave flew out, and it was late in the evening, more than 12 hours later, when Ray finally heard the sound of an aircraft returning. The sound of civilization. Of survival. Of escape. Exhausted, his heart soared in relief. It had been difficult just to keep ahead of the bugs. At last … but then he saw it was the float plane.

Chuck's role in the sampling program required that he alone use the float plane. With it, he broadly sampled all the sites which could be accessed easily from the water with floats. He studied the landscape from the air, taking note of the eskers, the direction of the ancient ice flows and the deposits of sand and gravel, plotting a course for the others to follow. When Chuck had called it quits for the day, and he and Jensen flew back to Desteffany, they learned from Dave that Ray was still out on the tundra. Quickly they threw some things into the plane and took off again.

It was eleven o'clock in the evening, the sun's rays slanting low over the land when they spotted Ray below them, desperately waving up at the plane. Chuck scribbled out instructions for Ray. There was simply no way they could pick up Ray off the tundra with a float plane. Chuck stuffed the instructions into a sleeping bag along with a new map and some supplies and tossed the bundle out the plane.

Ray ran to pick it up, ready to do anything to get off the tundra. As the plane circled overhead, he rolled out the package, and was dumbfounded when a small shovel and sample bags fell free. Around the handle of the shovel Chuck had tied his note. Ray studied it for a moment before he could make any sense of it. A meandering line was drawn across the land with several locations marked with *Xes* that Chuck wanted sampled.

Chuck had seen no reason to waste the opportunity that Ray's long overland traverse would provide, to collect some otherwise hard-to-get samples. Several kilometres away was a lake they could safely land on with the floats, and Chuck wrote that they would meet him there in the morning. That would give Ray plenty of time to walk the extra distance the samples required. With nothing further to accomplish, they straightened out and flew back to camp, while Ray, all alone once more, on the tundra, cursed wildly.

After a few fitful hours trying to sleep with his head tucked into his bag for protection from the mosquitoes, Ray began his long hike to the rendezvous. He wanted out. The land over which he hiked was a profusion of colourful mosses and lichens dotted with wildflowers. Each of the plants, Arctic rhododendrons, white heather, yellow poppies, and Arctic sorrel, different from their southern cousins, were miracles of adaptation to the environment. Exceptionally hardy, they suffered repeated summer freezes and thaws, yet continued to thrive and bloom without apparent ill-effect. Even their seeds endured. Those that had become trapped, frozen into the permafrost like the mammoths that had roamed here during the Pleistocene, remained as fresh after 10,000 years as though a single season had passed overtop. Arctic lupines grown from seeds that were that old raised intriguing questions about the very nature of life. If life could lie dormant for 10,000 years, then, a thousand thousand?

Uniquely, no true Arctic plant was poisonous to man. In fact, most, like sourdock, sandwort, bistwort and bilberry were exceptionally nourishing. Rich in vitamins and high in sugar and starch, they could sustain human life. It gave Ray some comfort, as he moved wearily over the land, to know that the flowers at least were on his side.

Contrasted with the stark harshness of the background in which they lived, each life form, even the rock lichens, took on a preciousness of being that highlighted the gulf between the living and the void. His own senses heightened, a loon crying out or a plover rising, startled, from the edge of the wet bog, caused Ray's heart to race madly, but he continued, walking, making intimate contact with this other life, united in spirit, through a land that was utterly barren.

Ray made it to the rendezvous – with the samples.

It was a summer in which the days blended into each other with a dreadful sameness, where the landscape over huge traverses remained unchanged and the work never varied. Hour after hour, day after day, they crossed the land by aircraft, boat or on foot, collecting samples and carrying them back. Only Jensen, the pilot, left every few days by himself with a load of samples, and returned with more gas. The rest of them remained behind, each alone with his private thoughts.

Chuck was at last closing in on his dreams, but the work did not bring him relief. They had not claimed the ground; it still remained open for the taking. For Dave, it was a time to contemplate life, the North, history and his own future. For Mark and Ray, the summer continued to be a battle with isolation, of internal spaces that craved release and found only the open tundra each morning, of almost unrelenting tedium, broken occasionally by moments of sheer terror. Ray's greatest fears were to be realized.

Ray had gone with Mark to collect a couple of samples several hundred metres from the plane, which remained on the water waiting for them, when he became aware of a third presence. Some sense caused him to turn around, and he saw a big boar grizzly stalking them. Somehow, stealthily, it had approached to within a hundred metres – in wide open country – before its cover had given out and it moved into the open. The bear was coming straight for them, rapidly closing the distance.

Instantly, Ray's mind bolted. Several hundred kilos of killing terror was descending on him. His instincts screamed at him to run for his life! Almost senseless with fear, he tried but couldn't move. Desperately, he struggled to break free of some incredibly powerful inertia which held him, immobilized, against his will. Mark seemed to be beside him, speaking something.

"Ray, don't run! DON'T RUN! IT'LL KILL US IF YOU RUN! RAY, LISTEN TO ME!"

Ray finally heard, understood words and became aware that it was Mark, gripping him tightly, holding him back. It was hard to think, harder to walk. The adrenaline surging through him had numbed all feeling. His legs weren't working. The grizzly was only 50 metres away.

"HOLY CHRIST!" Mark held onto him fiercely, with all his might. If he let go, Ray would fly or fall down.

"Walk, Ray! Walk!" Mark was pleading, trying to keep his own voice quiet, now that the bear was so close. "Don't run! Don't run, Ray!"

Mark kept up a constant stream of instructions as much to control himself as Ray. He knew also that the sound of a human voice, speaking calmly, was supposed to deter an attack. At least the bear would know they were not caribou.

As Mark marched Ray, still tightly gripped, quickly across the tundra towards the distant plane, the bear dogged them closely. It was pushing them, testing them, but perhaps unsure of them – prey ran – it stayed behind, waiting.

The sight of it, 50 metres away, following them across open ground, required a supreme exertion of will over instinct. Instinct shrieked at them to flee, while reason whispered they could never hope to outrun the bear. They were prey: dead if the bear wished it or they made a wrong move. The float plane was still half a kilometre away. As they closed the distance, even as they approached the pontoons, the grizzly stayed at their back. While they throttled the engine and took off, the bear stood at the edge of the lake like a silent sentinel, watching them leave.

Wolves were another concern. Large, long-legged animals, they ran with wide, loping strides and covered ground quickly. Strange creatures without apparent hostility or friendliness, the wolves exhibited a kind of detached interest in people and often followed the men around in packs as they worked, sometimes no more than a hundred metres off. One sensed that the order they lived under was a simple hierarchy: Creatures they could kill to eat, they did; creatures too dangerous to kill, they didn't.

Upon sighting a lone man on the land, they would move in rapidly and fan out around him, the way they circled any other prey. It was unnerving. Mark, again, had the closest contact. As it seemed to be human confidence that kept them at bay – the natural communication of a superior predator's power – Mark tried to show no fear, demonstrating his own strength with body language that they could read. They were alert to his every action.

Once, when a sample he had to get from a sandy gravel bank was close to a den area some wolves had dug out, he moved right in amongst them. The wolves, immobile, like boulders, held their ground. Mark marched in, took his sample from near the den and got out.

One learned to deal with fear as well as isolation in the tundra. Getting the samples became their only focus. The samples ranked supreme, and Mark, like his father, sometimes risked his life for them, but for entirely different reasons: the sooner they were finished, the sooner they could leave. With nothing else to do but sleep, eat and hide from the bugs, Chuck pushed them relentlessly.

Without money for a helicopter, they had to use labour-intensive sampling methods. Sometimes it took an entire day for one man, hiking an enormous distance, to collect a single sample. Twelve-hour workdays grew to 14 then 15 and sometimes 16, seven days a week, as the summer passed away. It was a difficult existence, and they all suffered it in their own ways.

With several hundred samples collected by the end of the season, Chuck finally decided they had done enough. They flew back to Yellowknife and had their first glimpse of strangers in two months. Away from the absolute stillness of the tundra and the deep calm the tractless emptiness created, they needed to get used to the "urban" environment again. There were more details and movements than a person could take in easily, and their senses, attuned to the soft whistling of the wind and the splash of a wave washing upon a rocky shore, were overwhelmed.

Dave Mackenzie flew back to the coast, Ray Dawson returned to New Zealand, and Mark went to work in the lab, concentrating the samples they had collected all summer. For Chuck, there was more than enough to do. With new contracts to run mineral surveys across the American Midwest and into Mexico, the lab continued to work non-stop. Although he was back to sleeping in his own bed at nights, it was another winter away from his family. Each sample from the Northwest Territories, once concentrated, took 12 hours to sift through, and although he had help, Chuck still had hundreds of samples to do. For security reasons, he did the final lab work himself. The fewer people who knew what he was up to, the easier he could sleep. The diamond pipes were still up for grabs.

By spring, the analysis was complete. In his secure office, plotting the results alone each night on large-scale maps of the Lac de Gras region, he began to see a picture of the diamond field emerge. It was still shadowy – certain features were well defined, others faded completely into the background – but without another season spent sampling, it was the best he could do.

The hottest sample of all remained the one he had collected years earlier at the base of the esker beside Exeter Lake, but they had not yet found the pipe that went with it. They had not yet found any pipes. Chuck did not know the exact dimensions of the field. The only boundary he was confident of was the eastern one, beyond which all hot indicator minerals ceased to exist, and the northern one, where again the indicators stopped cold. To the south, approaching Lac de Gras, there were indicators as far as they had looked. It was possible that there were even pipes under the big lake itself. How far the field extended to the west was anybody's guess. Diamond indicators were spread out there for hundreds of kilometres, as far away as Blackwater Lake.

All Chuck could do was apply the usual patterns of known pipe clusters world-wide to the area they had sampled, and then draw a wide circle around the area to be staked. Somewhere within the circle, were the pipes. *Should be*, he reasoned.

More importantly, the indicators were all hot. Their chemical compositions were as good as the best of the Russian pipes or any of DeBeers's. There was no question about it, the pipe cluster in the Northwest Territories was world-class, a treasure of the highest order. Even more important, the distribution of the indicator minerals over a wide plain suggested that the limits of the cluster were greater than any other grouping ever recorded. He couldn't be sure – the ice had smeared the indicators all over the surface – but there appeared to be more than a single pipe cluster. It looked like there were at least two of them, both rich in diamonds!

Chuck couldn't wait any longer. He had to begin staking.

CHAPTER FIFTY-NINE

STAKING THE NORTHWEST TERRITORIES

Above the high-water mark at the edge of the beach, about 200 metres from the esker at Exeter Lake, Mark struggled against the wind to put up a tent camp while Chuck drove in the first stake. All around them, rising above the thin layer of loose till, was the grey, exposed bedrock of the Slave Archean Craton, chunks of which had been ripped away by an ancient iceflow and strewn for hundreds of kilometres across the tundra, west to the Mackenzie River and the DeBeers claims.

Through a maze of private placements with the directors and staff of Dia Met and C. F. Mineral Research, their friends and relatives and new share sales, Dia Met had funds for one more season the: summer of 1989.

Starting from the beach Chuck's men moved out in all four directions. To avoid any information from leaking out at Yellowknife, 288 kilometres to the southwest, Chuck had had all the stakes made up in Kelowna and flown north. A local order for a mass of claim stakes delivered to the same airport the mining expediters used would raise questions he did not want asked. Chuck could not hide the fact he was staking – everything had to be registered publicly with the mining recorder's office – but he could minimize the chance of leaks. He filed the claim blocks under the name Shirley-Anne Eccott, the wife of a new director of Dia Met, Jim Eccott.

All the men working the staking project were trusted friends and family. Tight security was essential. Chuck's brother Wayne, also new to the Dia Met board, had come up to help with his own son. Dave Mackenzie was back. Paul Dirkson, Arnie Bauslaugh and Dan Tomlin, longtime employees of C. F. Minerals, were on the crew together with Dave Thompson, a geologist, and several other trustworthy employees from the lab.

With some exceptions, the men on the field crew thought they were staking a gold prospect. Most of the lab employees, even after all the years Chuck had been running diamond samples through the lab, had no idea that the samples they were processing were leads in a diamond hunt.

They christened their base Norm's Camp and then moved quickly out across the tundra, marking out claim boundaries and staking them. Now that Chuck was openly exposing his interest in the land, the need to proceed with haste spurred him on. Fear of discovery drove him now; the chance of being found out, however, was remote. In all the years he had been on the land – flying its breadth and its length from break-up until freeze-up – he had never once encountered northern people out on the tundra. Those who still hunted, and many of them did, stayed near their home territory. No one ventured this far out into the barrens.

Lac de Gras in particular, even in historical times, was a no-man's-land, too far into the tundra for the forest-dwelling Yellowknives and the Dogrib, and too far from the coast for the Copper and the Caribou Inuit. People of those tribes had sometimes crossed the Lac de Gras region and hunted over it, but it was their own frontier and no one was ever secure or safe here. Contact with their enemies usually meant death to whichever group was outnumbered, and the Yellowknives, whose entire population numbered less than 500 at the time of European contact and was spread thinly over a vast territory, were unable to muster the kind of force they needed to feel secure for long in the tundra.

Even aircraft were rarely sighted. A man could work for years in the Arctic without seeing another soul. It was unlikely, even with the size of his crew, that anyone would know they were there, but Chuck had to consider the possibility. Nobody was allowed to go back into Yellowknife. There were no breaks from the routine, no coming and going. When the men finished, they had to fly straight back to Kelowna, as far from curious eyes and ears as Chuck could keep them.

The men were excited by the work. Most of them were new to the far north, and staking was a novelty. The secrecy surrounding their staking of the "gold claims" made it even more so. They were all seated together in the cook tent when one of those who knew what they were really after caught Chuck's eye.

Surreptitiously he motioned Chuck outside. Still too close to the tent to talk, he inclined his head down the beach, leading Chuck far from the others and out toward a small point on the lake. The candle ice floating in large sheets up against the shore rose and fell gently with the waves, shearing off along the edges with high musical sounds like tinkling crystal bells. Chuck had no idea what was on the man's mind. In the most hushed and confidential tones possible the man told him. Barely able to control his own excitement, and nervously looking all around as though spying ears might somehow be listening from the open tundra, he dug into his pockets and, trembling, produced several large chunks of a clear, crystal rock. Chuck looked at them, nonplussed.

"I was staking around the lake and came upon these on the ground," the man told Chuck breathlessly. "They were just lying there! I'm sure there were some more around but I didn't want to draw attention to the area.... You know, like, in case somebody might see me?" He looked at Chuck expectantly.

Watching the man's expression, Chuck realized suddenly what he was talking about. Like giant strawberries waiting to be plucked from the ground, these were diamonds he believed. He thought he had found the diamond field. Chuck burst out laughing. Discovery fever was running high. The stones were very large quartz crystals. Chuck was pleased, though. Had the stones been diamonds, as the man believed, they would have been worth millions. The man was honest.

Chuck set up a tent for himself as a control centre with the maps and the base's radio. They were better-equipped than they had ever been. The men all wore bug suits, carried antibear spray and packed portable radios, although their range was limited to a few kilometres. Each morning Chuck gave the men their bearings and objectives, and every evening when they straggled in exhausted, on foot or by air, he debriefed them, plotting their progress. Daily the claim blocks grew, spreading out like an invisible web across the barrens. Although the territory he had decided to stake was huge, much larger than any gold deposit or uranium or copper field, they were forced to follow conventional staking rules. Around Blackwater Lake the government allowed concession blocks, areas that were many times larger than a claim block, but not here.

As in the previous summer they had encounters with wolves and bear, some close calls, but no attacks. While the main effort went into staking, to secure as much of the field as they could, Chuck explored, trying to determine the boundaries of the pipe clusters. The possibility that there were pipes under the waters of Lac de Gras itself continued to bother him. His crews were staking far from the big lake, covering the hottest areas first, and they would not be able to work their claims down to Lac de Gras at all before the end of the season, but he needed more information about the southern limits.

Dave Mackenzie had replaced the landing gear on his Super Cub after damaging it last summer. Instead of a rigid system, he had it fitted with a special structure designed to bend like a spring. Together with the tundra tires, it was the best aircraft system there was to fly the North. As velvety as the tundra appeared from the air, there were always rocks and holes around which to navigate when one got down to it, and landing was never a routine business.

Dave set out early in the morning with a list of locations Chuck wanted sampled around the north shore of Lac de Gras, in preparation for next year's staking program. The first, and furthest out, was the most important. It would probe the southern boundary.

Dave was a good pilot and cautious, although he was known to buzz the camp and loved flying low to the ground, where the sensation of speed was heightened. The blush of summer was on the land. All the living that normally occupied a year had to be squeezed into a couple of months, creating a richness and diversity of colour matched only by the eastern Canadian sugarbush in the fall. Even the lakes and boggy wetlands covering the surface were like shimmering pools of silver mercury which reflected light from the sky. Flying over it in the Super Cub, above the bugs, with colours splashed out below him like a Turner painting over the eternal and timeless qualities of the landforms, was the best of all worlds.

Arcing down to land near Lac de Gras, Dave banked his plane hard, enjoying the sensation of the forces that pressed him down into his seat as he studied the ground for a suitable place to land. With his flaps extended and his nose trimmed down, he glided in slowly, his engine coughing, just above stall speed. The great advantage of his aircraft was its lightness. He could land and take off just about anywhere. He levelled the plane, gliding a couple of metres above the ground as he pulled back on the throttle, and let the plane touch down naturally with its tail wheel. The Cub landed nose high; to see past the nose, Dave had to look rapidly from side-to-side, to steer around holes and rocks large enough to cause concern.

He didn't miss them all. While he was braking, his wheels struck a rock and the plane lurched. The nose dropped, the prop caught the ground, held fast, and the plane flipped over.

It took Dave a moment to collect himself. He was upside down, hanging from his seat belt. His chest ached and he had banged his head, but he was otherwise unhurt. He shut off the gas and the electrical system. Bracing himself for the fall, he unsnapped his belt and dropped down. The radio was useless. He was simply too far out. Grimly, he realized he had to walk back, nearly 50 kilometres.

Carefully he closed up the plane and set out across country. His head and chest still sore from the crash, he tried to pace himself for the effort that lay ahead, one step at a time. Walking was so much more difficult than flying. At first, he remained aware of the countryside, noticing clumps of purple saxifrage, and patches of lilies and licorice root, but he stopped seeing it at all after he waded across the first creek he came to. The water was numbingly cold and he had to concentrate on his footing to prevent a misstep. Having barely begun, he was already wet and tired and he had 45 kilometres to go.

It was late in the evening when Chuck noticed Dave floating on the horizon. He took it to mean that Dave was approaching on foot from a distance. In the tundra, without familiar visual references like buildings or even trees, perspective becomes distorted. A ridge of land that seemed only several hundred metres away might be several thousand. Sometimes, objects that appeared large and distant were small and close. The tundra is an easy place in which to become lost. But the familiar sight of a man instantly put everything around Dave into perspective: he didn't have his plane. As soon as he got within hailing distance, Chuck called out to him, "Dave, what the hell are you doing there?"

Dave's steps were heavy and laboured. He was exhausted. Weakly, he answered, "I crashed my plane. I got banged up. I've been walking all day to get here."

Chuck noticed a few scratches on Dave's face. They didn't look serious. More importantly, Dave was not carrying anything.

"Where's the sample?"

Dave just looked at him.

"Did you get the sample?" Chuck repeated, his voice rising. Perhaps Dave had cached it on the way back.

"No, I didn't get the sample," Dave replied flatly.

Chuck felt defeated. It was an important sample. "You go to all the trouble of flying out there, crashing your plane, and then walking all the way back and you don't even bring in one goddamned sample!" It was inexcusable.

Dave could only stare at him in disbelief. Chuck's nickname was One-More-Sample-Chuck. At that moment Dave could think of a couple more.

They had to leave the North when the money ran out. Chuck was not happy to go. Overall, they had staked less than half of what he thought was needed. And the southern boundary, where Dave had crashed his plane, was still completely fuzzy. With no samples from that area he had no way to determine what the southern limits of the field were. Having committed himself, the pressure to complete the work was intense. He could not wait until spring.

He needed more money. As soon as he got back he flew to Vancouver to see the managers of CMP, another investor fund, the last one in town left operating. His proposal for a cash-for-share trade was successful, and in the late fall of 1989, with Arctic gales blowing and the lakes stiffening up, he returned to the North with Mark.

They had little time. Chuck chartered a helicopter and they dropped down into billowing snow to work. Staking and chopping samples out of hardened ground, they moved rapidly across the land. Chuck made every second count.

There was no chance of being detected now. Nobody else dared to venture out. They camped in snow, and the temperature dropped so low their engine froze and the pilot used a gas heater under a tarp to thaw it. As the days disappeared into a consuming icy darkness, they continued staking until even Chuck was forced to concede defeat to the Arctic winter, retreating at last to the Explorer Hotel in Yellowknife and the nearly delirious pleasure of a hot shower.

Their field position was vastly improved and the claim blocks now encompassed nearly 160,000 hectares. But Chuck still wasn't satisfied. He had not sampled the southern boundary; it remained undefined.

Over the rest of the winter he processed the summer and fall samples, and by mid-March 1990 he had finished all the SEM analyses. The results were incredible, almost too good to believe. He sent the data to Rory Moore and John Gurney, asking them each for an independent assessment of the property. They confirmed Chuck's opinion. Gurney went so far as to tell Chuck it was the best data he had ever seen. The pipes the indicators came from were very good, but not all the pipes were within his claim blocks.

Chuck was worried. Sooner or later the word would get out, and when it did, the Arctic would be swarming with prospectors. The advantage he enjoyed of having the entire space to himself would not last. He had to secure as much of the field as he possibly could before he lost it to the human flood he knew would come rushing in.

In April, in Kelowna, the sailboats were out on Okanagan Lake, competing with jet-skis and sea-doos. The sun was already hot, the sage green, and the orchards in bloom. At Lac de Gras, the lakes were still under solid ice, the temperature, even in late afternoon, frequently below minus-20 degrees Celsius, and the grizzlies in hibernation, or hungry.

Chuck was back, doing all the navigating. He had new claim lines plotted out on the maps that he intended to fly in huge grid patterns across the land. Winter navigation presented new problems. In summer the crew had oriented themselves by reference to the lakes, whose bays and peninsulas corresponded to the shapes on their maps. Under the snow all their reference points disappeared beneath a blinding white sheet, that undulated in drift patterns left behind by the wind.

It took longer to set up the start of each staking line, but once they had it, they still managed to put down stakes at record rates. Sitting beside the pilot, Chuck had him fly full speed to each staking target. When the pilot pulled them up hard, Chuck called out the proper stake number to Mark, who sat in the back seat handing up the stakes. The instant the pilot touched down, Chuck, already leaning out the door, drove the stake into the ground between the skids. As soon as he felt it sink in, he yelled "GO!" and the pilot blasted off at full speed, low over the surface of the ground. They would be at their next spot before Chuck could even pull himself upright in his seat. It was an expensive way to stake, but very efficient.

They had one day of flying left before their money ran out when Chuck noticed an unusual feature and asked the pilot to do a quick circuit around it. It was a frozen lake, perhaps 20 hectares in size, that in summer was shaped like a teardrop, but now with the snowbanks blocking in the shore appeared perfectly ovoid. There was nothing unusual in that. Many of the smaller lakes, thousands of them, were circular depressions. Under some of them, no doubt, there were pipes – the softer kimberlite having been dug out by the action of the ice and the depressions later filled with water – but not under all of them.

Above the northern shoreline of this one, however, was an exposed windblown ridge, whose rock was foliated and had the appearance of bedding. Then it dropped down into a hole, the lake, rising up on the south side into another foliated ridge. The hole was unusual: not striking, but curious. What had created a round hole between two foliated bedrock ridges?

They continued staking – the few minutes he lost to circle the lake a major sacrifice of flying time – until dark. That night, the image of the lake swelled like a balloon in his mind. Unable to sleep, he dug out his flashlight and his secret maps onto which he had plotted the geochemistry results of all his sampling over the years.

Southwest of the ovoid lake towards Lac de Gras, some distance away, there was a barren sample with no indicators in it. Northwest of the lake, a sample had been taken which had numerous indicators. Most promising of all, a stream draining from the lake itself had been sampled. That one was loaded. Everything suggested one conclusion: this lake was over a pipe.

All night long he debated it: ice flows, chemistry, logic, geology and odds. It was a gamble. It might not be a pipe. The choice was to explore it or spend the last day staking. Over 500 square miles had been staked, not nearly enough to cover the field. He had one day left and desperately needed to spend it staking. But it was more important still to find a real pipe.

The claims were all expensive. It cost two dollars an acre just to maintain the claims in good standing, in total a million dollars he did not have. If that money was not spent on the claims in two years he would lose everything. Finding cash to stake the claims had been hard enough. Now, to keep the claims, he needed to find a partner with deep pockets. He knew how difficult that would be. "Diamonds in the Arctic" was still an oxymoron. Real mining companies were a lot more conservative than investment-fund agencies. All he had was a complicated chemistry that nobody else understood, except DeBeers and Hugo Dummett. He had nothing real to sell them – like a pipe.

Only a few months earlier, in the fall of 1989, Hugo had joined the Australian giant BHP, which had taken over Kennecott's old claims at Ok Tedi, now a large modern mining town that rivalled Bougainville, as Chuck had once hoped it would. Chuck had good memories of visiting Broken Hill and liked the company's philosophy. BHP was the second largest mining company in the world, after the Anglo American and DeBeers company group. More importantly, they wanted to be first. Hugo had been hired as the exploration manager for the company's operations in the United States and the Caribbean. He had not forgotten Chuck or the Northwest Territories, and before joining BHP, had tried to help Chuck obtain funding from other major players like CRA, but to no avail.

Chuck had called Hugo before Christmas and promised to fill him in on his progress if Hugo agreed to sign a confidentiality agreement. In the new year Hugo signed and Chuck brought him up-to-date showing him the results but not the location of the field. That was still confidential, even with the agreement. Chuck had hoped Hugo could bring in BHP and they were still talking, but as late as April 1990, as Chuck lay in his sleeping bag in his tent pitched on the snowbound northern plain, BHP might as well have stayed in the hot Australian desert, they were that far from any kind of agreement.

One of the problems with the project – the same problem he had faced from the beginning – was that it was all theory. Mining companies liked tangible results: if not diamonds, at least a pipe. Unless he could prove a pipe cluster was within his claim blocks, they would only believe he had staked a lot of frozen, barren land.

It was impossible to sleep. Weighing what he stood to gain and lose, he lay awake through the night, struggling with the issues until dawn when his direction suddenly became clear. He and his partners were out of money, and without better proof of what he had, he might never convince a major company that a worthwhile project lay under that snow. He needed to find a pipe. Everything depended on it.

Chuck had the pilot land them on the south shore of the frozen little lake, and he and Mark set to work while their pilot watched, vastly amused. The pilot still believed, as did all their pilots, that Norm's Manufacturing, which had chartered his helicopter, was out looking for gold. Nobody staked in the snow. Even the name was ridiculous: Norm's Manufacturing! Now they were digging down with small rock hammers through the snow and ice to find the lake bottom! He played along and followed orders – it was their money – but he could not take them seriously.

The snow had crusted and was over two metres deep at the shore. Chuck and Mark first dug a huge hole just to get down to the frozen surface and then began the exhausting task of chipping away to get through the ice.

It took them five hours. When they broke through at last, Chuck eagerly reached under the hole, feeling around for bottom sands. There were none. The bottom was composed entirely of large boulders deposited during the Ice Age and organics that had built up since then. In northern vernacular, *loon shit*.

It was all wasted effort. Chuck got up, stood back from the hole, oblivious to the numbness of his arm, and looked around the lake.

There had to be another way to prove there was a pipe under it. There was no point digging anywhere else – the bottom would be the same everywhere. Then he considered the direction in which the ice had flowed to the lake. The striations in the rock were its footprints, from the southeast to the northwest. He got back into the helicopter and had the pilot jump them across to the other side, down ice.

When the ice sheet had last covered this land, it slid slowly over the surface of the earth, ripping at the rock and dragging the surface layers along with its flow. When the era finally ended and the ice sheet melted, all the rock material that had been picked up fell to the ground, lying there, weathering, for 10,000 years.

Chuck walked with Mark up to an exposed point where the wind had blown the snow from the ground and studied the frozen till material underfoot. Whatever rock the ice had gouged out of the land 15 metres away, now concealed beneath the water, would have been dragged and deposited here, beside the lake, when the ice melted.

Chuck began chipping away at the frozen till with his rock pick, placing the frozen pieces into a plastic bag until he had collected a sample size. Mark replaced him, to fill the next sample bag. Bending low over the ground, Mark spotted an unusual tiny stone lying among the grey till.

It was bright emerald green and quite unlike anything else found on the tundra. Mark recognized it at once. It was like one of the diamond indicator minerals he had seen from his microscope work in the lab, only those had been microscopic fragments. This stone was large enough to mount in a ring! A chunk of chrome diopside, it had come from deep within the earth.

Attempting to display an outward appearance of calm, he casually picked it up and called out to his father, "Hey Dad, take a look at this!"

Chuck was a couple of metres away at the edge of the lake. The moment he saw the stone, a rush of excitement, a surge of adrenaline, pumped through him. At the same time, a feeling of such utter relief carried him to a state of near-bliss.

A large and perfectly shaped piece of soft crystal, the chrome diopside was pristine. The pilot was still watching, forcing Chuck to control his enthusiasm, but he was nearly intoxicated with the discovery. One centimetre in size, the stone was likely torn from the surface of the pipe while encased in kimberlite and deposited here. Over the aeons the softer kimberlite had weathered, eroding away to leave the crystal stone intact.

The lake was a crater infill. Beneath it had to be the kimberlite pipe which transported the mineral to the surface. To be certain, Chuck would have to take a sample up-ice from the lake to prove that this indicator mineral had come from a pipe which was under the lake and not somewhere up-ice from it, but he was confident he had found its source. The first pipe! After years on the trail, untold kilometres and effort, he had done it. He was ecstatic. There was much unstaked territory left to be claimed, weeks of work, but the gamble had paid off.

Once more he let his eye wander across the surface of the lake, frozen and snowbound. There was nothing to distinguish it from the rest of the Arctic. A buried pinprick. Yet it concealed the top of a pipe. Finding it validated everything. He was on the pinnacle. It was the highest peak he had ever achieved. The view was worth all the effort – and more.

The lake itself was unnamed. One of thousands in the area, it was in the centre of a large peninsula known as Point de Misere, which thrust out like the sharp point of a blade into Lac de Gras. Chuck decided to call the little lake Point Lake. He laughed. Like their cover name, Norm's Manufacturing, it would confuse the opposition – there was another Point Lake. A huge lake, it was northwest of the entire claims area, downstream from Lac de Gras and Exeter, but near enough to fool them.

Controlling their enthusiasm, Chuck and Mark quickly finished bagging three large samples of frozen till which they chipped from the ground – to the continued amusement of the pilot – and then flew straight through Yellowknife to Kelowna. As soon as they landed at the familiar little airport, Chuck set off at once for the lab.

With the windows open, the smell of the earth – a new season – was thick in the air. Baking like an oven in the heat of unobstructed sunshine, it felt like a midsummer's day. Miniskirts were making a comeback in 1990. Long legs and Harleys, bicycles and shorts were out on the streets everywhere.

Washing the dirt out of the samples, Chuck screened them and began processing them immediately, too excited to wait. As he expected, one after the other, the samples *smoked*. In each of the samples taken beside the lake, down-ice, there were thousands of diamond indicator minerals. More significantly, there were several tiny kimberlite chips mixed with the till – pieces of the pipe itself. He was floating again.

Point Lake was a hot pipe, and, he knew, it was only the first!

With Gurney's and Moore's reports, the new data from all the samples, and a probable pipe at Point Lake in hand, Chuck settled down to negotiate with BHP on behalf of his partners. The ownership of the claims involved Dia Met and the Blackwater Group, most of whose members had traded their original interests in the Northwest Territories project to Dia Met when it was formed, in return for shares in the company. Stu Blusson and Chuck had each retained their interests in the original Blackwater agreement, as well as their newer interests in Dia Met.

The first draft agreement with BHP was exhaustive, each potential issue explored, defined and arbitrated in advance, but they remained so far apart on the main terms it began to appear as though they would not reach an agreement after all.

In May, Chuck began scouting around for a new major partner. He approached Crystal Mines from Australia. They exchanged proposals with Chuck but their positions were even further apart than the last offer he had from BHP. Chuck contacted the Canadian mining company, Placer Dome in Vancouver, but could not get through to the top. None of his calls were returned.

Chris Smith from CRA in Australia had signed the confidentiality agreement and studied the data in mid-July, but he was taking his time. Time was something Chuck could not afford to lose. He needed to have an agreement signed quickly. The 1990 season was already half over, and nothing had been accomplished. If he failed to put in the money that mining law required he spend on the claims he had already staked, he would lose them all. It was that simple.

He had no time to waste. The more he shopped around, the more likely his carefully guarded secrets would leak out, confidentiality agreements or not.

Finally, on August 25, 1990, Hugo contacted Chuck with BHP's decision – they wanted in. BHP had agreed to meet Chuck's terms. Chuck's feelings of elation were nearly matched by Hugo's. Chuck was, at long last, getting his coveted contract with a major, and Hugo was officially getting back into the play.

Under the agreement, Chuck remained the operator, in sole control of the field and the program, while BHP would fund all the work – up to US$500,000 for the first year, and a million for the second. Another term provided for an increase of the annual exploration budget to US$2 million if Chuck found, and bulk sampled, a pipe with a diamond value of $60 per metric tonne over a minimum sample size of eight tonnes. Finally, BHP had the right under the agreement to earn a 51 percent interest in the claims – a controlling interest in the entire project – which would vest only upon BHP agreeing in writing to fund all feasibility costs and to finance the mine construction costs up to US$500 million. The remaining 49 percent interest was split between Dia Met, which would take 29 percent, and the last two partners of the Blackwater Group, Chuck and Blusson, each of whom would retain a 10 percent personal interest.

The parties also agreed that a buffer zone 22,500 feet wide, surrounding the core zone claims staked by Dia Met, would be staked by the BHP-Dia Met joint venture. Stu Blusson negotiated the right to dilute Dia Met's interest in the area surrounding the core and buffer zone claims by spending $750,000 on exploration and claims acquisition for diamonds.

Anticipating the formal signing of the agreement set for August 31st, Chuck mobilized the crews as soon as BHP gave them its decision and they left Kelowna the same day, flying through Calgary, Edmonton and Yellowknife before landing at the beach at Norm's Camp late in the afternoon. Chuck immediately took the crews out to stake claims and collect samples; Mark was assigned the responsibility of building them a permanent base.

Their tent camp of the previous season had proven unequal to the tundra's conditions. When the wind blew unobstructed across the land, it often moved with incredible speed and force. Small domed structures, in igloo-shapes, wide-based and low, hugging the ground like clamshells, could withstand the storms, but large, peaked tents, even under the protective wall of the esker, offered too much resistance.

Crawling out to stand over their collapsed shelters with their backs to the driving rain and sleet, whipped horizontally by the howling wind, lightning flashes and deep, rumbling thunder lighting up the night sky and shaking the ground under their feet, convinced the crew that a new camp was needed, something a little more solid.

Plywood bunkhouses with room to stand in, electric lights on generators and oil-drip heaters replaced the tent camp. It was a huge improvement. The cookhouse, christened the Taj Mahal, even had cold running water – and a professional cook. Chuck Richardson baked bread as well as he brewed coffee, although Chuck continued to prefer his boiled with the grinds. The Taj even had a sink for washing in and a hot shower, which Mark rigged with a coil heater inside an old steel drum set up in the rafters, that drained down through a faucet into a shower stall. Finally, to break the isolation, Mark rented some satellite space, hooked up a satellite transmitter and a receiving dish and gave them a phone link through Vancouver to the rest of the country.

The camp had all the comforts, except one. It was a dry camp. One of the conditions of employment was total abstention from alcohol while on the site. In wilderness workcamps alcohol led to excess. Last summer one of the men, who had brought in a .44 revolver as well as some gin, went bush-crazy and shot up the outhouse, trying to kill mosquitoes with bullets.

Chuck was back on the peak. BHP was funding the project and he had everything he wanted. Searing rock, *The Best of Cream*, playing on compact disc through the helicopter's expensive soft earphones, transported him into a mystical space of desire and anticipation. His nerves as well as his memories were ignited while the music drowned out everything else. They screamed low over the ground, brushing the crushed grey surfaces of the Earth littered with the debris from the last ice age, touched down to scoop up a sample, drive in a stake and roar off, racing through surreal images of music and tundra at record speeds.

Within the month, the perimeters of the claims had rapidly expanded. They had collected nearly 1,200 samples and were beginning to define a southern border to the field. A deliberate search for pipes had also begun.

At Point Lake, Chuck sampled a grid all around the lake, flying back to the lab to analyze it immediately. Results inhand, he again called John Gurney for his opinion. Gurney examined the data and predicted a grade greater than 60 carats per 100 metric tonnes.

It was all they could do. By late September, 1990, it was not horizontal rain that kept them huddled low to the ground but blinding blizzards. Even when it did not snow, the wind picked snow up off the ground and blew it around with such speed and in such density that the Taj Mahal itself could not be seen by men standing three metres away. They were the last to leave. The Arctic geese, the cranes and loons had long since fled the North, flying overhead in long waving lines, some from far above the Arctic Circle on their migration routes down the central Mississippi to the tropics. Only a couple of ravens remained behind, silently watching the men pack up.

CHAPTER SIXTY

POINT LAKE, SEPTEMBER, 1991

EVEN determined men could not prospect the Barren Lands in winter, but there were some things that could be done as the earth itself contracted and cracked in the deep freeze beneath them.

In January of 1991, BHP's Ray Ashley, a geophysicist, flew north with a "max-min" – a ground geophysical instrument that could read the electromagnetic frequencies of rock under two metres of ice. It was a technology that had not previously been applied to the search for kimberlites. Landing on the surface of Point Lake, Ashley dragged it back and forth across the ice, experimenting with several frequencies in order to establish an optimum reading of the rock. There was an anomaly under the lake.

When separated from the surrounding frequencies of the regional rock – the foliated bedrock ridges around the lake produced different frequencies than the rock type which existed under it – the instrument readings produced an image of a carrot-like shape beneath the water. Occupying the central core area of the lake was the top of a tube with a tapered root that snaked downward, disappearing deep into the earth: *the pipe*. Taking off, the plane flew back south. Men, moving silently on foot, would follow as soon as they were able.

In the early winter, even in sub-zero temperatures, with the land frozen and food scarce, grizzly wander the tundra. Perhaps the sik-siks living under the Taj Mahal attracted this bear. Perhaps it was the smell of Chuck Richardson's cooking, which had seeped into the walls. But when the bear came, it was hunting, and when it left, Norm's Camp was a ruin. Mark was dismayed. A pile of lumber inside a frame leaning above the beach was all that was left. He could have rebuilt it but for the wolverine who had made a home in it after the bear finished. The stink of the urine and gland secretions that had impregnated the wood forced Mark to burn the wreckage instead.

The old camp, built for eight men, never housed fewer than 15. The bright side of the situation was that Mark now had his chance to expand the camp. If he built it for 20, the men would have room to breath. The days were difficult enough without having to spend the evenings elbow-to-elbow. The new Taj had windows front and back to catch the light, the best views, an entrance porch where the men were required to leave their boots, and a back bedroom space for the cook. When Mark had finished, Chuck surprised him by flying in 30 men – the largest crew he had run in the North.

In spite of Richardson's noble efforts to turn the Taj Mahal into a real dining room, the reality of 30 men in crusty stocking feet, jammed together in the frame cookshack, wind and wolves howling and snow blowing outside, was impossible to overcome. Some men enjoyed the space, found it intensely challenging or deeply calming, while others hated it, saw nothing poetic or inspiring about the tundra, and fled on the next aircraft, stricken by the isolation and the emptiness.

They were all pressed into rows on the benches after supper, drinking mugs of tea and coffee to pass the time before sleeping, when the phone rang. Installed on a wall at the end of the table, it occupied the place of honour: their one link to the outside. Everyone stopped talking as the man nearest it picked up the receiver and then handed it to Chuck: "Your wife."

Bouncing from Earth to space and back, off the satellite, the transmission was accomplished by a slight delay and a pinging sound. Several men continued their own conversations, politely attempting to give him room, while others made no pretence whatsoever to being occupied and stared openly, listening intently to half the conversation and trying to guess the rest. Calls from the outside were entertaining, especially those from wives or girlfriends who wanted an intimate exchange to know how much they were being missed. Not surprisingly, the phone was not in constant use.

Marlene was at the luxurious Four Seasons Hotel in Vancouver, 2,400 kilometres away. It was the annual awards dinner for British Columbia's thoroughbred set, a formal affair, and Chuck had just won an award. His new horse, Travelling Spirit, from his mare Boldest Spirit, had been named British Columbia's Champion Two-Year-Old Colt. Chuck would have loved dearly to be there. He had had ambitions for horses even before he turned his mind to rocks. Marlene described her evening, the dinner, the guests, Russ Bennett's speech, the trophy and the photo session with the press.

It was all so far away, light-years from the Taj Mahal. Hurled by the wind, granular snow was driving at the windowpanes with the sound of spraying sand. From the top of the esker, above the ground squall, the air was dry and clear. Countless stars, a shower of diamonds, hung over the night. Washed across them, in surreal colours that took in the entire sky, touching the horizons, the northern lights danced as if the heavens themselves were walking on fire.

The summer of 1991 passed quickly in frantic, costly staking and sampling. By its end they had staked the buffer zones, the dimensions of which had been stipulated in the agreements and now had nearly a half-million hectares under claim, 3,000 samples filling all the storage space at the C. F. Minerals lab in Kelowna. A new focus on geophysics to locate pipes would later identify many new anomalies – most of them under water. Chuck was fairly confident they were pipes – they had all the right characteristics – but they remained mere drill targets.

Chuck wanted to prove them out – to drill them – but he was out of money, his million-dollar budget spent. And nothing had been proven yet – not even Point Lake. He needed results. Even with the agreement with BHP, Dia Met remained a small west coast company trading on the Vancouver Stock Exchange, and investors remained skeptical. A piece of kimberlite from a pipe would change everything for the company.

Hugo Dummett was as anxious as Chuck to go underground, to find a pipe and tap into it. It was September and the crews were leaving Norm's Camp as quickly as the light planes landing now on the esker, raked smooth for a runway, could ferry them south.

All summer, Hugo had been in a quandary over the pipes, unsure whether they even had a drill target. When he had studied the max-min data Ray Ashley had obtained in January from the Point Lake pipe, he agreed that Ray's test results had indeed identified something beneath the lake that was conducting, but he wasn't at all confident that the results pointed to a pipe. As far as anybody knew, kimberlites were not, generally, very conductive, and the positive results that all the geophysical tests produced might as well be explained by the deposit of other materials under the lakes, such as clay. The difficulty was that the partners were pioneering geophysical techniques in the field of diamond geology. There were, simply, no known geophysical tests to determine whether or not a kimberlite existed at a particular location. The established method was, as always, to drill. He was, however, reluctant to do so.

Hugo had brought BHP to the table with Chuck, and he had seen them through the contract, but he felt the company's support was soft. BHP might, at the last minute, decide that the budget might be better spent somewhere else and abandon the entire project. He had seen that happen before with Superior, and BHP, operating within the same strictures, had just shut down their diamond exploration programs in Australia because they were not getting results. He had to deliver something, yet this budget was already spent, and drilling in Arctic conditions was very expensive. If he ordered the target drilled – and Point Lake remained the best target they had – and the drilling didn't produce the expected results, not only would BHP quit the Northwest Territories, he might himself be looking for a new job.

It was late in the season and he was struggling with this dilemma when he learned that Echo Bay Mine, north of Norm's Camp, had just completed an airborne geophysical survey with Digem, a Toronto company that employed a helicopter-operated electro-magnetic survey system that Hugo felt would give them another, different perspective on the anomaly under Point Lake. To have them fly in with their instruments from Toronto cost more than Hugo was prepared to authorize, but Digem's crews were already in the vicinity and would fly right over the claims on their way home. Hugo called the company and spoke to John Buckle. Could they, Hugo asked John, fly a small survey for BHP over a couple of lakes at a bargain price?

John Buckle agreed, Hugo plotted out the course, and the instrument-heavy helicopter flew over Point Lake and then east over Lac du Sauvage, where Chuck's geochemistry results also seemed to point to another pipe under that lake.

John then called Hugo with the disappointing news: "All we found across the entire survey were a couple of small circular conductors, one under Point Lake, the other under Lac du Sauvage." Hugo said nothing, trying to reflect the disappointment he knew John was expecting him to feel. "Sorry," John added.

Believing that BHP was looking for a massive sulfide deposit of lead-zinc, John was looking for data produced by the instruments which would reveal the existence of a long, large anomalous showing. To him, the two bull's eyes that the data produced didn't indicate anything of economic value. To Hugo, however, the results were excellent. Not only did they confirm Ray Ashley's data on Point Lake and the geochemistry trails that led to these two lakes, Digem's survey had flown over numerous other lakes in its circuit and none of those lakes lit up. If the anomalies under Point Lake and now Lac du Sauvage were clay, all the other lakes ought to have had the same anomalies, but they didn't. Only those two lakes stood out.

Chuck now stood with Hugo at the edge of the ancient crater at Point Lake near the outcrop of rock that had yielded the chrome diopside. Chuck was reluctant to leave. The days and seasons were simply too short to accomplish everything he had to do. His inclination was that they should stay and work through the darkness of winter.

Both men wanted to drill Point Lake. It was their best target. They knew better than the rest that Point Lake should be a pipe. It was Hugo's call. Like Barney Barnato and Cecil Rhodes, who had stood at the edge of the Kimberley pipe over a century earlier, they, too, were trying to see into the future. They were now outside the agreement. Hugo was on his own and, if wrong, responsible to BHP for the consequences. For Hugo, as well as for Chuck, the Northwest Territories held a special interest. In another day, an earlier time, they had been partners in the hunt. It was Hugo who had put Chuck on this very track years ago, when he urged Chuck to find out what DeBeers was doing at Blackwater Lake.

The tundra appeared like the sea, the ground falling away from them along the edge of the horizon. With a few light clouds hugging the earth, moving rapidly through the air, the sensation was of the world spinning under a fixed sky. They were on their own ship.

Although the year's budget was exhausted, Hugo took a last look around, and then said firmly, "Drill it!"

The crews from Mid-West Drilling, based in Winnipeg, understood cold, but they had no love for it. As much as they could, they huddled inside the shack built around the drill rig. Inside, it was dark, deafening and filthy with lubricating oil and rock dust, but Chuck noticed none of that. He was watching the core. The rig was set up on shore and the drill angled at 45 degrees to bore down towards the centre of the lake. They could have set up on the ice, drilling straight down, but that presented the risk that the drill might cut down alongside the pipe and miss it. The odds of intersecting the pipe were better if the drill angled across the face.

After cutting through 30 metres of rock, the tension began to climb quickly. Chuck, Hugo and Ed Schiller were all inside, mentally counting the distance the drill had gone as the core slowly came up. Hugo's calculations put them under the lake and into the anomalous zone, but the rock core didn't change at all. It was all bedrock. The geophysical data Hugo had brought with him, stuffed into his pocket, suggested that the anomaly came to the edge of the lake, its buried perimeter roughly contiguous with the shoreline. Once under the lake, they should have hit the pipe. But there was nothing there.

At 60 metres they still hadn't hit kimberlite. Hugo and Chuck looked at each other but said nothing. They were barely breathing. The drill continued, mechanically, to eat into the Earth, beneath the lake. The noise in the shack drowned out everything but their feelings. Deeper. Ninety metres – well under the lake – and still nothing. The anxiety the men were feeling was intense. The tension was soaring. Everything hinged on proving a pipe, this pipe – their best target! The years, the effort, the hopes, the commitment, the technology, their lives, the past, present and future, all of it was now determined by this core, which continued to rise to the surface with no change at all in its composition. Grey, cratonic host rock. Deeper and deeper they went.

The drill bit, now 120 metres away, continued grinding slowly through the rock. It was impossible they could have missed the pipe – if it was there. The feelings the men had were complex and deep. At a depth of just over 120 metres, the drill bit suddenly chewed into something different, a softer rock. In the shack, the noise the spinning rods made changed. The pitch began to sing

Everyone heard it. To Chuck, the sight that followed, of the core from the narrow-bore drill being lifted to the surface in thin, broken, stone rods, returned him to the state of near-bliss he had felt when Mark found the chrome diopside only a few hundred metres away. The drillers didn't know what it was – they had never seen rock core like it – but they knew it was not gold ore. They had just intersected kimberlite. A composite of numerous minerals, rock fragments and magmatic components formed and picked up along the route this magma took in climbing from the deep mantle through the crust to the surface of the Earth, kimberlite's geological definition was as complex as its chemistry.

They shut down the rig when the distance from the bottom of the hole to the surface reached 456 feet. When the core was split in half over the shorter length of kimberlite that had been penetrated, what it yielded was 59 kilograms of raw kimberlite – straight from the pipe.

Chuck flew directly back to his lab with the most enticing sample he had ever had to examine. He was not looking for indicator minerals now – but for diamonds themselves.

Methodically, he began to run the core through his concentration processes. This was not a sample to rush through. After crushing the kimberlite, he ball-milled it, then washed and dried the ground rock, in preparation for separating the lighter elements from the heavier ones. The first was a separation of minerals with a specific gravity of 2.9. Next was a chemical separation of minerals with a specific gravity of 3.3. Then an electromagnetic separation. When the process was complete he had a small tray of heavy elements left. He couldn't wait any longer. Placing it on the counter under the microscope he peered down into it.

Brilliant points of light winked seductively up at him. Like a piece of star-filled sky, the tray was full of them: perfect, dazzling diamonds. The sight raised Chuck to new heights. Slowly, he began to pick through the concentrate, counting the diamonds. With each diamond his heart soared higher and higher.

Chuck counted 81 diamonds. Of those, 65 were microdiamonds and 16 were of a diameter greater than a half-millimetre, classifying them as macrodiamonds. Some were over a millimetre across.

Lightly, Chuck touched the diamonds. They were of a substance even more ancient than Pangaea, so ancient that their genesis revealed not only the origins of the Earth, but of the universe itself and the forces that had molded it. In that earlier, smaller universe, near the beginning of time, the elements that had filled space were primarily hydrogen and helium. It was out of those gases that the first generation of stars was born, the biggest and brightest of which burned out quickly, dying within a billion years. Yet while those giants lived, it was in their hearts that the universe burned the brightest. And it was in their hearts – forged in the hottest fires of the universe – that diamond matter was formed.

Bathed in the pure energy of temperatures of more than 100 million degrees, the hydrogen and helium elements were transformed in the centre of these stars, in a reaction known as the triple-alpha process, into new matter: carbon, nitrogen and oxygen.

Evolving from white stars into red giants, they burned out as they slowly shed mass, spinning carbon off into space, seeding the galaxy with the new elements – the stuff of diamonds and life. The Earth's sun was a second-or third-generation star, made up, like the Earth, of elements that had been created by the processes that went on before its time, but the secrets that diamonds held were important: they were sister diamonds, related to mankind. The carbon chain molecules upon which human life depends had come from the same source as the diamond: the heart of ancient stars. All things were connected.

Chuck had never been higher.

As soon as BHP saw the results of this 59-kilogram sample, it wanted a new agreement with Dia Met. BHP was not displeased by Hugo's initiative in drilling Point Lake, though the contract had limits on spending. They were thrilled. Chuck emerged from a meeting at BHP's San Francisco office with the company's full support to accelerate the exploration program. BHP, following the recommendation of Dr. John Gurney to adopt the DeBeers standard for sampling kimberlite, decided now to move as quickly as possible to take a 200-ton sample from Point Lake.

The only drawback was that the joint venture now had to go public. On November 5th, 1991, the partners issued a news release. The joint statement by Dia Met and BHP announcing the recovery of 81 diamonds from the Point Lake Pipe, and their decision to remain on the site over the winter to drill out a 200-ton bulk sample took the industry completely by surprise. There were diamonds in the Arctic!

Instantly, mining companies everywhere, their men and machines, sprang into action. It did not matter that it was winter in the Arctic, that they were unprepared or even that they had no idea what they were searching for – they moved with all haste to get into the action. Yellowknife went wild. Geologists, prospectors, drillers, pilots, cooks and samplers poured in from everywhere. Anybody who could pound a stake into the ground was hired. Money flowed faster than beer. The great Canadian diamond rush was on.

Almost overnight, DeBeers arrived on the scene, as Chuck knew they would. Staking as close to Dia Met's claims as they could, and working through its subsidiary Monopros, DeBeers threw all their resources into competing for a piece of the field. Hundreds of DeBeers men were out in the twilight haze working through the one-to two-hour windows the winter gave them, hammering stakes through the snow. Later, they could look to see what they had. Right now they were laying claim to anything they could get. And they were not alone.

Aber Resources, SouthernEra, Commonwealth Gold, Dentonia, Lytton, Bellex, Tyler, Tanqueray, Horseshoe Gold and Kettle River were all scrambling for positions. Kennecott, unable to resist the pressure, jumped into the play, backing Almaden, Williams Creek and the Troymin Group. Joint ventures mixed companies, talents and risks across the map. Kalahari Resources, Winspear, New Indigo, Camphor and dozens of other companies rushed in, jostling for room.

Yellowknife had never experienced anything like it. Neither had Canada. It was still early and the field was locked under some of the harshest conditions in the world. In spite of this, the diamond rush was already poised to overtake the Klondike Goldrush as the greatest in Canadian history. By spring, it was official. The discovery of the Point Lake Pipe and those 81 diamonds had created a staking rush that surpassed all others.

Until now the field had been exclusively the domain of Chuck and his crew, and the Explorer Hotel always had room for them. The news release changed everything. By January 1992, when Mark flew into Norm's Camp, still throwing off the competition by billing everything to "Norm's Manufacturing," Yellowknife was buzzing and new, huge claim blocks were spreading throughout the Lac de Gras region to the Arctic coastline. Everybody was watching everybody.

Chuck's longer history in the diamond search gave him several advantages over all the newcomers. He had been to the Sloan pipes at Fort Collins, Colorado years earlier and knew the problems its owners had had with it. After Sloan 1 and the other pipes they found in its cluster had proven uneconomical, the recovery plant the company had optimistically built on the site to process the kimberlite and recover the diamonds sat idle, gathering dust. Nobody was interested in it.

It was the only diamond processing plant in North America. Chuck snapped it up at a bargain price before anybody thought of the next step. As a result, Dia Met became the only company with facilities on the continent to bulk sample kimberlite.

As soon as Norm's Camp was thawed out, drillers from S.D.S. Drilling moved in to tackle Point Lake with a big rig that would produce a core size of 6⅝ inches in diameter. Their faces blackened under woolen balaclavas, wearing thick mittens and quilted suits against the minus-40 degrees Celsius weather, they were set up by Chuck on the ice. Rory Moore, who was on contract with C. F. Minerals, flew up to log the core with Chuck as it came out. Now that they knew where the pipe was, they were able to cut straight down into it, and once started, they did not shut down the rig until they had recovered 160 metric tonnes – as close to the 200 US-ton target as the men huddled in the rumbling little drill shack could estimate.

The drillers packed up and flew out and, in April, the bulk sample was trucked down to Dia Met's plant in Colorado. The results, made public, spurred the industry to an even greater frenzy – this sample contained diamonds weighing 101 carats. One quarter were gem quality, and several were in the one-to three-carat range. Point Lake looked good. New targets being identified by Chuck, however, looked even better.

The explosion of activity was a boon not only to Yellowknife but to all the specialized businesses that served the exploration and mining industries. Drillers and pilots were in great demand and everyone who could make his or her way to the northern city found employment. Helicopters were buzzing in from all around the country. The Arctic offered pilots easy flying, long days and good hourly rates. In two months one could make a year's income. Every aircraft that arrived at the territorial capital was picked up at its asking price by companies waiting in line.

The majors were not bothered by the local competition. They could afford to bring in their ground crews and their own aircraft. By spring, it was estimated that DeBeers alone was operating a fleet of 26 helicopters just for staking.

Chuck had managed to lay claim to an incredible one million acres – all the prime targets – but DeBeers, hoping to hit it lucky, soon surpassed that number. Their claims exceeded three million acres, and still they kept up the pace, desperately staking everything in reach. When they stopped, DeBeers had staked in excess of 10 million acres – all in the off-chance they might score.

It was gambling on a grand scale. Nor were they alone. The handful of companies that had flown in on their own aircraft at the first word of diamonds grew quickly to hundreds. All the majors came looking. The British conglomerate RTZ Corporation poured millions into the search. So, too, did Australia's Ashton Mining Company. Kennecott continued to spread itself around by signing option agreements with as many of the smaller players who had claims in the area as they could.

SouthernEra and Kalahari Resources both signed with Kennecott. Southern-Era had an advantage over most of its competitors. Its president was Chris Jennings, formerly with Falconbridge. Jennings had been in the diamond search in Africa for years and had previously gained access to some of the Falconbridge's joint venture diamond project results when it was partnered with Superior and Chuck, first at Golden, then at the Mountain Diatreme and finally at Blackwater Lake. Jennings understood the potential of the Arctic and was quick to position himself as close to Dia Met as he could get.

Tanqueray also had an advantage. It was Ed Schiller's company. As a member of Dia Met's board, Schiller had been privy to the results, which were now public, had supervised some of the work on the claims and knew all the boundaries. Tanqueray quickly staked a big block adjacent to Dia Met's claims.

Within days, Dia Met's claims were completely surrounded.

When Dia Met and BHP first made public the results of the initial core sample from Point Lake, the southern border of the diamond field remained undefined. It had never been explored or staked to Chuck's satisfaction. Dia Met's agreement with Stu Blusson gave Blusson the right to stake around the central and peripheral claim blocks. As soon as the Diamond Rush began, foreign claims tightly boxed Dia Met in. Among the companies staking land to the south of Dia Met's claims was Aber Resources. Like DeBeers and the others they staked what they could and hoped for the best.

Competition was fierce. It was more than a rush to reach treasure; it was an economic war. Whatever the players needed to do to improve their own positions, they did.

Yellowknife's resources were quickly exhausted. Companies that had not thought to bring their own supplies of wooden claim stakes with them were out of luck completely. There were none to be had in Yellowknife. Instead, they had to put in special rush orders to Edmonton, Vancouver, Winnipeg and the United States and then wait for them to arrive.

Most of the companies were too late. The land grab had become not only the largest in history, but the quickest and most expensive. Virtually everything staked was claimed without regard to what was in it. If the land was open, it was taken. Chuck had been proven right about the intensity of the rush. Many had no idea what they were looking for. Some only pretended interest in the land and made their money in the markets. Penny stocks soared as a result of rumours of mergers and options and then crashed when the hard news hit. Fortunes were made and lost in days. In the field – mostly on land Chuck had long ago looked at, sampled and left – companies raised money and began exploring their claims.

Chuck knew which claims were worthless and, early on, made public a simple statement, describing the country he knew to be barren as barren. It was good advice. Companies, ignoring it, raised capital on the markets from hopeful investors and went ahead anyway. One by one, as the truth dawned on them, they gave up, financially drained and bitter, coining a new expression to explain their failure: "Fipke's Curse." The press suggested he was arrogant.

Nobody could believe he knew the country as well as he did, not even DeBeers. But it was neither conceit nor a bond with the supernatural that informed his statements. It was simply the heavy-mineral surveys he had done – the methods he had patented – that and the fact he had spent years on this land, scouring it from the Mackenzie River to Hudson Bay. The only boundaries he had been unsure of were the southern ones, beginning at Lac de Gras, that he had left unstaked. They alone would prove to have pipes worth investigating.

It was a loss Dia Met could accept. Within their own claim boundaries, most of the best pipes of the diamond field were waiting to be unearthed. Better than Point Lake, was a pipe, Leslie, discovered by Mark. Dropped off on the tundra to collect samples, he was skirting a lake when he recognized a piece of kimberlite just over 16 centimetres in diameter, lying on the surface. There was little to distinguish it from the background rocks, but Mark had developed a keen eye. He put it in his pack, flagged the spot and went, up-ice, to the very edge of the water, where the shore was littered with chunks of kimberlite. The pipe was under the water.

Mark dragged a 90-kilogram sample from the helicopter to the operations shack at Norm's Camp, where Chuck was coordinating all the operations and presented the sack to his father. It was the first kimberlite sample collected by hand. Mark named the pipe Leslie after his wife.

The men working the diamond project, for Chuck and for BHP, were the best in the industry. The skills they brought to bear in the hunt for pipes so refined the techniques the partners had pioneered that they once more changed the nature of diamond exploration worldwide. Digem, the company that had flown the airborne survey over Point Lake at a discount price for BHP, now found themselves permanently engaged with the project. The second "bull's eye" anomaly their survey had turned up under Lac du Sauvage was, later, confirmed as a pipe and named simply, LSI. Geophysics was proving its worth. With the surveys done by Ray Ashley and Digem having proved that some pipes, at least, were conductors, airborne geophysical surveys became the new approach to the rapid identification of those pipes. When flown over the claims, "bull's eye" anomalies lit up everywhere. With the men, their skills and assorted instruments, numerous pipes were proven.

Koala, Misery, Fox and Panda were rich in diamonds. The groups of pipes known collectively as the "Falcon Pipes" and the "Caribou Pipes" were also diamondiferous, but drilling proved their grades too low to be economic. The search went on. The geochemistry techniques Chuck had helped design and geophysics identified the targets, while drilling proved them out. The claim area was so extensive that to explore it all, even with airborne instruments, would take years.

It was a dream with roots, spanning generations that, in Canada, had first found fertile ground in a homestead in Leduc, Alberta. Ed Fipke and his wife Anna both lived to see it realized. They had never moved from the farm on Trepanier Bench. Ed was happy there. He had always liked the land, and Chuck's discovery of the diamond fields was intensely satisfying to them. Whatever Ed had lost long ago, his son had found. Chuck had indeed made a future for himself in geology.

Chuck was basking in the glory of the spotlight. The entire mining world was watching, and he was at the centre of an international play worth billions. Jack Gower and Gunther Lishy were both gone, but his first mentor, Pat McBride, was still alive, and watching. Chuck was glad of that. It was to them he had most wanted to prove himself, years ago. Now, the feelings that had lingered were released at last.

Carried along by events, enjoying the rewards, he remained committed to the work. In charge, he was consumed by details as the field continued to expand and new dimensions were added to the project. BHP had taken the ceiling off the exploration budget, and no matter how fast he proceeded with the exploration of the claims and the economic assessment of each new pipe he found, it was never fast enough. It was the way Chuck liked to work: under pressure, with impossible standards to meet. He was in the centre of a maelstrom, and it was as exciting as anything he had ever experienced in his life.

Their drilling had some unexpected results. Once, the drill cut through an organic layer which had fallen into the crater when the pipe initially blew. Buried with the infill, preserved in the pipe, was a slice of ancient life. The paleontologist, Dr. Walter Nassichuk, a scientist emeritus with the Geological Survey of Canada, to whom Chuck gave the fossilized material, was ecstatic. It was new data that illuminated old theories, specifically that the Arctic has not always been a frozen wasteland. In the high Arctic untouched by the Ice Ages, there stands a fossil forest of trunks of huge metasequoia trees that date back to the late Paleocene Age. The material Chuck presented now established that the Lac de Gras area was the southern limit of that once-great forest. Fifty-two million years ago, the life around the rim of the crater had been lush. Metasequoia trees, turtles and a variety of plants growing on the surface fell into the crater after the explosion and remained sealed away for millions of years, until the drill bit cut through the crater and raised them once more to the surface.

The number of pipes grew by the month. Some, like Point Lake, rich as it was, were dropped. Its diamonds, although abundant enough, after evaluation were revealed to be a quality too low to justify the costs of processing the kimberlite. Each new pipe drilled had diamonds: some better than Point Lake, others worse.

Analysts worldwide were now rating the diamond field – whether it was, as Chuck had once suspected, two closely-related fields or one very large one – as having more diamond-bearing pipes than any other. More significantly, the diamond grades that followed the bulk sampling of several of the new pipes were being compared favorably to the best in the world. Famous names in diamonds were Finsch, Premier, Aikhal, Udachanaya, Argyle, Jagersfontein, Orapa, Kiffiefontein, Voorspoed and Jwaneng. Canadian pipes were joining that league. Sable, Fox, Misery, Koala, Leslie, Panda and other new pipes would become just as famous.

Chuck was not the only one in the spotlight. Hugo Dummett also rode the success of the discoveries to the top of the field. From chief diamond explorationist and head of exploration for BHP's U.S. interests, he was promoted first to head of exploration for all of North America and the Caribbean, and then to head of exploration for BHP worldwide. It was the world's premier exploration job. Although DeBeers was still more powerful, BHP's interests were far broader. With 48,000 employees, annual sales in excess of $16 billion and operations in more than 50 countries, BHP was a global force.

Like Kennecott, BHP had developed major assets in copper. They had followed Kennecott into New Guinea, taken over the Ok Tedi project, moved into Chile – its doors once more open to foreign investment – and discovered a huge porphyry copper deposit there. On the scale of Kennecott's former El Teniente mine, the Escondida mine was set up by Hugo's boss, Bob Hickman, at $320 million below projected cost and seven months earlier than anticipated. BHP promoted excellence. Hickman rose quickly to the top, becoming executive vice president of BHP Minerals.

Rory Moore, too, was rising. Filling the space vacated by Hugo, he became BHP's chief diamond explorationist and was also put in charge of industrial minerals. Ray Ashley and Larry Ott, reporting to Rory, were now in charge of BHP's interests in the Northwest Territories.

The changes within BHP had little effect on Chuck. Ashley and Ott were anxious to take over the field from him but, although the money was BHP's, the calls remained Chuck's. BHP was waiting for more results before exercising its full option and assuming control.

For three years, Chuck remained at the centre of activity. It was life on the peak. In 1992 he was named Mining Man of the Year. Dia Met obtained new listings on the Toronto Stock Exchange and the American Stock Exchange. Stock prices soared to more than $65 a share and stock splits followed. Dia Met bought their own helicopter, an AS350B2, one of the most powerful machines operating in the North. It gave Chuck complete mobility, with speed.

Across the whole Northwest Territories and south into the lower latitudes, from Alberta across to Quebec, the diamond rush that Chuck began would continue for years. Poking around the north shore of Lac de Gras, adjacent to the southern limit of the Dia Met-BHP claims, Aber Resources found some diamondiferous kimberlites going off under the big lake and was excitedly prospecting them. Further away, nearly 30 kilometres southeast of Dia Met's Lac de Gras property, Mountain Province, Glenmore Highlands and Camphor Ventures, all of Vancouver, were operating a joint venture on some pipes found there that they believed showed some promise, but the intense activity that Lac de Gras and Yellowknife had experienced would not be seen again. By 1994, the competition was giving up. One by one the other companies pulled up their stakes and went home. DeBeers, too, left, for the time being. It would be back in a joint venture signed with others, but its millions of acres had produced nothing. Aside from the claims Aber had staked along the shore of Lac de Gras, virtually everything of any value seemed to be inside Dia Met's claim blocks.

With the other companies gone and the land emptied of prospectors and aircraft, a state of natural quietude returned to prevail once more over the North, broken only by the haunting cry of a loon or the splash of a caribou high-stepping through the shallow waters along a beach front as the animals fled hordes of attacking flies. Exploration on Dia Met's claims continued unabated, but some pipes eluded their instruments. The hot samples from the esker at Norm's Camp were still without a known source. That pipe, perhaps the richest of all, remained curiously hidden. Whether the pipe was under Exeter Lake or the esker itself, the science of discovery was good, but far from perfect.

Chuck was flying high. The Central Selling Organization (CSO), DeBeers's marketing arm, controlled most of the world's diamond trade and was anxious to learn what marketing plans the joint venture partners had in mind. Chuck was invited to Europe as the guest of the cso's best customers, for lunch at Maxime's in Paris and dinner the same night in Antwerp, where he broke the rules of the diamond merchants' most exclusive black tie club by wearing baggy jeans and old sneakers. The merchants too, were anxious to learn how the Canadians intended to sell their diamonds. Would the Canadians join DeBeers's cartel or strike out on their own? Could they make some better deals? The contacts Chuck made were important, but he was not giving anything away.

And then it ended. On the 5th of May, 1994, Jim Eccott, the president of Dia Met, filed a major news release with the Toronto and Vancouver Stock Exchanges: "bhp Minerals Canada Ltd. announced today that bhp has given formal notice to Dia Met of bhp's commitment to prepare at its expense a feasibility study for the first diamond mine on joint venture property in the Northwest Territories. The effect of the notice under the joint venture agreement is to vest bhp with its 51% participating interest."

For Dia Met's shareholders, it was the news they were waiting to hear. For Chuck, it meant bhp was replacing Dia Met as the operator in the field. bhp now had the controlling interest.

Bob Hickman, Hugo Dummett's boss, delivered the message personally to Chuck. After 35 years of service to bhp, Hickman was only two years away from retirement, and two years after that he would join Dia Met as a member of the board of directors. He tried to be diplomatic. There were, he said, more important things for Chuck to do: development plans and marketing decisions. The reality: Chuck had no choice – that was the agreement. He was immediately relieved of all further responsibilities.

Chuck had been happy with the project. It had continued to evolve and, if he could have, he would have followed it – like following a trail into an unexplored jungle – to the very end, whatever that was, wherever it took him. With 10 percent of the property held by Chuck personally, and another 36.9 percent of Dia Met's equity held between Chuck and Dave MacKenzie, his stake was large. But still, bhp had control.

As the Brazilians always said after every expedition into the great unknown that they survived to talk about, it had been a good adventure. For Chuck, the Northwest Territories was over. He left the Arctic.

Once, long ago, he anticipated the conclusion of his projects. So consuming had been the effort of the past seventeen years, an unbroken chain of events that stretched back to his first contract with Chevron and his kitchen lab, that without the pressure of its constant demands, he now felt empty. He was drifting, unsure what to do next.

Slowly, with perspective, he began to see a new beginning. He realized what he loved most was what he had been doing: following his heart, doing whatever he wanted. The horizon was infinite; life short.

He could, if he wanted to, spend the rest of his life on the beaches of Rio. But

Chuck hated being idle. Treasure hunting in its purest form had always appealed to him: finding the ships that had gone down under the seas over the centuries. He could search for those ships. He could, instead, continue to push frontiers in his own field, with his own lab. He had new ideas for exploring the depths of the Earth through its gases. Anything was possible.

Now, he realized, he was free at last, and the true quest could begin. He drove out to Trepanier Bench where, years earlier, in another lifetime it seemed, he had wandered its open spaces struggling with questions that would decide his future.

The farm had changed little. The tar-papered shack looked the same but was empty, his parents having moved into another, better house on the property. They had kept intact his boyhood collection of wild birds' eggs from the prairie in a desk in the living room. A new highway, the Coquihalla, had cut a gash through a corner of the farm. But the forest had never been logged, the original homestead house was still standing, the cistern still worked, and his "collection" of cars was still parked where he had left them years before, out by the apple trees. In the field above, one of his new horses, in foal, was grazing.

He studied her a few minutes before slowly turning and driving to the top of the road, his back to the farm. Once, he had set speed records on the mountain with his '53 Ford, records no one had ever beaten. He looked at his watch, at the second hand. His new, fire engine red Dodge Viper had more power than the best of any two cars, combined, he had ever owned.

His foot hard on the brake, he raced the engine, and poised once more at the edge, he released the pressure, letting it fly.

EPILOGUE

THE EKATI DIAMOND MINE

AFTER Chuck left the Canadian Arctic, BHP moved ahead with its plans to commence mine construction and submitted its proposal to the federal government, requesting permission to proceed. In response, the minister of Indian Affairs and Northern Development, Ron Irwin, referred the project applications to the minister of the Environment, Sheila Copps.

With an investment of $160 million already in the field, BHP was anxious to proceed. Diamond mining, they pointed out, involved no chemical processes and was the cleanest of all mining operations. There was no better way to generate wealth for the country.

In her additional role as Deputy Prime Minister of Canada, Copps' statement that she would not be hurried by "big business" was heard in every boardroom of every major mining company in the world. With little political influence in Canada, BHP was a safe target, but its Australian roots were different from many of those old-world companies, including several in Canada, with their history of corruption, political involvement and blatant exploitation. The government's message, however, was clear, and it was quickly followed by an exodus of foreign mining capital – and the redirection of exploration budgets to more hospitable climates.

Most Northerners backed BHP, acutely aware that Alaska, next door, its treasury so enriched by successful oil and mineral investments, paid out handsome annual royalties to all of its citizens, while the Canadian north, with a different philosophy, remained an economic sinkhole. With the highest unemployment rates in the country, and an average of $16,000 paid out in federal support for every man, woman and child, the North was a collective welfare state on a grand scale. On the most basic level, Northerners wanted jobs. For many, the diamond project offered their first glimmer of hope.

BHP's mine proposal was to develop the five best diamondiferous pipes, commencing with open pit mining of Panda, followed by both open pit and underground mining of Misery, Koala, Fox and Sable, which, with better grades than Leslie, had replaced that pipe. The projected life of the mine was 25 years. Extensive exploration work had continued on the claims and further discoveries of commercial-grade pipes, considered likely, would extend the life of the project. Most importantly, the processing plant, centrally located on the claims southwest of the Koala pipe, would employ hundreds of people full-time, and BHP expected to generate annual revenues of between $400 million and $500 million.

The greatest proportion of this, by far, would be paid out in operation costs, salaries, royalties and taxation. The mine would directly and indirectly put billions into the territorial and federal treasuries.

Copps convened an Environmental Assessment Review Panel (EARP) in July of 1994 to consider the application at public meetings. The territorial government had recently passed a law, not without its critics, that required that all new projects also be subjected to the scrutiny of "traditional knowledge" before they would be permitted to proceed.

Travelling from village to village across the Northwest Territories, the panel sought out the opinions and concerns the people of the North had about the diamond mine proceeding. BHP found itself suddenly caught, politically, in the middle of historic internecine disputes. Much of the evidence the panel heard established that, in spite of random incursions into the Lac de Gras region, the area had never been occupied, being the frontier region between mutually antagonistic coastal Inuit and forest Natives; nevertheless, speakers from across the north tried to build cases for land claims and took the opportunity to make public speeches or vent feelings.

At the village of Dettah, Chief Darrell Beaulieu told the panel that the Yellowknives were not merely another "interest" group. "We are the landowners," he insisted, saying that therefore mining companies needed their permission to mine.

Elder Joe Migwi of the Rae Lakes Dogrib expressed the view that it was his own Dogrib Nation that needed to be consulted for approval.

Gary Bohnet, president of the Yellowknife Métis Nation, stood his ground in the battle for status: "We do not and will not, accept lesser recognition than any other aboriginal people in our homeland!" He wrote the panel: "There has been no recognition by BHP of the Métis in the North Slave region. If this indicates the quality of research conducted by the proponent, this could be a very long review process."

Indeed it became so. No group failed to stake their own claim on Chuck's discovery. Some argued that no development at all should be allowed to take place until the government had settled all northern claims. Others, like Harry Simpson, a Dogrib elder from Rae Lake, took a pragmatic approach in their alliances. "We are supporting the BHP group and I was hoping that they would support our claim with the federal government." Still others argued that the "traditional" use of the land for subsistence hunting, however intermittent, entitled them to ownership of mineral wealth anywhere their ancestors may have travelled.

The public hearings dragged on. For BHP the issue was simple: subject to legitimate environmental concerns and safeguards, they had the right to mine. The territorial and federal law was clear, and BHP had always been a model citizen. All else was political. The matter of royalties, like that of taxes, was not within its power to change. If it were to pay dues to a Native or to a Métis group, to the territorial government or to the federal government, the decision was not for BHP – or the panel – to make. The delay, however, cost them millions.

Talk of traditional ways did raise difficult truths. The number of Natives had never been large. Hunter-gatherers, they were neither environmentalists nor conservationists, rather, they were opportunistic hunters. Their numbers were only as large as the land was capable of supporting – never more than a few persons over a huge territory.

Like the Bushmen of the Kalahari, whose numbers across all of southern Africa had similarly been small, the cultures of the Native people were so intimately connected to the natural cycles and so utterly dependent upon the vagaries of wandering game for survival, that the slightest disturbances in the status quo were life-threatening. The consequences of change, whether in the caribou populations or their movements, or in human behavior, were often fatal for them. Life was lived forever on the edge. For the Natives, as for the Bushmen, the ability to adapt to change would determine their future.

Yet some aspects of Native culture remained in the hearts of Métis and Native alike: a need for the land, an abiding spirituality, a resistance to change, a vision that was still inherently conservative.

Not surprisingly, the panel everywhere met with concern for the caribou. It was the caribou more than any other creature that had historically sustained human life in the North. And still, most Northerners hunted and supplemented their diets with wild game, "country food," as it was now known. Once, not too long ago, when the caribou were late in arriving or the migration flow changed, the hunters who lived off them died. The memories and the relationships had, over thousands of years, become a central feature of the northern Native psyche: the caribou, the migrations. Now, came the changes associated with development: the winter roads, strangers.

The fear was not that the caribou themselves would suffer, but that the balance of nature would somehow be disturbed. The delicate harmonies that allowed the people to live might change. Then what? The fears offered up were profoundly deep. Bill Erasmus, National Chief of the Déné Nation, wrote to the EARP Panel, "When the caribou disappear, it is only a matter of time before we also disappear."

Nothing was certain with change, only that the BHP camp was a foreign creation in an ancient space. Change itself was threatening. And yet, the old life was already long gone. The northern communities, the villages themselves, were not sustainable. This land had never permitted settlements. The ancient people were nomadic. Living in small bands, they moved with the game and, in perfect balance, died when the game failed to feed them.

The new argument that Native people in the large settlements, which had evolved out of the old trading posts, now had an inherent right to live according to their traditional values and also to enjoy the same living standards as viable southern communities found little support. The panel listened politely. BHP was drawn into the issues unwillingly. Whatever their merits, there were no winnable arguments. Neither BHP nor Dia Met were in a position to settle anything. The hearings became a travelling spotlight on a myriad of northern myths, open sores and pipe dreams.

Not everyone demanded the impossible. Most understood that Chuck's discovery offered a chance at employment. For them, that was enough. Monica
Ayha, in the village of Deline, expressed her view that the development was a
major advantage for northern women: "Native women are finally getting a
chance. For years they were at the beck and call of men. Money will provide more
access to alcohol, but it also lets people improve themselves. If they're working at
least they're not out breaking and entering other people's homes. This mine is
going to help us socially. I like the feeling of independence."

Joe Migwi, of Rae Lake, also saw the development in positive terms: "The
world is changing. Now the trapping is not so good, and we have to turn to a
wage economy."

Seated behind the Native speakers were other faces, environmentalists from
the U.S., where virtually all the opposition to the mine was based, who had come
to express their views on the project. Pristine wildernesses, they proclaimed,
should not be developed. The very idea of diamonds, of wealth and luxury,
raised their ire. Coal mines, however debilitating was their work and damaging
was their product, at least had the dignity of historical usefulness. Diamonds
were not necessary. John Turner, former prime minister of Canada, now repre-
senting the World Wildlife Fund (WWF), went even further, and attempted to
block development of the project in the courts until the government first established a system of wilderness preserves throughout the North.

The British press reported a curious connection that the WWF had with
DeBeers. The South African diamond producer, if not directly a major contrib-
utor to WWF, was connected to it through the British Royal family which had
interests in both organizations. Turner, ultimately, withdrew WWF's opposition.

Although they also sought to align themselves with the Native groups, environmentalists were not successful there either. The Natives for the most part did
not want to be left alone. Far from it. If anything, their fear was that the diamond
fields had created an economic force that would, one day soon, leave them
behind, ignored again, out in the cold. Their values were more relationship-ori-
ented than those of the environmentalists. They did not want to stop the project;
they wanted a piece of it.

Across the tree line and into the Arctic, the people of the North, the Métis and
Natives, spoke of the need for a new approach. Poverty and subsistence living
seemed romantic only to those who did not experience it. There was no going
back. There was only the road ahead. Yet they did not want to exactly live like
people in "the Westernized world". That life, too, held little attraction for them.

Chuck, by means of the discovery, his company Dia Met and its association
with BHP, was able to offer them the only thing that really counted, the same gift
his father had given him: a future. Not platitudes, but employment. What they
chose to do with it was up to them.

The mine shifts would run two weeks "in", seven days a week, then two weeks
"out". They could live with a foot in both cultures, two weeks on the land, if they
wished, and two weeks in industry. To many, it seemed a good compromise. In a

modern world, people needed special skills to work, skills which would survive the life of the mines. BHP committed itself to hiring Northerners and to training them. It was a start. What the Northerners did, how they chose to live, was for them to decide. It was their future and their responsibility.

In the end, after interminable delays and an application of stricter environmental standards than had been applied to any other industry in the country – no polluting steel smelter, coal mine or paper mill – after promises by BHP to fund university scholarship programs, to safeguard the environment and to put controls on its employees that included severe measures against anyone caught feeding the wildlife, the government consented to allow the partners to proceed with the development of the diamond mine.

Ekati, the aboriginal name for the great lake, Lac de Gras, meant "fat lake." Fat was once one of the greatest treasures the land offered: life itself. Veins of white quartz crystal running through the surrounding rock like the marbling of fat in a healthy caribou had given the nearby lake its name, now given to the mine as well.

On the first of November, 1996, to a collective sigh of relief across the land, Ron Irwin, minister of Indian Affairs and Northern Development, issued the federal cabinet's final approval at an official signing ceremony in Yellowknife. On behalf of the government of Canada he said, "This diamond mining project is important to northerners, and to all of Canada. We all stand to reap the economic benefits of this important venture." The Ekati Diamond Mine was finally to become a reality. Construction began at once.

On the 14th of October, 1998, its construction complete, Ekati was officially opened with the enthusiastic attendance of representatives from the Native communities, Dia Met, BHP and both levels of government. Pleased with the intergrity that the partners had demonstrated, Don Morin, the Premier of the Government of the Northwest Territories, Jane Stewart, federal Minister of Indian and Northern Affairs, and Ralph Goodale, Minister of Natural Resources Canada, speaking for the future, gave the following commitment to the mining industry: Canada was open for business.

It marked the start of a new era for the Natives, the Métis, the North and the country. The diamond era had begun for them all.

At home in Kelowna, however, the new lifestyle had put pressure on Chuck's marriage that it had not known before. Marlene wanted Chuck to be closer to home. For Chuck – moving in the opposite direction – the rewards of success were not to quit the path of freedom but to embrace every opportunity that came his way. He and Marlene separated. They had much in common, a long history together and their children which would forever keep them connected, but their personal futures had become separate.

Nor had Chuck, since the takeover of the project by BHP in 1994, been waiting idly for the mine's opening. The Paul-Mike lead-zinc claims near Kimberley, British Columbia, that he had staked in 1979 while partnered with Superior and Falconbridge, finally got some attention: geochemical and geophysical surveys on the property indicated the existence of something with potential. New geo-chemical techniques, which he had patented, revealed anomalies buried deep beneath the surface, and the analysis of samples of deep, subsurface gases, which he had extracted from the earth, confirmed that the deposits warranted further investigation. Subsequent seismic testing had identified massive sulfide targets. Original geological reconstruction of the regional rock zones, located between the Kootenay King and the Sullivan mines, indicated that the Sullivan massive sulfide mine ore – famous for nearly a century for its rich lead-zinc-silver con-tent – also existed beneath the claims. The Sullivan mine was, after nearly a cen-tury of production for Cominco's mill, running out of ore. Exploration of the buried targets would take time. Drilling would have to prove it out; the shape and extent of the deposit would have to be determined and, if warranted, an eco-nomic assessment would follow, but if the claims did prove out, Chuck would find himself working once again with Cominco. This time, that prospect was an exciting one.

Nor was Chuck focusing on established claims; there were new lands to be explored. With the expertise he had developed in the Canadian Arctic, he moved across the sea to the tundra of northern Finland. Ray Ashley, the geophysical expert with BHP, who had designed the airborne electromagnetic system for locating pipes in the N.W.T., had joined Dia Met as its manager of exploration and was now running the program in a land where reindeer, domesticated cari-bou, had replaced their wilder Canadian cousins. In a huge survey that could only have been accomplished using Chuck's methods, nearly the entire country was sampled. The results, both geochemical and geophysical, were more than encouraging. In a matter of months, chemistries favorable for diamonds and diamond indicators themselves, narrowed the field of exploration and ultimately led to the discovery – and staking – of another pipe field. It was still early and, extensive exploration work was required, but it was beginning to look like Chuck had done it again. This time, Dia Met was not a small country player dependent upon handouts from investment fund managers or upon a major to finance drilling costs. This time, the playing field in central and northern Finland belonged entirely to Dia Met.

In their work across Finland, Chuck and Ray had found one other player in the field: Ashton Mining. The Australian company had been quietly searching for diamonds in Finland since 1986. As well as laying claim to its own discover-ies, Dia Met entered into a joint venture with Ashton in 1998 to do follow-up sampling of separate indicator mineral trains that Ashton had discovered in eastern Finland. Ashton, too, had located pipes, and preliminary sampling of those pipes had produced good results. Diamonds. And, if Dia Met was not ulti-mately successful in Finland, there was still Greenland.

DeBeers, through its subsidiary Monopros, had moved on after the diamond rush ended in the Northwest Territories and had begun prospecting in Green-land with Canadian geologists. There, in western Greenland, along the narrow band of coastal ground that was free of the island's massive ice cap, the geologists had detected indicator minerals favourable for diamonds. This time, DeBeers allied themselves with Dia Met. After Dia Met resampled the region, confirming the results, the two companies signed a joint-venture agreement. Chuck was now partnered with DeBeers in Greenland.

As they had in Finland, airborne magnetic surveys identified numerous circular magnetic anomalies: the targets. Further exploration work, sampling and drilling would take them well into the next millennium.

Chuck was flying once more.

His achievements attracted attention from other quarters as well. Fresh faces now entered Chuck's life. The world of academia was impressed with his accomplishments and, from it, new offers arrived. One, he accepted.

The University of British Columbia had for years maintained a regional college in the Okanagan valley. Students from Penticton and Kelowna could, locally, take UBC courses and graduate with UBC degrees. But the demands of a burgeoning population required the Okanagan to have its own independent university. In 1994, the college, with a new modern campus in Kelowna, received its charter, and in June of 1998 the students and staff of Okanagan University convocated for the first graduation ceremonies.

Among the sea of black robes was a single red gown. Dr. John Greenough, the speaker, turned to the university's president, Dr. Katy Bindon. "Madam President," he said, "I have the honour to present Charles Edgar Fipke for the degree of Doctor of Technology, *Honoris Causa.*"

It was, for Chuck, the realization of another dream. After Greenough read through a long list of Chuck's contributions to science – achievements that were deemed worthy of the highest academic recognition – Dr. Bindon draped a red, blue and gold trimmed hood over him and had him sign the register.

It was the first degree awarded by Okanagan University, and with it, Dr. Bindon established a standard of excellence the institution would thereafter strive to live up to. She then called upon Dr. Charles Edgar Fipke to deliver the convocation address.

In the audience were Ed and Anna Fipke. It was to them that Chuck first spoke. "I'd like to thank my father and my mother," he said warmly. It was as much their achievement as his, the struggle of generations.

Also in the audience were friends, old classmates and their children, now graduating. To them, his message was clear.

"Have the courage to live up to your potential ... And have fun!"

AR RUB' AL KHALI, SOUTHERN ARABIAN DESERT

Aт the edge of Ar Rub' al Khali, the southern Arabian desert was a welcome change from the hazy politics of Canada and the frozen tundra of Finland and Greenland. Under the afternoon sun, the desert appeared to undulate behind a shimmering curtain of baking heat, rising in waves under the white light.

In the west, towards the Red Sea, a massif rose up in a series of increasingly dramatic folds, heaved skyward by the action of plate tectonics five million years ago, when Africa began to break apart. The crack had shaken the continent from the Indian Ocean to the Mediterranean, widening until the waters of the Gulf of Aden and the Red Sea rushed in, forever separating Arabia from Africa. The desert itself was a sea of shifting sands, relieved only by the water of a deep well or a surface oasis. Hardy acacia and date palm, surviving precariously between infrequent rainstorms, grew along the dry wadis.

It was a land out of antiquity, that had once controlled the entrance to the Red Sea. Spices and scientific knowledge from Asia had created a coastal maritime commerce that ranged far beyond the areas known to the western Mediterranean world. Remnants of Jewish, Indian and Indonesian settlements, dating back beyond two millennia, were still to be found among the ethnic minorities of the Arabic majority – itself belonging to two distinct tribes with long recorded histories. One traced its ancestry to the biblical Joktan and the other to Ishmael, Abraham's elder son by his concubine Hagar, who had been turned out into the desert, after the birth of Isaac, to found a new nation.

Northwest of the ancient mountain city of San'a, the peak of An-Nabi Shu 'ayb, was the highest mountain in all of Arabia and at the centre of Chuck's latest endeavour. Chuck was flanked by men in traditional desert garb, wearing elaborately designed, silver filigree belts with curved, broad-bladed knives – jambiyah daggers – tucked into scabbards positioned over their groins. For the government of Yemen, a republic reunified by treaty in 1990 and known in Arabic as "Al-Jumhurijah al-Yamanijah," the success of Chuck's mission was as important as it was to him.

Chuck waited as the men finished their prayers, prostrating themselves in the direction of Mecca, the Kabah, built by Abraham and Ishmael, the first temple raised to God. Like the Jews, the Arabs, through Ishmael, were the children of Abraham, and they honored him no less.

Six hundred and sixty miles to the southeast of Mecca, on the southwestern edge of Arabia, the land upon which Chuck now stood was once part of the empire of Sheba, ruled by a queens known in Islamic tradition as Bilqis. When the queen of Sheba journeyed by caravan across Arabia to meet King Solomon in Jerusalem, the event was recorded.

The reign of Solomon, born in Israel, the Son of David, around the year 986 BC, marked the apogee of the kingdom of Israel. Renowned for his love of women, as well as for his wisdom and his wealth, Solomon took for a wife not only the daughter of the pharaoh of Egypt, but 700 other wives of royal rank. As if 700 women were not sufficient for his needs, Solomon had, additionally, 300 concubines. His reputation spread quickly.

Bilqis brought him gifts of immense values, and camels laden with "a hundred and twenty talents of gold." A talent was valued at 3,000 shekels. An Egyptian chariot could be purchased and imported for 600 shekels. The weight of gold mined yearly from Solomon's own sources was 666 talents. But where was this gold, which had maintained an empire, mined?

The search, for King Solomon's fabled "lost mines" had occupied treasure hunters for millennia. There were some clues, but unlike pathfinder minerals swept downstream from a deposit, they were far more obscure, buried in human history as well as geography. According to biblical lore: "King Solomon built a fleet of ships at E'zion-ge'ber, ... and they went to Ophir, and brought from there gold, to the amount of four hundred and twenty talents; and they brought it to King Solomon."

From Solomon's base at E'zion-ge'ber, a port on the northern shore of the Gulf of Aqabah, his Red Sea fleet regularly sailed south towards Sheba, which Assyrian records independently identified as an important trading centre. Ophir itself may have been in Sheba. Not only the historical texts, but recent geological research pointed to ancient Sheba as a promising field.

In November of 1996, a new listing had appeared on the Alberta Stock Exchange, Canadian Mountain Minerals, and in the spring of 1998 it merged with Goldtex to become Cantex – Chuck's new vehicle for exploration. Dia Met, now firmly established, would work with the new company and bring it into the Greenland diamond venture and the Paul-Mike lead-zinc project, among others, but Yemen was strictly a Cantex project, and Chuck was at its head. The agreement the new company had negotiated with the government of Yemen granted them exclusive exploration rights over a huge region of northwest Yemen – all of what had been ancient Sheba.

There were some who doubted that Chuck would find gold in Yemen. But he had no doubts of his own. The belief that the ancients had exhausted the deposits was as false as the notion that the 17th-century, Iron Age African miners had exhausted the mines they worked before European contact. In fact, when those early miners had reached the limits of their primitive technology they moved on, leaving the deeper deposits untouched. After centuries had passed, signs of the old works faded from the land, but Chuck knew where to look. Indeed he had already discovered the tailings of several of Queen Bilqis's mines.

Chuck was looking beyond the old prospects however, for new gold deposits of the type found in the Nevada Great Basin – something the ancients had had no knowledge about. The samples his crews had taken had produced several major hits near Hajjah and Bani Dhu Ayb, and in Wadi al Bir in the Kushar district.

Most promising of all was Al Hariqah. There, in a lost valley, honeycombed rock faces spoke of extensive ancient workings. Once, thousands of people had toiled in the ancient mines, now touched only by the searing wind. Sampling at Al Hariqah had confirmed the presence of a gold mineralized granitic rock zone with a continuous strike length of 1,700 metres. Early speculation was that Al Hariqah would again become the site of a new gold mine, now a modern heap-leach mine. Before that happened however, Chuck planned to bring in an archeological team. The members who were consulted were nearly breathless. The ancient mines were not the work of local tribesmen. An empire had been behind them – an empire like Solomon's.

As Chuck's small party, which included a military escort, began to collect, a group of Bedouin horsemen rode up on some of the finest animals he had ever seen. The two groups studied each other with equanimity. The modern thoroughbred bloodlines all traced back to here, to the ancient tribes of Yemen and their mounts. It was in Yemen that the "Arab" was born, the horse as much a part of the desert as the Bedouin themselves. There are Yemeni legends of great horses that have never been equalled, horses that were worth armies' lives.

The horses moved by, light as the wind.

Once there were ancient Chinese influences in Yemen, and Persian ones. Yemeni traders once competed with imperial Rome for the trade from southern Asia. In the countryside, especially along the fringes of the great desert, adobe villages that had remained unchanged for centuries rose like mud hives from the earth, while in San'a the Islamic mosques were among the finest achievements of Arabic architecture anywhere. Even the bird life was exciting and abundant.

As a field, Yemen offered it all – it was treasure hunting at its very best. Cantex was a junior company, just starting out, but it had an advantage now that put it into an entirely different league. It had the resources of a major, Dia Met, behind it, whenever necessary.

Loaded up and ready to move, Chuck's escort had one last detail to attend to before they climbed back into their jeep. The temperature in Fahrenheit under the roof with the windows open was in the mid-90s. It was bearable. Hot was nearer to a 110. Carefully unwrapping his supply of *qat* to prevent it from being contaminated by the desert sands, which even in the still of the afternoon penetrated every recess, one of the soldiers passed around the narcotic leaves. Stronger than a plug of tobacco, qat was chewed and savoured the same way.

Relaxing, one of the men began to joke and talk about women. In Yemen women were accessible only within marriage. But a man could have many wives.

"Is not the man with two wives better off than the man with only one?" he asked Chuck. The others encouraged him to agree. "If you stay, my friend," he added quickly, while Chuck was still considering the idea, "You will have three wives! I will arrange it myself!"

Chuck laughed and set to work. It was a gloriously bright day.

INDEX